Java™ For Dummies, 2nd Edition

Cheat Sheet

`<APPLET>` Tag

Tag Structure:

```
<APPLET attributes>
appletparameter tags
alternate HTML
</APPLET>
```

Example:

```
<APPLET CODE="LivingLinks.class"
WIDTH=100 HEIGHT=100>

<PARAM NAME="image"
VALUE="animalsButton.gif">

<PARAM NAME="effect" VALUE="Warp">

<PARAM NAME="soundDir" VALUE="audio/
animals/">

<PARAM NAME="inSound"
VALUE="dolphinSqueak.au | lionRoar.
au | rooster.au">

<PARAM NAME="links" VALUE= "Dolphins =
http://www.dolphin.com | Lions =
http://www.lion.com | Roosters =
http://www.rooster.com">

<B>If you can read this, you're
visiting without a Java-savvy browser!
</B>
```

This page requires a Java-savvy browser...

```
<A HREF="http://www.netscape.com">
GET ONE!</A>
</APPLET>
```

`<SCRIPT>` Tag Structure

Tag Structure:

```
<SCRIPT attributes>
<!— comments to hide script from
non-Java browsers

...JavaScript code goes here, inside
the comments above and below...

// closing comment —>
</SCRIPT>
```

Example:

```
<SCRIPT LANGUAGE="JavaScript">
<!—
todays_date=new Date();
document.write("The Current Date
and Time is: ")
document.write(todays_date)
//—>
</SCRIPT>
```

Five Fabulous JavaScript Sites

Netscape's JavaScript Developer site:
developer.netscape.com

Yahoo! JavaScript link:
www.yahoo.com/
Computers_and_Internet/
Languages/JavaScript

24 Hour JavaScripts:
www.javascripts.com/

Mantis JavaScript link:
www.mantiscorp.com/javascript

Gamelan's JavaScript site:
www.javascript.developer.com

Five Best Java Resources on the Web

Java For Dummies Support site:
www.mantiscorp.com/JavaForDummies

Java Applet Rating Service (JARS): www.jars.com

Mantis Java link: www.mantiscorp.com/java

Gamelan: www.gamelan.com

IDG's Java Resource site: www.idgbooks.com/
rc/java

...For Dummies: #1 Computer Book Series for Beginners

Java™ For Dummies, 2nd Edition

Cheat Sheet

Required and Optional Applet Attributes

Within your `<APPLET>` tags, some attributes are required, others give you room to play around. However, you'll never be able to use either of the two new Java 1.1 attributes when hooking up an original Java 1.0 applet since Java 1.1 attributes aren't supported by older Java 1.0 applets— so be careful when weaving your Java-powered pages!

Attribute	Description
Required Attributes	
CODE	This attribute specifies the name of the applet file to imbed in your page. (***Note:*** the CODE attribute is not used if the Java 1.1 OBJECT attribute described below is used.)
HEIGHT	This attribute specifies the height of your applet in pixels.
WIDTH	This attribute specifies the width of your applet in pixels.
Optional Attributes	
PARAM	Not an `<APPLET>` tag attribute, actually, but an optional tag that itself has two required attributes (NAME and VALUE). You may use any number of `<PARAM>` tags to customize an applet, as long as the applet you're dealing with supports them.
CODEBASE	This attribute specifies the base URL for your applet. The applet itself must be located relative to this URL. If CODEBASE isn't specified, the applet is expected to reside in the same directory as the Web page itself.
ALIGN	This attribute specifies where your applet is placed on the page in respect to the text around it; may be one of the following nine alignments: left, right, top, texttop, middle, absmiddle, baseline, bottom, and absbottom.
ALT	This attribute specifies alternate text to be displayed by Java-savvy browsers that are incapable of executing the applet for whatever reason. Note that this text is seen *only* by Java-savvy browsers, as it falls within the opening `<APPLET>` tag, which all non-Java browsers skip over. If you want to communicate with non-Java browsers, do so by using *alternate HTML*.
NAME	This attribute specifies the symbolic name of your applet, allowing other applets imbedded in the same page to locate your applet by name. This attribute is used only when applets on a page communicate with one another, something most applets don't do.
HSPACE	This attribute specifies the horizontal space surrounding your applet.
VSPACE	This attribute specifies the vertical space surrounding your applet.
Java 1.1 Attributes	
ARCHIVE	Available only with applets created using Java 1.1 or later, this attribute is used to specify one or more Java archives (JARs), assuming the applet actually takes advantage of JAR files (special-purpose archives introduced with Java 1.1). If multiple JAR files are required, they must be separated by a comma.
OBJECT	Available only with applets created using Java 1.1 or later, this attribute is used to specify the name of a "serialized" applet file, as opposed to the non-serialized applet file (standard Java class file) specified through the CODE attribute. Because serialized applet files are actually special versions of standard applets, the CODE attribute is not necessary when the OBJECT is used. When the CODE attribute is used, the OBJECT attribute is not used.

...For Dummies: #1 Computer Book Series for Beginners

JAVA™

FOR

DUMMIES®

2ND EDITION

JAVA™ FOR DUMMIES® 2ND EDITION

by Aaron E. Walsh

IDG Books Worldwide, Inc.
An International Data Group Company

Foster City, CA ♦ Chicago, IL ♦ Indianapolis, IN ♦ Southlake, TX

Java™ For Dummies®, 2nd Edition

Published by
IDG Books Worldwide, Inc.
An International Data Group Company
919 E. Hillsdale Blvd.
Suite 400
Foster City, CA 94404
www.idgbooks.com (IDG Books Worldwide Web Site)
www.dummies.com (Dummies Press Web Site)

Library of Congress Catalog Card No.: 97-80357

ISBN: 0-7645-0140-2

Printed in the United States of America

10 9 8 7 6 5 4 3 2 1

2E/RU/RQ/ZX/IN

Distributed in the United States by IDG Books Worldwide, Inc.

Distributed by Macmillan Canada for Canada; by Transworld Publishers Limited in the United Kingdom; by IDG Norge Books for Norway; by IDG Sweden Books for Sweden; by Woodslane Pty. Ltd. for Australia; by Woodslane Enterprises Ltd. for New Zealand; by Longman Singapore Publishers Ltd. for Singapore, Malaysia, Thailand, and Indonesia; by Simron Pty. Ltd. for South Africa; by Toppan Company Ltd. for Japan; by Distribuidora Cuspide for Argentina; by Livraria Cultura for Brazil; by Ediciencia S.A. for Ecuador; by Addison-Wesley Publishing Company for Korea; by Ediciones ZETA S.C.R. Ltda. for Peru; by WS Computer Publishing Corporation, Inc., for the Philippines; by Unalis Corporation for Taiwan; by Contemporanea de Ediciones for Venezuela; by Computer Book & Magazine Store for Puerto Rico; by Express Computer Distributors for the Caribbean and West Indies. Authorized Sales Agent: Anthony Rudkin Associates for the Middle East and North Africa.

For general information on IDG Books Worldwide's books in the U.S., please call our Consumer Customer Service department at 800-762-2974. For reseller information, including discounts and premium sales, please call our Reseller Customer Service department at 800-434-3422.

For information on where to purchase IDG Books Worldwide's books outside the U.S., please contact our International Sales department at 415-655-3200 or fax 415-655-3295.

For information on foreign language translations, please contact our Foreign & Subsidiary Rights department at 415-655-3021 or fax 415-655-3281.

For sales inquiries and special prices for bulk quantities, please contact our Sales department at 415-655-3200 or write to the address above.

For information on using IDG Books Worldwide's books in the classroom or for ordering examination copies, please contact our Educational Sales department at 800-434-2086 or fax 817-251-8174.

For press review copies, author interviews, or other publicity information, please contact our Public Relations department at 415-655-3000 or fax 415-655-3299.

For authorization to photocopy items for corporate, personal, or educational use, please contact Copyright Clearance Center, 222 Rosewood Drive, Danvers, MA 01923, or fax 508-750-4470.

is a trademark under exclusive license to IDG Books Worldwide, Inc., from International Data Group, Inc.

About the Author

Aaron E. Walsh is President and CEO of Mantis Development Corporation, a Boston-based software development firm specializing in advanced multimedia and network technologies, and an international best-selling author for IDG Books Worldwide, Inc.

Formerly the manager of Boston College's Advanced Technology Group (ATG), Aaron was lead software architect and engineer for a number of advanced technology projects developed at Boston College, including robust client/server technologies that pre-date the World Wide Web. While at Boston College, Aaron also wrote the core software system for Eagle Eyes, a research project that allows users to navigate their personal computer through eye movement alone. Under development for over four years, Eagle Eyes was selected as a finalist in Discover Magazine's 1994 Awards for Technical Innovation.

In 1992, Aaron co-founded Mantis Development Corporation, where he currently leads development of advanced software technologies based on the Java programming language developed by Sun Microsystems. He is the author of several articles for *MacTech Magazine* (formerly *MacTutor*) and *Dr. Dobb's Programming Journal,* and has written a number of books for IDG Books Worldwide, including *Destination Multimedia, Java For Dummies, Foundations of Java Programming for the World Wide Web,* as well as the forthcoming *Java Bible* and *Visual InterDev For Dummies.* In addition, Aaron is a regular columnist for *Java Report,* the leading print magazine for serious Java programmers, where he writes the Network Computing column.

Aaron is also the chairman of the Virtual Reality Modeling Language (VRML) Universal Media Library (UML) working group, a formal VRML Consortium research group. With an immediate mission to ". . . increase the realism of VRML worlds and decrease network downloads by defining a small, cross-platform library of locally resident media elements (textures, sounds and VRML objects) and a uniform mechanism by which VRML content creators can incorporate these media elements into their worlds," Aaron believes that the technology brought to fruition by his group will ultimately offer significant advantages to the entire World Wide Web.

ABOUT IDG BOOKS WORLDWIDE

Welcome to the world of IDG Books Worldwide.

IDG Books Worldwide, Inc., is a subsidiary of International Data Group, the world's largest publisher of computer-related information and the leading global provider of information services on information technology. IDG was founded more than 25 years ago and now employs more than 8,500 people worldwide. IDG publishes more than 275 computer publications in over 75 countries (see listing below). More than 60 million people read one or more IDG publications each month.

Launched in 1990, IDG Books Worldwide is today the #1 publisher of best-selling computer books in the United States. We are proud to have received eight awards from the Computer Press Association in recognition of editorial excellence and three from *Computer Currents'* First Annual Readers' Choice Awards. Our best-selling *...For Dummies®* series has more than 30 million copies in print with translations in 30 languages. IDG Books Worldwide, through a joint venture with IDG's Hi-Tech Beijing, became the first U.S. publisher to publish a computer book in the People's Republic of China. In record time, IDG Books Worldwide has become the first choice for millions of readers around the world who want to learn how to better manage their businesses.

Our mission is simple: Every one of our books is designed to bring extra value and skill-building instructions to the reader. Our books are written by experts who understand and care about our readers. The knowledge base of our editorial staff comes from years of experience in publishing, education, and journalism — experience we use to produce books for the '90s. In short, we care about books, so we attract the best people. We devote special attention to details such as audience, interior design, use of icons, and illustrations. And because we use an efficient process of authoring, editing, and desktop publishing our books electronically, we can spend more time ensuring superior content and spend less time on the technicalities of making books.

You can count on our commitment to deliver high-quality books at competitive prices on topics you want to read about. At IDG Books Worldwide, we continue in the IDG tradition of delivering quality for more than 25 years. You'll find no better book on a subject than one from IDG Books Worldwide.

John Kilcullen
CEO
IDG Books Worldwide, Inc.

Steven Berkowitz
President and Publisher
IDG Books Worldwide, Inc.

Eighth Annual Computer Press Awards ≥ 1992

Ninth Annual Computer Press Awards ≥ 1993

Tenth Annual Computer Press Awards ≥ 1994

Eleventh Annual Computer Press Awards ≥ 1995

IDG Books Worldwide, Inc., is a subsidiary of International Data Group, the world's largest publisher of computer-related information and the leading global provider of information services on information technology. International Data Group publishes over 275 computer publications in over 75 countries. Sixty million people read one or more International Data Group publications each month. International Data Group's publications include: **ARGENTINA:** Buyer's Guide, Computerworld Argentina, PC World Argentina; **AUSTRALIA:** Australian Macworld, Australian PC World, Australian Reseller News, Computerworld, IT Casebook, Network World, Publish, Webmaster; **AUSTRIA:** Computerwelt Österreich, Networks Austria, PC Tip Austria; **BANGLADESH:** PC World Bangladesh; **BELARUS:** PC World Belarus; **BELGIUM:** Data News; **BRAZIL:** Annuario de Informática, Computerworld, Connections, Macworld, PC Player, PC World, Publish, Reseller News, Supergamepower; **BULGARIA:** Computerworld Bulgaria, Network World Bulgaria, PC & MacWorld Bulgaria; **CANADA:** CIO Canada, Client/Server World, ComputerWorld Canada, InfoWorld Canada, NetworkWorld Canada, WebWorld; **CHILE:** Computerworld Chile, PC World Chile; **COLOMBIA:** Computerworld Colombia, PC World Colombia; **COSTA RICA:** PC World Centro America; **THE CZECH AND SLOVAK REPUBLICS:** Computerworld Czechoslovakia, Macworld Czech Republic, PC World Czechoslovakia; **DENMARK:** Communications World Danmark, Computerworld Danmark, Macworld Danmark, PC World Danmark, Techworld Denmark; **DOMINICAN REPUBLIC:** PC World Republica Dominicana; **ECUADOR:** PC World Ecuador; **EGYPT:** Computerworld Middle East, PC World Middle East; **EL SALVADOR:** PC World Centro America; **FINLAND:** MikroPC, Tietoverkko, Tietoviikko; **FRANCE:** Distributique, Hebdo, Info PC, Le Monde Informatique, Macworld, Reseaux & Telecoms, WebMaster France; **GERMANY:** Computer Partner, Computerwoche, Computerwoche Extra, Computerwoche FOCUS, Global Online, Macwelt, PC Welt; **GREECE:** Amiga Computing, GamePro Greece, Multimedia World; **GUATEMALA:** PC World Centro America; **HONDURAS:** PC World Centro America; **HONG KONG:** Computerworld Hong Kong, PC World Hong Kong, Publish in Asia; **HUNGARY:** ABCD CD-ROM, Computerworld Szamitastechnika, Internetto online Magazine, PC World Hungary, PC-X Magazin Hungary; **ICELAND:** Tolvuheimur PC World Island; **INDIA:** Information Communications World, Information Systems Computerworld, PC World India, Publish in Asia; **INDONESIA:** InfoKomputer PC World, Komputek Computerworld, Publish in Asia; **IRELAND:** ComputerScope, PC Live!; **ISRAEL:** Macworld Israel, People & Computers/Computerworld; **ITALY:** Computerworld Italia, Macworld Italia, Networking Italia, PC World Italia; **JAPAN:** DTP World, Macworld Japan, Nikkei Personal Computing, OS/2 World Japan, SunWorld Japan, Windows NT World, Windows World Japan; **KENYA:** PC World East African; **KOREA:** Hi-Tech Information, Macworld Korea, PC World Korea; **MACEDONIA:** PC World Macedonia; **MALAYSIA:** Computerworld Malaysia, PC World Malaysia, Publish in Asia; **MALTA:** PC World Malta; **MEXICO:** Computerworld Mexico, PC World Mexico; **MYANMAR:** PC World Myanmar; **NETHERLANDS:** Computer! Totaal, LAN Internetworking Magazine, LAN World Buyers Guide, Macworld Netherlands, Net, WebWereld; **NEW ZEALAND:** Absolute Beginners Guide and Plain & Simple Series, Computer Buyer, Computer Industry Directory, Computerworld New Zealand, MTB, Network World, PC World New Zealand; **NICARAGUA:** PC World Centro America; **NORWAY:** Computerworld Norge, CW Rapport, Datamagasinet, Financial Rapport, Kursguide Norge, Macworld Norge, Multimediaworld Norge, PC World Ekspress Norge, PC World Nettverk, PC World Norge, PC World ProduktGuide Norge; **PAKISTAN:** Computerworld Pakistan; **PANAMA:** PC World Panama; **PEOPLE'S REPUBLIC OF CHINA:** China Computer Users, China Computerworld, China InfoWorld, China Telecom World Weekly, Computer & Communication, Electronic Design China, Electronics Today, Electronics Weekly, Game Software, PC World China, Popular Computer Week, Software Weekly, Software World, Telecom World; **PERU:** Computerworld Peru, PC World Profesional Peru, PC World SoHo Peru; **PHILIPPINES:** Click!, Computerworld Philippines, PC World Philippines, Publish in Asia; **POLAND:** Computerworld Poland, Computerworld Special Report Poland, Cyber, Macworld Poland, Networld Poland, PC World Komputer; **PORTUGAL:** Cerebro/PC World, Computerworld/Correio Informatico, Dealer World Portugal, Mac*In/PC*In Portugal, Multimedia World; **PUERTO RICO:** PC World Puerto Rico; **ROMANIA:** Computerworld Romania, PC World Romania, Telecom Romania; **RUSSIA:** Computerworld Russia, Mir PK, Publish, Seti; **SINGAPORE:** Computerworld Singapore, PC World Singapore, Publish in Asia; **SLOVENIA:** Monitor; **SOUTH AFRICA:** Computing SA, Network World SA, Software World SA; **SPAIN:** Communicaciones World España, Computerworld España, Dealer World España, Macworld España, PC World España; **SRI LANKA:** Infolink PC World; **SWEDEN:** CAP&Design, Computer Sweden, Corporate Computing Sweden, Internetworld Sweden, it branschen, Macworld Sweden, MaxiData Sweden, MikroDatorn, Natverk & Kommunikation, PC World Sweden, PCaktiv, Windows World Sweden; **SWITZERLAND:** Computerworld Schweiz, Macworld Schweiz, PCtip; **TAIWAN:** Computerworld Taiwan, Macworld Taiwan, NEW ViSiON/Publish, PC World Taiwan, Windows World Taiwan; **THAILAND:** Publish in Asia, Thai Computerworld; **TURKEY:** Computerworld Turkiye, Macworld Turkiye, Network World Turkiye, PC World Turkiye; **UKRAINE:** Computerworld Kiev, Multimedia World Ukraine, PC World Ukraine; **UNITED KINGDOM:** Acorn User UK, Amiga Action UK, Amiga Computing UK, Apple Talk UK, Computing, Macworld, Parents and Computers UK, PC Advisor, PC Home, PSX Pro, The WEB; **UNITED STATES:** Cable in the Classroom, CIO Magazine, Computerworld, DOS World, Federal Computer Week, GamePro Magazine, InfoWorld, I-Way, Macworld, Network World, PC Games, PC World, Publish, Video Event, THE WEB Magazine, and WebMaster; online webzines: JavaWorld, NetscapeWorld, and SunWorld Online; **URUGUAY:** InfoWorld Uruguay; **VENEZUELA:** Computerworld Venezuela, PC World Venezuela; and **VIETNAM:** PC World Vietnam.
3/24/97

Dedication

To my nephew Dane, with love.

Author's Acknowledgments

With thanks to Tim Berners-Lee for inventing the World Wide Web, and to Sun Microsystems for giving it a serious jolt of life with Java.

Special thanks to Barbara Mikolajczak, whose dedicated research and work on the CD-ROM made both the original *Java For Dummies* book and this revision of it possible, and to everyone at Mantis Development Corporation (www.mantiscorp.com). In particular I'd like to thank Robert Wade, who wrote the majority of JavaScript code found in Part III, as well as David Ruxton, Igor Svibilskiy, and Jeff Orkin for their significant contributions to LivingLinks and several other Java applets provided on CD-ROM (with additional thanks to Jeff Orkin for "Celebrity Painter").

To Bill Wellington, Adam Gupta and Yeji Hong for their work on the Java "CookBook" Web pages provided on CD-ROM, and Baiju Paul Mathews, Sanjeev Dasgupta and Scott Clark for creating special effect plug-ins for the LivingLinks applet. Thanks to Alex Garbagnati for the Marquee applet, and to Aaron deMello for his work as technical editor on this book.

I'd also like to extend special thanks to Dr. Gary P. Kearney, and Paul R. Gupta for their continued support and contribution to Mantis Development Corporation, as well as Talbott and Pradeepa Crowell.

To the good folks at IDG Books and Dummies Press (www.dummies.com) for making this book possible in the first place. In particular I'd like to thank Tere Drenth, the editor of this *Java For Dummies* revision, for bearing with me as I pushed the concept of "drop dead" deadlines as far as possible, and Bill McManus, for applying his keen eyes and quick mouse to my draft manuscript. To Mary Bednarek for giving the thumbs-up to my original *Java For Dummies* proposal, and to Ellen Camm for helping me whip the game plan for this second revision into place. I'd also like to thank Joyce Pepple, Kevin Spencer, and Heather Dismore for all their work on the CD-ROM, and Darren Meiss for taking most of the screen shots that appear in this book.

Finally, I'd like to thank my family in Colorado, for everything, and my fiancée Basia, who became the center of my "new" family in Boston on October 11, 1997.

Publisher's Acknowledgments

We're proud of this book; please register your comments through our IDG Books Worldwide Online Registration Form located at http://my2cents.dummies.com.

Some of the people who helped bring this book to market include the following:

Acquisitions, Development, and Editorial

Project Editor: Tere Drenth

Acquisitions Editor: Ellen Camm

Copy Editor: William F. McManus

Media Development Manager: Joyce Pepple

Associate Permissions Editor: Heather Dismore

Technical Editors: Aaron deMello and Garrett Pease

CD-ROM Reviewers: Kevin Spencer, Joell Smith

Editorial Manager: Colleen Rainsberger

Editorial Assistant: Darren Meiss

Production

Project Coordinator: Sherry Gomoll

Layout and Graphics: Steve Arany, Cameron Booker, Lou Boudreau, Linda M. Boyer, Angela Bush-Sisson, Maridee V. Ennis, Todd Klemme, Drew R. Moore, Mark C. Owens, M. Anne Sipahimalani, Kate Snell

Proofreaders: Michael Bolinger, Christine Berman, Kelli Botta, Michelle Croninger, Rachel Garvey, Nancy Price, Rebecca Senninger, Janet M. Withers

Indexer: Christine Spina

Special Help: Access Technology, Inc.; Stephanie Koutek, Proof Editor

General and Administrative

IDG Books Worldwide, Inc.: John Kilcullen, CEO; Steven Berkowitz, President and Publisher

IDG Books Technology Publishing: Brenda McLaughlin, Senior Vice President and Group Publisher

Dummies Technology Press and Dummies Editorial: Diane Graves Steele, Vice President and Associate Publisher; Kristin A. Cocks, Editorial Director; Mary Bednarek, Acquisitions and Product Development Director

Dummies Trade Press: Kathleen A. Welton, Vice President and Publisher; Kevin Thornton, Acquisitions Manager

IDG Books Production for Dummies Press: Beth Jenkins, Production Director; Cindy L. Phipps, Manager of Project Coordination, Production Proofreading, and Indexing; Kathie S. Schutte, Supervisor of Page Layout; Shelley Lea, Supervisor of Graphics and Design; Debbie J. Gates, Production Systems Specialist; Robert Springer, Supervisor of Proofreading; Debbie Stailey, Special Projects Coordinator; Tony Augsburger, Supervisor of Reprints and Bluelines; Leslie Popplewell, Media Archive Coordinator

Dummies Packaging and Book Design: Patti Crane, Packaging Specialist; Lance Kayser, Packaging Assistant; Kavish + Kavish, Cover Design

♦

The publisher would like to give special thanks to Patrick J. McGovern, without whom this book would not have been possible.

♦

Contents at a Glance

Cartoons at a Glance

By Rich Tennant

page 73

page 235

page 301

page 7

page 325

Fax: 508-546-7747 • E-mail: the5wave@tiac.net

Table of Contents

Introduction

· ·

As if the World Wide Web weren't reason enough to do cartwheels down the street, the globe is ablaze with the fire of a brand-new invention: *Java.* Nope, I'm not talking about the life-giving beverage (without which this book would not have been possible). I'm referring to the Java that has tens of millions of people around the world abuzz — a fresh blend of technology that brings the Web to life with dazzling animation, pulse-pounding sound, and full-blown interactivity, the likes of which the online community has never seen. With this book, you're poised to plunge headfirst into the most exciting craze ever to sweep the face of the Earth.

About This Book

One of the wonderful things about Java is its universal appeal; all Web surfers can add a dash or two of Java to their Web pages, bringing their Web sites to life with very little effort. And that's exactly what this book shows you how to do — create state-of-the-art Web pages using Java.

This book tells you where Java fits into the Internet, why Java has exploded onto the Web, and how Java promises to change the way you learn, work, and play. Of course, discovering this neat stuff about Java is just the beginning. The real purpose of this book is to show you how to give your Web pages a serious jolt of Java, electrifying them with the two forms of Java now on the market:

- ✔ **Java applets:** miniature applications that bring your Web pages to life with sound, action, and interactivity

- ✔ **JavaScript:** English-like commands that cause browsers to act a certain way

Yep, this book has everything you need to know to inject your pages with both flavors of Java. As icing on the cake (or cream in your coffee, if you will), I show you the best places on the Web to satisfy the constant Java cravings you're sure to get. Brace yourself — you stand a good chance of becoming a serious Java addict. After you have your first taste of Java, getting hooked is inevitable!

Foolish Assumptions

Although the title of this book says ...*For Dummies,* I'll bet dimes to donuts that you're no fool. You wouldn't be reading this book if you were. This book helps you make sense of Java and assumes that you already know a little bit about using the Web and creating Web pages. But don't worry if you're not a major Web-head.

Even if you've never seen Java in action before, you'll be just fine. If that's the case, the only thing you really need is a computer that can run a Java-savvy Web browser (for details, see Chapter 3). Assuming that you are comfortable using your computer, you'll soon be surfing the seas of Java on the World Wide Web and creating your very own Java-powered pages. To use this book, I assume that you are comfortable:

- ✔ Copying files and creating directories (or *folders*)
- ✔ Using an online service or a direct Internet connection
- ✔ Browsing and creating pages on the World Wide Web

The CD-ROM that comes with this book contains a directory of Internet Service Providers (ISPs) that support Java-savvy browsers, as well as a special ISP "kit" that will get you up and running with AT&T WorldNet Service — a national, well-respected, Java-loving ISP — in no time flat (see Appendix A for a guide to using this CD-ROM). And Chapter 3 shows you how to set yourself up with a Java-savvy browser even if the online service you already use doesn't offer one.

How to Use This Book

I wrote this book to make creating Java-powered Web pages easy. Because you have your own comfort level with using the Web, creating Web pages, and Java's role in the whole scope of things (or even with talking about these things at a dinner party), I try to cover all the bases. Aren't I thoughtful?

You betcha. I organized the book in a modular fashion, making it easy to find the information you need without having to read the entire book from start to finish. Instead, you can just cruise through the Table of Contents for specific information that interests you. For example, if you're comfortable using the Web already, but don't have a Java-savvy browser, you can jump right to Chapter 3.

However, if you're already surfing the Web with a Java-ready browser, you needn't bother with Chapter 3 at all. Instead, you may jump to Part II, where you actually hook up your own Java-powered pages, starting with a crash course in HTML. Now, if you don't want to deal with applets at all, you can always start with Part III and begin hooking up JavaScripts. If you're hard core, you may just leap into Chapter 13 and begin weaving both applets and scripts into your pages at the same time. Think of it as a double shot of espresso with a cappuccino chaser; you'll be wired for days.

However, if you're brand-spanking-new to Java, or if you want a nice, detailed overview of everything from soup to nuts, then consider starting at the very beginning (always a good place to start) and working your way through the book from there. Not only is this approach easier on the heart, but you'll also discover many cool things about the Internet, the Web, and Java. You're sure to impress friends, relatives, and in-laws at your next backyard barbecue.

Regardless of where you begin or where you end, from time to time, you're going to stumble upon text that `looks like this`. I use this style to represent code or other text exactly as you'll find it on-screen. Such text may be a Web address or code that you type to weave Java into your own Web page. In both cases, be careful to enter the text exactly as shown — even your use of uppercase and lowercase letters must match the text I provide to you, unless I tell you otherwise!

At times, where you're required to type in text other than code, it'll look **like this.**

Also, because I assume that you're already comfortable surfing the Web, I thought it'd be nice to remove "http://" from Web addresses altogether — today's browsers don't actually need it. Why clutter things up with "`http://`" if it isn't even necessary?

How This Book Is Organized

This book is organized into five parts, each part capable of standing on its own. However, if you want to, you can read through one part and into the next one. Heck, you can even read this book from front to back, if you're so inclined. Although this book follows a modular design, meaning each chapter can stand on its own, reading straight through is a lot of fun. Take your pick!

Part I: Caught in a Web of Intrigue

In Part I, you find out exactly why everyone on the Web these days seems to be scrambling for a taste of Java. You discover what the Web really is and its relationship to the Internet and Java. Here you'll find out how to get your hands on a Java-savvy browser, how to take it for a spin to see some of the coolest Java sites on the Web, and how to stay current with the fast and furiously changing world of Java. You'll realize that the best Java-powered Web sites and search engines are only a click away, so you can get a quick Java fix any time you start to feel out of touch with the rest of the Java technogeeks living in Java-induced bliss.

Part II: It's Applet Pickin' Time!

In Part II, you get your hands on Java applets, the most powerful form of Java you can find. I show you how to find and distinguish between the original Java 1.0 applets and the latest crop of Java 1.1 applets, and how to weave both types of applets into your Web page, customizing them to fit your needs. In this part, you create dazzling, living Web pages for the world to see.

Part III: A Sip of JavaScript without the Bitter Aftertaste of Programming

In Part III, you find out about scripts, Java's alternative to applets. Discover how scripting languages differ from more complex programming languages (like the one used to create applets). In this part, you discover how to use JavaScript to customize existing scripts and to fine-tune your Java-powered pages.

You'll also discover how to combine both applets and scripts, bringing the best of both Java flavors to your Web pages, and how sniffer scripts can give your pages the utmost Java-power, allowing you to dynamically generate scripts and applets on the fly, fully customizing your pages specifically for the make, model, and versions of browsers that visit your pages. Finally, you'll find out what the future holds for applets and scripts, and what HTML 4.0 and JavaBeans are all about.

Part IV: The Part of Tens

Part IV lists the top places on the Web to find Java help when you need it most, Java applets to pick and place into your Web pages, and the top sites for finding scripts. With the very best Java joints on the Net, your cup will runneth over. And just in case your Java percolator goes on the fritz, Part V describes the top Java snafus you may face at one time or another.

Part V: Appendixes

Okay, I know what you're thinking: "Where does this guy get off calling a glossary and some appendixes a *part?*"

Sure, Part V doesn't have any chapters in it, but it's packed with useful information nonetheless!

- ✔ Appendix A is your road map to the CD-ROM that comes with this book. Look here for all the information you need to locate the applets, scripts, sample Web pages, utilities, and other goodies included on the CD-ROM. Not bad, huh?

- ✔ Appendix B takes you to Java 1.1 and beyond! Since Java 1.0 was first poured onto the Web, things have changed a little (boy, have they). Appendix B serves up the perfect recipe for weaving Java 1.0 and Java 1.1 into your Web pages and prepares you for the future when you will be using HTML 4.0.

Icons Used in This Book

If you're like me, reading nothing but straight text is a killer. After a while, your eyes start to twitch and your mind starts to wander. That's why many books are full of illustrations — to break up the text and give you something to look at as you're reading.

This book is no different. Each chapter contains pictures to help you make sense of the material (and to keep your eyes from bugging out). But this book has another important graphical element: Each chapter is brimming with icons designed to highlight specific information. In fact, the icons used in this book are organized so that you can skim through the book and find much of the most important information at a glance!

The information beside this icon can save you time, money, or both.

This icon alerts you to other *...For Dummies* books that relate directly to the discussion at hand, books that are worth taking a gander at if you want to learn more about the current topic.

This icon marks stuff you should tuck away in the back of your mind — you'll need it at some point in the near future.

If you're interested in the nitty gritty, if you like tech talk, or if you're really into the material you're reading, check out the information marked with the Technical Stuff icons. Although this info isn't necessary to get the job done, it does make interesting bedtime reading.

Whenever the discussion involves stuff that you can find on the CD-ROM that comes with this book, you see this icon. When you find this icon, you can put down the book (if you can tear yourself away from the thrill-a-minute pace) and pop in the CD-ROM to get your hands on the subject of the moment. Can life get any better than this?

What good would a book dealing with the Web be without a goodly supply of Web addresses? Not much, which is why this icon appears from time to time to supply you with the freshest and most exhilarating Web nuggets related to Java and JavaScript. Don't be shy: Fire up your Web browser and give 'em a whirl.

Never ignore this icon! Even if you skip the other icons, this is one you don't want to miss. Trust me.

So, Off You Go!

You're still reading this Intro? Jeez, get the lead out and get on with it! A dazzling, exciting new world awaits, and you're holding the key. So what are you waiting for? Go get your jolt of Java!

Part I
Caught in a Web of Intrigue

The 5th Wave   By Rich Tennant

"HONEY! OUR WEB BROWSER GOT OUT LAST NIGHT AND DUMPED THE TRASH ALL OVER MR. BELCHER'S HOME PAGE!"

In this part . . .

Tired of feeling left out of the online craze? Starting to suspect that keeping up with Internet buzzwords is a full-time job? Want to know exactly what Java is and how it fits into the whole World Wide Web? If so, then Part I is the place for you to get your feet wet. This part brings you quickly up to speed on Java and its role on the Web and even shows you how to get ahold of a Java-savvy browser so that you can view Java-powered pages for yourself. And because Java is such a rapidly changing technology, I tell you how to stay on the cutting edge with some of the best online Java resources and searching utilities.

Chapter 1
A Thirst for Java

*F*irst it was the Internet. Then the World Wide Web. And just when you thought it was safe to remove the cotton from your ears, there's another buzzword — Java — ringing loud and clear. Java has exploded onto the scene, promising to change the way you learn, work, and play. But what is Java? And to be just a tad bit cynical, aren't all the other buzzwords promising the same thing, too?

For answers to these questions, you must take a closer look at each buzzword and be able to separate fact from fiction when it comes to the surrounding hype. As luck would have it, I happen to have my official technology tour guide hat and buzzword microscope handy. Follow me.

The Internet: Where It All Started

Before the hysteria surrounding the World Wide Web and Java surfaced, the Internet was all the rage. Although it skyrocketed in popularity in the past five years, the Internet happens to be nearly 30 years old!

The Internet was developed shortly after World War II to provide U.S. government officials with a reliable means of communication capable of transmitting electronic messages, even in the midst of a nuclear attack. From there, Internet has grown into today's granddaddy of computer networks — a vast, globally connected system of computers and people. Unfortunately, the Internet has always been a royal pain to use.

Because the Internet originally required a significant amount of computer expertise, it was off-limits to the masses for the first 20 years or so. Most folks could only sit idly by and listen half-heartedly as others gushed about the joys of being connected to the Internet. Zap! as they sent electronic mail to their more savvy friends on the other side of the globe. Zing! as they scoured the data-rich ether, digging up timely nuggets of information that consistently impressed their bosses. Pow! as they bought and sold countless and varied items over the wire without leaving the comfort of their home computers. Crunch! as they shed pounds of excess weight thanks to the delicious, fat-free recipes to which only those on the Internet were privy.

And so it went. Zap! Zing! Pow! Crunch! The Internet was tremendously exciting and paid great dividends to those who had access and knew how to use it, but offered squat to the rest of us.

The Doors Creak Open with Online Services

Initially, the terms *cyberspace* and *Net* referred only to the formal Internet — a global assortment of smaller, specially interconnected computer networks acting as one giant, seamless network. In recent years, however, the scope of these terms has expanded to include all computer networks that are attached to the Internet, regardless of how limited that connection may be. Consider, for example, commercial online services such as America Online, CompuServe, and Prodigy. Only within the past few years have these independent networks given their members access to the Internet; originally, commercial online services were entirely self-contained and isolated from the rest of the electronic world. Up until a few years ago, users of these services could only access information that was specific to the service. America Online users could only access information residing on America Online, CompuServe users could only access information residing on CompuServe, and Prodigy users could only access information residing on Prodigy. Such restrictions prevented commercial online services from being considered part of cyberspace; their users weren't *really* on the Net.

The commercial online services quickly responded to the piercing screams of their members demanding Internet access. Having ripped open the floodgates that once prevented access to outside information, most online service providers now allow millions of members daily to spill out into the open seas of the Internet. As tributaries of the Internet, these services are now considered part of cyberspace. If you're on America Online, CompuServe, Prodigy, or any other service connected to the Internet in any way, you're part of the Net.

At about the same time, online services opened up access to the Internet, and the term *Information Superhighway* was coined. Banking on the promise of computer information becoming as easy to access and navigate as television, politicians furiously began to hype the coming revolution. While visions of lightning-fast connections to every conceivable type of information danced in our heads, the realization that this would take years to become a reality forced those who previously hyped the Information Superhighway to confront the pivotal question: *When?*

If the hype surrounding the Information Superhighway held true, by now you'd be surfing the Internet with a remote control from the comfort of your living-room Lazy Boy. You would bank, shop, order food, go to school, chat face-to-face with friends and family, and find your soul mate, all with the same ease as tuning in to your favorite television shows. Unfortunately, you're not doing anything of the sort — are you? Don't worry; almost nobody is at the moment unless they have WebTV. Instead, most of us are perched in front of our personal computers absorbed in the closest thing available: the World Wide Web.

WebTV is a nifty little box that attaches to your television set, allowing you to connect to the World Wide Web using nothing more than a remote control. If you usually sit in front of a computer to connect to the World Wide Web, imagine making that connection from the comfort of your couch at home. That's what WebTV is all about — it lets you connect to the Web easily, at home (from your living room or bedroom), without having to bother with a computer.

Welcome to the Web

The World Wide Web, commonly known as *the Web,* is to the Internet what hot fudge, whipped cream, and sprinkles are to vanilla ice cream: sheer heaven. The traditional, plain vanilla Internet is cryptic and difficult to navigate. Although it offers a world of information, you need a suite of special software programs and detailed knowledge of each program just to scratch the surface of what's out there. The World Wide Web, however, sits on top of the plain vanilla Internet, turning it into a sumptuous, decadent treat.

Using the Web, you now can instantly access and easily understand what was once nearly impossible to find and terribly confusing to use. Instead of forcing you to learn a new tool for each type of information out there, the Web gives you access to everything through one simple tool. And where the Internet is cryptic and text-based, the Web is a rich and attractive blend of text, images, and sound. The difference between the two is like night and day or, more accurately, like the difference between newspaper and television. Essentially, the same information is available regardless of how you get it. The Web just makes getting it easier.

But even the World Wide Web doesn't come close to fulfilling everyone's expectations of the Internet. Even with hot fudge and whipped cream, ice cream is still ice cream. But add a touch of Java, and that's another story. To truly appreciate the significance of Java, you first must understand the environment for which Java was designed — the World Wide Web — and what the Web was like before Java came onto the scene.

Hyperlinking through the Web

The easiest way to describe the Web is to call it a graphical doorway to the Internet. Whereas the traditional Internet was text-based, requiring users to memorize and type cryptic commands in order to do anything, the Web is entirely graphics-based. When you enter the Web, you don't have to type a thing. Using the mouse to navigate, you can click your way through scads of information quickly and easily. Instead of memorizing commands and typing them into the computer, you simply point and click on *hyperlinks* — images (hypermedia) or words (hypertext) that you can select to access new information automatically.

A remote control for your computer

To understand how hyperlinks work, think for a moment about your television's remote control. Using a remote control to channel surf is the closest some folks have ever come to surfing the Web:

✔ **With both the remote control and the Web, you click a button or two, and bingo! You're viewing information.** When you're channel surfing, you don't have to put much thought into it: You just click buttons on the remote control and off you go. You can cycle through all of the stations by pressing the up or down buttons or tune in to a specific channel by pressing the appropriate button or combination of buttons.

Clicking on hyperlinks with your mouse is like pressing the up or down button on a remote control. You don't have to know exactly where you're headed; you can just sit back and let the channels roll by. What appears may be exactly what you were expecting or a complete surprise. You also can type in the location (typically known as an *address* or *URL — Uniform Resource Locator*) of a specific piece of information to view it. Using the Web this way is more like punching in a specific channel on your television's remote control — in both cases, you know exactly where you want to go and you supply the proper information to get there.

✔ **Both your TV's remote and the Web isolate you from the details of what's going on behind the scenes.** Watching television doesn't require any special knowledge about the technology. You don't have to know how the programs are broadcast, who produces them, how they are created, or any other technological details to tune into your favorite shows. Do the signals carrying the broadcast travel through the airwaves, cable, or satellite? What type of film is used to record the scenes, and how is that film converted into a television signal? None of this matters to you. You simply press buttons, tune in, and relax.

Accessing information on the World Wide Web is similar. You don't have to know any of the gory details about the sea of data swirling around out there. Simply select a hyperlink with your mouse, and away you go.

Of course, the Web isn't *exactly* like your television — if it were, you wouldn't be reading this book! The following are some important ways in which these technologies differ:

✔ **Channels galore:** With TV, you're limited in the number of channels you can access. Even those lucky viewers with cable or a satellite dish are still choosing from a finite number of channels. But with the Web, the number of hyperlinks is nearly limitless. You could spend every second of your life, from birth to death, clicking on hyperlinks and never get to them all. When you choose a hyperlink, it almost always takes you to more hyperlinks! Amazing as it may seem, hundreds of millions of hyperlinks exist on the Web, with thousands more being added every hour.

✔ **Global access:** Depending on what town you're in, the numbers you punch into a television's remote control don't always take you to the same station. Plus, what's playing on a given station depends on what time it is when you tune in! Not so on the Web. True, the information in a link is subject to change from time to time depending on who put it there and why, but what you find on the Web doesn't revolve around a programming schedule the way television shows do. And not only is the Web independent of time, but it's also independent of space. People around the world get the very same information when they click on the same hyperlink.

✔ **Trick or treat?** With television, you generally know what you're going to run into. Sure, you don't know what's on *every* station at *every* moment of the day, but you know more or less what types of shows you're going to find when you begin flipping though channels. In fact, this is one of the major gripes of television viewers: Between the reruns, the boring and unappealing shows, and the commercials, you can find yourself surfing stations in vain for something worth watching!

With the Web, however, you're afloat in a vast sea of information —
more information than you probably know what to do with, actually.
When you click on a hyperlink, you don't always know what you're
getting into. In fact, not knowing what's likely to happen when you
select a hyperlink is part of the thrill of using the Web. Most of the time,
you receive information in line with what you are expecting. Sometimes,
however, hyperlinks point to stuff you'd never anticipate.

In many ways, using the Web is like a giant Easter egg hunt. If the
information connected to a hyperlink is particularly interesting, useful,
or enjoyable, you're said to have stumbled onto an *Easter egg*. If the
Web site is distasteful or otherwise undesirable, consider it a bad egg
and move on. By simply following a trail of hyperlinks, I stumble onto
many glorious Easter eggs on the Web. Occasionally, however, I run into
the digital equivalent of a rotten egg and must retreat in another
direction with my nose firmly pinched shut. This is all part of the game
of selecting hyperlinks with no particular destination in mind. Sometimes you win; sometimes you lose.

Hypertext — using words as a launch pad

Hypertext is the most common type of hyperlink found on the Web.
Hypertext is either a word or a phrase that appears in electronic documents
and is linked to information in other documents. When you select hypertext,
your screen automatically displays the document and information linked to
that word or phrase. You aren't stuck viewing this new information, of
course; you can easily return to the document containing the original
hyperlink by using a Back or Return option. Or if another hyperlink is
available, you can just keep linking to new pages.

If you've used the Web before, you know what hypertext looks like. Typically, hypertext is distinguished from standard text by its color and style.
The *browser* software you use to connect to the Web, such as Netscape
Navigator or Internet Explorer, determines what the hypertext you encounter looks like. Take a look at Figure 1-1. This document contains several
hypertext items, which clearly stand out from the rest of the text (especially
if this book were printed in color).

The browser that is used to display the document in Figure 1-1 identifies
hypertext items by coloring them blue and underlining them. Although
underlined blue text is a convention used by this particular browser, others
may use different colors and styles to identify hypertext items. In all cases,
however, a unique color and style makes hypertext items easy to distinguish
from standard text.

Although most Web browsers allow you to choose the color and/or style in
which you want hypertext to appear, you almost always must specify at
least one unique feature. That is, most browsers won't allow you to make
hypertext look like normal text; at the very least, you must give it either a

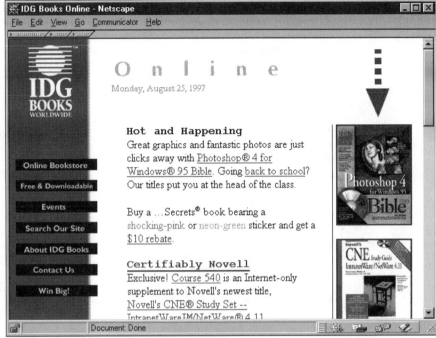

IDG Books Online - Netscape

File Edit View Go Communicator Help

O n l i n e
Monday, August 25, 1997

Hot and Happening
Great graphics and fantastic photos are just
clicks away with Photoshop® 4 for
Windows® 95 Bible. Going back to school?
Our titles put you at the head of the class.

Buy a ...Secrets® book bearing a
shocking-pink or neon-green sticker and get a
$10 rebate.

Certifiably Novell
Exclusive! Course 540 is an Internet-only
supplement to Novell's newest title,
Novell's CNE® Study Set --
IntranetWare IM/NetWare® 4.11

Online Bookstore
Free & Downloadable
Events
Search Our Site
About IDG Books
Contact Us
Win Big!

Document: Done

Figure 1-1:
You can
easily
distinguish
hypertext
from
standard
text by its
color and/or
style.

unique color or style. Personally, I prefer that my browser display hypertext
in both a unique color *and* style. After all, what good is hypertext if you can't
tell that it's hypertext?

Hypermedia — springboarding from images

Take the concept of hypertext one step farther and apply it to both still and
moving images. What you have now is *hypermedia,* another type of hyperlink
technology that you can find in nearly all Web documents. Instead of linking
a text blurb to additional information, hypermedia enables you to connect
to that information from images and animation. As a result, anything you see
on-screen can potentially link you to more information.

In many cases, all you find in Web documents are images. Take Figure 1-2, for
example. This document displays only images. The words appearing under
some of these images happen to be part of the images; they aren't hypertext
or even standard text. Nope, in this case, everything you see is an image.
And, thanks to hypermedia, each image is linked to information.

Years ago, the term *hypermedia* didn't actually mean the images were linked
to information or that they were capable of being used as part of the navigation process. Before the Web was invented, it was enough that hypertext
items merely be *linked* to images and animations. In this sense, just the

capability to easily navigate to different types of media (images, animation, sound, and so on) using text was enough to justify the term *hypermedia*. Today, however, the term has expanded to mean that the media itself can be linked to information.

What are you getting into?

Exactly what type of information can hypertext and hypermedia be linked to, anyway? In the preceding section, I proclaim that these items provide links to documents full of information, but I haven't said one word about what a document is or what type of information it may contain. (You may want to grab a cup of coffee before tackling this stuff!)

Web pages — the building blocks

All the information that is accessible using the Web is actually stored in documents, or *files*. You're probably familiar with the concept of files already; you use them on your personal computer all the time. Whenever you use a word processor, send an electronic mail message (e-mail), or draw a picture using a computer graphics program, you're dealing with files.

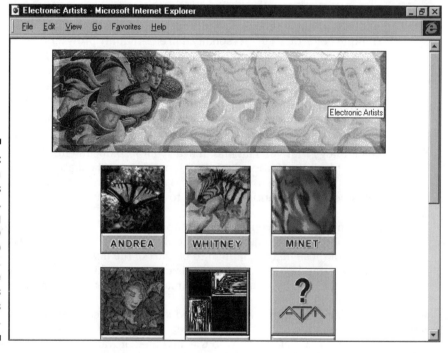

Figure 1-2: Hypermedia allows images, both moving and still, to be linked to information. Every image in this document is a hyperlink.

With standard computer programs (such as word processors and graphics design programs), you typically view the information (be it graphics, text, or whatever) one file at a time in each window. On the Web, however, you can have access to many different files at once from within a single window. A special file known as a *Web page* may point to (or *reference*) other files that contain any combination of text, images, animation, and sound.

Web pages don't just appear all by themselves. Just as you need a word processor to view text files and a graphics program to view image files, you need a Web program to view Web files. This program, called a *Web browser,* is responsible for displaying the files and hyperlinks that abound on the Web, allowing you to navigate the Web's vast contents. You may say that the browser is your surfboard for surfing the Web. (Chapter 3 covers Web browsers in mind-boggling depth.)

Typically, hyperlinks point to Web pages. However, they may also point to individual pieces of information, such as a single image or a sound clip. Usually, when you select a hyperlink, the browser discards the current page and displays a new one that contains the associated information. But this rule is not without exceptions. In particular, when you select a hyperlink to a sound clip, the browser doesn't bother to discard the current page and display a new one. Instead, the browser remains at the page containing the hyperlink and simply plays the sound.

The greatest advantage of the World Wide Web over the traditional Internet is the way in which the Web organizes information. The Internet simply stores information in directories scattered around the world. If you want something on the Internet, you have to find and download it before you can actually use it. The Web, on the other hand, uses hyperlinks to organize multiple files containing different pieces of information that reside on the Internet into larger, special files called *Web pages.* A Web page can contain text, graphics, animation, and sound, which you view all at once using a browser.

Web pages can be any width or height, extending infinitely in either direction. Of course, you only see the portion that fits on your computer screen — when viewing a large page in a browser window, you can scroll horizontally or vertically as needed. This process is similar to how you view a text document using a word processor: When you get to the bottom of the page, you scroll down to see more text. When you want to return to the top, you scroll up. If text extends horizontally beyond the margin, you can scroll sideways to see it. Scrolling is nothing new, even if Web pages are.

Web pages are created by people like you and me. If you've been on the Web before, you know how different each page is. The author of a page decides what to include in it, how it looks or sounds, and what hyperlinks to create. The author even determines what information the hypertext and hypermedia links are attached to.

Surveying Web sites

Web sites are collections of interlinked Web pages, much as a book is a collection of printed pages held together by a binding. Note that the pages contained in a site need not contain related information. The subject matter a page contains has nothing to do with its capability to be linked to other pages. As a result, the pages of a Web site can cover a diverse array of subjects.

For instance, although a soccer site is likely to be dedicated entirely to that sport, and a corporate site, such as a clothing store, is likely to contain pages relating to its product line, whether all the pages in a site stick to that topic is up to whoever creates the site (or whoever owns the company). The soccer site can just as easily contain pages about knitting and macramé. For that matter, a clothing store site may contain a few pages describing how to throw a memorable cocktail party.

Think of the Web as a giant filing cabinet, with each site being a manila folder inside it. Web pages, in turn, are documents inside these manila folders. Nothing prevents a mishmash of unrelated documents from being stuffed inside the folder, and nothing prevents a site from containing a bizarre combination of pages. This is the nature of the Web. It's a beautiful thing.

The home page is where the heart is

So how do you connect to a Web site if it is merely a collection of interlinked pages? Simple: through the home page. Each site has an official access point called a *home page*. From the home page, you get an overview of the site and can begin exploring its associated pages. A properly designed home page is, in essence, like a hospitable host or hostess. It invites you in and tells you all about the things you can see and do during your visit.

The home page is the most important page of any site. It is the starting point for your journey, and it sets the tone for what to expect within that site. In addition, the home page supplies links to the major pages in the site. As such, the home page is usually the most attractive and well-designed of the pages in a site.

Uniform resource locators

The concept of pages and sites is all well and good, but if you haven't used the Web before, you're probably wondering how in the world you connect to the sites in the first place. Do you just fire up the browser and scream "Pepsi!" at the top of your lungs in hopes of reaching the Pepsi site's home page? And how do you change directions in midstream? Suppose you get to the Pepsi Web site, but decide that you'd rather be at the Coke site instead. Certainly Pepsi won't provide a hyperlink to its competition. So how do you tell your browser to view the Coke site without a hyperlink?

In my reverie about the World Wide Web earlier in this chapter, I indicate that, with the advent of the Web on the Internet, you'll never have to type again. I lied. In reality, you do end up typing now and then on the Web. Sure, once connected to the Web, you can navigate entirely by clicking on hyperlinks with your mouse button. But to make the most efficient use of your time, you'll occasionally need to type *Uniform Resource Locators* (*URLs*).

A *URL* is nothing more than a special address that tells your browser how to find and use the billions of files scattered across the Web. Files on the Web include pages, word processing files, spreadsheet files, graphics files, audio files, and even executable software programs. Because every file on the Web has a unique URL associated with it, typing a URL into your browser takes you directly to the one page you want to view. For example, if you know the URL for the Coke home page, you can view that page at any time by typing its URL into your browser (you do this by typing the URL into your browser's Location Area, described in more detail in Chapter 3).

What's in a name?

URLs are organized in a very specific way. You read them from left to right, just like a telephone number. The first piece of information in a URL describes what type of protocol the browser must use to retrieve a given file. (A *protocol* is a set of rules the browser must follow to successfully locate and retrieve a file. See the section in this chapter entitled "Protocols: Computers have manners, too!" for the lowdown on protocols.) Common protocols used in URLs are http, ftp, and gopher.

Although all URLs begin with a protocol, the manner in which the protocol appears may vary. Depending on the protocol itself, it will be followed by either a colon and two slashes (`://`) or simply a colon (`:`). For example, the http protocol is specified in a URL by using a colon and two slashes (`http://`), whereas the news protocol is specified with only a colon (`news:`). Fortunately, you don't have to memorize every protocol out there to use them with your browser. As it turns out, every protocol is represented using a colon and two slashes with the exception of news (`news:`) and mailto (`mailto:`).

The news protocol is used to access newsgroups, which can be thought of as Internet discussion areas (I discuss newsgroups in Chapter 4). The mailto protocol, on the other hand, lurks behind every hyperlink that you click, opening an e-mail form within your Web browser. Unlike the news or http protocols, mailto isn't something that you actually type into a browser yourself. Instead, mailto works behind the scenes, allowing some hyperlinks to deliver e-mail messages.

What follows the protocol depends on the protocol itself. With the exception of the news and mailto protocols, the second part of most URLs is the name of the computer storing the file (the second part of a news URL specifies a newsgroup, and the second part of a mailto URL specifies an e-mail address). This isn't a name you or I might use when referring to our personal computers. Not even close! It's a name used to identify computers whose contents are available on the Web, and it is formally called a *host.* As a result, you won't see names like "Humphry," "WickedFast," or "Aaron's Little Buddy" used in this portion of a URL. Instead, you'll see rather cryptic names typically separated by periods into two or three different parts, like so:

- ✔ `www.mantiscorp.com` (Mantis Development Corporation)
- ✔ `www.toysfortots.org` (Toys For Tots organization)
- ✔ `www.bc.edu` (Boston College)
- ✔ `www.whitehouse.gov` (The White House)

The third and final part of a URL is the *directory path* leading to the file and the name of the file itself. This path identifies a hierarchy of directories (or *folders,* if you're a Macintosh or Windows 95 user) on the computer that is specified in the preceding part of the URL. Each level of the hierarchy is separated by a slash. The browser looks inside each directory, one at a time, until it reaches the file specified at the end.

The path may be quite complex, containing a number of directories, or terribly simple. Sometimes, no directories are specified in the path, only files. And sometimes, not even the filename is specified. When no directory path is specified, the browser knows to look for the file the moment it connects to the computer; it doesn't have to burrow down into a directory. When no filename is specified, a default filename is used. In the case of the http protocol, the most popular on the Web, the default filename is index.html. If you ever specify an http URL without supplying a filename, the browser automatically looks for an index.html file. Notice the various complexities of directory paths in the following URLs:

- ✔ `http://www.mantiscorp.com/index.html`
- ✔ `http://www.mantiscorp.com`
- ✔ `http://www.toysfortots.org/index.html`
- ✔ `http://www.bc.edu/bc_org/evp/iir/fb/factbook.html`
- ✔ `http://www.whitehouse.gov/WH/welcome.html`
- ✔ `http://www.whitehouse.gov/WH/EOP/html/principals.html`

In the preceding examples, the last piece of information you see is the name of a Web page itself. You can easily identify this name by looking for the .html extension. All Web pages have this extension because all Web pages are actually Hypertext Markup Language (HTML) documents. The only exception is when the computer on which the page is stored isn't capable of using more than three character extensions when naming files — then the URL ends with .htm instead.

In the case of the second URL (www.mantiscorp.com), no name is specified. As a result, the browser automatically looks for index.html. Because this is functionally equivalent to the URL above it, most folks simply leave off the name of the file when entering an http URL that leads to an index.html file.

Because index.html is the default filename for http URLs, most folks name their home pages index.html. As a result, when they give out a URL leading to their home page, they need supply only the protocol and directory and don't have to bother including the filename.

URL overload

Remember, you don't have to memorize scads of URLs to use the Web. Even though you may not know the URL for a particular file, the hyperlinks to that page do. Behind every hyperlink is a URL ready to be put to use. When you select a hyperlink, you're actually giving your browser the URL associated with that link; your browser then retrieves and displays the file that URL identifies.

Sometimes, a hyperlink to a Web page that you want to visit isn't immediately available. However, if you know the URL of that particular destination, you can type it in.

Kicking .asp and taking names

Occasionally you run into Web pages that end in .asp instead of the standard .html or .htm, which might lead you to think that a new standard is emerging. Not so! The .asp extension was invented by Microsoft Corporation and is used to indicate that the page is an "Active Server Page" (ASP). Active Server Pages are actually standard HTML pages that contain special nonstandard commands, making it necessary to clearly distinguish them from plain old-fashioned HTML Web pages. As a result, the .asp extension is used to make these pages easy to identify and to prevent potential confusion.

Fortunately, you can tell your browser to save URLs so that you don't have to remember them — like adding a telephone number to the speed-dial feature on a modern phone. For example, you can tell the browser to save the preceding URL after you enter it the first time. Then, whenever you feel like visiting the Toys For Tots page in the future, you just choose it from the list of URLs saved in your browser. This process, known as *bookmarking* or *hotlinking* a URL, is supported by all browsers and is a tremendous time-saver!

How you enter a URL into a browser, tell the browser to remember a URL, and visit a site that you've previously saved depends entirely on the browser software you use. Because I'm dealing with the Web in very general terms in this chapter, I keep the discussion about browsers general as well. For a more detailed understanding of how to enter and save a URL in the various browsers, turn to Chapter 3. There, you discover how to find and install a browser capable of dealing with Java, something not all browsers are equipped to handle, and how to save URLs of your favorite sites (many of which are sure to be injected with Java!).

Hypertext Markup Language (HTML)

All Web pages are created using a special language known as *Hypertext Markup Language* (HTML), which allows you to organize text, graphics, animation, and sound into documents that a browser can understand. HTML is the glue that holds the Web together; it is the language that makes hypertext and hypermedia possible.

Although HTML is indeed a language, it is not the type of programming language typically associated with computers and software development. You don't have to study for years or have a college degree to learn it. Instead, HTML is a relatively friendly markup language that practically everyone can begin using within a day or two.

Markup languages define a formal set of rules and procedures for preparing text to be electronically interpreted and presented; with HTML, you surround text and references to files with special directives known as *tags*. Tags are used to specify how the text or files are supposed to appear when viewed with a Web browser; they are used to "mark up" the document in a way that the Web browser understands.

Using tags to mark up a document for electronic publication is easy. You can take a standard word processor document, add a dash or two of HTML, and voilà — you've created a Web page. Not bad, considering that creating a simple page can take less than 15 minutes.

In truth, a Web page is nothing more than a text file that contains references to any number of image, animation, and sound files that the browser retrieves, assembles, and displays when that page is accessed. All files are stored independently of the pages in which they appear; that is, files aren't stored inside of the Web pages that display them. Instead, HTML merely *references,* or points to, these files, telling the browser exactly where they're located so it can go out and get them when the time comes for the page to be displayed.

Figure 1-3 shows a portion of the HTML source code used to create a Web page appearing earlier in this chapter (refer to Figure 1-2). Although HTML may seem like gibberish at first, after a few days learning the language, it all makes perfect sense. But if mastering the language seems like too daunting a task for you, you'll be happy to know that special-purpose tools exist that let you create Web pages without knowing a spec of HTML. But if you want a really dazzling Web page — one enhanced with the glory of Java — you have to know a bit more about HTML. Check out Chapter 4.

Protocols: Computers have manners, too!

If you think the idea of a Web browser being able to access and display pages containing information stored on computers scattered around the world is a bit magical, join the crowd. It is indeed a tremendous feat, made possible by a number of innovative technologies.

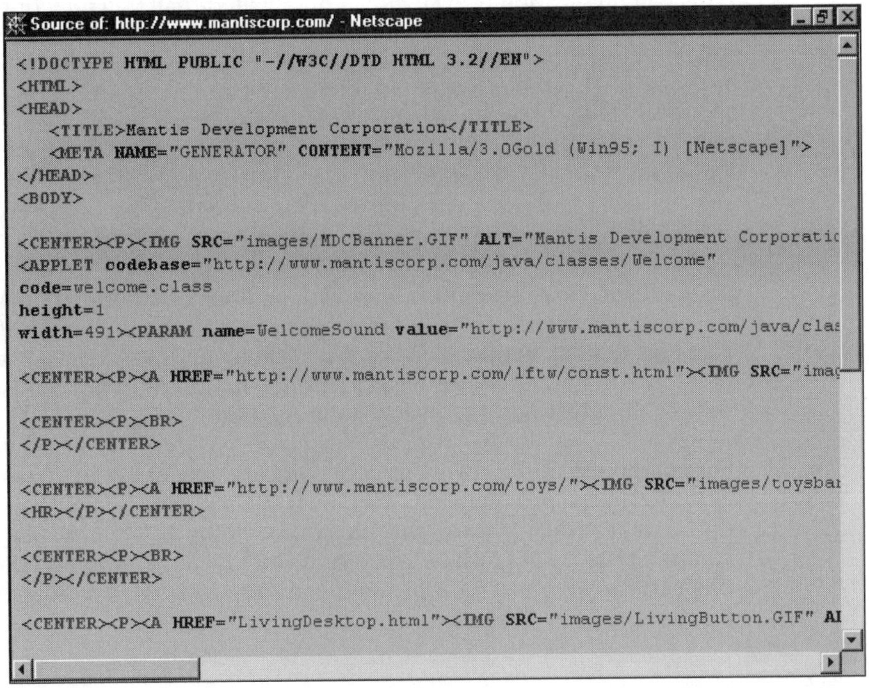

Figure 1-3:
Hypertext
Markup
Language
(HTML) is
the glue
that holds
the Web
together;
every page
on the Web
is created
using
HTML.

```
<!DOCTYPE HTML PUBLIC "-//W3C//DTD HTML 3.2//EN">
<HTML>
<HEAD>
    <TITLE>Mantis Development Corporation</TITLE>
    <META NAME="GENERATOR" CONTENT="Mozilla/3.0Gold (Win95; I) [Netscape]">
</HEAD>
<BODY>

<CENTER><P><IMG SRC="images/MDCBanner.GIF" ALT="Mantis Development Corporatic
<APPLET codebase="http://www.mantiscorp.com/java/classes/Welcome"
code=welcome.class
height=1
width=491><PARAM name=WelcomeSound value="http://www.mantiscorp.com/java/clas

<CENTER><P><A HREF="http://www.mantiscorp.com/lftw/const.html"><IMG SRC="imag

<CENTER><P><BR>
</P></CENTER>

<CENTER><P><A HREF="http://www.mantiscorp.com/toys/"><IMG SRC="images/toysbar
<HR></P></CENTER>

<CENTER><P><BR>
</P></CENTER>

<CENTER><P><A HREF="LivingDesktop.html"><IMG SRC="images/LivingButton.GIF" AI
```

In particular, computers must be able to talk with one another for such sharing of information to take place. In essence, a browser must be able to ask, "May I have this piece of information?" to which the computer having the piece of information can say, "You bet, here it is," or "Are you nuts? This is confidential information. Get your grubby mitts off!"

If the browser is given access to the information it requests, it must then retrieve that information. This begins another conversation between the browser and the computer, which is quite different from the previous one. In this case, the computer having the information begins spitting it out at the browser as a continuous stream of data. The browser catches the information as it comes flying down the wire and displays that information to the user as it comes. This process, called *downloading* a page, continues until there's no more information to send, at which point the computer says, "All done," and the browser replies, "Thanks — much appreciated."

Although you may never know that this process is taking place, it's essentially what happens every time you surf the Web. Browsers are constantly asking for information, and computers on the Web are constantly supplying the information to them. In fact, this process is so common that it has its own name: *client-server relationship*. The browser is the client, asking for stuff all the time, and the computer is the server; it delivers, or *serves*, information.

This communication is even more complicated than you may think. Such conversations don't necessarily take place directly between the browsers and the computer. Heavens, no! That would be too easy. Remember, the Internet is a vast network of interconnected computers. What are the chances of your computer being directly connected to one located halfway around the world? Or in the next city, for that matter? Zilch. It's like having a direct telephone connection with someone: Unless you're the President of the United States and have a nifty red phone with an exclusive connection to the Kremlin, it's just not gonna happen, my friend.

Instead, you share telephone lines with millions of other people. When you dial, special computers help direct your call through the tangle of wires. The same basic thing happens on the Web. When your browser asks for a piece of information, the request passes through hundreds, if not thousands, of other computers before it reaches the right one.

For computers on a network to communicate effectively and pass requests along to the proper recipient, they must use a common language. If they don't, what results is the digital equivalent of the Tower of Babel: Every computer speaks its own language and can't be understood by the others. In this case, any request your browser makes is doomed; it won't get past the first computer on the network.

However, by using a common language, or *protocol,* networked computers are able to send and receive messages smoothly. As a message comes through, the computers check to see whether the message is for them. If it is, they respond. If it's not, they pass it along. This process continues until the message reaches its intended recipient, at which point a response is generally sent back.

Although this sounds time-consuming, it happens in a flash. Within seconds, the request message sent by your browser makes its way to the computer having the information it needs. And, just as quickly, your browser receives the response. If all goes well, the information is on its way in less time than it takes to scratch your head. Both your browser's request and the server's response rocket through the network, past scores of other computers along the way, a digital feat that is nothing short of astonishing. But, thanks to protocols, this terribly complicated process is something most folks take for granted.

Where the Web Falls Short

Although the Web is an incredible invention, unlike anything the world has seen before, it does have shortcomings. As the Web matures, myriad innovations will come along to address these shortcomings. Because Java is one such innovation that addresses many of the Web's current failings, it has become a red-hot topic.

Over the years, the Web has been refined in many ways. Eventually, it grew out of the control of its original creator and into the hands of companies eager to make it look and act as they wanted. For example, many folks wanted to include animation on Web pages. But the original Web standard didn't provide for animation, meaning that you couldn't add animation to a page and remain in compliance with the standards originally put forth by the Web's governing bodies.

If you wanted to add animation to a Web page a few years ago, you had to break the standard. Pure and simple. This wouldn't have been so bad if all browsers had supported nonstandard features such as this, but they didn't. Back then, there was no guarantee that a browser would understand the animation in your Web page. And because animation wasn't supported by most browsers, you couldn't be certain that everyone who visited your page would see the animation. It was entirely up to the browser to support or ignore nonstandard features — and you had no way of knowing what browser someone would use to access your page.

But the problem didn't end with animation. The Web lacked a number of other features that were simply too complex to add to the HTML standard at the rate people wanted to see them adopted. Tables, colored text, background images, and multiple-choice hyperlinks were just a few of the features the original HTML standard didn't support. As a result, each of these problems spawned different nonstandard solutions — solutions that are enhancements to HTML that haven't been approved by the Web's governing bodies (you find out more about HTML and the organizations that work to make it a standard in Chapter 5). But again, the solution you chose may or may not have been supported by every browser on the market. You simply couldn't guarantee that every visitor to your site would see the same thing unless the feature was part of the standard Web.

Fortunately, many of the best nonstandard features have been adopted as official Web standards over the past year or so, meaning that all modern browsers support them in the same way so you no longer have to worry whether end users will experience your site in its full glory. However, because the Web is still quite new, it needs more time to mature.

Unfortunately, users around the world continue to clamor for features that are difficult to add to the standard in time to satisfy everyone. As a result, the software companies that develop Web browsers must decide whether their products will support or ignore each new nonstandard feature.

Although Java is also a nonstandard addition to the Web, it is so powerful and flexible that it addresses many of the issues that were previously addressed by a host of nonstandard features. As a result, when a browser supports Java, it kills many nonstandard birds with one stone. Rather than attempting to include all nonstandard features as soon as they are dreamed up (the rough equivalent of finding all the needles in all the haystacks in the world), the simple addition of Java to a browser provides a far more powerful and elegant solution.

Chapter 2

Java: Caffeine for the World Wide Web

About the time the World Wide Web was hatching in a particle physics lab in Switzerland (way back in the early 1990s), a California-based company called Sun Microsystems was embarking on an advanced technology odyssey of its own. Although developed separately and, initially, for entirely different purposes, the World Wide Web and Sun's Java would come together nearly four years later, jointly holding the promise of a second information revolution: a truly interactive Web.

Java is a programming language that enables software developers to create special little programs called *applets*. Unlike the software programs that you use on your personal computer, applets live inside Web pages. When a Web *browser,* the program that allows you to navigate the World Wide Web and view the pages that abound on it, encounters a page that contains applets, something special happens. If the browser is *Java-savvy* (that is, if it understands what applets are and knows how to deal with them), it downloads the applet and hands it off to your computer to run it. If the browser isn't Java-savvy, it simply ignores all the applets it encounters and displays Web pages as usual.

Because applets are actually little software programs, they can be programmed to do just about anything. How a given applet behaves is up to the software developer who creates it. For example, Java applets can play sounds, animate images, and allow you to interact in ways that were impossible before Java.

Thanks to these miraculous little Java applets, pages can contain interactive games, spreadsheets, graphics capabilities, and just about anything else you now do on your computer. But the magic is that you don't do these things using software programs residing on your home computer; instead, you do them across the World Wide Web, along with millions of other people who are free to access the same Web pages at exactly the same time.

Brewed at Sun Microsystems; Served around the World

Although millions of Web surfers are chanting the Java mantra day in and day out ("Java . . . Java . . . Java . . . Java . . . Java . . ."), you may be surprised to hear that Java started out in a completely different direction but veered off course, colliding with the Web at precisely the right moment. In fact, Java was initially positioned as a key technology in several different industries, none of which it successfully penetrated.

And then, as if out of nowhere, Shazam! The Web hit the big time, setting the global Internet ablaze. Almost overnight, Java became a buzzword dancing on the tip of the world's information-hungry tongue. After staggering through years of profound struggle, Java found a soul mate in the Web. Although it was just a few years ago that the dimly flickering light of Java was nearly extinguished by its very creators (see Chapter 1), Java today is red hot, on fire, and burning with the intensity of a thousand suns. It's revolutionizing the Web and the computer industry itself.

A Tonic for All Web Ills?

Today's Web is just the beginning of the world's relationship with Java. Tomorrow, you'll see Java spilling out of the Web into all aspects of your life. Because the Java technology is so rich in breadth and depth, it's not limited to the Web alone. You're likely to see it everywhere in the future: TVs, VCRs, appliances, and all other electronic consumer devices are candidates for the coming Java invasion. The Web just happens to be an ideal place to get it off the ground; but I guarantee that Java will spill over into the consumer-electronics market.

So if the Web is just the tip of the iceberg when it comes to realizing the potential of Java, why don't you hear about Java in other contexts? What's so special about the Web that Java found its home there? Well, the Web revolutionizes the way folks deal with information and provides a framework for Java to operate in — a framework with astounding global appeal. Because millions of people use the Web every day, it's the ideal way to inject Java technology into the mainstream marketplace.

However, a massive, international base of users isn't the only reason the Web is ideal for Java. Java has become a smash hit thanks to the Web's own limitations. As if made for each other, Java complements the Web perfectly, and the Web provides Java with the nurturing environment it needs to thrive. To understand why the Web makes an ideal mate for Java, consider the two areas where the Web is inherently weak without Java: dynamic content and interactivity.

Delivering dynamic content

The Web without Java is inherently limited to *static content*. By static, I mean that the Web was designed to display information that doesn't change as you look at it. Of course, static content is ideal for information such as magazine articles, recipes, tax forms, and the like, but it's woefully inadequate for dynamic content, such as constantly changing stock market prices, live news coverage, graphics and text animation, and other information that evolves over time.

Java overcomes this natural limitation of the Web because it easily and efficiently delivers dynamic content on the Web, making once-lifeless pages come alive. Without Java, Web pages are best described as snazzy electronic magazines and brochures. You can see images and text, but nothing changes or moves.

With Java-injected Web pages, however, pages truly come to life: Regularly updated stock market ticker tapes slide across pages, buttons dance and sing, images jump around, and sound and music pour over the ether and out of your computer speaker.

Because applets are tiny programs that live in Web pages, they can do just about anything that standard software programs can. Viewed with a Java-savvy Web browser (check out Chapter 3 for more on browsers), the applets inside a page spring into action and do their magic. This magic, of course, is determined by the individual (or group of individuals) who create the applet by using the Java programming language. Although the capabilities of applets range far and wide, just as the capabilities of standard software programs do, Java applets all have one thing in common: They enhance the traditional Web as it stands built upon standard HTML alone, bringing an otherwise static medium to life!

Introducing interactivity

Dynamic content is only half the battle against the war on static information. With dynamic content alone, you have little more than a computerized (and considerably slower) version of television and radio. To be of real use in the information age, information must be interactive.

Alternative routes to interactivity

Although a few nonstandard ways exist for providing interactivity on the Web, the only *standard* mechanism is known as the *Common Gateway Interface* (CGI). Unfortunately, CGI is difficult to weave into Web pages and terribly limited in its capability to deliver interactivity — so limited, in fact, that most people don't consider CGI-enhanced pages truly interactive at all.

The main use of CGI is to allow you to enter text information on the Web through *forms.* With CGI, you can type information into forms, such as when you're using a search engine (like Yahoo!, Lycos, or AltaVista) or registering for a product. Although forms such as these aren't at all interactive, CGI is also used for a more interactive purpose: It makes image maps possible. *Image maps* are images whose different areas are hyperlinked to separate URLs, allowing you to click on various sections of an image to get to different places. Image maps are often used as navigation toolbars in Web sites.

Although such capabilities are useful, that's about all CGI can do when it comes to interactivity: forms and image maps. Java, on the other hand, can do forms, image maps, and much more. As a result, Java is expected to make CGI obsolete in the near future.

If the traditional Web, created using only standard HTML, doesn't support dynamic content, you can bet your sweet sanity that the content it does deliver isn't interactive. No, the best the Javaless Web has to offer is hyperlinked content. You can click on a hypertext or hypermedia item and jump to another page of information. But that's a far cry from interactive content, my friend.

Without Java, you can only view information and click on hyperlinked text and images to visit more information on the Web. You have no way of interacting with the information, however. And interactivity is the key to compelling content. You don't want to merely *see* cool stuff coming across the wire — you want to add to it, change it, work with it. You want to interact with it.

Interactivity is nothing new to you and your personal computer, although you may not have thought much about it. Have you ever played a video game, drawn or painted an image, created an electronic slide show in a presentation package, recorded or altered sound or music, or done anything other than read, view, or listen to data on your personal computer? If so, you've been interacting with that data.

Interacting with data is something that everyone who uses a personal computer takes for granted. But the standard Web itself, without enhancements, is incapable of providing an interactive experience, relegating you to the role of passive viewer. With Java, which is the ultimate Web enhancement, you're in control — you're part of the action.

Okay, So It's Not Perfect — Yet!

Okay, so I'm a Java zealot. I'll admit that. But I'm also open minded enough to admit that Java isn't 100 percent perfect (shhh . . . it'll be our little secret).

In truth, Java has a long way to go. Currently, for example, applets can't print. Yes, it's sad but true: Applets have no way of sending information to a printer! They simply weren't given that kind of power — at least not yet.

You see, Java was designed with security in mind, so its applets aren't given all the power that full-blown applications are. Here's why: Do you really know who's behind every Web page you visit? Of course not; that's the beauty of the Web – you can click yourself dizzy, visiting countless sites using little more than your mouse, without ever having to ask yourself questions such as "Who created this page?" and "Can I trust the people behind this site?"

The reason you're able to surf the Web just as freely as a hippie lived during the '60s — we're talking serious freedom here — comes down to one thing: lack of privilege. Web pages have no right, or capability, to do anything at all with your computer. They can only be displayed by a Web browser, and that's about it. When you print a Web page today, it's actually your Web browser that does the work — the page itself has no clue what's going on. It just sits around looking pretty.

The engineers at Sun made Java as limited in its knowledge of your computer as a Web page itself. That is, they effectively lobotomized Java applets when it comes to doing anything beyond running inside a Java-savvy browser. However, smarter capabilities are currently being built into Java, so you should soon encounter applets that can print, store files on your computer, and read the contents of files residing on your own hard drive. But don't freak out quite yet! The kind engineers who are building these capabilities into Java understand how such privileges might be abused and the damage a rogue applet can wreak on an unsuspecting system.

When these capabilities come to Java applets — probably sometime in 1998 — only you will be able to grant applets such intimate access to your computer. If you don't give an applet explicit access to your computer, it has no way of doing damage. And, because you're likely to only give applets such access if you really trust the party on whose Web page they appear, the chance of granting a potentially dangerous applet access to your computer is pretty low.

Spilling the Beans — Java Everywhere

Even though the combination of Java and the World Wide Web is relatively new, it's such a perfect mix that it's destined to revolutionize the world of communications as we know it, as millions of Web users, or *Webbers,* will eagerly tell you. The excitement is particularly amazing considering the fact that the first wave of Java-powered Web pages is rather primitive compared to what's really possible.

Whenever someone asks me, "Hey, Aaron, what are the chances of the Boston Red Sox winning the World Series in your lifetime, and just out of curiosity, what does Java hold in store for the Web?" I have a canned answer waiting in the wings: "None and everything."

The Red Sox don't seem to have much hope. But where Java's concerned, you're dealing with a fresh technology and facing an absolutely unlimited field of dreams. Most of the Java applets you find on the Web today are primarily from the first crop to hit the Net, with only a small portion — a second generation of applets — actually showing Java's potential. In fact, most of the applets that you run into today aren't mind blowing. But those new applets are becoming more compelling every day, and literally hundreds of thousands — and soon millions — of people from around the world are diving into Java.

By the time 1999 rolls around, the vast majority of Web pages will look and act nothing like they did a few years ago, or even today for that matter. By then, you can expect many pages to have the same visual appeal as the best CD-ROM titles on the market today. And you can expect the same degree of interactivity, if not more. Despite what some consider primitive examples of the technology at work, when you see Java on the Web and imagine the possibilities this new technology offers, you can see that Java clearly has what it takes to transform the Web and computing as we know it. It's already doing just that, and the best is still to come.

To use my favorite analogy, comparing the Web today to the state of television when it was first invented is fair. When television first reached into homes, it was terribly crude by today's standards. The picture quality was poor at best and wasn't even in color. To change the station, you had to extract yourself from the cozy couch cushions and shuffle over and turn the knob. There wasn't even much of a selection compared to the hundreds of channels you can get today through cable and satellite.

From a futurist's point of view, the same can be said for today's Java and the World Wide Web. They're terribly crude compared to what's in store, but they are going to explode in complexity overnight — guaranteed. Computer technology advances at an astounding, sometimes unbelievable, rate. Approximately every two years, computers double in speed and power while the software you run on them becomes more sophisticated, more appealing, and more packed full of features. Astonishing as it may seem, Java's been moving at an even faster pace thanks to a global initiative and breakneck effort under way by millions of developers to make the Web as fast, smooth, and attractive as television, yet with the interactivity you'd expect from today's best CD-ROM titles.

Martian Java

On July 4, 1997, Java landed on Mars — literally. The mobile Mars rover, called Pathfinder, landed on the surface of the red planet that day, powered in part by Java. Thanks to Java-powered applets on the Web, some 40 million earthlings peeked in on the rover each day during the first few weeks of our visit to the Martian planet. And, thanks again to Java, you had the amazing ability to remotely control a Pathfinder simulator set against Mars' surface and send photographs sent back to earth from the real Pathfinder. You could, in essence, drive your own little rover around Mars, checking out the terrain from the comfort of your office cubicle.

If you have an itchin' to see the red planet for yourself, check out `java.sun.com/features/1997/july/mars.html`

By merely reading this book, you're standing at the edge of a true revolution. You will see great gains and enormous changes taking place over the next few years, and this book shows you how to contribute your own musket to the charge by adding Java to your very own Web pages. As you begin to add Java to your own pages, you may become aware of other pages on the Web that also make use of this irresistible technology. Already, the combination of Java and the Web is changing the way people learn, work, and play.

Java Delivers Executable Content

The key to Java's success is its ability to deliver executable content over the Web. *Executable content* is what allows Web pages to contain dynamic and interactive content, where once everything was static. To understand executable content, you must understand what execution means. In the real world, executions are rare; life without parole is much more common. In the computer world, however, executions happen all the time.

Whenever you run a computer program, you're said to be "executing a piece of software." To write a letter, you must execute a word processor. To send electronic mail, you execute an e-mail package. Want to play a game? Paint a graphics image? Crunch a spreadsheet? Execute. Execute. Execute. There's no getting around it; to do anything on your personal computer, you must first execute the software program you need to do it.

When you execute a program, you effectively tell your computer to follow all the instructions that make up the program itself. *Programs* are really nothing more than a bunch of instructions that tell the computer how to present information and handle user input. Every program has its own set of instructions, specific to the task or set of tasks it performs. When you execute a program, its instructions are carried out by the computer. Javaless Web pages of yesterday contained only static information such as text and graphics; they had no way of providing special instructions for the computer to follow. Without Java, a Web page just displays the text or images and then sits around waiting for you to visit another page of information.

Java, on the other hand, allows pages to contain executable content. You can think of Java Web pages as having one or more tiny programs embedded inside of them. Your browser recognizes these little programs, formally known as *applets,* as being something much more than static content. Rather than try to display an applet, the browser hands it off to the personal computer and says, "Here's a little program — execute it!" Executable content is what Java is really all about. With executable content, you can embed tiny programs in your Web pages so that, when someone accesses your page, the programs execute normally. As a result, dynamic and interactive content is a reality.

Although you may think that applets provide the perfect opportunity to invade your system with viruses, worms, or Trojan horses (all of which are designed to infiltrate your computer system and cause you and your system grief in one way or another), Java has been designed from the get-go with security in mind. True, it's not foolproof (never say never!), but it would be incredibly difficult to circumvent the various security checks Java applets must pass through before they are allowed to execute on your computer. As a result, creating malicious or deceitful applets would be quite a feat. For more information about applets and security issues, see Chapter 6.

Because Java applets are downloaded directly to a user's personal computer and are executed as actual software programs, applets can do just about anything. Think of how many different programs are available for your personal computer. Now, consider that Java allows the same type of programs to be embedded in Web pages and you can understand why such a buzz surrounds this new technology. Suddenly, anything you can imagine — and much of what you can't imagine — becomes possible.

The Rush Is On

Today, the Java rush is on. Unlike any previous technology, other than the Web itself, Java has ignited the world in a blaze of excitement and anticipation. Every day, thousands of programmers around the globe are creating new and exciting Web pages that feature content never before possible. And millions of people just like you and me are loading pre-made Java applets into their pages, adding fuel to the Java fire.

Soon, the majority of Web pages will take advantage of Java's executable content capabilities. After all, why have dead pages when you can bring your Web site to life?

Chapter 3

Java-Savvy Browsers

*B*efore you dive head first into Java, you have to obtain and install a *browser* — the software that connects you to the Web. This chapter answers all of your lingering questions about browsers: What's the difference between an ordinary browser and a Java-savvy browser? Which browser should I use? And how do I enable Java in my browser?

Browser, Smowser: What's the Big Deal?

Without a Web browser, you have to navigate the Internet the old-fashioned way — by using a specialized tool for each type of information that you want to retrieve. You have no way of viewing graphical Web pages without a browser, which means that you don't have the benefit of hyperlinks — hypertext (words with links to other Web pages) and hypermedia (images with links) — to make navigation a snap. And, if you can't use hyperlinks, you have to manually retrieve each piece of information that you want, which means that you have to find out where the information is located and then figure out how to get there. Chances are, without a Web browser, you won't even bother to surf the Web because it takes so much time and effort — which is exactly what prevented so many people from using the Internet in its early days. Before Web browsers, which provide fast and easy access to tremendous stockpiles of information, the Internet was just too difficult and time-consuming for most people to bother with.

Not only is finding the specific piece of information you want nearly impossible without a browser, but you also have to know what tool to use to retrieve the document, if you actually locate it. And after you manage to copy (or *download*) the document to your own computer, you have to figure out which program to view it with. And even if you have a rough idea of what format the document is in, you have to own a software program that is capable of displaying documents in that particular format.

Thanks to Web browsers, you don't have to worry about such difficulties. Instead of needing to know exactly where a file is located, you can follow a hyperlink to it, or better yet, you can use a sophisticated tool (called a *search engine* — see Chapter 4) to find what you're looking for instantly. And when the link or search engine locates the information you want, the browser displays that information immediately — you don't have to bother downloading and saving files to your computer for use with yet another piece of software. A browser displays text, graphics, and animation and plays sounds as it encounters them.

You also can save information to your own computer for later use, if you want to. However, you can access information on the Web by navigating from hyperlink to hyperlink without ever having to manually download anything to your computer. And, because Web browsers combine the functionality of several traditional Internet software programs, you don't have to understand a whole set of tools to get the information you need. Just select a hyperlink and let the browser do the rest.

Okay, So I Need a Web Browser. But What's a Java-Savvy Browser?

You should be thoroughly convinced by now that you can't surf the Web if you don't have a browser — but all browsers are not the same. To view pages containing Java applets, you need to obtain and install a *Java-savvy* browser. Because Java applets are actually tiny programs embedded inside Web pages (see Chapter 2), the browser you use must understand how to deal with such unique content. When a Java-savvy browser accesses Web pages, it automatically downloads and executes all Java applets embedded inside the page. When you use a non-Java-savvy browser to view a page containing Java, the browser simply ignores the applets. After all, only Java-savvy browsers recognize applets and know how to download and execute them. When a non-Java-savvy browser comes across an applet, it goes "Huh?" and skips right over it.

Without a Java-savvy browser, you'll be sorely disappointed when visiting Web sites that are enhanced with Java applets, because you won't be able to see or interact with the applet-enhanced portions of the page. When you're armed with a Java-savvy browser, however, a dazzling world of Web-page wonders is just a few mouse clicks away.

Not all computer systems can run Java-savvy browsers, though. Currently, users of the following systems can cash in on the Java craze:

- ✔ Intel-based machines running Microsoft Windows NT, Windows 95, or Windows 3.1
- ✔ Apple Macintosh (and Power Macintosh) machines running System 7.5 or later
- ✔ Sun SPARC-based machines running Solaris 2.3 or later
- ✔ Silicon Graphics machines running Irix 5.2 or later
- ✔ Systems running IBM's AIX
- ✔ Systems running DEC's Digital Unix
- ✔ Systems running Linux

The Many Flavors of Java-Savvy Browsers

A few years ago, Java-savvy browsers were scarce — Java was brand-spanking-new at that time. Today, however, it's a different story — several Java-savvy browsers are currently available. Java is an incredibly hot commodity these days, with just about everyone who uses the Web clamoring for access to it. As a result, most companies that make browsers have added support for Java to their products. The question of the day is, "What flavor of Java-savvy browser is best for me?"

Choosing a Java-savvy browser is a little like choosing a pet — it's largely a personal decision. You have several browsers to choose from, each slightly different from the others in features and appearance. There currently are three leading Java-savvy browsers to choose from:

- ✔ Netscape Navigator
- ✔ Microsoft Internet Explorer
- ✔ Sun Microsystems' HotJava

If you have a choice, you may consider using the latest version of Netscape Navigator. Because Navigator is still the most popular browser in the world (although Explorer is catching up fast), you can't go wrong by choosing this market leader. Not only will you get the most advanced browser on the market, but chances are good that a bunch of your fellow Webbers are using it too.

In some cases, you don't have a choice of browsers. If you're connecting to the Web through a commercial online service, such as America Online, CompuServe, or Prodigy, you may not have the option of choosing a browser other than the one your service provides (which, right now, is usually Internet Explorer).

Regardless of the browser you choose, as long as it's Java-savvy (that is, as long it can detect Java applets embedded in Web pages), you don't have to worry about having the right tool for the job — if your browser is Java-savvy, it's up to the task at hand.

HotJava

The world's first Java-savvy browser, HotJava (see Figure 3-1), was created by the same company that created Java — HotJava was developed by Sun Microsystems' Java division, specifically to showcase its Java technology. For Sun, creating the first Java-savvy browser was, in fact, a necessity.

After Sun developed Java, it built a brand-new Web browser, one capable of displaying non-Java Web pages as well as those embedded with Java applets. Written entirely in Java (see the sidebar entitled, "Applets versus applications"), HotJava was a technological marvel at the time it was released. It displayed standard Web pages, and it was capable of handling the executable content delivered in applet form.

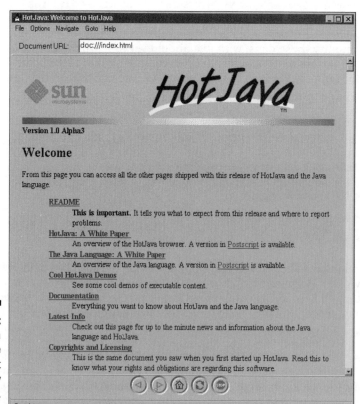

Figure 3-1:
HotJava
was the
world's first
Java-savvy
browser.

HotJava was the first browser to be capable of *learning* about the Web as it browses, which means that when HotJava encounters information or protocols it doesn't understand, it dynamically learns how to deal with them. Instead of requiring a browser software upgrade every time new technology comes along — which seems to happen nearly every day — HotJava extends itself on the fly through an innovative feature called *handlers*. Handlers are kinda like brain implants that Java-savvy browsers call upon to handle new information or protocols. Here's how handlers work: Whenever a new protocol or type of content is developed for the Web, a corresponding Java handler is also developed (see Chapter 1 for details on Web protocols). Then, when a Java-savvy browser comes across the unknown content or protocol, it instantly learns how to cope with it by using the corresponding handler.

Although HotJava was the first Java-savvy browser, it certainly is not the most popular. Netscape Navigator and Microsoft Internet Explorer are, by far, the most widely used browsers. But HotJava remains significant nonetheless.

Applets versus applications

The Java technology, rich in breadth and depth, isn't limited to bringing Web pages to life (check out Chapter 2). Java can, in fact, do much more.

In essence, Java is a new software-development language. With Java, any software program that you can imagine, and many that you can't begin to dream of, can be created. In fact, the HotJava browser was developed through use of the Java language!

HotJava is an application, not an applet, meaning that it doesn't exist inside a Web page. Unlike applets, which are tiny programs embedded in Web pages, Java applications are just like any other software program that you use. You execute Java applications in the same way that you execute any of the other programs on your computer.

Unlike standard applications, however, Java applications are often deeply enmeshed with the Internet, because the Java language makes developing networked products, such as HotJava, relatively easy. Standard software-development languages, such as C and Pascal, were invented long before the Internet exploded in popularity. As a result, creating network-capable products with such languages is painstaking and tedious compared to what the Java programming language offers.

The Java language, invented only a handful of years ago, was designed with networks in mind. As a result, programs that are developed with Java automatically understand how to connect to the Internet, retrieve information from it, and send information over it. This is why applets and applications, the two types of software programs that can be created with the Java language, are so deeply intertwined with the Internet and the World Wide Web.

Sun never intended to have HotJava compete head-to-head with mainstream browsers. HotJava was originally intended to be (and has remained) a *concept browser,* designed to showcase the Java technology and to prompt other browser vendors to include support for Java in their products. Clearly, the concept was a hit. After HotJava was introduced, all major browser vendors rushed back to the drawing table to make their products Java-savvy. Today, HotJava continues to lead the pack in terms of pure technological Java prowess, and the other browsers continue to follow along.

Netscape Communicator and Navigator

Netscape Navigator was developed by Netscape Communications Corporation, which is consistently on the cutting edge of browser technology — Navigator is largely responsible for the massive buzz surrounding the Web. In the good old days (about a year ago!), Netscape's primary claim to fame was its Navigator browser. Today, things are a little different. Navigator has given way to a product called Communicator, which has more bells and whistles than you can shake an electric stick at.

Communicator is actually a set of products, of which the Navigator browser is one part. Using Communicator, you can browse the Web with the latest, very slick version of Navigator; create and publish your own Web pages, courtesy of Composer; send and receive e-mail by using Messenger; conduct live chats over the Internet; and much more. Undoubtedly, Communicator is an impressive collection of software products, created expressly for communicating over the Internet. In fact, Netscape Communicator provides so many cool ways to communicate, it makes me wish I had more friends and a larger family.

To get Navigator up and running, you need to understand the three different groups of controls that are visible at the top of the browser window, as shown in Figure 3-2:

Navigator: Blowing past Mosaic

When Netscape Navigator was introduced in December 1994, it was several times faster than the predominant browser of the time, NCSA Mosaic. In addition, it was more flexible in the types of data and protocols it understood. Without a doubt, Navigator was the Cadillac of Web browsers. Bursting ahead of NCSA Mosaic, Navigator took an early lead in the browser race and never looked back. Within the first nine months of its release, over ten million people were using the Navigator to browse the Web. Millions more have made Navigator their browser of choice since then, thanks to its superior speed and flexibility.

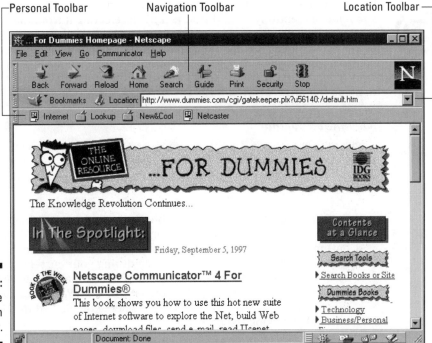

Personal Toolbar ┌ Navigation Toolbar Location Toolbar ┐

Figure 3-2:
The three
toolbars in
Navigator.

> ✔ **Navigation Toolbar:** Buttons corresponding to the most frequently used Navigator commands.
>
> ✔ **Location Toolbar:** The Location Toolbar lets you view addresses (URLs) or type in URLs manually, enabling you to connect directly to a Web page if you know its corresponding URL. The Bookmark button provides quick and easy access to your favorite Web sites. Using this button, you also can *bookmark* a specific site when you visit it, which then allows you to return to it at a later time without having to remember, or type in, the entire URL. The Location area is a simple text area for typing in URLs, enabling you to connect directly to a Web page.
>
> ✔ **Personal Toolbar:** Buttons that provide quick access to a few of the most useful sites on the Web, helping you to navigate its vast contents.

These controls appear in order of significance; you are likely to use the Navigation Toolbar the most, followed by the Location Toolbar and then the Personal Toolbar. Of course, this rule isn't set in stone; it's just an educated guess based on experience and what each feature offers.

If you find that you aren't using one (or more) of the Navigator controls, you can remove it entirely from the screen by deselecting it from the Options menu. Removing a group of controls from the screen gives you more space to view Web pages. For the most space possible, remove all three groups of controls from the screen. Because all features are accessible via keyboard or menu commands, you don't lose their functionality at all, you just can't see them on the browser window.

Navigation Toolbar

Navigator's Navigation Toolbar is composed of several buttons that correspond to the browser's most commonly used commands. Each of these items is also available through a menu item, so you can access them either way.

- ✔ **Back and Forward:** Of the available Navigation Toolbar buttons, the Back and Forward buttons probably are used the most. Clicking these buttons (which correspond to options in the Go menu) enables you to revisit pages that you've encountered during your current Web-surfing session. To return to the page you visited immediately before the one you are currently viewing, click the Back button. When you arrive at that page, you can return to the page where you clicked the Back button by clicking the Forward button.

  You can click Back and Forward several times in a row to revisit pages farther back (or forward) in your current surfing session. For example, if you want to revisit a page that you encountered five pages ago, just click the Back button five times. But you're better off simply selecting that page from the Go menu rather than clicking Back over and over! The Go menu takes you directly to the page that you select, whereas the Back button stops at each page in between the one you want to view and the one you are currently viewing.

- ✔ **Reload:** Clicking the Reload button reloads the current page, retrieving it from the Web as if you are connecting to the page for the first time. This option helps when you're viewing a page that is jumbled because not all of its data transmitted properly. Simply click on Reload, and presto — the page comes in fresh from the Web.

- ✔ **Home:** Clicking the Home button takes you directly to the start-up Web page. By default, this page is the Netscape Communications Corporation home page, although you can set it to any page you want (in the Edit⇨Preferences dialog box).

- ✔ **Search:** Clicking the Search button takes you to Navigator's search engines, which allow you to search the Web for topics you're interested in. You can search for Web pages relevant to the information that you're looking for by typing in keywords (such as **car**, or **iguana**, or **Pig Latin**) and then clicking the Search button. You can also use the category hyperlinks to help narrow down your search, or even search the online Yellow Pages by clicking on that link.

✔ **Guide:** Clicking the Guide button reveals a popup menu containing five items: Yellow Pages, People, Net Search, What's New, and What's Cool. Depending on which item you choose, Navigator takes you to different guide areas that provide detailed information and links related to that topic. If you're new to the Web, the Guide button is a great place to start exploring.

 ✔ **Print:** Clicking the Print button is equivalent to choosing File⇨Print. Both actions enable you to send a Web page to your printer (if you have a printer).

 ✔ **Security:** Clicking the Security button shows you detailed information related to the security features of Navigator, something most novice users should avoid. To find out more about security, select Help Contents from the Navigator Help menu and then click the Security link that appears.

 ✔ **Stop:** One of the most often used buttons on the toolbar, Stop instructs the browser to stop loading the current page. If you find that a page is taking an excessive amount of time to load, you can click the Stop button and then choose Reload, forcing the browser to establish a brand-new connection to the page.

Location Toolbar

Navigator's Location Toolbar (see Figure 3-3) appears, by default, just below the Navigation Toolbar. The Bookmarks button, as you may have guessed, is used to save *bookmarks,* or shortcuts, to your favorite Web pages. When you encounter a page that you want to bookmark, just click this button and select the Add Bookmark item that appears. The name of the page is then *bookmarked,* appearing alongside any other pages that you may have previously bookmarked. To visit a bookmarked page, simply click the Bookmarks button and choose it from the names of Web pages that appear.

Figure 3-3:
The
Location
Toolbar
features the
Bookmarks
button and
the Location
area.

| 📖 Bookmarks ⚡ Location: http://www.dummies.com/cgi/gatekeeper.plx?u56140:/default.htm ▼ |

To the right of the Bookmarks button is the Location area, which serves two purposes: It tells you where you are by displaying the URL of the current page, and it allows you to quickly access a page by typing in the page's URL. To connect to a Web page by using the Location area, simply type in the URL for that page and press Return (or Enter) on your keyboard.

Personal Toolbar

Navigator's Personal Toolbar, shown in Figure 3-4, provides quick access to some of the more useful sites on the Web, helping you to navigate the Web's vast contents. Although each of these buttons connects you to a valuable site, perhaps the most interesting is the New&Cool button. Clicking this button reveals two menu items: New and Cool. Need I say more?

Figure 3-4:
The Personal Toolbar includes cool links to useful sites.

If you're new to Navigator, or want to find out more about the Navigator product, you should use the Help menu, located in the main menu bar. The Help Contents item that is located in the Help menu is the first place to

---

Customizing your browser

To get the most out of your new Java-savvy browser, you can customize it to fit your personal needs and interests. To customize Navigator or Explorer, use the various items that appear in the dialog box when you choose Edit⇨Preferences (Navigator) or View⇨ Options (Explorer). These items include ways to customize your browser, from changing the color and style of hyperlinks to setting a start-up Web page and even to disabling the automatic loading of images for a dramatic speed increase when browsing the Web.

To find out about the many ways in which you can customize your browser, click the Help menu and select Help Contents from the items that appear. This displays the online help manual, where you'll find everything you ever wanted to know about your browser!

start, and it even contains detailed instructions on how to use Java within Navigator. But don't bother with the Help menu if you're anxious to get going with Java; just read on.

Microsoft Internet Explorer

Although Navigator has reigned supreme since it first exploded onto the Web scene, Microsoft is hard at work trying to steal a little of the thunder, if not the entire storm, that Navigator has generated.

Microsoft Internet Explorer has become a major player in the Java-savvy browser market in the past year or so, since Internet Explorer 3.0 was introduced. Every new Windows 95 computer comes with Internet Explorer built in, which means that millions of new computer buyers become new Internet Explorer users at the same time. What else would you expect from the company that brought you Windows, Word, Excel, PowerPoint, Encarta, and a raft of other award-winning software products?

Due to ship at about the time you read this book, Version 4.0 of Microsoft's Internet Explorer will compete head-to-head with Netscape Navigator. (I'm using a preview version of IE 4.0 for several of the screen shots throughout this book, which makes me a guinea pig for the testing phase of the new version.) Thanks to the muscle Microsoft has available to flex when it comes to striking deals, Explorer is beginning to replace the non-Java-savvy browsers provided by many online services.

The fact is, Internet Explorer is quite a good browser. When it comes to Java support, Internet Explorer 4.0 claims to be significantly faster than Navigator when running applets. I tend to believe this claim because the Java-powered Web pages that I've viewed while using Internet Explorer seem to download faster and run at a slightly higher speed (applets that produce animations, for example, appear faster and are smoother looking when viewed with Internet Explorer 4.0 than they are with Navigator 4.0). However, Navigator is no slouch either — the difference between the two is almost negligible, and you probably won't notice increased performance in Internet Explorer unless you're paying close attention.

The user interface for Internet Explorer 4.0 is much the same as that of Netscape Navigator 4.0, although the terminology used by each browser is slightly different (see Figure 3-5). For example, Navigator uses "Navigation Toolbar" to describe the toolbar that contains navigational buttons, such as Back, Forward, and Stop, while Internet Explorer uses "Standard buttons Toolbar" instead. Functionally, these two toolbars are more or less the same, with only minor differences between the two. But first, take a moment to review Table 3-1, which lists the names of the three basic toolbars available in each browser.

Standard buttons Toolbar   Address Toolbar   Links Toolbar

Figure 3-5:
Internet
Explorer
contains
several
toolbars
that are
similar to
Navigator's
toolbars.

Table 3-1	The Three Basic Toolbars
Netscape Navigator 4.0	*Internet Explorer 4.0*
Navigation Toolbar	Standard buttons Toolbar
Location Toolbar	Address Toolbar
Personal Toolbar	Links Toolbar

Just as with Navigator, Internet Explorer's toolbars appear in order of
significance; you are likely to use the Standard buttons Toolbar most often,
followed by the Address Toolbar, and then the Links Toolbar. Of course, how
you use these toolbars is entirely up to you. You might find the Address
Toolbar to be the most useful to you, or even the Links Toolbar. As a result,
you can arrange Internet Explorer's toolbars in the order that best fits your
needs. To arrange your toolbars, simply click on the thin vertical line that
appears on the far left of a toolbar and drag it to the position where you
want it located. When you unclick the mouse, the toolbar moves to that
place on the screen; other toolbars automatically reposition to accommodate the one you move.

If you find that you really don't use one (or more) of the Internet Explorer
toolbars, you may remove it from the screen entirely. From the View⇨
Toolbars menu, simply deselect the toolbar you want to remove. Removing
a toolbar from the screen gives you more space to view Web pages. For the

most space possible, remove all three toolbars from the screen. Because the features each toolbar offers are accessible via keyboard or menu commands too, you don't lose their functionality at all; you just can't see them on the browser window.

Netscape Navigator 4.0 and Internet Explorer 4.0 look very much the same, and each browser offers a similar set of toolbars for navigating the Web. However, while the toolbars each browser uses are very similar, they're not exactly the same. Because Navigator's toolbars are discussed earlier in this chapter, I give you a closer look at the toolbars offered by Internet Explorer to see where the differences are.

Standard buttons Toolbar

Internet Explorer's Standard buttons Toolbar is comprised of several buttons that correspond to the browser's most commonly used commands. Each of these commands also is available through a menu item, so you can access them either way.

✔ **Back and Forward:** Of the buttons on the Standard buttons Toolbar, the Back and Forward buttons are probably used the most. You can click these buttons (which correspond to options in the Go menu) to revisit pages that you've already seen during your current Web-surfing session. To return to the page you visited immediately before the one you are currently viewing, click Back. When you arrive at that page, you can return to the page where you clicked the Back button by clicking Forward.

You can click Back and Forward several times in a row to revisit pages farther back (or forward) in your current surfing session. For example, if you want to revisit a page that you saw five pages ago, just click the Back button five times. But you're better off simply selecting that page from the Go menu rather than clicking on Back over and over! The Go menu takes you directly to the page you select, whereas the Back button stops at each page in between the one you want and the one you are currently viewing.

✔ **Stop:** One of the most often used buttons on the toolbar, Stop instructs the browser to stop loading the current page. If you are at a page that is taking too long to load, click on the Stop button and then choose Refresh, which forces the browser to establish a brand-new connection to the page.

✔ **Refresh:** Clicking the Refresh button reloads the current page, retrieving it from the Web as if connecting to it for the first time. This option helps when you're viewing a page that is jumbled because the data it contains didn't transmit entirely. In this case, simply click on Refresh, and presto — the page comes in fresh from the Web.

✔ **Home:** Clicking the Home button takes you directly to the start-up Web page. By default, this page is the Microsoft home page, although you're can set it to any page you want (in the View⊄Options dialog box).

 ✔ **Search:** Clicking the Search button displays Internet Explorer's search engines, which enable you to search the Web for topics that you're interested in. You can search for Web pages that are relevant to the information you're looking for by typing in keywords (such as **car**, or **iguana**, or **Pig Latin**) and then clicking the Find button. You can choose from several different search engines to conduct your search by using the Select provider popup menu that appears after you click the Search button.

 ✔ **Favorites:** Internet Explorer Favorites are the equivalent of Netscape Navigator bookmarks. Clicking the Favorites button lets you view and access all the Web addresses (URLs) that you have added to this menu, if any. (Note that clicking on the Favorites buttons only lets you view and access Web sites. To add a new favorite, you must choose Add to Favorites from the Favorites menu, located on the menu bar.)

 ✔ **History:** Clicking the History button shows a listing of all the Web pages you recently visited, enabling you to quickly return to a previously visited site, even if you haven't bothered to add it to your Favorites. To visit a Web page that appears in the History list, simply click on it.

 ✔ **Channels:** Clicking the Channels button displays the various Web sites that may be broadcast directly to your personal computer. In the same way that television shows are broadcast over the airwaves, Internet Explorer gives Web site developers the capability to customize their pages for broadcast over the Internet. By clicking the Channels button, you can view and subscribe to these Web broadcasts.

 ✔ **Print:** Clicking the Print button is equivalent to choosing File⊄Print. Both actions send a Web page to your printer (if you have a printer).

 ✔ **Font:** Clicking the Font button displays a popup menu that lets you either increase or decrease the text size used by Internet Explorer to display Web pages. If Web pages are too difficult to read due to the size of the text, click the Font button and increase or decrease the font size accordingly. The popup menu that appears also contains items that let you specify a particular alphabet to use when displaying Web page text (the default is a font called Western alphabet).

 ✔ **Mail:** Clicking the Mail button displays a popup menu from which you can choose to send or read e-mail (assuming that Internet Explorer is configured to deal with e-mail. If it's not, click the Mail button, which leads you through the process of hooking up Internet Explorer's e-mail capabilities).

Address Toolbar

Internet Explorer's Address Toolbar (shown in Figure 3-6) appears, by default, just below the Standard buttons Toolbar. Just like the Location area found in Netscape Navigator's Location Toolbar, Internet Explorer's Address Toolbar serves two purposes: It tells you where you are by displaying the URL of the current page, and it allows you to quickly access a page by typing in the page's URL. To connect to a Web page by using the Address Toolbar, simply type in the URL for that page and press Return (or Enter) on your keyboard.

Figure 3-6:
The Address Toolbar displays the current URL.

Links Toolbar

Similar to Navigator's Personal Toolbar, Internet Explorer's Links Toolbar contains a variety of buttons that give you quick access to some of the more useful sites on the Web to help you navigate the Web's vast contents (see Figure 3-7). Although each of these buttons connects to a valuable site, perhaps the most interesting button is Best of the Web. Clicking this button takes you to some of the, well, best sites on the World Wide Web.

 If you're new to Internet Explorer 4.0, or if you want to find out more about the product, try using the Help menu, located in the main menu. I strongly suggest that you check out the Help menu first: It is, without a doubt, the first feature of Internet Explorer to become familiar with, because it provides direct access to all the online help documents and guides that you need to get the most out of Internet Explorer.

Figure 3-7:
The Links Toolbar connects you to valuable Web sites.

The demise of PowerBrowser

When Oracle entered the Java-savvy browser market a few years ago with its PowerBrowser product, Oracle expected PowerBrowser to carve out a nice niche for itself among corporate users who already utilized Oracle's database products. Unfortunately, PowerBrowser was officially yanked from Oracle's product line in 1996, buried in a vast technology graveyard among the bones and shadows of countless other computer hardware and software products that held great promise but failed to grab market share.

Finding a Browser on the Web

If you already use the Web, you won't have any problem getting your hands on a Java-savvy browser. Because all the browsers are available on the Web, simply connect to one of the sites listed in Table 3-2 to download your Java-savvy browser of choice. After you download the new browser to your personal computer, installing it is a snap.

Browser vendors give away their products online to get customers like you to use them; they make their money by licensing the same products to large companies (such as Internet Service Providers — ISPs). The catch, however, is that technical support usually isn't provided for free. If you want to be able to call or e-mail the vendor with questions or problems, you usually have to pay a fee. As a general rule, browsers are trouble-free, so before you slap down cold, hard cash for technical support, test-drive the puppy for a while to see whether you really need any support.

Table 3-2	Java-Savvy Browsers on the World Wide Web		
Browser	**Version**	**Supported Platforms**	**Web Address**
Netscape Navigator	2.0, 3.0, 4.0	Windows NT/95, Macintosh, Sun Solaris, Silicon Graphics, and most flavors of UNIX	(home page) `home.netscape.com/` (download page) `home.netscape.com/ comprod/mirror/ client_download. html`
Microsoft Internet Explorer	3.0, 4.0	Windows NT/95, Macintosh	(home page) `www.microsoft.com/` (download page) `www.microsoft.com/ ie/msie.htm`

Browser	Version	Supported Platforms	Web Address
HotJava	1.0	Windows NT/95, Sun Solaris SPARC-based machines	`java.sun.com/ products/hotjava/`

If you don't already use the Web, you have to set up an Internet account at some point. After all, how can you create Java-powered Web pages if you don't first have access to the Web itself? In general, you can gain access to the World Wide Web in either of two ways:

- ✔ Through an ISP
- ✔ Through a commercial online service, such as America Online, CompuServe, or Prodigy

If you're in the market for an ISP, it's terribly important that you choose one that not only gives you access to the Web but also allows you to create your own Web pages. Although most service providers automatically grant their customers the right to create personal Web pages, not all providers do.

Providing access to the Internet is a booming business. With literally thousands of service providers to choose from, making sense of the myriad offerings can be a bit daunting. To help cut to the chase and get you on the Web in short order, the CD-ROM that comes with this book includes a listing of several top-rated service providers. (See Appendix A for details about using the *Java For Dummies,* 2nd Edition, CD-ROM.)

Pedal to the Metal — Enabling Java

To get off the ground and get cooking with Java, you must ensure that your browser is properly configured to deal with Java applets. Although Navigator and Explorer both come with Java already turned on, future versions of these browsers may not have this option all ready to go (Java is always enabled in HotJava, so it's not possible to disable Java support when using HotJava). And if you share your computer with others, someone may accidentally disable Java!

You may begin to suspect that Java is disabled if everything seems dead when you surf the Web. Because applets don't execute when your browser has Java support turned off, Java-powered pages appear dull and lifeless. If you ever happen upon pages that you're sure contain Java applets, yet nothing exciting or cool happens, there's a good chance that your browser's Java option is disabled.

✔ If you're using Netscape Navigator 4.0, the only way to know for sure whether Java has been disabled on your browser is to choose Edit⇨ Preferences. The Preferences dialog box appears, allowing you to customize various settings.

To view your Java settings, choose the Advanced item, located on the left side on the Preference dialog box — you see several options appear in the right side of the Preferences dialog box (see Figure 3-8), including two check boxes that allow you to enable or disable Java and JavaScript. If you want to tap into the full power of Java, make sure that both of these two items are selected! (For more on JavaScript, skip to Part III of this book.)

✔ Internet Explorer 4.0 users, on the other hand, can find out whether their browser is ready to view Java-powered pages through the browser's Security Zones settings. You find these settings by selecting View⇨Options. From the Options dialog box, shown in Figure 3-9, select the Security Zones tab, choose the Custom option, and then click the Settings button. Scroll down the list of settings options that you see (shown in Figure 3-10) until Java appears in the list; click on the Java item. You should see an option to disable Java, which you can use to turn support for Java on or off (clicking this radio button disables Java).

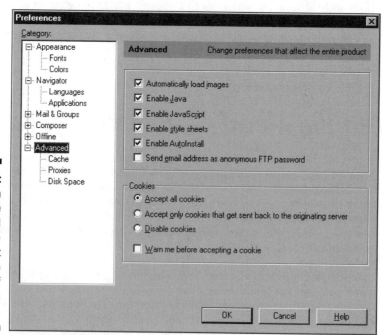

Figure 3-8:
Click both
the Enable
Java and
Enable
JavaScript
boxes to
see all of
the goodies
on the Web.

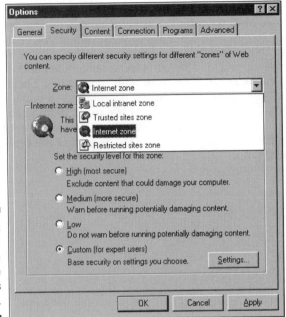

Figure 3-9:
The
Security tab
of the
Options
dialog box.

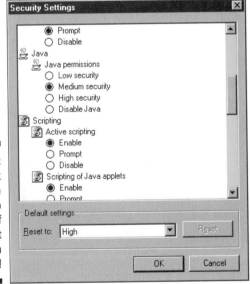

Figure 3-10:
Don't click
the Disable
Java radio
button if
you want
Java
support!

If you use Internet Explorer 4.0, keep in mind that options settings are based on zones of Web content — general categories that Internet Explorer uses to describe the types of Web content you're likely to encounter. (Figure 3-9 shows the four zones.) The Internet zone is the default zone when you view Internet Explorer options, although you can specify unique settings for three additional zones: Local intranet zone, Trusted sites zone, and Restricted sites zone. If you want to completely disable Java support, you have to do so for each zone (that is, you have to disable Java, as just described, four different times — one for each zone that appears under the Security Zones tab of the Options dialog box).

Chapter 4

Staying Hip to That Java Noise

. . . .

In This Chapter

▶ Surfing the Web for Java applets, scripts, and source code

▶ Visiting Java repositories

▶ Rummaging through Javazines

▶ Discovering Java support areas

▶ Using search engines to look for Java goodies

▶ Joining a Java newsgroup

. . . .

*T*he CD-ROM in the back of this book contains a bunch of applets and scripts to kick-start your Java habit. But the CD-ROM is just the beginning. You can find literally thousands of applets and scripts on the Web, free for the taking, and hundreds more are added every day.

Because the number of Java-powered pages is increasing so rapidly, the demand for comprehensive Java support has gone through the roof. You now can find a number of sites dedicated to assisting Java developers and people who create Java-powered sites. To get your Java fix, you only have to look in the right places. And even if you don't know exactly where to look for that special nugget of Java information, you can always turn to traditional search engines to light the way.

In an attempt to make sense of the different types of sites you may visit on the road to Java enlightenment, I break them down into five categories:

✔ **Repository:** Contains bunches (a technical term) of Java applets and JavaScripts as well as oodles (another technical term) of hyperlinks to other Java sites.

✔ **Electronic magazine:** Generally targeted at Java developers and high-end users. An *e-zine* is the digital equivalent of a paperbound periodical, in which you can usually find material about the latest and greatest happenings in the world of Java.

- ✔ **Support area:** Targeted almost exclusively at Java developers, a support area typically contains Java source code and example applets that demonstrate special features of the Java programming language.

- ✔ **Search engine:** Lets you search the Web for information about any subject, from chocolate-chip cookies to Java.

- ✔ **Newsgroup:** The electronic equivalent of a town meeting, a Java newsgroup allows you to participate in ongoing online conversations with fellow Javaites from around the world.

Repositories: Jam-Packed with Applets, Scripts, and Source Code

If you want to get your mitts on a specific Java applet or script and you're hoping also to get its *source code* (the body of computer instructions that a programmer writes to create an applet or script — consider it the DNA of an applet or script), be sure to drop by a repository first. A *repository,* in essence, is a Web site containing centrally maintained links to Java applets and scripts. A great deal of source code is also available in repositories, which is a welcome bonus if you want to learn how the applets and scripts in a repository were created.

Mantis Java Links

www.mantiscorp.com/java

Mantis Java Links, the code repository established for this book (and other Java publications produced by the Mantis Development Corporation), is shown in Figure 4-1. The applets and scripts at this site also serve as an upgrade to the CD-ROM in the back of this book. This site is regularly maintained and updated; not only are the contents of the CD-ROM available at this site, but more goodies will also have been added by the time you visit!

The Mantis Java Links site is a self-contained repository, which means that all applets and scripts are located and managed on the Mantis Development Corporation server. As a result, none of the links are dependent on *external* sites, or sites other than the Mantis server. In this controlled approach to maintaining a repository, you don't need hyperlinks to an external site in order to view applets or scripts, so you won't head into deeper waters unless you specifically choose to link to another repository.

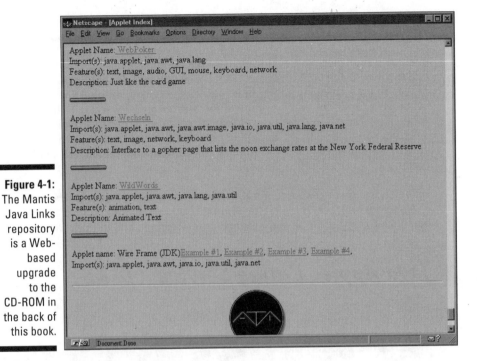

Figure 4-1:
The Mantis
Java Links
repository
is a Web-
based
upgrade
to the
CD-ROM in
the back of
this book.

Not only is the site controlled in a physical sense, but the applets and scripts also are controlled. Unlike other repositories, which attempt to provide as many applets and scripts as possible, Mantis Java Links attempts to separate the wheat from the chaff so that you don't waste time sifting through unwanted links. For that reason, Mantis Java Links is a good place to begin your quest.

Gamelan

www.gamelan.com

Not many people would argue about whether Gamelan is the most compre-hensive Java repository on the Web — it's the hands-down favorite of many Java developers. Gamelan is a *reference repository:* It provides links to external pages maintained by the applet and script authors rather than store and maintain them on the Gamelan Web server. Although Gamelan may not sound like a *true* repository because it doesn't act as a central storage area, it really is a repository — just not in the traditional sense. However, when you view the Web as one gigantic hard disk (which is what it really is), any site that maintains links to its contents is considered a repository.

Maintaining links is what Gamelan does best! Gamelan is a wonderful site, offering hyperlinks to tons of applets, scripts, and even source code, as shown in Figure 4-2. Gamelan doesn't stop at merely providing links, however: At Gamelan, Java developers register themselves as resources — you can retrieve the profile of an individual or group who is responsible for developing a particular applet or script that you like, and you can retrieve other Java products they have developed. Alternatively, if you're looking exclusively for custom Java-development services, you can search the developer resource list to find that special individual or group who can meet your Java-related development needs. In this sense, Gamelan also acts as a registry of Java resources.

Gamelan is a great resource not only for locating applets, scripts, source code, and resources, but also for finding anything related to Java. Gamelan has links to electronic Java magazines, newsgroups, and support areas.

Java Applet Rating Service (JARS)

www.jars.com

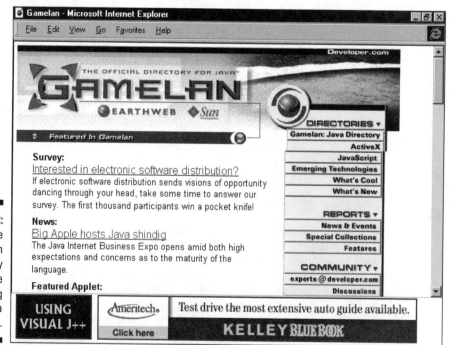

Figure 4-2:
The
Gamelan
repository
is a favorite
among
many Java
developers.

While Gamelan is a repository of immense proportions, the Java Applet Rating System (JARS) is lean and mean in comparison. JARS reduces the number of links it maintains by employing a rating system for the applets and scripts it references. JARS maintains hyperlinks to external Java-powered pages, as Gamelan does, and also ranks the applets in each page it points to.

Keep in mind that the JARS I'm talking about here is simply an acronym for Java Applet Rating System, and has no relation whatsoever to Java Archives (JARs).

Because all JARS applets are rated by a large panel of judges, rest assured that only the cream of the crop is offered when you look at the "JARS Top 1%" applets (as shown in Figure 4-3).

JARS also does a good job of differentiating between applets that come with source code and those that don't. Many Java developers are more than happy to give away their applets; they even encourage people to make use of them. But giving away an applet and giving away its source code are two different things altogether. If a developer gives away an applet, you can embed it only in your own Web pages. If a developer gives away the source

Figure 4-3: JARS uses a rating system to keep its offerings pared down: It takes a "best of breed" approach rather than attempting to maintain links to everything out there.

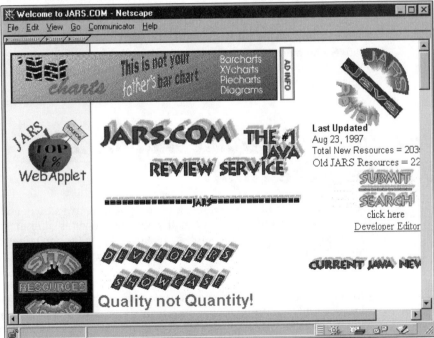

code for an applet, however, you can change the way the applet works internally and then redistribute your own version of it. If you use this approach, it's always cool to credit the developer who wrote the original source code.

Before using the source code of an applet (or a script, for that matter) that you find on the Web, it's a good idea to make certain that the author hasn't provided it as "reference only." Any available copyright information is usually at the top of a source code file. If the source code doesn't list a copyright anywhere, and if you didn't see a copyright in any of the files that came with the applet, chances are good that you can use the code for your own purposes. If you have any doubts about an author's intent, however, your best bet is to contact that person for permission or to simply use the source code to learn how to write your own code. Think of it as a free tutorial, but — just to be on the safe side — be sure to create your own code from scratch in this case.

Because applets often take a long time to develop, authors generally want — understandably — to keep their source code to themselves. When you're on the hunt for source code, it can be frustrating trying to locate applets that fit the bill and that have the corresponding source code. You can always contact the applet author by e-mail to request the source code, but you're not likely to get anywhere. If the source code isn't already available, chances are good that the author doesn't want you to have it.

Thanks to the easily identified images JARS uses, however, you can tell at a glance which applets are provided with source code and which are not (see Figure 4-4). If all you want is source code, don't link to the applets for which the source code is not provided.

Javazines: Electronic Magazines on a Caffeine High

Electronic magazines, commonly known as *e-zines,* are slowly coming out of the woodwork. Similar to traditional magazines, e-zines offer articles to inform you about a specific subject. In Java e-zines (or *Javazines,* as I like to call them), that subject matter revolves exclusively around — surprise, surprise — Java!

Although you can now find scores of e-zines on the Web that cover a gamut of topics, only a handful focused exclusively on Java a few years ago. Today, however, with a quick spin of your mouse, you can find scores of e-zines that cover cooking, nightclubs, macramé, and body piercing, and nearly as many that focus on Java. In the short amount of time that it has been in the public eye, Java has spawned e-zines of all stripes and colors.

Figure 4-4:
These simple icons help tell you at a glance which JARS applets are provided with source code and which aren't.

E-zines can be categorized into two general groups: professional and independent. Professional e-zines are usually consistent, well-written publications that are published on a regular schedule. Independent e-zines, on the other hand, may not be as reliable, well thought out, or rich in breadth and depth when it comes to the material they offer, but they are usually much more creative, irreverent, exciting, and visceral in their approach to delivering information. This refreshing perspective is most likely the result of not being bound to a corporate culture or concerned about conforming to standards or regulations imposed on professional publishers. Without a doubt, independent e-zines are the free spirits of the publishing world.

If you're looking for something fresh and exciting to read, independent e-zines are wonderful, but they usually have a tough time attracting professional writers. In many cases, this difficulty doesn't make a bit of difference, but it does matter where Java is concerned. For independent e-zines dedicated to Java, the caliber of content is likely to pale in comparison to their professional counterparts. I suspect that this situation will eventually change, however, as more and more Webbers willing to contribute to independent e-zines become fluent in Java. In the meantime, you'll probably find that the professional e-zines are much more valuable.

JavaWorld

www.javaworld.com

JavaWorld is an online magazine published by International Data Group (IDG). Updated bimonthly, *JavaWorld* is packed with comprehensive, well-written articles targeted at Java developers and high-end users (see Figure 4-5).

Figure 4-5: JavaWorld is full of interactive articles written expressly for Java developers.

You not only can read about Java technology but also see it working right in front of your face. With nothing more than a click of your mouse, you can see the source code used to create each applet and JavaScript you see in action.

If you really want to push the envelope of what Java can do for you, check out this site. At a minimum, you will find articles related to JavaScript. For ambitious types, *JavaWorld* has plenty of applet source code to go around. Dig in and don't be shy.

TIP

Bookmarking your favorite Java sites

For fast and easy access to these sites the next time around, you can *bookmark,* or *hotlink,* them the first time you visit. To save even more time, bookmark the Mantis Java Links site (www.mantiscorp.com/java), which keeps track of these sites so that you don't have to (Web addresses occasionally change). This site maintains hyperlinks to all sites mentioned in this book; the links it offers are updated regularly (with new ones added as they emerge) and are categorized for fast and easy access. If you don't feel like typing the address of a site that appears in this book or if you just want to see what's new, this is the place to visit.

The Kilroy of the '90s

If you're like me, it will be virtually impossible to tear yourself away from your computer after you actively begin prowling the Web to look for Java applets and scripts. There's *always* another link to try or another site to visit. You will soon while away your waking hours basking in the warm, comfortable glow of your computer monitor.

Your relationships with friends, relatives, and loved ones will soon give way to the eternal bond you form with Duke, the official Java mascot. A surprising number of Java developers use this adorable little creature when they need a graphics image and don't have one handy. Looking something like a Corn Nut carrying a red beach ball, Duke is sure to appear somewhere in your quest for fire.

This rakish devil appears to have taken over the Web. He has been spotted dancing, tumbling, waving, and operating a jackhammer, among other things. And lucky for us: Early mornings, long days, late nights, and weekends spent Java-surfing — mastering the subtle art of cruising the Web in search of cool Java applets and scripts — might otherwise be a solitary endeavor. Thanks to Duke, though, you have a friend on the Web (and a Java-induced friend, at that).

The Java Resource Center

www.idgbooks.com/rc/java

The *Java Resource Center* flowed into the ether less than a year ago, but has fast become a favorite pit stop of Java junkies around the globe. Owned and operated by IDG Books Worldwide, Inc. (the same company responsible for this very book), the Java Resource Center has information about all the company's Java publications. In addition, sample chapters, applets, scripts, and other Java materials are available at this site.

Support Areas: Where Java Developers Dare to Tread

Unlike repositories, Java support areas are targeted almost exclusively at developers. Support areas attempt to provide you with the tools and information you need to *develop* Java applets and scripts, not just to use them in your Web pages. These areas may also supply applets, scripts, and source code, although that's not their focus. Instead, you're more likely to find Java software development tools, documentation, technical support, Frequently Asked Questions (FAQs), and other Java-related information that programmers need to create top-notch applets and scripts.

Although support areas are targeted mainly at developers, they often contain applets and scripts for the taking. With this in mind, you may want to visit these areas even if you have no intention of writing your own applets or JavaScripts: You never know where you might find that nugget of information or applet that pulls your page together.

JavaSoft

java.sun.com

Perhaps the most popular Java support area is Sun Microsystems' own JavaSoft Web site, the official home of Java (see Figure 4-6). If you're interested in becoming a Java developer, this is the place to begin. Here, you can find everything you need to get started in developing your own Java applets: the Java Development Kit (JDK), extensive documentation, FAQ documents, source code samples, and links to other Java resources.

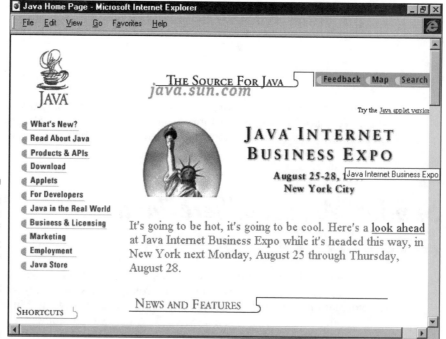

Figure 4-6:
JavaSoft is one of the most popular Java support areas on the Web.

Be warned! The process of programming Java applets is no trivial task. It requires significant software-development skills and a heavy dose of geek appeal. Even if you don't have an interest in creating your own applets, however, JavaSoft may be of interest to you.

JavaSoft also offers a large number of applets, which are available for free. Unfortunately, the only way to get these applets is to download the Java Development Kit (JDK) and install it on your system. The JDK is about 8MB or so in size and, depending on the speed of your connection to the Internet, can take a long time to download (if you're using a modem, expect to put aside more than an hour!).

If you decide to download and install the JDK, you are rewarded with more than 25 nifty little applets, ranging from animation to tic-tac-toe to hangman and more. You can plug in most of these applets directly to your own Web site, using your own graphics and sound files where appropriate, or use them as the basis for your own development efforts.

Writing Java applets is no simple trick; it makes writing JavaScripts seem like a carefree walk in the park on a lazy summer afternoon. If you want the full power of Java at your fingertips, however, there's no other way to go. If you want to try your hand at developing Java applets, I highly recommend that you get a copy of *Java Programming For Dummies,* 2nd Edition, by Donald J. Koosis and David Koosis (IDG Books Worldwide, Inc.) — it's a great book for mastering the ins and outs of the Java programming language without losing your mind in the process.

The Netscape JavaScript support area

```
developer.netscape.com
```

and

```
home.netscape.com/eng/mozilla/3.0/handbook/javascript
```

If the thought of writing applets from scratch makes your stomach turn and your head spin (Maalox, anyone?), JavaScript may be more your style. Although it's not nearly as complex as the Java programming language, which is used to create applets, JavaScript is considered a "lightweight" alternative to writing applets from scratch. You can't do all the things with JavaScript that you can do with Java, but JavaScript is nonetheless extremely powerful and is a great place to begin if you really want to customize your Web pages. (For details about Java and JavaScript, see Part III.)

If Part III isn't quite enough information for you, check out *JavaScript For Dummies,* 2nd Edition, by Emily A. Vander Veer (IDG Books Worldwide, Inc.). Because *JavaScript For Dummies* is focused 100 percent on JavaScript, starting with the very basics and moving all the way through some of the more complicated scripting issues, you'll find it invaluable if you want to get the most out of the scripting language.

Even though it was introduced a year or so after Java originally hit the Internet, JavaScript (a joint-development product of Netscape Communications Corporation and Sun Microsystems) has grown greatly in popularity among Web developers. As a less intimidating and easy-to-use alternative to Java, JavaScript is popular among programmers and nonprogrammers alike. If you're interested in writing your own scripts, check out Netscape's JavaScript support area. Here, you can find out about JavaScript in detail and learn how to write your own scripts from scratch. In addition, this site has links to several JavaScript-powered sites on the Web that can help you to generate ideas about how you can apply this flexible and powerful scripting language to your own pages.

The Java FAQ Archives

www-net.com/java/faq

Frequently Asked Questions, or *FAQs,* are text documents packed full of questions and their corresponding answers; they're a fantastic resource if you find yourself asking, well, *questions* about applets or scripts.

The Java FAQ Archives is actually a FAQ document repository that maintains links to scores of different Java-related FAQs available on the Web. If you have a question about applets or scripts, chances are good that someone else has already asked it. If your question *has* been asked more than once, it — and its answer! — are likely to have made their way into a FAQ document. Because FAQs are nothing more than text documents, you can download them to your computer, where you can read through them whenever you have a question related to applets or scripts.

You can save yourself much of the time you spend scanning through FAQ documents by simply using a text-search tool (such as your browser, word processor or the Find utility built into your computer) to search the contents of FAQ documents that you have downloaded from the Net.

Although FAQs of all flavors exist, you may be happy to know that scores of Java-related FAQs are available from the Java FAQ Archives site, as shown in Figure 4-7. Simply connect to this site with your Web browser and then download all the FAQs you want. Be sure to return to the site often: New FAQs are generated all the time!

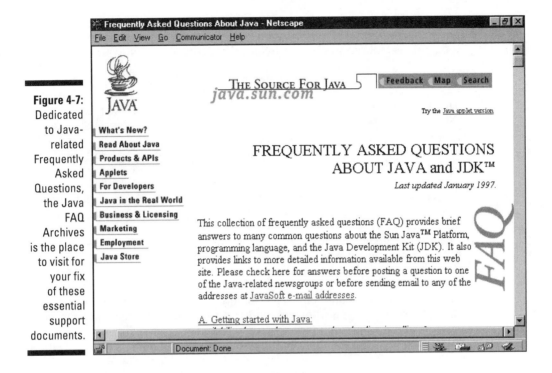

Figure 4-7:
Dedicated
to Java-
related
Frequently
Asked
Questions,
the Java
FAQ
Archives
is the place
to visit for
your fix
of these
essential
support
documents.

Search Engines: Scouring the Web for Java Nuggets

Although you're likely to find everything you need Java-wise by visiting the sites in the preceding section, sometimes you may come up empty-handed when looking for a specific applet or script. In these cases, it's time to turn to search engines — sites dedicated to helping you find information available on the Web.

Search engines use what's known as a *spider,* also called an *agent* or *robot* (don't computer people know how to make things sound cool?), which is a special little program that scours the Web night and day looking for new pages and information to report to the home base.

By returning information to the search engine in the form of hyperlinks (along with a little information about the page to which it points), spiders help a search engine build a gigantic database full of Web links. When you're looking for a specific piece of information, you can visit a search engine and type a keyword or two that are related to your question. The engine compares the keyword or keywords you give it to the massive database of links it maintains and reports back the links that it thinks match your query.

By searching for the keyword **applet**, for example, a search engine shows you all the hyperlinks it finds in its database that contain the word **applet**. The links, and a brief description of the pages they point to, act as a tiny, pinpointed table of contents for the Web — they let you know what's out there as it applies to your query, as shown in Figure 4-8. Because these links are hyperlinks, you can click on any of the items to visit a site and see it in its full splendor.

Search engines are a great boon to Web surfing because you would be in a pickle if you had to find a specific piece of information without them. (How long would it take, using your browser, to search tens of millions of pages? Chances are good that you would run out of steam — and coffee — long before you came close to finding what you were looking for.) Search engines do have a downside, however.

The problem with search engines is simply the vast amount of information that they report to you when you perform a search. Sure, you can be more specific about what you're looking for and qualify your search criteria in an attempt to limit the number of potential matches, but you still end up with a

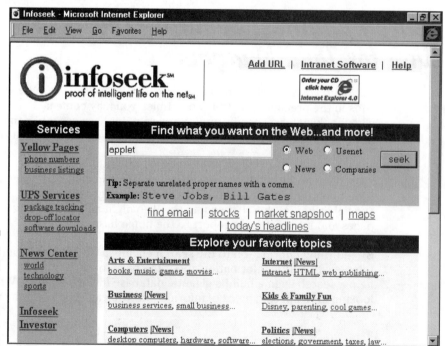

Figure 4-8:
Results of your search come in hyperlink form.

large number of links to filter through. (A recent search for the words **Java applets**, using a popular search engine, reported several hundred thousand matches!) The biggest drawback, of course, is that you have to visit each link before you know for sure what it contains. For this reason alone, I rarely use search engines when I'm looking for applets and scripts; I would rather spend my time prowling around repositories, Javazines, and newsgroups.

In addition to providing newsgroup access, most search engines also categorize their databases so that you can see all the best links that pertain to a specific topic (such as Java). You can then bypass altogether a standard keyword search and head directly to the category in which you're interested. Yahoo!, for example, offers a Java category that consists only of links to useful Java sites (see Figure 4-9). Thankfully, you don't have to waste your time running down dead-end links; Yahoo! (www.yahoo.com) does the work for you by ensuring that each link in the category is something you can use.

Although most search engines are more or less the same when it comes to helping you find information on the Web, one stands apart from the crowd when it comes to finding Java applets. The AltaVista search engine (www.altavista.digital.com), from Digital Equipment Corporation, brings a new and powerful search capability to the Web: the capability to search for applets by name.

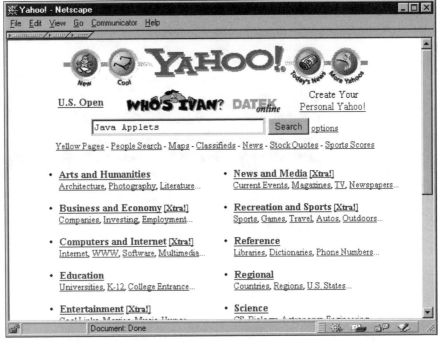

Figure 4-9:
Most search engines categorize their database to save you time and effort.

AltaVista enables you to search for the *name* of the applet .class file; you can search inside the `<APPLET>` tag! If you want to find all the pages that have an applet named "tickertape" embedded in them, for example, you can do just that (see Figure 4-10). With AltaVista, you simply type **applet:** in front of the applet name:

```
applet:tickertape
```

Other search engines would return every link that has the word *tickertape* in it, even if the pages have nothing to do with applets or Java (ticker tape parade, anyone?). Thanks to AltaVista, however, you don't have to separate the needles from the haystack — AltaVista does it for you.

Although the AltaVista search engine can save you a great deal of time in looking for a specific applet, be careful when you type the name of the applet to search for: AltaVista matches it exactly, including lowercase and uppercase letters! If you search for **Tickertape**, for example, AltaVista finds only a hundred or so applets. Change your search to **tickertape**, however, and it reports several thousand matches.

Although AltaVista is currently unique among search engines, thanks to this nifty feature, it won't be for long. Other search engines will eventually offer the same capability. It's not that I can tell the future, mind you — it's just that the capability to search for applets by name is an extremely useful

Figure 4-10:
Using AltaVista, you can search for applets embedded in Web pages; here, it looks inside the `<APPLET>` tag!

feature, and one that AltaVista's competition won't sit on their heels forever and wait to implement. The search engine market is cutthroat, and every competitive edge counts. When one engine comes out on the market with a new feature such as this one, it doesn't take long for the others to pounce on it.

Newsgroups: Electronic Town Meetings

If after searching the Web, you cannot find the Java information that you're looking for, you might consider joining a Java newsgroup. *Newsgroups* are online discussion groups in which people get together electronically to talk and share information. Although newsgroups are not standard Web pages, you can nonetheless access the newsgroups through your Web browser by typing in the newsgroup address into your browser's location area (where you'd normally type in a Web address, although newsgroup addresses begin with `news:` instead of `http://`). Following are two of the more popular Java newsgroups:

✔ `news:comp.lang.java` — Although primarily populated by Java programmers, this newsgroup is worth visiting if only to hear some of the lively and often passionate debates that surface from time to time. You may also find this newsgroup worthwhile if you're interested in more technical Java discussions, especially those related to the Java programming language.

✔ `news:alt.www.hotjava` — Although less technical than the `comp.lang.java` newsgroup, `alt.www.hotjava` is still plenty techni-cal. In this newsgroup, however, you're likely to find discussions revolving around non-programming related issues, such as Java-savvy browsers.

For details on joining a newsgroup, contact your Internet Service Provider or network administrator. To be able to access newsgroups, your browser must be configured correctly, which requires special information about your connection to the Internet. Simply ask your ISP what you need to do to participate in Java newsgroups, and they'll lead you through the process.

Although newsgroups are generally a great place to congregate and ask questions when you hit a sticking point in finding a topic, the Java newsgroups are overloaded with people asking questions. The problem is that everyone seems to be asking questions and only a few answers are being given. As a result, many questions go unanswered and become little more than digital roadkill that newsgroup participants speed by while looking for help with their own problems.

By this time, you might consider posting a question anyway, in the hope that someone will help you out. After you've truly exhausted all avenues, your question is likely to be taken seriously. Because your request isn't easily answered by doing a little legwork, others in the newsgroup might recognize that you aren't being lazy but are truly in need. With luck, someone will respond to your post with a solution.

Many search engines enable you to search newsgroups — if you don't want to wade manually through the messages in a newsgroup, you can use a search engine instead. In particular, you might consider visiting DejaNews (www.dejanews.com), a search engine dedicated entirely to finding information related to newsgroups.

Part II
It's Applet Pickin' Time!

The 5th Wave

By Rich Tennant

"Naaah, he's not that smart. He never uses quote marks, forgets to consistently name his files, and drools all over the keyboard."

In this part . . .

Ready to apply the latest Java applets to your own Web page? Part II walks you through designing a Java-powered Web page, finding suitable applets, and customizing them to meet your needs. You don't need to learn the ins and outs of Java programming to be the proud owner of a sleek, personalized Java-powered Web site. This part explains how you can benefit from the labor of others — legally! You can also find out what makes an applet an applet, and pick up just enough HTML to put applets on your Web page and to create Web pages that satisfy nonJava-savvy Web surfers as well.

Chapter 5

HTML and the <APPLET> Tag

*I*n order to weave Java applets into your Web pages, you must first know the basics of the Hypertext Markup Language (HTML). Although you can now find software tools that enable you to create incredibly sophisticated Web pages without knowing a thing about HTML, if you want a *Java-powered* Web page, you still need to know a thing or two about HTML. Here's why:

✔ Most of today's HTML-generation tools aren't designed with Java in mind. Instead of allowing you to drag and drop applets right into your pages (as they do with images), most HTML-generation tools can deal with applets only the old-fashioned way — they force you to type in the applet information by hand (as explained later in this chapter).

✔ Your Java-powered pages will invariably be visited by Webbers using non-Java browsers. In this case, the non-Java browser has no idea how to deal with applets and shows the user nothing but blank, empty space instead of your wonderful applet. This chapter tells you how to use HTML to provide content for these poor souls.

HTML Basics

Hypertext Markup Language is the glue that holds all Web pages together; without it, Web pages wouldn't exist. Although the name *Hypertext Markup Language* sounds a little intimidating, HTML is really a cream puff. It's something everyone can learn to use in a day or two. If you know how to use a word processor, you can create Web pages with HTML. In essence, Web pages are really nothing more than text documents that have been enhanced with HTML.

This chapter covers HTML just enough to wet your whistle, giving you the information you need to inject Java in your Web pages. If you really want to get the most HTML has to offer, I highly recommend that you sashay on down to your local bookstore and plunk a few bucks on the counter for *HTML For Dummies,* 3rd Edition, by Ed Tittel and Steve James (IDG Books Worldwide, Inc.). Because HTML and Java go hand-in-hand, *HTML For Dummies* is the perfect companion to this book.

Marking it up

With HTML, you can convert any blasé text document into a hypermedia tour de force, complete with hypertext and hypermedia links to any object residing on the World Wide Web. But you're not limited to enhancing existing text documents — you can create razzle-dazzle Web pages from scratch using this flexible markup language.

Markup language? Yes indeed. HTML is a *markup language,* meaning that it's not one of those complex programming languages computer scientists discuss, using cryptic jargon and lots of math. HTML is not something you use to create a software program, such as a word processor or a video game. Instead, it's a friendly language with the express purpose of creating Web pages.

Marking up text is nothing new, really. Think for a moment about how you highlight a word or phrase in a word processor document and then apply a special format to it. You can change the font type and size; specify bold, italic, or underlined; and even change the color of the highlighted text. In essence, you are *marking up* a document. But, rather than going onto the Web where browsers view them, word processor documents usually remain on a personal computer to be viewed by word processors.

Generally speaking, a *markup language* is a formal set of rules and procedures for preparing text to be electronically interpreted and presented. In the case of HTML, you create documents to present on the World Wide Web, where they're interpreted by browsers. When preparing documents for the Web, you apply special keywords, or *tags,* to portions of the text.

Playing tag

Tags are the fundamental building blocks of HTML. You apply tags to parts of a text document to specify how browsers should interpret that text and the document itself. Do you want portions of the text to appear big, small, bold, or italicized? How about making a word or phrase hyperlink to another Web page? And don't forget hypermedia. Why not add a few nice-looking graphics to the document to jazz it up a bit, and make a few of these graphics link to other places on the Web? With HTML tags, you can do all this and more.

HTML tags are very easy to create and use. They're nothing more than a keyword (or even a single letter) inside a pair of less-than (<) and greater-than (>) characters. For example, to indicate the beginning of bold text, HTML uses the tag <B>. You simply type the *opening tag* <B> at the beginning of any text that you want browsers to display as bold:

```
This text isn't bold ... <B> but this text is!
```

Easy enough, huh? When viewed with a browser, all the text appearing after the <B> tag is bold.

But how about turning *off* the bold format? That's easy too; simply create a *closing tag* by putting a forward slash mark before the HTML keyword you want to turn off. For example, to turn off the bold format, you place the tag </B> after the last piece of text you want to appear bold:

```
This text isn't bold ... <B> but this </B> text is!
```

In the preceding code line, I specified that the words *but this* should be bold. All the other words appear in normal text because they fall before the opening <B> tag or after the closing </B> tag. Pretty simple stuff, isn't it? This structure forms the basis of HTML:

- ✔ The opening tag is specified with the keyword inside <>.
- ✔ The closing tag (assuming that particular tag even requires a closing tag — not all do) is the same keyword, but with a slash before it </>.

Although you're free to enter tags in uppercase or lowercase, I recommend always using uppercase letters to make the tags easier for you to read. For example, although <b> and <B> mean the same thing to your browser, the tag in uppercase stands out more. When you're reading through reams of HTML code; lowercase tags have a way of disappearing into the text, whereas those in uppercase seem to jump right out at you.

In HTML, you cannot include any spaces between the <> characters and the text inside them. If you type < B>, the browser won't know what you mean because a space appears before the B. To create a tag, squish the <> characters right up against whatever you put inside them. No spaces allowed!

Specifying an HTML document

If a Web page is nothing more than a text document marked up with a bunch of HTML tags, how does the Web browser know the difference between the two? What happens, for example, when a browser comes across a regular text file? And, better yet, what happens when a browser encounters a document full of HTML tags?

Consider, if you will, the following poem:

```
Mountain Twilight

Iron clouds
have moved east.
The mountain is
a black silhouette
the lake
a gold and lavender
bowl of twilight.
                -TFW
```

Clearly, the preceding poem has no HTML tags, making this nothing more than standard text. Suppose a browser comes across the document containing this poem. How will it display the document? The answer to that question depends on the browser that is viewing the document. Depending on how they're designed, browsers have two different methods of identifying an HTML document:

- ✔ By checking the document's filename for an .html or .htm extension
- ✔ By determining whether the document contains HTML tags

Because you have no surefire way of knowing which method a particular browser will use to view your Web document, you should use both methods of identification.

If the preceding poem (which contains no HTML tags) is stored in a file having a .txt extension, for example, every browser recognizes it as a plain text document and displays the contents as plain text (see Figure 5-1). In fact, even if this file's extension is .abc, its contents are treated as plain text because the text itself contains nothing special to tell the browser otherwise. If, however, the file contains more than just text, and instead is marked up with HTML tags, some browsers actually disregard the extension and display the document as if it has an .html extension.

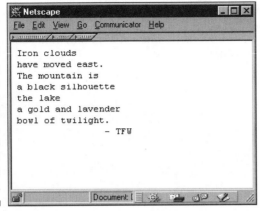

Figure 5-1:
This
document's
file
extension,
.txt, tells
browsers to
expect plain
text.

Because not all browsers go the extra distance and bother to look inside the files they display for the presence of HTML tags, giving your pages the proper extension is critical. Whenever your Web files contain HTML tags (which they almost always do, unless you need to display plain text), they should also have the .html extension (or .htm, for computers that can only handle three-letter extensions). The .html file extension is the standard way of telling browsers to expect HTML code inside.

When plain text resides in a file having the .html extension, browsers treat that text as if it is marked up with HTML. But in the case of the preceding poem, no HTML tags are present. As a result, when this document has the .html extension, everything is jumbled together, as shown in Figure 5-2.

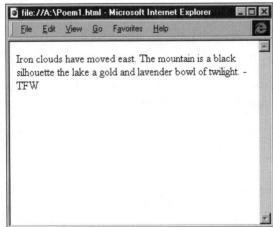

Figure 5-2:
Giving a
document
containing
no HTML
tags the
.html
extension is
like giving
suntan
lotion to a
mole — it
won't do
much good.

Creating an HTML document involves more than just saving text in a file that has an .html extension. For a text file to be truly considered an HTML document, the text in that document must, at a minimum, be enclosed in opening <HTML> and closing </HTML> tags:

```
<HTML>

Mountain Twilight

Iron clouds
have moved east.
The mountain is
a black silhouette
the lake
a gold and lavender
bowl of twilight.
                -TFW


</HTML>
```

When these two tags are present, together with an .html extension, any browser knows immediately that it should treat whatever's between these tags as HTML instead of plain text.

Although HTML documents technically don't have to be stored in files having the .html (or .htm) extension, they almost always are. Rarely, if ever, do you encounter an HTML document on the Web that has a different extension. Because extensions are a way of identifying the file they are appended to, storing HTML documents in files having anything other than an .html (or .htm) extension doesn't make much sense.

Getting the text in order

Now you may think that the presence of the opening and closing <HTML> tags should make a big difference in how a browser displays your document, but it doesn't! The opening <HTML> tag just tells the browser "Hey, you're dealing with an HTML file — keep your eyes peeled for more tags from now on." The closing </HTML> tag, on the other hand, just says "Okay, you've reached the end of the HTML file — you won't see any tags from here on out."

In effect, the opening <HTML> and closing </HTML> tags just define the beginning and ending of the file. What falls between these two tags is what matters. And because nothing but plain text falls between these two tags in the poem example, the browser doesn't do anything special with it. HTML doesn't even recognize *carriage returns* (that is, paragraph marks) the way that your word processor does. Instead, you must supply carriage returns the HTML way — as tags.

You can indicate carriage returns in two ways in HTML. If you want the browser to recognize the carriage returns as they actually occur in the text, you can surround the entire poem (between the opening and closing HTML tags) with the opening <PRE> and closing </PRE> tags. These tags, which mark text as *preformatted information,* tell the browser to expect word processor-style carriage returns:

```
<HTML>

<PRE>

Mountain Twilight

Iron clouds
have moved east.
The mountain is
a black silhouette
the lake
a gold and lavender
bowl of twilight.
                    -TFW

</PRE>

</HTML>
```

Although this approach does the trick, as shown in Figure 5-3, it may not give you exactly what you were hoping for. Because the browser assumes that preformatted information is special text, it displays it in a special font. As a result, text appearing between the opening <PRE> and closing </PRE> tags looks different than other HTML text.

Figure 5-3:
Browsers recognize standard carriage returns and display them properly in preformatted text, but they display the text itself in a special font.

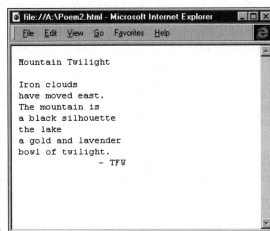

Because of this font variation, Web page authors often scrap the <PRE> tags and use the *line-break*
 tag or the *paragraph-break* <P> tag instead. A line break acts much like a single carriage return, forcing the text following it to begin on a new line; a paragraph break acts like a couple of carriage returns, adding a line of blank space between it and the text following it. (These two tags don't require a closing companion tag because they simply tell the browser to insert a paragraph break or line break wherever they appear.)

Here's how the poem looks when you use the line- and paragraph-break tags instead of the <PRE> tag:

```
<HTML>Mountain Twilight <P>Iron clouds <BR>have moved
          east.<BR>The mountain is<BR>a black
          silhouette<BR>the lake<BR>a gold and
          lavender<BR>bowl of twilight.<BR>-TFW</HTML>
```

Notice in this code example that I've removed the word processor style carriage returns that previously came between the lines of the poem. Because the poem is no longer marked up as preformatted information, browsers ignore all word processor style carriage returns anyway. However, you're free to include them in your HTML *source code* — that's what these lines of commands, or code, are called — just to make it easier for you to read:

```
<HTML>
Mountain Twilight <P>

Iron clouds <BR>
have moved east.<BR>
The mountain is<BR>
a black silhouette<BR>
the lake<BR>
a gold and lavender<BR>
bowl of twilight.<BR>
                    -TFW
</HTML>
```

The results of both examples (with or without carriage returns) look the same, as shown in Figure 5-4. But take a look at the last line. Instead of appearing to the far right, the text (-TFW) is left aligned, just as the other text is. The browser has disregarded the spaces before the text.

By marking the last line as preformatted information, browsers keep the spaces intact (see Figure 5-5). And because this last line is not part of the poem, but rather the initials of the author, having it appear in a different font is actually desired in this case:

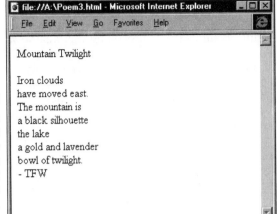

Figure 5-4:
You can't
use multiple
spaces to
align text
without the
<PRE> tag.

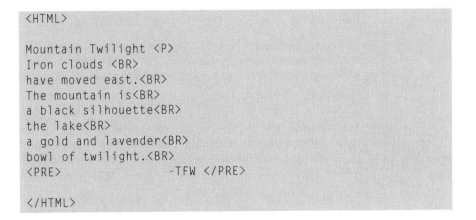

```
<HTML>

Mountain Twilight <P>
Iron clouds <BR>
have moved east.<BR>
The mountain is<BR>
a black silhouette<BR>
the lake<BR>
a gold and lavender<BR>
bowl of twilight.<BR>
<PRE>                    -TFW </PRE>

</HTML>
```

Figure 5-5:
When
marked as
preformatted
information,
the spaces
preceding
"–TFW" are
displayed
exactly as
they appear
in the HTML
source
code.

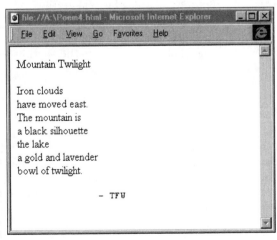

Standard HTML's more advanced features

The "Mountain Twilight" example in the preceding section shows how HTML markup tags function to format text so browsers can view it. HTML has many tags and structures (other than the ones discussed) that you can use to create cool Web pages. The following bulleted list gives you an idea of some other important HTML functions and characteristics:

- ✔ You can use nested tags (one set of opening and closing tags, such as `<I>` and `</I>` to denote italics, placed inside a different set of opening and closing tags, such as `<B>` and `</B>` for bold) to apply more than one type of formatting to the same text. For both bold and italic:

  ```
  <B><I>moved east</I></B>
  ```

- ✔ You can organize your text into logical, easy-to-read sections by using tags for different levels of headings. For a bold, italic level 3 heading:

  ```
  <H3><B><I>moved east</I></B></H3>
  ```

- ✔ You can supply certain HTML tags with *attributes* (special keywords that help qualify how the tag acts). To include a graphic image on your Web page, use the image tag `<IMG>` with the source (`SRC`) attribute:

  ```
  <IMG SRC="coolgraphic.gif">
  ```

- ✔ You can include hyperlinks to any other type of object residing on the Web. (See the sidebar "Linking to relative and absolute URLs.") For a link to another Web document, include the URL for the document inside the anchor tag `<A>`. To make the word "lakes" a hyperlink to a lake Web site:

  ```
  <A HREF="http://www.water.org/lakes.html"> lakes </A>
  ```

- ✔ You can further format your Web page by grouping items into bulleted lists, aligning text and images, creating special characters (like copyright and trademark symbols), and including horizontal rules.

- ✔ And, of course, you can include exciting Java applets in your Web page by using the `<APPLET>` tag. (I show you how in the section "Introducing the <APPLET> tag.")

The evolution of HTML

HTML is a constantly evolving language, with new tags added all the time to keep up with the demands of Web publishers and Webbers. When it was first invented, HTML offered a relatively small set of tags. But millions of Web page developers around the world quickly outgrew those initial offerings, requiring that new features be added to the language.

TECHNICAL STUFF

Linking to relative and absolute URLs

You can use HTML to create hyperlinked text and images — words and pictures that you can click on to call new information to the screen. (Many Java applets use nonstandard HTML to create hyperlinked animations, as well.) You need only two things to create hyperlinks:

✔ The object that will serve as your link (for example, a word, phrase, image, or animation)

✔ The location of the object to which you want the link to lead

Suppose you want to link the word "lakes" to a distant Web site dedicated to large bodies of water. As long as you know the URL for the site, you're all set. Your code may look like this:

```
<A HREF="http://www.water.org/
    lakes.html"> lakes </A>
```

Here, the word "lakes" has been associated with a Web page by combining the <A> anchor tag with a *hypertext reference* attribute (HREF="") containing a URL (http://www.water.org/lakes.html). As a result, the opening <A> tag is enhanced with the special information that is required to create a hyperlink, making it much longer than most other tags.

Even though this tag is quite long, the browser treats it as just another opening tag. This tag, however, creates a hyperlink reference for the text that follows. All text following this opening tag is treated as a hyperlink until the browser encounters a closing </A> tag. In this example, only the word "lakes" is marked as a hyperlink, although I could just as easily have placed an entire chunk of text such as "Check out my awesome lake photo, dudes!" inside the <A> and </A> tags instead. Hey, this is HTML — we can mark up any amount of text that we'd like.

Whenever a Webber selects the word "lakes," the browser connects to the associated Web page. This is known as an *absolute reference* because the exact (or *absolute*) URL for the information it refers to is supplied. However, both text and image hyperlinks are capable of utilizing *relative* references.

Relative references, sometimes referred to as *partial addresses* because they're not complete URLs, create links to information that is found relative to the location of the Web page containing the reference itself. Objects specified using a relative URL are expected to be in the same directory as the Web page containing the HTML code itself. Thus, when you use a relative URL reference, you don't specify the URL in your tag. If the lakes.html document to which you want to link the word "lakes" is housed in the same directory as your Web page, you may use the following relative reference instead:

```
<A HREF="lakes.html">lakes</A>
```

In many respects, you can think of HTML as a software product: New features (tags) are added, problematic and unused ones are eliminated, and a new release is prepared for public consumption. Unlike a software product, however, HTML doesn't simply become available (or *go golden*) based on one company's belief that it is ready for release. Instead, each new version of HTML goes through a rigorous evaluation process before it becomes a standard.

The HTML tags discussed in this chapter are a fraction, a very small fraction, of the ones available for use. And not all browsers support all tags.

To accommodate users with browsers that don't support all tags, you should enhance your applets with standard HTML (see the section "Alternate HTML" in the following discussion of the <APPLET> tag). Including standard HTML in your Java-powered Web pages enables both Webbers who are using Java-savvy browsers and those who aren't so fortunate to get the most out of your site. If you don't provide such an alternative, those with non-Java browsers may turn away from your site, thinking that you just don't know how to create cool Web pages.

If an applet normally animates a series of images, you can provide alternate HTML code that displays just one of those images for Webbers without access to Java. You may even consider hyperlinking an alternative image for non-Java browsers to Netscape's home page, giving those users one-click access to their own Java-savvy browser!

Introducing the <APPLET> Tag

The <APPLET> tag, used to embed Java applets in Web pages, is the mother of all nonstandard tags. Depending on the applet that you're embedding, and to what extent you choose to customize that applet for your page (see Chapters 8 and 9), the <APPLET> tag you construct can be relatively simple or exceptionally complex.

The <APPLET> tag, like all other *compound* tags, is comprised of several parts. That is, additional information related to the tag may be included between the first portion of the opening tag (<APPLET) and the closing brace of the opening tag (>). However, only a few of these pieces of information are required. Whether you have to provide anything other than the absolute bare minimum depends entirely on the applet you are configuring. Some applets make heavy use of all parts of the <APPLET> tag; others need only the required parts.

The following code gives a simplified look at the four main parts of the <APPLET> tag:

```
<APPLET attributes>
applet-parameters
alternate-HTML
</APPLET>
```

TECHNICAL STUFF

HTML 4.0: The latest and greatest

A brand-spanking-new version of HTML — 4.0 — is in the works. HTML 4.0 is the latest and greatest revision of the hypertext markup language and it incorporates a large number of the most popular non-standard tags in a noble effort to bring browsers into *parity* with one another, meaning they all support the same suite of HTML tags and therefore all display the same Web page in exactly the same way (provided, of course, that all browsers support HTML 4.0 when it becomes official). In fact, HTML 4.0 supports a new tag called <OBJECT> that is expected to

eventually replace the <APPLET> tag, because it's designed specifically to weave executable content into Web pages.

Unfortunately, it will be a while before Web browsers support HTML 4.0 and the <OBJECT> tag. HTML 4.0 is still under development, after all, and must first be completed before browser vendors can incorporate it into their products. As a result, our good friend <APPLET> is still the only way to go when it comes to weaving Java applets into Web pages.

The opening <APPLET> tag

As with all tags, both standard and nonstandard, the <APPLET> tag begins with an opening tag. And like many other tags, the applet tag supports a number of *attributes* — information that enhances the way the applet looks or acts when a browser runs it.

Placing the required attributes

Attributes are keywords that tell browsers to do something special when they encounter a tag; in the case of the <APPLET> opening tag, this *something* is a bit more complex than with other tags. Although many opening tags consist of nothing more than a letter or two (<B>, <I>, <BR>, and so forth) and no attributes whatsoever, the <APPLET> tag requires that you provide the initial part of the opening tag (<APPLET>) *and* at least three attributes that together tell the browser the name of the applet and how much space the applet will take up when displayed:

```
<APPLET CODE="Marquee" HEIGHT=25 WIDTH=450>
```

In this example, an applet named Marquee has been specified. The CODE attribute of the opening tag identifies the file containing the applet. The HEIGHT and WIDTH attributes of the opening tag, on the other hand, are used to tell the browser how much space in the Web page the applet requires. In this case, the applet takes up 25 pixels in height and 450 pixels in width.

Squeezing applets into tiny JARs

Some applets rely on a number of files, such as images, sounds, and even other bytecode files created by a programmer — each of which you must download over the network to your computer before you can use them. As you may suspect, downloading each of the files needed by an applet takes time, especially because the browser has to make a *network connection* — a special request — for each one. When Java was first introduced to the world, there was no way around this; every file an applet needed had to be downloaded one at a time by the browser, meaning a network connection had to be created and then closed for each file.

Java has matured quite a bit since it was first introduced to the Web. Today, the most current crop of Java-savvy browsers can download all the files an applet needs by using a single network connection. There's a catch, however: These files first must be assembled by the developer and then compressed into a *Java Archive*, or JAR for short. A JAR file is essentially a compressed archive that contains the files an applet uses. It requires considerably less time to download than if each of the files had to be downloaded separately.

JAR files are an option that an applet developer may not choose to take advantage of because JARs are understood only by the latest versions of browsers. JARs will likely become more popular as time goes on — why download every file an applet needs one at a time when you can download them all at once in a fraction of the time?

Of course, JAR files don't come for free as far as the `<APPLET>` tag is concerned. You must specify every JAR file an applet needs via the `ARCHIVE` attribute, (which I cover at the end of this chapter). When an applet makes use of a JAR, or more than one JAR (yep, applets can use multiple JARs), the `ARCHIVE` attribute comes into play. If you don't properly specify the JAR by using the `ARCHIVE` attribute, the browser has no way of knowing what to download — other than the bytecode class file specified in the `CODE` attribute. The `ARCHIVE` attribute does not replace the `CODE` attribute; rather, they work hand-in-hand (as this chapter explains).

Using quotation marks

Notice that the name of the applet file, `Marquee`, is surrounded by quotes, but the height and width values aren't. While quotes are not absolutely necessary when dealing with the `CODE` attribute, you often see strings of characters enclosed in quotes because of the potential for spaces in applet names. An applet Background Color, for example, contains a space in its name, as opposed to an applet called BackgroundColor, which doesn't. (Numeric values, such as height and width, never have spaces in them — that is, the number one hundred is always represented by 100, not 10 0, 1 00, or even 1 0 0.)

Surrounding strings with quotes ensures that the browser knows exactly what to look for, even if spaces are included. For example, if you leave off the quotes on an applet *parameter* — a piece of information that modifies how an applet looks or acts — named Background Color, the browser sees only the characters leading up to the first space. In this case, the browser sees only the first word, Background, and doesn't find the applet you specify.

Be extremely careful to balance your quotes. If you start a piece of text with a quote, you must supply a corresponding end quote. Furthermore, you must be sure not to include any extra quotes. Improper use of quotes is deadly to Java-savvy browsers and may cause them to crash! The following two examples would, at best, confuse the browser; at worst, they could cause the browser to shut down:

- ✔ Missing quote: <PARAM NAME="speed" VALUE="500>
- ✔ Extra quote: <PARAM NAME="speed" VALUE="500"">

You also must be careful not to use curly quotes when creating hyperlinks. Browsers don't recognize curly quotes (sometimes called *smart quotes*) as real quotes, so using them will prevent your hyperlink from working properly. Avoid them like the plague when creating Web pages and you'll be a happy camper.

Although you don't have to place quotes around numeric parameters, it's a good idea to get into the habit of surrounding everything in quotes. Quotes don't do any harm when surrounding numbers or strings that don't have spaces, and ensure that you never make the mistake of omitting quotes where they're really needed (around strings having spaces). Do yourself a favor, and surround all numbers and strings with quotes. It's better to be quote-rich than quote-poor when it comes to applets!

If your applet filenames don't contain spaces (and they rarely will), you don't have to bother using quotation marks. However, because omitting quotes when they are needed is one of the most common mistakes people make when hooking up applets, I highly recommend always surrounding non-numeric values with quotes — better to be safe than sorry!

Case matters! When supplying the name of an applet file, be sure to type the name exactly, matching each letter case for case. For example, if an applet is named Marquee, you must specify that name exactly in the CODE attribute. If you type in **marquee** (lowercase "m") instead, the browser won't be able to find the applet!

A class act

Almost all applets are stored in files having a .class extension. This is a result of the software development process, the final step of which involves converting human-readable Java code into machine-readable code (see the sidebar "Cracking the code"). Once converted, the file has the .class extension.

As a result, the `Marquee` applet is actually stored in a file named Marquee.class. Although you're free to include the .class extension when specifying your applets, you don't have to. Java-savvy browsers know to look for a file with that extension. You must, however, provide the extension if the applet is anything other than .class. Thus, the following opening `<APPLET>` tag is functionally equivalent to the one shown previously, although slightly more precise when it comes to the applet file name:

```
<APPLET CODE="Marquee.class" HEIGHT=25 WIDTH=450>
```

Attribute alley

At a bare minimum, all opening `<APPLET>` tags must contain the three attributes shown in the preceding examples: `CODE`, `HEIGHT`, and `WIDTH`. These are known as *required attributes* (see Table 5-1) because you can't include applets in Web pages without them. In addition to the three required attributes, you can use a number of *optional attributes* to control how an applet appears in your pages.

Cracking the code

Applets are tiny programs written in the Java programming language by software developers. The special instructions a developer writes using this language is known as *source code*, which can be thought of as the recipe for an applet. After a developer writes the source code for an applet, the applet goes though a special tool known as a compiler. The compiler converts the human-readable source code into a form the computer can read, known as *bytecode*, which results in the creation of the applet (think of a compiler as an oven; it bakes the source code "ingredients" into a delectable treat known as an applet).

The resulting applet is really what you weave into your Web pages; you specify the name of this file in the `CODE` attribute of the opening `<APPLET>` tag. After you understand that applets are stored in files comprised of computer-readable bytecode, using the word `CODE` in the opening tag to identify the applet makes sense — you're telling the browser the name of the applet bytecode file to look for.

Table 5-1	Required Applet Attributes
Attribute	**Description**
CODE	Specifies the name of the applet file
HEIGHT	Specifies the height of your applet in pixels
WIDTH	Specifies the width of your applet in pixels

You may also include optional attributes, listed in Table 5-2, anywhere within the opening tag. I recommend that you specify optional attributes after the three required ones in order to increase the readability of your HTML source code.

```
<APPLET CODE="Marquee" HEIGHT=25 WIDTH=450 ALT="This is a
         cool applet — too bad you can't see it!"
         HSPACE=10
         VSPACE=25>
```

The exception to this rule is CODEBASE, which should come before the CODE attribute if you use it at all (see the "Getting to base" section, later in this chapter).

Table 5-2	Optional Applet Attributes
Attribute	**Description**
ALIGN	This attribute specifies where your applet is placed on the page in respect to the text around it; it may be one of the following nine alignments: left, right, top, texttop, middle, absmiddle, baseline, bottom, and absbottom.
ALT	This attribute specifies alternative text to be displayed by Java-savvy browsers that are incapable of executing the applet for whatever reason. Note that this text is seen only by Java-savvy browsers, as it falls within the opening <APPLET> tag, which all non-Java browsers skip over. If you want to communicate with non-Java browsers, do so by using *alternate HTML* – plain old fashioned HTML that appears immediately before the closing </APPLET> tag (see the section entitled "Alternate HTML" for more details).
CODEBASE	This attribute specifies the base URL for your applet. The applet must be located relative to this URL. If CODEBASE isn't specified, the applet is expected to reside in the same directory as the Web page.
HSPACE	This attribute specifies the horizontal space surrounding your applet.

(continued)

Table 5-2 *(continued)*

Attribute	Description
NAME	This attribute specifies the symbolic name of your applet, allowing other applets embedded in the same page to locate your applet by name. This attribute is used only when applets on a page communicate with one another, something most applets don't do.
VSPACE	This attribute specifies the vertical space surrounding your applet.

After you begin adding optional attributes to the mix, the opening tag can become quite difficult to read. To further increase the readability of your HTML source code, I recommend placing any optional attributes on their own line:

```
<APPLET CODE="Marquee" HEIGHT=25 WIDTH=450
ALT="This is a cool applet — too bad you can't see it!"
HSPACE=10
VSPACE=25>
```

The browser doesn't care how the tag appears, as long as it begins with < and ends with >. As a result, you can format your opening tag in any way you want.

Getting to base

Under normal circumstances, the browser expects to find the applet file inside the same directory as the Web page. In this case, you must ensure that the applet file and the Web page in which it is embedded share the same directory (flip to Chapter 7 for details).

However, keeping the applet and the Web page in the same directory isn't always possible. What if the applet you want to embed in your page resides halfway around the world (a *distributed* applet, described in Chapter 7)? In this case, it's physically impossible for your Web page and the applet to reside in the same directory.

And what if you want a bunch of different pages on your Web site to use the same applet? What a profound waste of time and Web server space it would be to upload a copy of the applet into every directory containing a Web page that used it. A better idea is to have the applet reside in a central location on your server where all pages can get to it. But how?

Fortunately, the optional CODEBASE tag does just that. It enables you to specify a URL that points to the directory containing your applet. When a Java-savvy browser encounters the CODEBASE attribute, it automatically knows to look for the applet in whatever directory that attribute points to. The URL you supply for CODEBASE may point to a directory on your server or one on any other server on the Web:

```
<APPLET CODEBASE="http://www.mantiscorp.com/applets/"
CODE="Marquee" HEIGHT=25 WIDTH=450>
```

In this example, browsers won't look for the Marquee applet inside the same directory as the Web page containing this <APPLET> tag. Instead, browsers expect the applet to be located on the Mantis Development Corporation server (www.mantiscorp.com), inside the applets directory.

The CODEBASE tag is particularly helpful when a number of pages on your site use the same applet. Rather than having multiple copies of the same applet scattered all around your server, you can place a single copy of the applet in one directory and specify the appropriate CODEBASE attribute in all pages. This eliminates the headache of creating these pages because you don't have to upload a copy of the applet for every page that uses it and it makes upgrading the applet a cinch: Simply upgrade the single applet and you're done.

The URL you supply for CODEBASE can be either relative or absolute (refer to the sidebar "Linking to relative and absolute URLs").

Applet parameters

The second major part of the <APPLET> tag, *applet parameters,* is where you can really customize an applet. To make an applet look or act as you want it to, you use a special <PARAM> tag that has two of its very own attributes: NAME and VALUE. Although not all applets are customizable, those that are allow you to supply information by using one or more <PARAM> tags according to the following format:

```
<PARAM NAME="parameter name" VALUE="parameter value">
```

For example, an applet may allow you to provide a sound track that plays in the background when the applet is running. To tell the applet the name of the sound file to use and where that file is located, you could supply the following <PARAM> tag:

```
<PARAM NAME="sndTrack" VALUE="audio/sinatra/summerwind.au">
```

In this example, the name of the parameter is sndTrack. The value associated with this parameter, audio/sinatra/summerwind.au, is a *relative URL* (a partial URL pointing to a file or image located relative to the Web page in which the applet itself appears) leading to a sound file. Some applets may also accept an absolute URL (complete URL provided) for this parameter:

```
<PARAM NAME="sndTrack" VALUE="http://www.music.org/beatles/
          HeyJude.au">
```

Because the author of an applet must write the programming code that allows the applet to deal with parameters, each applet is unique in so far as the parameters it accepts. For example, another applet may also allow you to specify a sound track. Depending on how it was written, however, the applet may not understand URLs at all — the applet may insist that the sound file reside in the same directory as the applet itself, meaning you supply only a filename:

```
<PARAM NAME="music" VALUE="nirvana.au">
```

Here, the applet just looks for the sound file named nirvana.au, expecting to find it in the same directory in which the applet resides. Not only that, but the parameter name isn't sndTrack. Because the programmer decides what features you can customize, as well as the parameter names that correspond to these features, you may find a number of different names used for the same thing. Whereas this applet uses "music" as the parameter name that corresponds to the file with a background sound track, others may use the name background, back music, sound_Track, sound, or just about anything else a programmer can think of!

Applets can play only sounds that are stored in a very specific format, which is why each of the sound files specified here have the .au extension. For details on this sound format, see Chapter 6.

Good, solid values

Different applets may support any number of different parameters. It's not unusual, for example, to come across applets that support several different parameters, giving you great flexibility when it comes to configuring them. To supply more than one parameter, all you have to do is enter the parameters one after another.

The Marquee applet, for example, enables you to customize the text that scrolls across the screen. You can specify the font, style, and point size the text should appear in. All you have to do is provide a parameter tag for each of the parameters that you wish to supply to the applet when it's executed:

```
<PARAM NAME="font_face" VALUE="Helvetica">
<PARAM NAME="font_size" VALUE="24">
<PARAM NAME="font_italic" VALUE="yes">
<PARAM NAME="font_bold" VALUE="yes">
<PARAM NAME="marquee" VALUE="Yo! The text you are now
          reading will scroll across the screen when
          this applet is executed...">
```

There are a number of ways to customize the preceding applet, although you don't necessarily have to supply a parameter for each and every parameter the applet supports. Marquee, like many applets, supplies a default parameter if you don't bother to supply one. If, for example, you don't supply any information about the font, Marquee uses Times, 18-point by default. Of course, it's up to the programmer whether an applet provides a default. Some applets force you to supply parameters; others are written to supply default values if you leave parameters out.

The Marquee applet is provided on the CD-ROM that comes with this book, so you can weave it into your own Web pages. For more details on how to configure the Marquee applet using parameter tags, see Chapter 8.

Just as with opening <APPLET> tag attributes, any parameter value that contains a space character (or many spaces) must be surrounded by quotes. Of course, when parameters require numeric values, you don't need to use quotes at all.

Multiple values

Some applets don't stop at having just one value associated with a given parameter name. In many cases, you can supply several values at once. When this is possible, each value must be separated from the others so as not to confuse the applet. Typically, the | character is used:

```
<PARAM NAME="sounds"
        VALUE="sinatra.au|HeyJude.au|nirvana.au">
```

In this case, the applet receives three sound files as one parameter. Not all applets accept multiple parameters, of course, but those that do accept multiple parameters insist that you separate each with a special character. Although the | character — sometimes called the *pipe character* — is the most common, it's up to the developer of the applet to decide what character you supply. As a result, don't be surprised to find commas, colons, and even spaces used to separate multiple values:

```
<PARAM NAME="sounds"
        VALUE="sinatra.au,HeyJude.au,nirvana.au">
<PARAM NAME="images" VALUE="shark.gif:pig.gif:tiger.au">
<PARAM NAME="images" VALUE="shark.gif;pig.gif;tiger.au">
<PARAM NAME="speeds" VALUE="100 355 23 0 535">
```

Alternate HTML

Following any parameter tags that you may use, but before the closing </APPLET> tag, there is a special area where you can supply what's known as *alternate HTML*. Here, you may enter any amount of HTML code you want; such code will be displayed only by non-Java browsers.

Although applets completely ignore alternate HTML, it's an important part of the ⟨APPLET⟩ tag nonetheless. Alternate HTML gives you an opportunity to create Web pages that are useful to Webbers regardless of the browser they happen to use. If you don't supply alternate HTML for non-Java browsers, you run the risk of alienating users with those browsers.

Take, for example, Figure 5-6. Here, frozen in time, is a screen shot of a Java-powered page as viewed by a Java-savvy browser. Although you can't tell by looking at this figure, the buttons on this page are all courtesy of applets. When this page is viewed though a Java-savvy browser, each applet executes and begins animating its respective button. As a result, a page full of living, animated buttons is displayed.

Each of the buttons on this page uses an applet tag similar to the following:

```
<APPLET CODE="LivingLinks" WIDTH=100 HEIGHT=100>
<PARAM NAME="image" VALUE="animalsButton.gif">
<PARAM NAME="effect" VALUE="ripple">
<PARAM NAME="sound" VALUE="dolphinSqueak.au">
<PARAM NAME="URL" VALUE="http://www.mantiscorp.com /">
</APPLET>
```

These buttons were brought to life with the LivingLinks applet, provided on the CD-ROM that comes with this book. This flexible, general-purpose applet provides you with a means to animate buttons and play sounds in your pages.

If you view the page in Figure 5-6 using a non-Java browser, you won't see any of the applets! And because no alternate HTML is provided to compensate for their loss, nothing is displayed in place of these applets. The result, shown in Figure 5-7, is a pathetic excuse for a Web page: Nobody will find it useful because all the buttons are missing.

Fortunately, this nightmare is entirely avoidable. Just be sure to provide the corresponding alternate HTML code for each applet and the buttons will be visible to users of non-Java browsers:

```
<APPLET CODE="LivingLinks" WIDTH=100 HEIGHT=100>
<PARAM NAME="image" VALUE="animalsButton.gif">
<PARAM NAME="effect" VALUE="ripple">
<PARAM NAME="sound" VALUE="dolphinSqueak.au">
<PARAM NAME="URL" VALUE="http://www.mantiscorp.com/">
<IMG SRC="animalsButton.gif">
</APPLET>
```

Although a carriage return between the last ⟨PARAM⟩ tag and the alternate HTML isn't necessary, it makes the code easier to read.

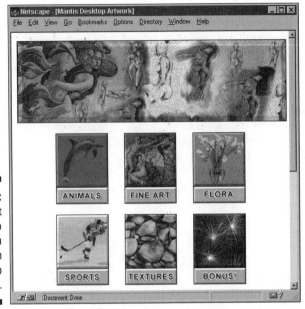

Figure 5-6:
An applet
is used to
place each
button on
this Web
page.

Figure 5-7:
Without
alternate
HTML,
non-Java
browsers
won't
display
anything in
place of
the applets
they can't
execute!

If displayed using alternate HTML (`<IMG SRC="animalsButton.gif">` in this case), the buttons aren't alive the way they are under Java's steam, but it's a far cry from having nothing at all on the Web page. In fact, because any HTML code may be supplied in the alternate HTML area, these buttons need not appear merely as decoration. Instead, each can be a fully functional hyperlink:

```
<APPLET CODE="LivingLinks" WIDTH=100 HEIGHT=100>
<PARAM NAME="image" VALUE="animalsButton.gif">
<PARAM NAME="effect" VALUE="ripple">
<PARAM NAME="sound" VALUE="dolphinSqueak.au">
<PARAM NAME="URL" VALUE="http://www.mantiscorp.com/">
<A HREF="http://www.mantiscorp.com/">
<IMG SRC="animalsButton.gif">
</A>
</APPLET>
```

It's always a good idea to provide alternate HTML code for your applets whenever possible. Of course, there are some things applets do that you can't mimic with standard HTML. However, whenever you can provide alternate HTML code that approximates an applet's visual appearance (as in the button example in this section), you should do it — users of both non-Java and Java-powered browsers will benefit from your site.

The closing </APPLET> tag

The fourth and final part of the `<APPLET>` tag brings the entire tag to a close. To properly form an `<APPLET>` tag, you must balance the opening tag with a closing `</APPLET>` tag. When the browser sees `</APPLET>`, it knows there is no more to the applet: That's all she wrote!

Putting Your <APPLET> Tag to Work

Although many applets are quite easy to use, others are extremely complex. The only way to learn how to construct an appropriate `<APPLET>` tag for a given applet is to read the information that comes with the applet, assuming documentation of some sort is supplied. Otherwise, you can always look at the tag as it appears in an existing Web page (see Chapter 6 for details).

In all cases, you're free to ignore the alternate HTML portion of an `<APPLET>` tag when you are constructing your own tag. And, in many cases, you won't have to bother with parameter tags at all: Not all applets are customizable. However, you always need to use at least the opening and closing `<APPLET>` tags, regardless of the applet itself. And within the opening tag, you're required to supply three attributes: `CODE`, `HEIGHT`, and `WIDTH`.

As a result, the most simplistic tag possible looks something like this:

```
<APPLET CODE="AnyApplet" HEIGHT=50 WIDTH=100>
</APPLET>
```

Although this example is certainly bare-boned, it's not uncommon. Many applets don't support the use of parameter tags, so such tags will be ignored if you supply them.

When an applet allows you to customize it, remember to use PARAM tags. Although each applet is different in the number and name of parameters it accepts, be sure to provide all of the parameters immediately after the opening tag but before the first line of alternate HTML. Although this can make the tag difficult to read, especially if there are a number of parameters, you're free to indent the code as you see fit. Personally, I prefer to indent all the parameter tags and place a carriage return between the very last one and the first line of alternate HTML:

```
<APPLET CODE="Marquee" WIDTH=500 HEIGHT=40>
    <PARAM NAME="font_face" VALUE="TimesRoman">
    <PARAM NAME="font_size" VALUE="24">
    <PARAM NAME="font_italic" VALUE="yes">
    <PARAM NAME="font_bold" VALUE="yes">
    <PARAM NAME="marquee" VALUE="Yo! I'm scrolling!">

Gee, you can't see the scrolling text can you?
That's because this page requires a Java-savvy browser...
<A HREF="http://www.netscape.com">GET ONE!</A>!
</APPLET>
```

When viewed in a Java-savvy browser, the applet comes to life and scrolls the words "Yo! I'm scrolling!" across the screen (see Figure 5-8). Those with non-Java browsers, however, are teased a bit and offered a link to Netscape's home page, where they can get their hands on a Java-savvy browser (see Figure 5-9).

Figure 5-8:
Applets execute only if their <APPLET> tag is properly constructed.

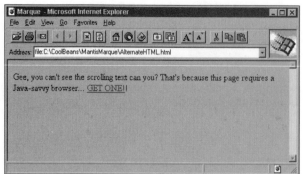

Figure 5-9: Alternate HTML allows users on non-Java browsers to view your pages.

Java 1.1: There's a New <APPLET> Tag in Town

Today there's a new and improved <APPLET> tag that you really need to understand before wading too deep in the Java waters. Actually, it's not so much a new <APPLET> tag as it is an *enhancement* to the earlier version — two <APPLET> tag attributes that are available *only* to browsers that support Java 1.1. Fine, you say, but what exactly does that mean? And what's the big deal with these two attributes anyway that they need their own introduction?

Because you're new to Java applets and the <APPLET> tag used to weave them into Web pages, chances are pretty good that these new attributes may freak you out. Don't panic! I start out easy, sharing only the absolute minimum, and ease into the more complicated aspects of the <APPLET> tag in Chapter 8. Sound fair?

It's easy to get overwhelmed when looking at the <APPLET> tag from a "what's it got" view. If you look at the tag only in terms of braces, tags, attributes, and alternate HTML, you'll probably go bonkers. So don't do that, please.

Instead, think in terms of what the applet needs in order to operate. Don't try to memorize everything about the <APPLET> tag at once; just familiarize yourself with the parts needed to put applets into your pages. If you start with a simple applet, such as the Marquee applet provided on the CD-ROM accompanying this book, you learn the basics from the get-go and can graduate to more complicated parts of the <APPLET> tag at your own pace.

Consider the two new attributes supported by the Java 1.1 <APPLET> tags, explained in Table 5-3. Remember, you don't need to memorize them now. You only need a general idea of what they do and why you may eventually use them.

Table 5-3	Java 1.1 Optional Applet Attributes
Attribute	*Description*
ARCHIVE	This attribute is used to describe one or more Java archives (JARs). JAR files may contain images, sound files, or any other resources that the applet requires to operate properly. If multiple JAR files are required by the applet, they must be separated by a comma. This attribute works hand-in-hand with the required CODE attribute (see Table 1.1) because a Java archive may actually contain the class file specified with CODE. (The class file specified by CODE may reside alternatively outside the archive, depending on how the applet developer decides to implement the applet.)
OBJECT	This attribute specifies the name of a serialized applet file, as opposed to the non-serialized applet file (standard Java class) specified through the CODE attribute. *Serialized* applet files are an advanced feature of Java 1.1 that enable developers to store applet information in a way that makes it easy to send applets and their internal data over the network or save them to disk. Because serialized applet files are actually special versions of standard applets, the CODE attribute is not necessary when the OBJECT attribute is used. If the CODE attribute is used, however, the OBJECT attribute is not used. The best way to determine whether an applet uses CODE or OBJECT is to consult the documentation that comes with it or peek at an <APPLET> tag contained in an example Web page, if available. However, because serialized applets typically have a .ser extension, as opposed to the standard .class extension traditional applets have, you can usually determine if an applet supports the OBJECT attribute simply by looking at the applet's file extension.

The many faces of Java

It may come as a surprise to you that Java 1.0, 1.01, and 1.02 are all considered "Java 1.0." Likewise, Java 1.1, along with all minor changes to that version (Java 1.1.1, 1.1.2, and 1.1.3, to be exact), are considered "Java 1.1." What gives? Certainly, software engineers can see that 1.1 and 1.1.1 aren't equal, so why call them the same name? To make life a little easier on you and me, it turns out.

Would you rather remember major version numbers, such as 1.0, 1.1, and 1.2, or all the major and minor versions in between? Personally, I'm happy to reserve my already feeble memory for more important things, such as when I last fed my cat Harley and my wedding date and time (October 11, 1997 at 3:00 p.m., thank you — no need to send a card), and so I'm perfectly content to remember only the major Java version "families" rather than all the little itty-bitty members that come in between.

When Java 1.0 was first introduced to the World Wide Web, it was a fresh, invigorating technology that held tremendous promise. And, as you may suspect, the `<APPLET>` tag was designed especially for Java 1.0.

Java 1.1 is, at the very moment I write these words, the latest and greatest version of Java. However, even as I type, another version of Java is in the works. By the time you read this book, Java 1.2 will be the latest and greatest and Java 1.1 will be old news. As anyone who has seen Disney's *The Lion King* will tell you, this is the circle of life: old is replaced by new, over and over and over again.

Thanks to major changes already made to Java and others soon to come, it's no wonder the original `<APPLET>` tag has been enhanced. Thankfully, we don't have to discover very much in order to take advantage of Java 1.1 applets. The enhancements to the `<APPLET>` tag are minor and well worth understanding because of the advantages they offer. In fact, all you have to do is learn about two new attributes. Everything else stays the same. How's that for simplicity?

Because Java 1.1 is a major enhancement to the original version of Java, Web browser manufacturers are just now starting to build support for it into their products. By the time you read this, the most popular Web browsers in the world will understand the new `ARCHIVE` and `OBJECT` attributes that have recently been added to the `<APPLET>` tag.

Catch me if you can!

Because Web browser vendors are always playing "catch up" with Java, it usually takes a while before the latest and greatest features of the language are built into browsers. In fact, the only commercial browser that supports Java 1.1 at the time I am writing this book is Netscape Navigator 4.0. However, even Navigator 4.0 doesn't fully support all the features of Java 1.1 — it only supports a few features, which means that I have to wait for an upgrade to Navigator before I can be certain that all Java 1.1 applets run properly in this browser!

By the time you read this, however, Navigator may well be updated to support Java 1.1. But be warned — millions of users are likely to forego the upgrade (for any number of reasons, not the least of which is that most folks don't realize that full Java 1.1 support isn't built into this first release of Navigator), which means that applets written to take full advantage of Java 1.1 won't work properly when viewed by these people. As a result, it's important to take into account all the various capabilities of Web browsers being used around the world if you want your Java-powered Web pages to be accessible to the widest possible audience. Fortunately, we do just that in Chapter 13. In that chapter, you figure out how to create Java-powered Web pages that can accommodate Web browsers of all stripes and colors.

Using the ARCHIVE attribute

A Java archive, better known as a JAR, is nothing more than a compressed collection of files that an applet needs in order to run. JARs are meant to make your job a little easier. Instead of dealing with a bunch of applet files, such as .class files, image files, and sound files (each of which has to be uploaded to your Web site to be of any practical use to a Java-powered Web page), you only need to deal with a single archive.

Because the files in a JAR are compressed, they take up less hard drive space and take less time to transfer over the network. Consequently, Webbers don't have as long to wait before an applet starts running. In many cases, JAR files cut applet download times almost in half — not bad, especially considering JAR files also make uploading applets to the Web much easier. (Wouldn't you rather upload one Java archive than a dozen or more individual files? I know I would.)

When using JAR files, you have to let the browser know what's going on — browsers aren't mind readers. Luckily, telling a browser that it needs to download a JAR file isn't very difficult thanks to the ARCHIVE attribute. Consider the following example:

```
<APPLET CODE="Marquee" ARCHIVE="Marquee.jar" WIDTH=500
        HEIGHT=40>
</APPLET>
```

In the prior example, the browser downloads the JAR file named Marquee.jar. It then looks inside that archive for a file named Marquee.class, because that's the full name of the file specified in the CODE attribute.

The .class file extension is implied when dealing with the CODE attribute, so you actually don't have to include it. However, just for fun, take a look at the following example:

```
<APPLET CODE="Marquee.class" ARCHIVE="Marquee.jar"
        WIDTH=500 HEIGHT=40>
</APPLET>
```

This example is functionally equivalent to the one shown earlier — they both tell the browser to download the Marquee.jar archive file and then look inside it for an applet .class file named Marquee.class. In most cases, the JAR file contains the actual Java applet .class file, but not always. If the applet .class file isn't inside the JAR, the browser downloads it separately. Whether or not the applet .class file is contained inside the Java .jar archive file is entirely dependent on the software developer who created the applet.

Including the .class file inside a JAR file is not an absolute requirement, although it does make things a little easier for us as we only have to deal with one file (the JAR file) if the .class file is inside of it. If not, we have to deal with the .class file and .jar file separately. Come to think of it, there's no hard-and-fast rule saying what exactly goes into a JAR. Developers are free to place any files they want inside a JAR, and can even split the various files an applet requires over more than one JAR. Consider the following variation on the theme I have going here:

```
<APPLET CODE="Marquee.class" ARCHIVE="MarqueeClasses.jar",
        "MarqueeSounds.jar", "MarqueeImages.jar"
        WIDTH=500 HEIGHT=40>
</APPLET>
```

In this example, three distinct JARs are specified in the ARCHIVE attribute, each separated by a comma. While this isn't a real <APPLET> tag (the Marquee applet included on the CD-ROM accompanying this book doesn't have any use for images or sounds — it only scrolls a text message across the screen), it illustrates the concept that multiple JAR files are sometimes used by applets. Again, the number of JARs an applet requires depends on how the developer chooses to implement the applet.

Of course, just because an applet may use JAR files doesn't mean it can't also take advantage of the flexibility that parameters offer. In each of these examples, I've intentionally omitted PARAM attributes because the focus has been on the ARCHIVE attribute. However, applets that use JAR files are just as likely to use PARAM attributes as those that don't, as the following <APPLET> tag illustrates:

```
<APPLET CODE="Marquee.class" ARCHIVE="Marquee.jar"
        WIDTH=500 HEIGHT=40>
    <PARAM NAME="font_face" VALUE="TimesRoman">
    <PARAM NAME="font_size" VALUE="24">
    <PARAM NAME="font_italic" VALUE="yes">
    <PARAM NAME="font_bold" VALUE="yes">
    <PARAM NAME="marquee" VALUE="Yo! I'm scrolling!">
Gee, you can't see the scrolling text can you?
That's because this page requires a Java-savvy browser...
<A HREF="http://www.netscape.com">GET ONE!</A>!
</APPLET>
```

Again, the PARAM attributes that an applet supports is entirely dependent on the developer who creates it. Different applets use different PARAM attributes, allowing us to customize them in different ways (Chapter 8 has more information for you).

However, alternate HTML is supported in the same way for every applet, regardless of who develops it. As the above example shows, alternate HTML always appears just before the closing </APPLET> tag. If a Web browser isn't Java-savvy, the alternate HTML is used. If not, the applet is run.

Using the OBJECT attribute

Serialized applets are a feature of Java 1.1 that makes life easier on the developer. Serialized applets are internally represented in such as way that they're easier to send over a network or save to a hard drive — they're essentially the same as normal applets, meaning you won't really be able to tell the difference between normal and serialized applets even though serialized applets fundamentally different on the inside. On the outside, they're no different from other applets.

Serialization is a feature of the Java 1.1 language that relates directly to how a developer actually writes programming code — you can think of it, in terms of cooking, as a special-purpose spice that a chef has the option of using at his discretion. Not all dishes benefit from a particular spice, and those that may aren't guaranteed to get a dash or two of it. It's the chef's choice. Such is the case with serialization; not all applets need it and even those that could use serialization aren't guaranteed to take advantage of it. It's up to the individual developer. You say tomato, I say tomaauhtow.

Java 1.1 serialization enables developers to create applets that are more easily transferred over a network and/or saved to disk. This enhanced ease isn't realized from an end-user's point of view, but instead from a programmer's perspective. If you're interested in creating your own applets from scratch, check out *Java Programming For Dummies,* 2nd Edition by Donald and David Koosis (IDG Books Worldwide, Inc.). *Serialization* is a powerful new feature of the Java language that gives developers special programming capabilities, a feature that greatly advances the state-of-the-art in applets. Fortunately, you don't have to sweat the details of serialization other than to simply use the OBJECT attribute. It's the programmer's job to work out the details of applet serialization. You just sit back and take it easy. Maybe that's why programmers are generally an edgy bunch?

For those applets that do take advantage of serialization, however, the OBJECT attribute is necessary. In fact, serialized applets have no need at all for the CODE attribute. Unlike ARCHIVE, which works closely with CODE, the OBJECT attribute replaces it lock, stock, and barrel:

```
<APPLET OBJECT="Marquee.ser" WIDTH=500 HEIGHT=40>
</APPLET>
```

The OBJECT attribute entirely eliminates the need for the CODE attribute. Simply put, the two just don't get along. If CODE is used, OBJECT shouldn't be used, and vice versa. Of course, which attribute you use depends on the applet itself. To find out which attribute you should use for an applet, you have to either explore the documentation that comes with the applet or take a look at an example <APPLET> tag already woven into a Web page. Alternatively, you can peek at the applet's file extension. Traditional applets that rely on the CODE attribute have the .class file extension, while serialized applets usually have a .ser extension (not always, mind you, because the extension given to a serialized applet is also up to the developer!).

Chapter 6

Designing Your Own Java-Powered Web Page

*I*f you've spent any amount of time on the Web with a Java-savvy browser, you're probably just itching to add this addictive technology to your own Web pages. After all, playing with Java-powered pages is only half the fun. Finding applets to put on your own Web pages is where it's really at. So let your hair down, kick off your shoes, slip into something more comfortable, and turn up the tunes. Prepare to get wired — it's Java time!

The first step is deciding what you want your Java-powered pages to be like and then getting your hands on the applets that will make such pages possible. After all, without applets, your thirst for Java can't be quenched. Luckily, finding Java applets is easier than locating a Starbucks coffee shop in Seattle; they're everywhere.

To be perfectly honest, applets aren't the only route to jazzing up your pages with Java. JavaScript, discussed in more detail in Part III, is another way to add a Java jolt. However, JavaScript is like a watered-down version of applets. Think of JavaScript as a cup of Folgers (if you can stand yet another coffee analogy) and applets as a double shot of espresso straight up.

Landing the Perfect Applet

You're all ready to jazz up your Web site with some really spiffy Java applets, when you stop in your tracks and ask, "Where do applets come from?"

Time to sit down and have a little talk . . .

Don't sweat it

How you go about finding applets to use in your Web page plays a big part in your overall planning process. When trying to decide what Java applets to include in your Web site (as well as the overall design of your pages), you can employ either of two essential techniques:

- **Inspiration surfing:** The easiest way to generate ideas for your Web site is to look at what other people have done. By surfing the Web, you can find pages and applets that will inspire you. This is a process I call *inspiration surfing,* and it's perhaps the most direct and enjoyable way to generate ideas for your Web pages.

- **Perspiration working:** If you're a glutton for punishment, you can come up with the ideas on your own, in relative isolation, as a direct response to your site's specific requirements. This technique is much less enjoyable, requires a significant amount of mental energy, and forces Web page authors to sweat out the details of a site without taking advantage of the hundreds of thousands of hours that others have put into developing state-of-the-art Java sites.

  The worst part of this approach is that after you've figured out what you want the applets to do, you have to build them or get them built. Sure, if you have a Ph.D. in Computer Nerdology, you can program your own applet from scratch (or you can take the easy way out and flip through *Java Programming For Dummies,* 2nd Edition, by Donald and David Koosis [IDG Books Worldwide, Inc.]). But if you're just starting out, you're much better off taking the easy route and customizing pre-existing applets.

Personally speaking, I'd rather be inspired than perspire. How about you?

To really get a feel for what your Web pages can and should do, you need to spend a considerable amount of time online looking at what's out there. Only after you've spent a great deal of time navigating these hypermedia documents can you really understand and appreciate good Web page design.

Unfortunately, many folks rush onto the Web without truly understanding what it's all about in an attempt to get in on the excitement. This eager-beaver approach leads to the condition of *perspiration working,* sweating out the details of developing Web pages for no good reason, when even a little time spent surfing would make the process a whole lot easier. Making this mistake can be fatal for your Web site; publishing Java-powered pages on the World Wide Web without first giving yourself the time and experience to know good from bad page design will drive a stake right through the heart of your site.

To understand why this is true, consider the culture of the Web. Tens of millions of people are surfing every day, spending their time and money basking in the warm glow of a computer monitor. Today, the pipelines for delivering data across the Web are narrow and congested with traffic. The more people that are on the Web, the slower navigating it becomes — just like a department store the day after Christmas.

One of the top reasons folks connect to the Web is for the "Eureka!" experience it delivers. You can go anywhere, see anything, and travel for eternity, it seems, without retracing your steps. Unfortunately, every time you come to a page, you have to wait for it to download over the Net. The Web isn't an instant-delivery information system the way that television is; it takes time for the page's source code, images, sounds, and applets to download to your computer. And on the Web, time is money.

Web design is even more important when you use Java because applets take a long time to load, especially if they use images and sounds (which many do). Because Java is so cool, many Webbers will hang out long enough to check out a Java-powered page. But what if the site they've been waiting around for turns out to be completely bogus, a total waste of their time and money? You can bet they'll grab their surfboards and beat a path to another Web page before you can say "pork chop express." And the longer they have to wait, the more hostile an impression of the offending site will be burned into their memory. If, on the other hand, a site is really useful or cool, visitors will stick around — they may even bookmark it for instant access later on, meaning that the site gets repeat visitors.

There's only one way for you to know good design from bad: You have to experience them both in vast quantities. And the only way to do that is to surf the Web. If you haven't surfed the Web much or don't think you know good sites from bad ones, there's no time like the present to take the plunge. Not only is this preparation necessary, but it's also an absolute blast. Think of it as a homework assignment that's really nothing more than a trip around the world, with instructions to take photographs and notes at every stop — that's all you have to do. Just surf the Web and keep track of the sites you really like and the ones that turn you off. Check out the section "A Quest for the Best Applets in CyberLand" (in this chapter) to find out how to surf for Web sites, keep track of them for fast access in the future, search them for applets, and save the source code for future reference.

I don't mean to suggest that you should put off hooking applets up to your own pages until you've searched the Web far and wide and distilled out the quintessential Web page. In fact, honing your applet-embedding skills at the same time that you are cultivating a taste for page design is a good idea.

Because you create Web pages on your local computer, you are the only one who can view them, until you upload to a Web server. Thus, your Web site can be a work in progress right on your own hard drive. You and you alone decide when a page is ready for prime time, so you can refine it as you go along.

Getting permission to pick

When you come across an applet on the Web that you want to weave into your own page, investigate to see whether you're allowed to use the applet. Be aware that some applets are completely out of your reach — many Web pages are chock-full of scrumptious applets that simply aren't available for the picking.

You can tell when an applet is entirely off limits to the public because the site doesn't provide any information explaining how to use the applet in your own pages. Of course, it's a good idea to navigate around the entire site before giving up. But if such details aren't provided, you have no choice but to move on.

If the Web page that contains the "applet of your eye" doesn't explicitly offer its applets to you, move on to another orchard. If you pilfer applets from a page that doesn't say something to the effect of, "Howdy, I'm an applet free for the taking — use me on your own Web page!" you stand a good chance of catching a shotgun blast of legal buckshot right in the rump.

Applets are little software programs, and taking them without permission is just as illegal as walking into a store and swiping a box of software off the shelf. Of course, you can always contact the author of an applet you desire and ask for permission to use it. Depending on who wrote the applet, and what its author thinks about the idea of giving away the result of his or her blood, sweat, and tears (or at least a long night at the keyboard), you may or may not get a blessing to use it. But don't let the idea of being turned down by a software developer discourage you — it's worth a shot if only to get a personal "Bug OFF!" e-mail from the author!

Fortunately, truckloads of applets on the Web are free for the taking, with bushels more arriving every day. And most of these applets describe in clear detail exactly how you can weave them into your own pages. So unless you're in the market for some exotic applet, chances are you can find exactly what you need by surfing the Web (see Chapter 4).

Ordering a custom-grown applet

If you search the whole wide Web and still don't find an available applet that you like, you can always have an applet custom-developed to fit your needs (see Figure 6-1). But be warned, custom-written applets aren't cheap; depending on the work involved, you can expect to spend anywhere from $50 to $1,000 for the most basic work!

An overwhelming number of self-proclaimed Java experts have surfaced on the Web lately, each promising to create top-notch applets at a fair price. If you decide to have a custom Java applet created for you, play it safe and follow these tips:

✔ **Only choose a firm with experience.** Look for companies that have customer references and examples of their work prominently displayed on the site (or those willing to furnish these items immediately upon request).

✔ **Don't accept references at face value.** Contact each reference and ask pointed questions, such as "What work was done?", "How long did it take?", "How much did it cost?", and "Would you recommend hiring this company for my job?"

✔ **Shop around.** What one company may charge $500 to develop, another company may develop for $100 or less. But keep in mind that price isn't everything; a developer's reputation is, in my opinion, the most important part of the equation.

Figure 6-1:
Custom applet-programming services are surfacing everywhere on the Web these days, but be wary: Not all developers are created equal.

The Web provides a forum in which all its users who have a computer and a modem can proclaim themselves Java-development experts. Don't be taken for a ride.

A Quest for the Best Applets in CyberLand

One of the most challenging aspects of injecting your Web pages with Java is the dizzying spectrum of choices you have when you're finally ready to pick an applet (or applets!) to weave into your pages. If you take a spin, even a quick spin, on the Web with a Java-savvy browser, you know exactly what I mean: At every twist and turn in the ether, new and enticing applets appear, begging to be adapted for use in your very own pages.

You can weave any number of applets into a single Web page. But don't go crazy; each applet takes time to download from the Internet. As a result, anyone visiting an applet-saturated page may have to wait a long time for the applets to finally kick into high gear — which may actually drive folks away from your site rather than attract them. With applets, as with Web pages in general, you should consider the overall design of the page *before* you actually create it.

Setting sail in search of great applets

If you're not sure where to start your applet search, don't worry. You can begin surfing with any page, letting your mouse lead you in any number of directions. You can progress from page to page, site to site, at any pace you choose. However, I suggest surfing slowly in the beginning because you need to cultivate a taste for Web page design.

Check out Chapter 4 for a discussion of a variety of different surfing styles, all of which I strongly suggest you try on different occasions. Keep in mind that you need to cultivate your Web-page design skills, and that requires you to see pages the way other Web travelers do. And because there are different approaches to surfing the Web, check out pages that use a variety of approaches.

As you surf, you develop a taste for Web page design. You begin to understand what you like and don't like, which will influence your design decisions later. What makes a Java-powered site especially strong or weak is a matter of personal taste, but a great Web site usually has the following qualities:

✔ **It's fresh.** The applets on the site aren't the same old applets that everybody uses. If an applet appears on half the Java sites, will your site grab anyone's attention by using it? Probably not. But if you can't get your hands on unique applets, consider configuring the ones you do have in a way that sets them apart from the pack.

✔ **It's attractive.** The site itself isn't overcrowded with applets, images, and so on. Faced with an ugly screen, users will probably back out of the page before you can show your magic.

✔ **It's cool.** Nothing beats a page that makes the surfer say, "Wow!"

✔ **It's useful.** In addition to being attractive and cool, your page should be something that people can use. People who surf the Web love finding things they can use. If you build it, they will come.

✔ **It's interactive.** Finally, your site should interact with its users. If they can *do something* with the applets at your site as they play, learn, or work, the site becomes both useful and fun. After all, wouldn't you rather do something useful *and* fun than just useful?

Several Web sites are dedicated to exposing the worst sites and pages out there, and many more are dedicated to honoring the best ones. To find the best and worst sites on the Web, simply use a search engine (see Chapter 4 for details) and enter the keywords **worst Web** and **best Web** in your query.

Dropping anchor with bookmarks

When marking your place in a printed book like this one, you may rip off a piece of paper and slip it between two pages. You may even write something on the piece of paper to remind you why you put it there. When you use the Web, you do the same thing. No, don't worry about getting out a piece of paper and a pen. Remember — this is the electronic age, so you use a virtual bookmark.

When you come upon a Java-powered Web page that appeals to you, bookmark it! Every Web browser allows you to bookmark, or *hotlink,* Web pages for instant access later on. In Netscape Navigator, the feature is called *bookmarking;* In Microsoft Internet Explorer, it's called *Favorites.* When you bookmark a page, you can return to it quickly to refresh your memory, which is certain to become clouded after you see a few hundred Java-injected pages.

As you search the Web for Java inspiration, take notes about the bookmarks you make. Fortunately, most browsers allow you to enter notes at the same time that you make bookmarks, as I did in Figure 6-2. Be sure to record your first impressions of a page the moment you actually bookmark it. First impressions of a site are the ones that count the most because these can make or break a site; most Webbers decide within a matter of seconds whether a site is worth sticking around or if they should head elsewhere. You need to develop a feel for what attracts and repels Webbers, and the only way you can do that is to get in touch with your inner Web child.

In addition to recording your first impressions of a site, consider ranking the site and recording its score along with your notes (see Figure 6-2). You can choose any ranking system you like, as long as you have a way to distinguish between the good and the bad sites. For a rather mundane example, you might choose a 1–10 ranking system, where a low number represents bad sites, a higher number represents a good site, and a 10 is reserved for the best of the best. Whatever floats your boat, as long as you have a way to distinguish between the good, the bad, and the ugly sites.

Figure 6-2:
Recording notes inside your bookmarks helps you remember your first impressions of Web pages that you visit.

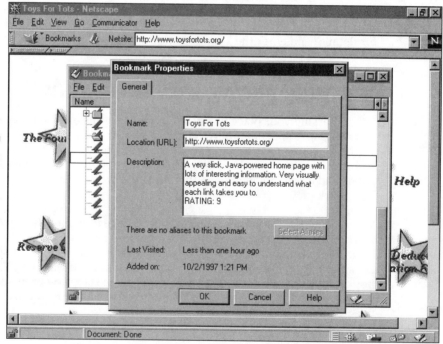

Page courtesy of Toys For Tots (www.toysfortots.org)

Digging for buried treasure in source code

Setting bookmarks alone isn't enough. You also want to peek behind the curtains and take a look at the HTML code used to create the pages that turn your crank.

By taking a look at the HTML source code someone else used to create the pages that inspire you, you're effectively looking at the recipes for tasty Web pages. All Web browsers have a built-in function that makes peeking at the source code behind Web pages easy: Choose either View⇨Page Source or View⇨Source, depending on which browser you use, as shown in Figure 6-3.

As you view the source code of a Web page, you can find out just about everything you need to know regarding how the page was created. You are, after all, looking at the recipe used to create the page from scratch! In particular, you'll want to see what applets, if any, the page uses, which is a simple procedure. You need only invoke the browser's Find feature and search for the word *applet.*

Figure 6-3:
Sneaking a peek at the HTML source code used to create Web pages is easy; every Web browser lets you look under the covers of a Web page.

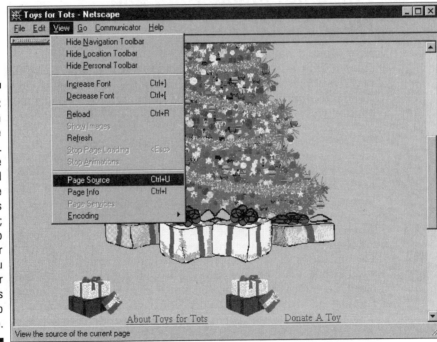

*Page courtesy of Toys For Tots (*www.toysfortots.org*)*

Keep in mind that the word *applet* may appear in the <APPLET> tag in either upper– or lowercase letters, even though I suggest you always use upper-case when weaving applets into your own Web pages for the sake of read-ability. Luckily, by default, the Find feature in most browsers ignores case (if yours doesn't, look for an option in the Find window that lets you specify that case should be ignored). As a result, you find all <APPLET> tags in a document, whether you search for the word *applet* or *APPLET.*

Of course, just *looking at* the source of a document online doesn't do you too much good and may end up costing a small fortune in online fees if you pay for your connection to the Internet by the hour (as opposed to the "all you can eat for $19.95" deal that most ISPs offer). You'd have to connect to the Web and view the source each time you needed to see the details of how the page was created. Fortunately, you don't need to have Einstein's memory to recall the specifics of the <APPLET> tag format; your computer already does. It's called *local storage* — better known as saving a file onto your hard drive.

Pillaging, plundering, and bringing home the loot

After you find a page that inspires you, why not download to your personal computer the HTML source code used to create it, where you can view it countless times without bothering to surf the Web? After all, there's no reason to connect to the Web to peek at source code when you have the page on your very own system!

Saving the source code of a Web page is easy. All you have to do is choose your browser's Save option, which is usually found under File on the browser's menu. Note that, in some browsers, you must choose the Save As option while viewing the Web page itself, not when viewing the source code, because no menu options are available when viewing source code.

When saving a Web page, be sure to give the page a descriptive name, followed by the .html (or .htm) extension, as shown in Figure 6-4. Saving the document this way enables you to easily recognize that it contains Web-page source code. Also, be sure to save the Web page in HTML format, if you're given the choice; otherwise, you may end up saving the document as plain text instead of as source code! (Although some browsers automatically default to HTML format when you save Web pages to disk, other browsers may not.) If you're unsure of what format your browser is saving a page in, simply open up the document with a word processor (or any program capable of viewing plain text files). If the format is HTML, you see the source code right off the bat. If not, return to your browser and save the page again — this time using the HTML format.

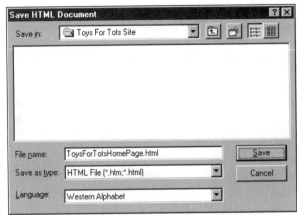

Figure 6-4:
Be sure to
save Web
pages in
the HTML
format;
otherwise,
you won't
be able to
read the
source
code!

As with any other document, when you save a Web page, you have to choose a location on your hard drive to store it. Personally, I prefer to create a new directory for each site I save pages from and store the pages in that directory. Of course, you're free to save the source code anywhere on your computer that you'd like. Just make sure to make a note of where you place it so that you can find it later.

After downloading the source code of a Web page to your personal computer, you can view the source code with your browser by accessing the appropriate option under the File menu — usually something like Open or Open Page.

When you open a Web page residing on your computer, you can bookmark it just as you do a Web page that exists online, giving you instant access to it the next time you want to view it. And, just as with Web pages in cyberspace, you can use your browser to view the source code of the pages you save on your computer — but with these local pages, you don't have to rush yourself, concerned that, with every passing moment, you're tying up your phone line. With Web pages stored in local files, there is no online time.

Downloading More Than Source Code

The first time you download a page for local access, you may be surprised to find that none of the images, sounds, or applets associated with that page are available. That fact can make for a radical change in appearance from the page you viewed on the Web and happens because you only downloaded the source and nothing more. But you shouldn't have a problem because the source code of Web pages is what's most important — it's the source you use as a recipe for your own pages.

Don't let your thirst for Java put you behind bars!

Although the idea of millions of Web pages floating around in cyberspace (with source code and images seemingly free for the taking) may seem like just the ticket to get your site up and running in record time, be careful; what you download may not be "free" at all. Using these materials in your own site without permission could end up costing you a small fortune in lawyers' fees!

The contents of most Web pages are intended for access only through a Web browser, not for downloading to your personal computer. However, as long as you download such information for your own personal use and don't republish it, you're safe. The second you publish (on the Web or elsewhere) words, images, sounds, music, or applets created by other people without their express permission, you're in danger of being slapped with a copyright infringement lawsuit.

For this reason, I strongly suggest that you download Web page source code and images only to learn how others went about creating them. Think of source code and images as

digital blueprints: You're free to use the source as the basis for your own work, as long as you substitute your own text and images. But never (ever!) use the text or images created by another in your own pages, no matter how tempting, unless you first receive permission from the author or know for a fact that what you're using is in the public domain or falls under the legal umbrella of *fair use*.

Were it not for the fact that browsers intentionally provide a mechanism for saving Web page source code and images to your personal computer, I would never have suggested that you do it. Lawsuits simply aren't my cup of tea, and I'm sure if the screws were put to you by a high-pressured legal dream team, you'd sing like a canary: "Aaron told me to do it. I swear!" But because browsers give you everything you need to save source code and images to disk in the blink of an eye, I'm willing to take that risk. Under heavy Spanish Inquisition-style interrogation and fear for my very life, I, too, will crack and chirp like a finch: "Netscape made me do it. I swear!"

But Java-powered Web pages aren't made up of HTML source code and images alone, the way most standard pages are. Fortunately, saving Web page images to your computer is a breeze; however, saving the other elements a page may contain, such as sounds and applets, isn't so easy. In Chapter 7, I show you how to save applets and their support files.

Wouldn't it be nice to save the *entire* page (source code, graphics, sound, and applets) to your hard drive all at once? Saving *all* the elements that a page contains, although technically possible, is a rather tedious process when compared to saving images. In fact, the way to go about saving all the elements is a fairly well-kept secret that I'm afraid I can't share. You see, not only is it unethical to retrieve an entire page to your local computer, doing so may be illegal!

The law in this area is a light shade of gray because the Web is a public entity used to publish material for the public at large. The underlying elements that make up publications, however, may not be intended for you to download and use in your own Web pages. In fact, some lawyers insist that it's illegal for you to do anything but look at a Web page, suggesting that copying any contents of a page to your own computer is grounds for a lawsuit. Because the Web is so new, this debate remains a gray area until a precedent is set, and wouldn't you just hate to be the one caught in the middle of such a high-profile lawsuit? My advice? Unless an applet is freely offered by a Web page, don't bother with it — it's just not worth the effort and risk.

Saving images

At times, you may want to save more than just the source code of a Web page to your computer. This is particularly true when you come across a page that contains images intended to be used in conjunction with Java applets, something you'll probably encounter quite often as you scour the Web in search of inspiration for your own pages.

Fortunately, images often are made available free of charge and without restriction through Web pages, meaning that you can use them in your own pages without fear of being slapped with a lawsuit. Borrowing images is a real time saver and is particularly helpful, because slick-looking images are extremely difficult to create from scratch. Instead, you can pluck really cool images right off the Web for use with your Java applets, without the pain of creating images yourself. I'm assuming, of course, that the page from which you take these images explicitly states that they are free for the taking, without restriction.

With most Java-savvy browsers, saving images is a cinch. All you have to do is click on the image in a special way. Simply clicking on an image normally takes you to whatever item it may be linked to, assuming that the image is indeed a hyperlink. A slight variation on this theme allows you to save the image to disk:

- ✔ If you're a Macintosh user, the trick lies in *not* releasing the mouse button after you click. All you have to do is press and hold down the mouse button while your cursor is over the image and a pop-up menu appears with an option for saving it to disk.

- ✔ For Windows users, simply right-click the image and a pop-up menu appears. Cool, huh?

After you click on each of the graphics in a page, using the appropriate mouse technique for your system, choose Save Image from the menu that appears. The only fatal flaw to this plan is broken links.

Dealing with broken links

Because Web pages can contain images that reside in different directories or even on different Web servers, you may have to update the source code for the page after you save any images it contains to your computer. Say, for example, that you save a page and all its images into a single directory on your computer, as I typically do. Unless the images are located in the same directory on the Web as the page itself, the links to the images are broken. As a result, you won't see the images when opening the page on your computer using your browser because the images now reside in the same directory as the page rather than the location that the Web page specifies.

The solution is to either update the source code or create a directory structure on your computer that parallels that of the Web site from which the source came. I recommend that you update the source code. To change the source code, load the HTML into a text editor, such as the Windows Notepad (or the Macintosh SimpleText application), and update the HTML references.

You can deal with relative URLs (flip to Chapter 5) simply by creating the equivalent directory path on your computer. With absolute URLs, you're in over your head unless all the absolute URLs pass through the same directory as the page itself, which is highly unlikely. In this case, you have no choice but to change the source code of the page so that it uses a relative URL, because you can't mimic entire Web servers on your computer by using simple directory structures.

Battling Bandwidth Bottlenecks

It's easy to get lost in the excitement of creating Java-powered Web pages full of sophisticated animation and sounds. Souping up your site with animated, high-resolution images and injecting long, heart-pounding audio clips into the mix is terribly tempting! And even though everything may seem just dandy as you develop such pages on your personal computer, you may be cruising for a rude awakening when the time comes to bring your pages to life on the Web.

You see, when you create pages locally with the HTML source code, images, applets, and support files (usually images and sounds used by the applet) that reside on your hard drive, everything is smooth as silk. All the pieces of your page already exist on your computer, so there's no delay whatsoever waiting for them to come over the wire — everything loads into your browser almost instantly. But when you upload the page and all its parts onto the Web (as Chapter 10 shows you how to do), you're dealing with a completely different beast, the beast called bandwidth.

Anyone who visits pages that reside on the World Wide Web is at the mercy of *bandwidth* — how fast things can travel down the wire (a hip way of saying "over the network") into the user's computer. Plainly put, limited bandwidth is one of the biggest problems on the Web today. The vast majority of Webbers connect to the Internet at speeds too slow to make viewing Web pages jam-packed with images and sounds an enjoyable experience. Instead of surfing through your pages, as you do when the pages reside entirely on your personal computer, visitors to your site will probably feel as if they're swimming in quicksand as they wait for everything to download before the fun can begin.

Because bandwidth is a major issue with the majority of Webbers, you must consider the lowest common denominator. Although you may try to convince yourself that 56 Kbps modems are the norm — perhaps with dreams of high-speed ISDN and cable modem access not far behind — many folks are connecting to the Internet at speeds of 28.8 Kbps, 14.4 Kbps, or even less! To deliver a decent experience to visitors of your Web site, offering your Java-powered pages to everyone, without penalizing those with slower access, you must take extra care when planning your pages: You must take bandwidth into consideration.

Although applets are quite small and come across the wire in a hurry, the graphics and audio files that applets utilize are tremendous by comparison. You can do several things to decrease transmission time and prevent serious bottlenecks when downloading these files over the network. The following sections tell you how.

Sizing up sound files

When dealing with sound files, Java supports only Sun's AU sound format. Files using this format have an extension of .au. If you have a sound file that isn't stored in this format, like a Windows .wav file, you have to convert the sound file to the AU format in a very specific way if you intend to use the sound file with an applet.

Although the AU format creates sound files that typically are smaller in size than other formats, the sound quality isn't the best of the lot. As a result, you may have to fiddle with various sound editing functions in your conversion tool (if you own one) to try to eliminate the hiss you hear when converting higher-quality sounds to this format.

A bevy of sounds, each in the AU format, reside on the CD-ROM included with this book — giving you a wide assortment of choices for using audio in your Java-powered pages.

However, if you want to use your own sound files, you first must convert them into the AU format. Not only must you convert the file to AU format, but you must be sure to apply a uLaw compression to the sound in the conversion process (AU is the format, while uLaw is a special way of compressing AU sound files). Because AU files may be compressed using different uLaw settings, you must be careful to convert your sounds exactly as Java requires: 8-bit, 8000 Hz, single-channel (mono) AU uLaw settings.

To help you convert your existing sound files into this very specific AU format, the CD-ROM packaged with this book contains a special utility for just this purpose. Macintosh users can use the SoundApp program and Windows users can use the GoldWave utility. For details on where these files are located, refer to Appendix A.

Although the GoldWave conversion utility (for Windows users) includes a number of sound-editing features such as Smooth and Fade effects, the SoundApp program (for Macintosh users) is only capable of converting files — it can't edit them. If you're a Macintosh user and find that the sounds you convert contain excessive hissing, consider investing in a commercial-quality tool capable of both editing sounds and saving them in the AU format supported by Java. But before you run out and plunk down your hard earned shekels, you might first check the stockpiles of Macintosh shareware that abound on the Web.

Cutting the silence

To reduce the size of sound files as much as possible when converting them for use with Java, you should keep only the absolutely essential portions of the sound file. Cut out any preceding or trailing silence. In doing so, you reduce the size of the file without adversely affecting the sound.

Because cutting out all preceding and trailing silence in a sound tends to result in playback that begins and ends abruptly, you may be tempted to keep a second or two of silence on either end just to make the sound more natural. Luckily, you can achieve the same effect by applying a *fade-in* to the beginning of the sound and a *fade-out* to the end. These effects give smooth transitions to a sound that may otherwise start and stop abruptly. Not only is the result a more professional and appealing sound, but you also trim precious seconds of download time in the process.

A few seconds may not seem like much, but every single second counts when it comes to bandwidth. This is especially true if you happen to use several sounds in a Web page. Seconds add up to minutes . . . which, if you're paying for every hour of time spent online, add up to dollars.

Creating sound loops

Because sound is such an effective way to grab attention and add impact to a Web page, and because Java applets make using sound so easy, many folks tend to overuse sounds on their Web pages. Unfortunately, doing so creates bandwidth bottlenecks that can turn your Web page viewers off.

Rather than playing a large number of audio clips with your Java applets, consider whether *looping* may be a reasonable alternative. When you loop a sound file, it repeats continuously until you tell it to stop. The effect can be quite powerful, especially if the sound you loop is subtle. Looping can be a great alternative to bombarding your visitors with sound after sound and sucking up bandwidth in the process.

Thanks to Java's audio support flexibility, you can play any number of sounds at once; you don't have to stop a sound loop in order to play another sound file. Unless you specify otherwise (assuming the applet you use allows you to), all sounds you play at the same time are mixed together, resulting in a rich audio experience.

Making the most of images and colors

Java supports only GIF (Graphics Interchange Format) and JPEG (Joint Photographic Experts Group) images, meaning that you have a limited choice when using images with your applets. However, the format you should choose relates directly to the quality of images you have.

The JPEG format enables you to utilize 24-bit color (near photographic quality) images with your applets. With GIF, however, you're limited to a much smaller selection of colors — no more than 256 colors, to be exact.

Although you may be tempted to use full-color JPEG images with your applets because this format supports a much larger spectrum of colors than GIF, don't do it! Instead, try to reduce the number of colors in your images to 256 or less; in doing so, you greatly reduce the amount of time your file takes to come across the wire. Of course, getting your images down to 256 colors or less is the trick. When you accomplish this feat of minimalism, you still have to decide upon a file format to save them in: Will it be GIF or JPEG? The next section helps you decide.

Choosing GIF or JPEG

When you add images to your Web page, you eventually have to decide on a format to support. Java supports both GIF and JPEG formats, but a number of factors may make one of these formats preferable to you over the other.

Using GIF images has several benefits. For starters, most graphics programs, including shareware utilities, support this popular format, so you're never at a loss for tools to help you create and edit images in this format. In fact, GIF is the most common graphic format in use on the Web today. In addition, the GIF format is highly efficient and has built-in compression that makes for relatively small images, as long as you're not dealing with photographs. (The GIF format is great at compressing cartoon-like artwork, but not nearly as good as JPEG for compressing photographic-quality images.) Finally, GIF supports *transparency* and *interlacing,* which can greatly enhance the visual appeal of your applet.

Getting transparency with GIF

Transparency enables the graphic artist to specify any color in an image as being transparent. When rendered on the screen, this color isn't actually displayed. Instead, whatever is underneath it shows through (typically the background color, although other images — such as Web page background images — may be placed underneath transparent portions of a GIF image, as well).

Without transparency, images are displayed using all colors in the palette, including portions of the images that you'd prefer were see-through. As a result, the images are often unattractive — unless portions of the images that should be transparent are in colors that match exactly the underlying backgrounds (see Figure 6-5). Therefore, the GIF format is the only choice for images that must have "see-through" portions.

Figure 6-5:
Transparency allows you to specify a color in an image as being see-through. The top image of this figure uses transparency; the one underneath does not.

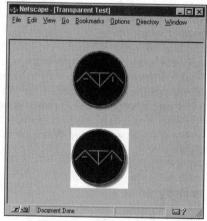

Unfortunately, not all Java applets know how to deal with transparent images. As a result, even if you've gone through the hassle of creating transparent GIF images (something you need a special graphics utility to do), your images may be displayed with the background colors showing, depending on what applets you use them with. As a result, you should use applets that support transparent images when you have a choice. How do you know if an applet supports transparent images? You have to ask the person who wrote the applet or check any documentation that comes with the applet. Alternatively, you can just try it out and see for yourself.

Sometimes you don't have a choice — perhaps the only applet you can find that does exactly what you want, whatever that may be, doesn't support transparent images. In this case, the solution is to use a graphics program to alter the images the applet will use, setting a background color that is exactly the same as the color of the Web page on which it will be displayed. This way, when each image is displayed, it appears to be transparent even though it really isn't — it just has a background color that happens to be the same color as the Web page on which it is displayed.

Setting a color to be transparent and choosing a background color for your image are both functions of the graphics program you happen to use. To find out how to create a transparent image or set a particular background color for it, consult your documentation for the program or the corresponding ...*For Dummies* book.

In time, all applets will support transparent images. Because the Java programming language didn't originally provide an easy way for programmers to support transparency in their applets, many programmers simply didn't bother. Today, however, the Java programming language has been greatly enhanced and offers many more features than it did originally — all applets created can easily support transparent images. What a glorious time to be a Java programmer!

Interlacing with GIF

Interlacing is another feature unique to the GIF format, but unlike transparency, which is supported on an applet-by-applet basis, interlacing is supported by *all* applets. *Interlacing* enables images to be incrementally drawn on-screen as they come across the wire, so viewers don't have to wait until the entire image is transmitted. The effect is similar to watching a Polaroid photograph develop before your eyes; you have an idea of what the image is before it is completely developed.

Because interlacing gives Webbers something to watch as the image becomes clearer, those viewers aren't as likely to abort the process and go elsewhere. Instead, many will stick around and watch the image materialize, mesmerized by the magic.

Getting more colors with JPEG

Because the GIF format supports both transparency and interlacing, in addition to being the default format for Web graphics in general, it's more often than not a better choice than JPEG for your applets.

However, GIF images are currently limited to 256 (8-bit) colors. Although an update to the format is due out any day now, at the time of this writing you can't use GIF images to display any more colors than that. The JPEG format, on the other hand, supports over 16 million (24-bit) different colors. In cases where you absolutely must have more than 256 colors in an image, you must use the JPEG format.

Taking up less space with JPEG

As a general rule, you should keep the total amount of material to be downloaded per page (text, graphics, sound files, applets, and so on) under 250K. How do you find out how large a file is?

- ✔ Macintosh users can go to the Finder, highlight the file, and select File⇨Get Info.
- ✔ Windows 95 users can go to Windows Explorer, click on the file with the right mouse button, and select Properties from the pop-up menu that appears.

Of course, these techniques only give you the size of one file; you have to repeat the process for each file that appears on your Web page and then add up all the figures.

Alternatively, you can choose Get Info (Macs) or Properties (Windows) on the directory that contains your page, the applet, and all graphics and sound files it uses (assuming that they all reside in the same directory). Just be sure that the directory only contains files that are used in the page and that the size reported includes every file contained in the directory.

If you have a large number of graphics and more than 250K in total Web page material, consider using the JPEG format simply to gain the highest degree of compression possible. Because images with more than 100 colors tend to compress more efficiently in the JPEG format than with GIF, target those images with the most colors first for JPEG.

After reducing the palette and compressing each image that will appear in your page (whether as part of the standard page using HTML or to be used only by an applet), calculate the total amount of memory your page will take up. If the combined size of your page is over 250K, seriously consider reducing the overall amount of material on it. You can also reduce the dimensions of the images, cropping excess material out altogether.

How JPEG works

JPEG images use a *lossy* compression algorithm, allowing the artist to specify a trade-off between image quality and storage size. When you select the highest level of compression, some image information is lost (hence the term *lossy*) in exchange for the tightest possible compression. Future versions of the JPEG format may include support for transparency and interlacing, although, at the moment, neither are available for use with Java applets.

In fact, a new version of the JPEG format, called JPEG Progressive Download, is similar in nature to an interlaced GIF. As images in this format come across the wire, they are displayed incrementally. At first they look blurry but become sharper and sharper until finally the entire image is clearly visible. Unfortunately, this new JPEG format is not supported by the current version of Java.

And, of course, you can always use the JPEG format with the highest degree of compression for *all* your images. Just be aware that if you use the JPEG format, you lose both the transparency and interlacing features available with the GIF format.

Considering your visitors' systems

Your final consideration when choosing a format is the users' equipment. If you're still tempted to use images that contain more than 256 colors in your Web pages and applets, consider for a moment that the vast majority of Webbers don't have computers that display more than 256 colors. In fact, many systems connected to the Web can't even display as many as 16 colors. As a result, your beautiful full-color images will be reduced to ugly, pitiful creations on these systems. To avoid this potential disaster, take the time to reduce the palette of your images as much as possible from the very start.

Although I don't recommend that you spend a great deal of time attempting to accommodate users with really old computer systems, I do highly recommend that you assume the majority of Webbers can see only up to 256 colors. If you do so, the choice between JPEG and GIF becomes even easier.

Java runtime system: The applet cop

What's to stop distributed applets from using the support files on your computer? Can't you just tell a distributed applet where your files are located on the server? Sure, you can try; but it won't do any good. If the applet attempts to access your files, the Java runtime system smacks it with a rolled-up newspaper and sends it off with its tail between its legs. The *Java runtime system* (the underlying, invisible system on your computer that runs applets that the browser passes to it) simply doesn't allow applets to get files from other servers. Period.

The Java runtime system, also known as the *Java Virtual Machine,* is automatically installed on your computer system when you install a Java-savvy browser. Without the Java runtime system, your computer is incapable of executing applets. The Java runtime system exists on your machine inside a directory called Java, which is inside the same directory that contains your Java-savvy browser. In the Java directory are all the special programs and files that comprise the Java runtime system, which acts as a middleman between applets and your personal computer. When you download an applet from the Web, the browser hands it off to the Java runtime system. This runtime system works hand in hand with your personal computer, allowing the applet to execute as though it is just another software program on your system.

In fact, not all applets even bother with support files. Take, for example, the various ticker tape applets — little Java programs that allow text to scroll across the viewer's screen — that abound on the Web. The vast majority of the ticker tape applets available are self-contained; they don't rely on support files at all (although the `Marquee` ticker-tape applet supplied on the CD-ROM that accompanies this book does have the option of retrieving messages from text files — you can find out how to retrieve messages in Chapter 8). To customize a ticker tape applet, you need to supply only the words that scroll across the screen, as the following HTML snippet shows, along with the details of what the text should look like:

```
<APPLET
  CODEBASE = "http://www.mantiscorp.com"
  CODE="Ticker"
  HEIGHT=25 WIDTH=300>
  <PARAM NAME="message" VALUE="Welcome to my page!">
  <PARAM NAME="font" VALUE="Courier">
  <PARAM NAME="fontsize" VALUE="14">
  <PARAM NAME="fontcolor" VALUE="red">
</APPLET>
```

Chapter 7

Weaving Applets into Your Web Pages

In This Chapter

▶ Embedding applets in HTML documents

▶ Choosing between distributed and server-bound applets

▶ Creating a directory structure

▶ Installing applets and support files

▶ Hooking up the `<APPLET>` tag

▶ Testing and troubleshooting Java-powered pages

*W*eb pages don't just spring to life on their own with Java; someone (maybe you!) has to weave one or more applets into the HTML code of the page. The process is very similar to that of adding graphics to Web pages: After you decide which graphic you want to add, you must obtain the graphic and then embed it into the HTML code of your Web page. Applets, however, are a wee bit more complicated to hook up than graphics because they often require that you configure a number of settings in the body of the `<APPLET>` tag before they'll work properly.

Just as with any aspect of Web-page development, the bulk of the work in weaving applets into your page takes place *locally;* that is, you weave applets into pages on your personal computer and upload them to the Web only after ensuring that they look and act exactly as you want them to. Depending on the applet itself and how simple or complex the applet is to configure, this process can take anywhere from minutes to hours. Typically, however, weaving applets into Web pages takes no more than 30 minutes or so; you usually can have an applet hooked up and running before your cup of coffee cools down.

All you need in order to pour lava-hot Java content into your Web pages are a Java-savvy browser (see Chapter 3) and some degree of comfort dabbling in HTML (see Chapter 5).

Will That Be for Here or to Go?

When picking an applet, you have a choice to make. No, not golden versus red delicious — *distributed* or *server-bound* applets.

If you want to add a Java-powered applet to your Web page, you have to go get the applet and put it on your page, right? Not necessarily. In some cases, you don't need to get the applet to make use of it on your Web page! Amazing as it may seem, you can use many applets *remotely*, without ever having to deal with them directly. All you have to do is make a reference to the applet in your Web page, specifying where the applet resides, and you're set. When others load your page, their browsers see that the applet is located on another Web server and go retrieve it.

Applets that you actually download to your own Web server are called *server-bound applets*. Applets that you can add to your Web pages without ever plucking them from their original sites on the Web are called *distributed applets*.

The distinction between distributed and server-bound applets is due to a security restriction imposed on all applets. Because an applet may access only files that reside on the same Web server as the applet resides, you must upload on your own server those applets that allow you to supply your own sound and image files (hence the term *server-bound*). If an applet is self-sufficient, meaning that you don't need to provide it with your own files, it can be made available in a distributed mode. Distributed applets, however, are often provided in server-bound form as well, allowing you to upload them to your own Web site.

Distributed applets and support files

The advantage of distributed applets is obvious: You don't have to bother installing the sucker to take advantage of it. That is, you don't have to upload to your Web server the applet and its associated *support files* (any files an applet makes use of when it is executing — usually sound or image files). Because distributed applets are already installed on the Web and can be accessed remotely, the only thing you have to worry about is constructing an <APPLET> tag in your Web page to reference it. For their sheer ease of use alone, distributed applets are a blessing.

Although your Web pages can reference any applet on the World Wide Web, a distributed applet can't use anything other than what's on its own server. That is, you can't supply your own graphics and sounds for a distributed applet to use. Unless someone gives you special access to the Web server on which an applet resides, which is highly unlikely, there's no way for you to customize the applet with your own support files.

Actually, everything on the Web is distributed!

If you want to be nitpicky about it, you can argue that all Java applets are distributed because they ultimately reside on the World Wide Web and are downloaded to your computer before they execute. In this sense, they are *distributed* from the Web servers to personal computers. However, in terms of categorizing the overall functionality of applets, I consider *distributed* to mean those applets that can be invoked, or woven into Web pages, from a remote location. Any number of Web pages can then make use of an applet without requiring that the Web pages reside on the same server as the applet itself.

Information distribution is a fundamental capability of the World Wide Web and is not unique to applets. Think for a moment about your ability to create pages that contain graphics. Your pages can display graphics that are located on your own server or those that

exist somewhere else. All you have to do is specify the location of the image (either on your own server or out on the Web), and the browser takes care of the rest. (Check out the discussion of absolute and relative references later in this chapter to find out how files on the Web are referenced in Web pages.) This is the beauty of a distributed system.

Applets, however, have a security restriction imposed on them that graphics do not. This restriction makes sense, considering that applets are actually little software programs that *do something*, whereas graphics don't do anything other than sit around and look good (not a bad gig). In particular, applets aren't allowed to access files that don't reside on the same server as they do. All graphics, sounds, and any other support files an applet requires must therefore be on the same server as the applet.

And herein lies the crux of your Web-page planning. Will the applets be expected to use support files (such as sound and image files) from your own server? If so, you have no choice but to install the applet on your own server. If not, you're free to use distributed applets.

Configuring distributed applets

Of course, distributed applets are configured by using <APPLET> tag parameters, just as their server-bound counterparts are. You can configure distributed applets to your heart's content, as long as the parameter information you supply doesn't reference files on any server other than the one the applet comes from. And this setup should be just fine because well-designed distributed applets will have all the support files they need installed on the same server.

In this example, the distributed Ticker applet resides on the `mantiscorp.com` Web server, which the `CODEBASE` parameter points to with a URL. All I do is specify the following:

- ✔ The size of the applet as it should appear on my page (25 pixels high and 300 pixels wide)
- ✔ The message to be scrolled ("Welcome to my page!")
- ✔ The specifics of the font to be used (14-point Courier, in a nice shade of red)

I make no reference whatsoever to support files because this applet doesn't make use of them. If it did use support files, however, they would have to reside on the `anywhere.org` Web server for this applet to be able to access them. Either way, when your browser executes the applet, it is displayed using the various parameters that I specify (see Figure 7-1).

Figure 7-1:
You can't tell just by looking whether an applet is distributed or server-bound. To find out, you must take a peek at the `<APPLET>` tag.

How you construct your `<APPLET>` tag is up to you. I prefer to use all uppercase letters for each tag (APPLET, PARAM, and so on) and any attributes I supply (CODE, HEIGHT, WIDTH, NAME, VALUE, and so on). I also like to enclose all the parameter names and values in quotes, even though doing so is necessary only when you specify something with a space in it (such as "font color"). For details on constructing the `<APPLET>` tag, refer to Chapters 5 and 8.

Be careful about which fonts you choose for your text. Because you can't be sure which fonts will be installed on the machines on which your applet will be executed, it's a good idea to stick with fonts that are likely to be available on most users' systems. If you use a font that isn't installed on a visitor's computer, a font substitution will take place that may ruin the visual effect you planned. Play it safe and try to keep your font choices to a bare minimum. Times Roman, Courier, and Helvetica, for example, are good choices because they are installed on most Macintosh and Windows computer systems. With other fonts, you just can't be sure.

Okay, it's confession time: There really is no applet named Ticker on the `mantiscorp.com` Web server! I just said that as an example of how distributed applets work; if you try this example, it will fail. Can you ever forgive me? Tell you what — let me make it up to you by providing the Marquee applet on the `mantiscorp.com` site instead (`www.mantiscorp.com/java/applets/marquee`, to be precise) so that you can use it in a distributed fashion. Sound fair? To find out how to tap into the Marquee applet in this way, keep reading.

The pros and cons of server-bound applets

Although distributed applets are a breeze to deal with (because you don't have to bother uploading anything to your server to use them), they have one major downside: You can't rely on them to always be available. Distributed applets don't reside on your server, so you have absolutely no control over their availability. One day your page may be able to access the applet, and the next it may not. What if the server on which a given applet resides becomes overloaded with activity, preventing your browsers from making a connection? Or the applet itself may have been relocated or removed entirely. Whatever the case, you're in no position to complain.

You have much more control over server-bound applets than over their distributed brethren. You can place server-bound applets wherever you choose on your server and configure them to take advantage of your own graphics and sound files (or any other support file, for that matter).

Not only are server-bound applets more flexible than distributed applets in this respect, but you also don't have to worry about whether your pages will be able to access server-bound applets. Because they reside on the same server as the Web pages that use them, server-bound applets aren't in danger of being relocated or moved without you knowing. As a result, they won't disappear out from under you the way a distributed applet might.

Despite these advantages, server-bound applets do have a minor downside: They're slightly more time-consuming to configure. As their name implies, server-bound applets must be "bound" to your server. Although the act of binding an applet to your server sounds impressive and perhaps even difficult, it's not; all you have to do is upload it to your Web server (see Chapter 8). As soon as an applet is uploaded to your Web server, it is *bound* to that server and can access only files that reside there. And, because the applet then resides on your own server, you can customize it with your own support files, which is something you can't do with distributed applets.

However, uploading an applet to your Web server is a small (if not entirely insignificant) price to pay for the benefits you enjoy in return. With server-bound applets, you're free to choose support files, such as graphics and sounds, for the applets to use. Whereas distributed applets restrict you to the support files that someone else decides to make available, server-bound applets give you complete control.

Keep in mind that all applets, whether distributed or server-bound, are capable of accessing only those files that reside on the same server as they do. For this reason, you can't customize distributed applets with your own support files, which leaves server-bound applets as the only option if you intend to use your own images or sounds.

Making the choice

Generally speaking, I prefer server-bound applets over distributed ones (can you tell?). Not only do I get to supply my own support files with server-bound applets (an absolute necessity in many cases), but I can also rely on these applets being available 24 hours a day, 7 days a week, 365 days a year (give or take a few days here and there — Internet Service Providers aren't 100 percent reliable and occasionally become unavailable due to routine maintenance).

However, there are occasions when only a distributed applet will do. For example, every time the Fortune Cookie ticker tape applet runs, a new message scrolls across the screen — so every visitor to a page with this applet gets a new "fortune." This ticker tape does use a support file, unlike most of the other available ticker tapes, but it's not a graphics or sound file, as you might expect. Instead, Fortune Cookie requires the use of a plain text file containing different messages (or fortunes).

Because I wouldn't want to bother thinking up a bunch of fortunes to place in the text file — and the whole point of a fortune cookie is that you get an unexpected message — this applet works well as a distributed applet.

Someone else maintains the support file this applet uses, so I never have to bother inventing my own fortunes. As a result, a new fortune is displayed each time the applet is run, just as you'd expect a new fortune from each new fortune cookie you break open.

Having the choice made for you

Of course, the entire process of deciding whether to use a distributed or server-bound applet assumes that you have a choice. If an applet is available only through someone else's Web server (that is, if the applet program isn't made available for you to upload to your own server), you don't have a choice. Not only that, but very few server-bound applets are also available in distributed form. And it's no wonder: Giving everyone in the world distributed access to the applets on your Web server tends to put quite a load on your site.

So how do you know whether an applet you stumble across on the Web is available in server-bound or distributed form? That all depends on where you find the applet and what type of access you're given to it. You may use any applet as a distributed applet, provided that it's made available on the Web for you to reference in your own pages. In fact, I tell you how to reference distributed applets later in this chapter, in the section titled "Tapping into distributed applets." If you can download the applet, however, you can use it in a server-bound manner by placing it on your own Web site.

The CD-ROM that comes with this book contains a bunch of applets, free for the taking. All of these applets may be used as server-bound applets; that is, you can put them on your own Web site. If you want to make an applet on your Web site available to the world (distributed), all you have to do is provide information in a page on your site that tells folks exactly where it's located and how it may be configured.

If you don't find the applet you want on the CD-ROM, don't worry. Thousands of applets are available on the Web now, with more added every day. In fact, the disc has a hyperlink that takes you to the perfect starting place on the Web for your applet hunt — see Appendix A for details.

Applet Harvesting

"Great, so applets are everywhere — but how do I get them onto my own pages?" you ask. "After all, finding a cool applet on someone else's Web pages is one thing, but hooking it up on my own page is quite another."

Distributed applets are the easiest to use on your page because they remain exactly where they are — you don't have to bother downloading distributed applets to your own computer, leaving the applet on the tree, if you will. With distributed applets, all you have to do is hook up your <APPLET> tag in such a way that it *points* to the applet by providing its URL.

Server-bound applets, however, are a mite more complicated. Because server-bound applets must physically reside on the same Web server as the pages in which they are embedded, you must download the applets from the Internet onto your personal computer. When these applets are on your computer, you can weave them into your Web page and then upload the page, the applet, and any support files the applet uses (sound and image files, for example) onto *your* Web site.

When you see an applet that you want to add to your Web site as a server-bound applet, and it is free for the taking, you must know how to get the applet and all its support files into your mitts and onto your page. Every Web page author has their own way of explaining how to go about doing this, but the process of harvesting applets is about the same, no matter what the applet.

Time to download

Whereas distributed applets are a cinch to use because you need only configure the <APPLET> tag before you're up and running, if you want a server-bound applet, you must first download it to your computer. This means that you must physically initiate a download with your Web browser, which copies the applet from the Web to your computer a little at a time. Depending on the size of the applet, this process usually takes no more than a few minutes.

The trick isn't in the downloading. Any page that offers you its applets makes downloading a snap: All you do is click on the appropriate hyperlink to initiate the download and then choose the directory on your computer to place the incoming applet (see Figure 7-2). Just as with any other download, you're free to choose any location on your computer to store the applet (including the desktop).

 Personally, I like to place all the applets I download from the Web in a master directory on my computer called Web Applets. When choosing a location on my system to place an applet being downloaded, I simply navigate to my Web Applets directory and then create a new subdirectory for the incoming applet. This way, each applet I pluck off the Web has its own little home on my computer, so I don't have to worry about it rubbing up against the others I have previously downloaded. This setup doesn't just make for healthy and happy applets, it also makes for a healthy and happy me; I'd lose my mind trying to keep track of my applets if I stored them all in the same directory!

Figure 7-2:
To begin a
download,
first choose
a place
on your
computer
to save
the file.

The first step, of course, is initiating the download. That step starts the compressed archive on its way, sending it a little at a time over the network until it has been completely transferred to your computer.

Downloading archives

When the archive arrives, you typically need to decompress it. You can think of a compressed archive as a nice little bundle of goodies — a package that has been tightly wrapped to survive the journey. When that bundle arrives on your system, you need to unwrap (or *decompress*) it. Unfortunately, not all files are bundled in the same way, making the process of decompression a little more complicated in some cases.

Depending on what computer system the applet and associated files were compressed on and what compression tool was used to do the job, the archive that arrives on your computer may be in any of several formats. Although a number of formats exist, three particular types are most commonly used on the Web. You can distinguish these types by the three-character extension following the archive's filename:

- ✔ **archivename.zip:** The ZIP archive is popular in the Windows community.

- ✔ **archivename.sit:** The StuffIt (SIT) archive is popular in the Macintosh world.

- ✔ **archivename.tar:** The TAR archive is popular among UNIX users.

To decompress an archive, you must use a tool that understands the format in which the archive was created. To decompress a ZIP archive, for example, you need to use a decompression tool capable of handling the ZIP format. Likewise, if you come across a SIT archive, you have to use a tool capable of decompressing the SIT format. And, lest I leave anybody out, if you happen to download a TAR archive, you must unwrap it using a tool that understands the TAR format — TAR archives aren't compressed; rather, they are simply wrapped up in a single package, in their original size.

The frustration comes when you finally stumble on that perfect, plump, ripe little applet on the Web, the one sitting out there seemingly just for you, the one practically begging to become part of your site. After downloading an archive containing the applet (and any files it comes with), you realize that it's in a format that you can't decompress. You have no way to get the files out of the bundle!

Your predicament with the archive is just a temporary one, however. As soon as you find a decompression tool that understands that formula, you're back in business. The solution, of course, is to amass all the decompression tools you could ever need, building a digital war chest for just such times. If the first tool doesn't understand the format, try the second one, then the third, then the . . . well, you get the idea.

Because decompression tools are quite small by comparison to most software programs today — they typically weigh-in at a svelte 1MB or less — you can easily fit several such tools on your computer as long as you have even a smidgen of hard drive space available. And even if you went crazy and decided to download every decompression tool you could get your hands on, you'd probably only suck up around 50MB of hard drive space or so (you'd be hard pressed to find more than fifty decompression tools for each computing platform in use today). Of course, you don't need to download every tool you come upon. In fact, to fully round out your arsenal of decompression tools, you need only have a tool capable of decompressing the most popular type of archive formats used on the Web today.

To compress, or not to compress — that is the question

In truth, not all archives are compressed. In some cases, files are just assembled into an archive to bundle them for easy transfer over the Internet. The person who assembles the archive decides what files are in it and whether compression should be used to reduce their size. The TAR format, in fact, is never really compressed; it's just a convenient way to bundle up files for distribution over the

Net. You can apply compression to an existing TAR archive, however. That is, you can compress the entire archive after all the files have been added to it. Standard compression utilities, on the other hand, compress each file as it is added to the archive. The result is a ZIP file, which you can decompress by using most utilities that handle the ZIP format.

If you choose the right decompression tool in the first place, you rarely need to fall back on others in your arsenal. A good decompression tool is like a Swiss army knife (complete with scissors, screwdriver, corkscrew, nail file, and jet-propulsion engine) in that it understands a variety of formats and can give you access to 90 percent or more of the archives you come across. So which decompression tools are the good ones?

If you're a Windows user, I suggest WinZip, by Nico Mak Computing, shown in Figure 7-3. This fantastic ZIP tool understands the TAR format as well. However, WinZip doesn't understand SIT archives. To deal with the SIT format, Windows users have to get their hands on a copy of StuffIt Expander (the Windows version of this tool, of course, as shown in Figure 7-4).

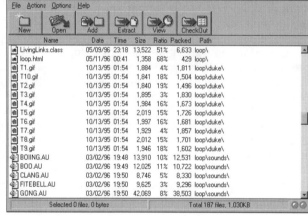

Figure 7-3:
WinZip
is an
invaluable
compression
tool that no
Windows
user should
be without.

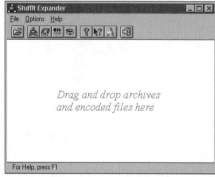

Figure 7-4:
StuffIt
Expander
for
Windows
gives you
access to
archives in
the SIT
format,
which is
wildly
popular
in the
Macintosh
community.

If, on the other hand, you're a Macintosh user, you should start off with the Mac version of StuffIt Expander (see Figure 7-5). This versatile decompression tool understands the SIT format as well as archives stored in CPT *(Compact)*, HQX *(BinHex),* and other popular Macintosh archive formats. Because the applet orchards are thick with ZIP archives, you should also get your mitts on a copy of ZipIt, shown in Figure 7-6.

Figure 7-5:
StuffIt
Expander is
the ideal
decom-
pression
tool for
Macs.

Figure 7-6:
To
decompress
ZIP files,
Macintosh
users
require a
tool such as
ZipIt.

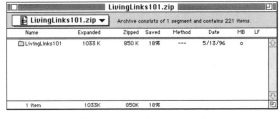

As luck would have it, all of the utilities that I mention in this section (WinZip, ZipIt, and the StuffIt Expander for Windows and Macs) are packed into the CD-ROM that comes with this book. Simply copy the Goodies directory to your computer (see Appendix A for details about the directory structure of this disc), and you're set to take on the world — or at least to decompress it.

An enhancement to StuffIt Expander, appropriately named the StuffIt Expander Enhancer, adds ZIP format capabilities to this utility. The CD that comes with this book contains a trial version of the StuffIt Expander Enhancer.

If you don't want to bother manually decompressing archives that you download from the Web, consider configuring your browser to do the decompression automatically. For details, check the documentation for your browser. Netscape Navigator users should consult the online handbook available through Netscape's home page (`www.netscape.com`); Microsoft Internet Explorer users can visit the Internet Explorer home page (`www.microsoft.com/ie`) and navigate to the Internet Explorer documentation from there.

Although you may have a tool capable of recognizing a particular format, you may encounter different flavors of the format that the tool can't deal with. In this case, you should contact the person who made the archive available and ask which tool they recommend for decompressing it. E-mail is always the best route for contacting these individuals; hunt for an e-mail address on the Web page where you found the archive and then drop a line or two explaining your predicament. Chances are, you'll receive a reply telling you exactly which tool to use.

Decompression: Tricky, tricky

The trick to using server-bound applets isn't in the download process itself, it's accessing the applet *after* you've downloaded it. After all, you're not just down-loading an applet; you're getting a compressed archive that may contain all of the following:

- ✔ The applet
- ✔ Any support files the applet requires
- ✔ Installation instructions
- ✔ An example Web page or two with the applet already woven in

Because most applets provided on the Web come with a handful of companion files such as those listed above, figuring out how to decompress the archive can be a bear. If you've haven't downloaded files from the Web, the first few times can be a bit tricky. But after you have the process down, it's a breeze.

Keep your hands out of JARs

Keep in mind that when I talk about decompressing, I'm not referring to *Java archives* or *JARs* (which I talk about in Chapter 5). JAR files are a feature of Java 1.1 that allows applet developers to place support files in a compressed archive — and that archive is supposed to stay compressed! Don't try to extract JARs; instead, keep all the files together inside the archive they come in and use the `ARCHIVE` attribute of the `<APPLET>` tag to tell the latest crop of browsers how to deal with a JAR. (See the section further on in this chapter called "Let the Weaving Begin!" to find out how to weave JARs into Web pages.)

So, how do you know if you're dealing with a JAR file that's supposed to stay compressed, or a compressed archive that you're supposed to decompress after you've downloaded it? As a vintage comedian might say, "very carefully."

Actually, determining what type of archive you're dealing with isn't all that difficult. If the archive file name has the .jar extension, you're dealing with a JAR file that should not be decompressed once you get it. Any other extension is fair game, but there's one in particular that might cause you problems: .zip.

If I've said it once, I've said it a thousand times: ZIP it!

If you've spent much time on the Web, chances are pretty good that you've come upon files having the .zip extension. *ZIP archives,* as they're called, are quite common on the Web because compressing and decompressing files using the ZIP technique is easy. However, as convenient as ZIP is for compressing files and sending them over the Internet, downloading applets can get a little hairy if you assume that every ZIP file containing applets should be decompressed.

You see, long before the latest version of Java introduced JAR files (which are really just special-purpose ZIP archives created specially for applets), some developers turned to ZIP in an effort to shave time off how long it takes a browser to run their applets. Instead of using ZIP archives to give *you* easy access to the various files that comprise an applet, these developers use them in the same way that JAR files are used: To allow the Web browser to download and run the applet and its associated files as fast as possible. As with JAR files, these particular ZIP archives are not supposed to be decompressed ever! Instead, simply upload the ZIP archive to your own Web site (see Chapter 10 for details on uploading files to your site) and then construct a unique `<APPLET>` tag that tells the browser how to deal with the archive. Fortunately, JAR files eliminate the need for such uses of ZIP archives, so you'll probably never have to deal with this potential confusion.

As long as you pay attention to the download instructions that appear on a Web page containing ZIP archives, you know what kind of ZIPs you're downloading.

The private life of ZIP archives

Although I refer to ZIP as a compression technique, it's actually an algorithm, or computer "recipe," that describes the exact steps necessary to create a ZIP archive file. Conversely, ZIP archives can be decompressed with tools that apply the algorithm in reverse. If you're a computer buff, you may be interested to know that the ZIP algorithm was invented by two individuals whose last names contributed in part to the "ZIP" acronym.

Cool Beans! — hand-picked applets

If the prospect of hunting down applets on the Web, downloading them to your computer, and decompressing the archives in which they'll likely be wrapped doesn't appeal to you, take heart: Right on the CD-ROM that comes with this book, you can find a number of the hottest applets available. Of course, this probably comes as no surprise to you because the book's very cover announces this fact with pride.

To use any one of these applets, all you have to do is copy it (and any files it may require) from the CD-ROM onto your own computer. After you copy an applet to your computer, you can simply embed it directly into your Web pages (see the upcoming section, "Let the Weaving Begin!"), bypassing the whole downloading and decompression rigmarole.

For details regarding the applets available on this disc, check out Appendix A. There, you'll find a description of the contents of the CD-ROM along with a layout of the various directories on it. And although the Cool Beans! folder is reason enough to jam the disc into your CD-ROM drive this very moment, you'll want to click into another folder as soon as the disc spins up: CookBook. The CookBook folder contains a number of Java-powered Web pages you can use as the basis for your own page.

Let the Weaving Begin!

Weaving applets into Web pages is really quite simple and can be broken down into a few easy steps. These steps are essentially the same regardless of whether you're dealing with distributed applets or those that are bound to your own server:

1. **Obtain the applet you want to use (or a URL pointing to it in the case of distributed applets).**

2. **Choose the page to which you want to add the applet (if the applet will be server-bound, copy it into the same folder as the Web page).**

3. **Construct an appropriate `<APPLET>` tag, typing it directly into the HTML source code of your page.**

4. **Test the page.**

After you pick, download, and decompress an applet (or copy it from the CD-ROM, as described in Appendix A) or, in the case of distributed applets, obtain the URL leading to it (see the section "Tapping into distributed applets," later in this chapter, for details), you're ready to embed it into your own Web page. Depending on the applet, the process of embedding and configuring, which I like to call *weaving,* may take as little as a few minutes or over an hour. Yet in all cases, no matter how simple or complex the applet, whether distributed or server-bound, you ultimately end up typing an <APPLET> tag into the HTML page that will contain the applet.

Without the <APPLET> tag, described in detail in Chapter 5, you have no mechanism for embedding an applet in your Web pages. The <APPLET> tag tells Java-savvy browsers that an applet is embedded in a page, where that applet is located, and how that applet should look and act after it's activated. Without the <APPLET> tag, you would be weaving without a loom, stitching without a needle, sewing without thread.

Although the <APPLET> tag can be quite complex depending on the applet you're dealing with, it can also be incredibly simplistic. In truth, you must supply only three pieces of information (attributes) to your HTML code. Applet *attributes* are settings you provide within the opening <APPLET> tag that allow you to control such things as how the applet is positioned on the Web page, whether it's referenced from your own site (server-bound) or someone else's (distributed), and whether it will be capable of communicating with other applets on the same page. Although you can choose from a number of attributes, only three of them are mandatory for applets created using the original version of Java. These attributes, which are required for both server-bound and distributed applets, are as follows:

- ✔ CODE (or OBJECT): The name of the applet file
- ✔ HEIGHT: How tall the applet will be, measured in pixels
- ✔ WIDTH: How wide the applet will be, measured in pixels

Depending on the applet and what it does, the HEIGHT and WIDTH settings you provide may or may not affect how the applet appears on your page or how it performs when running. Because you can't be sure what an applet requires when it comes to these attributes, however, you should take a look at the documentation that comes with the applet (see Chapter 8). If the documentation doesn't note the applet's size requirements, you have to resort to the ol' trial-and-error method. Keep trying different sizes until the applet looks the way you want it to. There's no magic formula for computing height and width; you have to fiddle with each applet you use to get the right values for your pages (that is, you alone decide how large or small an applet will appear in your Web page).

Additionally, the applets created using Java 1.1 may take advantage of the new `<APPLET>` tag attributes, specifically the `ARCHIVE` and `OBJECT` attributes described in detail in Chapter 5. Of course, only the most modern Java-savvy browsers understand these new attributes, meaning you run the risk of alienating all other browsers unless you take the time to accommodate less powerful browsers (I describe how to do this in Chapter 13).

In any case, the only way to know whether an applet requires that you use either of these two new attributes is to read the documentation that comes with it. If you want to play it safe, and don't want to bother with the extra work involved in accommodating both Java 1.0 and Java 1.1 browsers, you can opt to work with only Java 1.0 applets. Because Java 1.1-compatible browsers understand Java 1.0 applets, you can be sure that all Java-savvy browsers will be able to run your pages. If you weave Java 1.1 applets into your Web pages, on the other hand, you either have to take the time to accommodate older browsers (see Chapter 13 for details), or live with the fact that millions of people will never be able to experience your page as those with more modern browsers can.

The remaining attributes depend on the applet itself and how you intend it to appear in your page. But at the very least, you must supply the opening and closing parts of the tag (`<APPLET>` and `</APPLET>`) and these three attributes, like this:

```
<APPLET CODE="Wildapplet.class" HEIGHT=100 WIDTH=350>
</APPLET>
```

Assuming that the Wildapplet requires no more than these basic components, which is the case with many server-bound applets, the preceding tag is complete and ready to go. A Java-savvy browser that encounters this tag looks for the applet named Wildapplet inside the same directory as the Web page in which it is embedded and will display this applet in an area on that page that is exactly 100 pixels high and 350 pixels wide. What goes on inside this area is the applet's business because an applet is free to do as it likes.

This same applet may use a JAR file, as the following example illustrates, although the `ARCHIVE` attribute necessary to identify the JAR is still considered optional, while the `CODE` attribute must be included whether or not a JAR is used. In the following example, the JAR file is named "wild.jar," although it could just as easily have been named "wildapplet.jar," — or just about anything else for that matter — because the developer chooses names for both the applet ("Wildapplet," in this case) and any JAR that might be associated with it:

```
<APPLET CODE="Wildapplet.class" ARCHIVE="wild.jar"
            HEIGHT=100 WIDTH=350>
</APPLET>
```

While an applet is loading and preparing to do its magic, a gray rectangle appears as a placeholder, as shown in Figure 7-7. The rectangle is located where your applet will be shown, and the height and width of this rectangle are the values you specify in the HEIGHT and WIDTH attributes in the <APPLET> tag.

Figure 7-7:
A gray
rectangle
appears
while an
applet is
loading,
acting as a
placeholder
as the
applet
prepares to
execute.

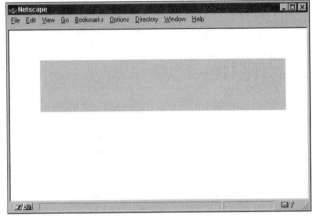

Applets, whether distributed or server-bound, are stored in files that have a unique four-character .class extension. When specifying an applet in the CODE attribute of an <APPLET> tag, you're specifying the name of the file that contains the applet. And although you don't have to include the .class extension of the file, doing so is a good idea. Referring to applet files in your Web pages by their full name (that is, by providing both the filename and the .class extension to the CODE attribute) as I've done here, reinforces for you that applets are contained in .class files, making them easier to identify and manage as you quickly become immersed in Java.

Although you often can get away with using just the three basic attributes, most applets require that you specify more than just the dimensions of the rectangle in which the applet will appear. Exactly what information an applet requires depends entirely on what it was built to do. A few optional parameters you may want to include to position the applet precisely in your Web page are outlined in Chapter 5, in Table 5-2.

Some applets written in Java 1.1 ignore the CODE attribute altogether. Specifically, serialized applets — applets whose internal code is *serialized,* or arranged in such a way that makes it a cinch for the applet to be sent over a network or saved to a hard drive — use the OBJECT attribute instead of CODE, which non-serialized (traditional) applets use. This is the only case where CODE isn't mandatory:

```
<APPLET OBJECT="Wildapplet.ser" HEIGHT=100 WIDTH=350>
</APPLET>
```

Regardless of whether you're working with 1.0 or 1.1 applets, however, you may find that one of the most important applet options isn't really an option at all — it's full-blown HTML! Between the `<APPLET>` and `</APPLET>` tags, you can specify HTML that will appear only when the page is viewed in browsers that are *not* Java-savvy. I cover this option, called *alternate HTML,* in the next section.

Alternate HTML

Perhaps the most important thing you can do when weaving applets into Web pages, aside from configuring the applet itself, is to provide what's known as *alternate HTML* or *alternate context* — HTML code that is used when the page is loaded by a browser that doesn't understand Java. Because not every Webber has the luxury of using a Java-savvy browser to visit your Java-powered site, you must be sensitive to the fact that many will never see the wonderful applets adorning your pages.

When Java-ignorant browsers see an opening `<APPLET>` tag, they skip right over it and go on to the next tag. Because the browsers don't understand Java, they ignore everything that falls between the `<` and `>` in the opening tag. The entire opening tag, attributes and all, then gets overlooked. The same goes for `<PARAM>` tags (discussed in Chapter 5), used to configure an applet — every single one is ignored!

However, just before the closing `</APPLET>` tag (which, by the way, is also ignored by Java-ignorant browsers), is a special area in which you can provide HTML code. This area, called the *alternate HTML area* (or the *alternate context area*), is not ignored by non-Java browsers. Whatever you put in this area gets displayed in place of the applet, as an *alternative* to the applet. An applet that uses several parameters, for example, would require any alternate HTML you provide to appear after the last `<PARAM>` tag but before the closing `</APPLET>` tags:

```
<APPLET CODE="Wildapplet.class" ARCHIVE="wild.jar"
        HEIGHT=100 WIDTH=350>
<PARAM NAME=param1Name VALUE=param1Value>
<PARAM NAME=param2Name VALUE=param2Value>
<PARAM NAME=param3Name VALUE=param3Value>
This is the alternate HTML area, which is displayed only by
        non-Java browsers!
</APPLET>
```

In the *alternate HTML area* in the preceding <APPLET> tag, you provide the HTML code that you want to communicate to Webbers using browsers incapable of displaying Java applets. You can include any type of HTML you choose, as though this were a regular part of your Web page. You can enter plain text, hyperlinked text, and even images and hyperlinked images here; this area can handle anything that non-Java browsers can handle. Java-savvy browsers, on the other hand, ignore this space entirely because it's intended for non-Java browsers. As a result, this is just the place to put a line or two of information telling Webbers that they're missing out on something cool:

```
<APPLET CODE="LivingLinks" WIDTH=100 HEIGHT=100>
<PARAM NAME="image" VALUE="animalsButton.gif">
<PARAM NAME="effect" VALUE="Melt">
<PARAM NAME="soundDir" VALUE="audio/animals/">
<PARAM NAME="inSound" VALUE="dolphinSqueak.au|lionRoar.au
          |rooster.au">
<PARAM NAME="links" VALUE= "Dolphins = http://anywhere.com
              |Lions = http://anywhere.com | Rooster = http://
              anywhere.com">
<B>If you can read this, you're not using a Java-savvy
          browser! <B>
</APPLET>
```

In fact, you may even want to include a hyperlink to help these unfortunate souls find the truth and the light of Java: Point them to a site that offers a Java-savvy browser (such as the Netscape Navigator home page on the Web at www.netscape.com, or Microsoft's Internet Explorer home page at www.microsoft.com/ie). This way, any Webber who visits your page with an inadequate browser will be only one click away from nirvana:

```
<APPLET CODE="LivingLinks" WIDTH=100 HEIGHT=100>
<PARAM NAME="image" VALUE="animalsButton.gif">
<PARAM NAME="effect" VALUE="Melt">
<PARAM NAME="soundDir " VALUE="audio/animals/">
<PARAM NAME="inSound " VALUE="dolphinSqueak.au |
          lionRoar.au | rooster.au">
<PARAM NAME="links" VALUE= "Dolphins = http://anywhere.com
              |Lions = http://anywhere.com | Rooster = http://
              anywhere.com">
<B>If you can read this, you're visiting without a Java-
          savvy browser! <B>
This page requires a Java-savvy browser... GET ONE:
<A HREF="http://www.netscape.com">Get Netscape Navigator</
          A>
<br>
<A HREF="http://www.microsoft.com/ie/">Get Internet
          Explorer</A>
</APPLET>
```

When Web surfers riding Java-savvy browsers view a page containing an
<APPLET> tag, they see the applet, assuming that Java is in fact enabled.
Non-Java browsers, however, as well as Java-savvy browsers that happen to
have Java support turned off (which both Netscape Navigator and Internet
Explorer allow, as described in Chapter 3) are clued in to the fact that
they're missing out on something good and are provided with a hyperlink to
cure their wicked ways (see Figure 7-8).

Figure 7-8:
You can use
alternate
HTML to
alert those
with
non-Java
browsers
that they're
missing
out on
something
cool.

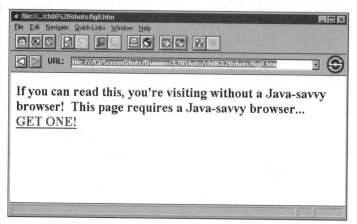

If you can read this, you're visiting without a Java-savvy
browser! This page requires a Java-savvy browser...
GET ONE!

Of course, displaying a "Shame on you! Get with it and get a Java-savvy
browser" message as an alternative to your applets is not always appropriate. In many cases, you use an applet to enhance the visual appeal of a Web
page, and displaying such a message would disrupt the entire design of the
page. Don't worry — you're free to provide anything your heart desires in
the alternate HTML area; as long as it's HTML code, that is.

Often, you end up using the alternate HTML area in an attempt to display
whatever content the applet enhances, such as animated images or image
maps. But because standard HTML produces documents that are entirely
static by nature, the content is no longer vibrant, dynamic, fluid . . . in a
word, *alive,* when viewed by non-Java browsers. Although that's just the way
the Web cookie crumbles, the important thing to realize is that both types of
browsers will visit your site, which you must accommodate as best you can
by using alternate HTML. Bring your site to life with Java, but provide for
those using dead (non-Java) browsers as well.

Thanks to the following <APPLET> tag and alternate HTML, the button at the
bottom of Figure 7-9 is alive when viewed by Java-savvy browsers, pulsing
with life. When the same page is viewed by a non-Java browser, however, the
applet isn't activated and only the alternate HTML inside the <APPLET> tag
is displayed. In this case, the button is still visible and is a hyperlink as well.
It's just not pulsating with life for these Webbers.

Figure 7-9:
When viewed with a Java-savvy browser, this button is animated with a series of images that are slightly different from one moment to the next. Non-Java browsers will see only one image in the series and will miss out on the pulsating effect.

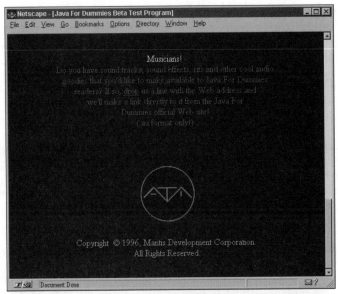

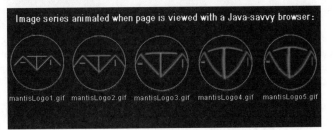

```
<APPLET CODE="LivingLinks" WIDTH=115 HEIGHT=115>
<PARAM NAME="imagesDir" VALUE="images/">
<PARAM NAME="imagesName" VALUE="mantisLogo">
<PARAM NAME="imagesExt" VALUE="gif">
<PARAM NAME="imagesCount" VALUE="5">
<PARAM NAME="speed" VALUE="15">
<PARAM NAME="backgroundColor" VALUE="black">
<PARAM NAME="reverse" VALUE="yes">
<A HREF="http://www.mantiscorp.com"> <IMG SRC="images/
          logo1.gif">
</A>
</APPLET>
```

Tapping into distributed applets

Embedding distributed applets in your Web pages is as easy as spotting Ted Kennedy at an all-you-can-eat dinner buffet — it's painfully obvious. All you have to know is where the applet resides and what attributes and parameters (if any) it requires. As soon as you have this information, you can tap into distributed applets faster than you can say "Would you like a second helping, Senator?"

The information that you need to weave a distributed applet into your Web pages typically is provided on the same page on which you find the applet. If the information doesn't appear directly on that page, hunt around the site. If after scouring the site you still can't find out the exact information you need, chances are that the applet is off limits. You should cut your losses and look for another applet.

To see how such information is usually presented with an available distributed applet, consider the page located at www.mantiscorp.com/java/applets/marquee, which is shown in Figure 7-10. Here, the applet is running on-screen, with a brief description of the <APPLET> tag directly below it. In this case, you don't even need to type the tag into your own page; simply copy and paste it! In fact, you can always save the HTML source code of the page to your computer for later reference, which is a good idea if your memory is as fleeting as mine. For more information on saving the HTML source code of a Web page, check out the section "Digging for buried treasure in source code" in Chapter 6.

Whether you choose to type the <APPLET> tag shown in Figure 7-10 into your own page or to copy and paste it instead, you end up with the same thing:

```
<APPLET CODEBASE="http://www.mantiscorp.com/java/applets/
          marquee/"
CODE="Marquee"
WIDTH=493 HEIGHT=26>
<PARAM NAME="font_face" VALUE="TimesRoman">
<PARAM NAME="font_size" VALUE="18">
<PARAM NAME="font_italic" VALUE="yes">
<PARAM NAME="font_bold" VALUE="yes">
<PARAM NAME="marquee" VALUE="Am I scrolling, or what?
          Wheeeee!!">
<B> This line is alternate HTML — if you can read this, you
          don't have a Java-savvy browser! <B>
</APPLET>
```

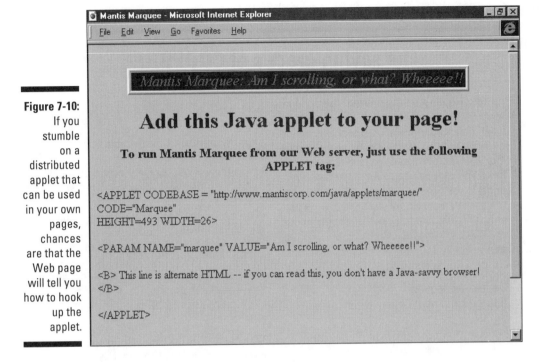

Figure 7-10:
If you
stumble
on a
distributed
applet that
can be used
in your own
pages,
chances
are that the
Web page
will tell you
how to hook
up the
applet.

The most significant part of this tag (in the context of this discussion, at least) is the CODEBASE attribute. Without CODEBASE, browsers assume that the applet resides within the same directory as the Web page that references it. Thanks to CODEBASE, however, you can embed in your pages applets that are physically located on the other side of the world!

CODEBASE is the key to all distributed applets; without it, you would have no way of telling Java-savvy browsers where to find these applets. Without the CODEBASE attribute, all applets would be server-bound and forced to reside in the same directory as the pages that reference them.

Places, everyone

When weaving applets into your pages, you must, of course, decide where they appear. As with all HTML tags, an applet appears on a page in relation to where you enter the <APPLET> tag into the HTML source code: Tags appearing at the top of the page result in your applet appearing at the top, and tags at the bottom appear at (surprise!) the bottom. In fact, positioning an applet on your page is nearly identical to positioning an image; you simply decide where it should appear and then enter the <APPLET> tag in the appropriate place in the HTML source code.

TECHNICAL STUFF

The saving graces of CODEBASE

CODEBASE isn't used exclusively to access applets residing on other Web sites. If you have a server-bound applet that appears in many different pages at your site, you would normally have to upload a copy of that applet into the directory of each page that references it. Or you can use CODEBASE so that every page at your site references the same, centrally located applet. All you have to do is provide the URL leading to the applet in the CODEBASE attribute of the <APPLET> tag, and you're set!

Consider the <APPLET> tag used to display the Marquee applet, especially the opening tag:

```
<APPLET CODEBASE="http://
    www.mantiscorp.com/java/
    applets/marquee"
CODE="Marquee"
WIDTH=493 HEIGHT=26>
```

Which, if it happened to be a serialized applet (which it's not, but work with me here — I'm on a roll), would use the OBJECT attribute instead of CODE:

```
<APPLET CODEBASE="http://
    www.mantiscorp.com/java/
    applets/marquee"
```

```
OBJECT="Marquee.ser"
WIDTH=493 HEIGHT=26>
```

The first example actually appears in several pages of the Mantis Development Corporation Web site. It references the Marquee applet, which resides on the same server as the site (www.mantiscorp.com) but does so in a distributed manner. Now, thanks to CODEBASE, you don't need to have a copy of the Marquee applet inside the directory of each page at the Mantis site that makes use of the applet. Instead, all pages reference the same one — the Marquee applet located in the directory pointed to by CODEBASE (www.mantiscorp.com/java/applets/marquee).

This feature is particularly useful when it comes to managing all the applets you'll eventually have at your site. Using CODEBASE, you have to keep track of only a single applet instead of bothering to manage all the copies of the applet that would otherwise need to be uploaded into each Web page directory that references it. As a result, upgrading the applet is a snap: Just replace the one applet pointed to by CODEBASE and you're done!

Any number of applets can be included on a Web page. In Figure 7-11, for example, every item displayed on-screen appears courtesy of an applet. When viewed with a Java-savvy browser, this page literally comes to life. The logo at the top glows as though it's on fire, while the images below it seem to be continually pushed from behind with the end of a broom handle — they expand and retract, begging to be clicked.

Of course, positioning applets on a page can be tricky if you're not comfortable writing HTML code. In particular, you must know how to position images; if you can do that, you can place applets on your page with the same precision. The only difference is that, instead of entering image tags, you enter applet tags.

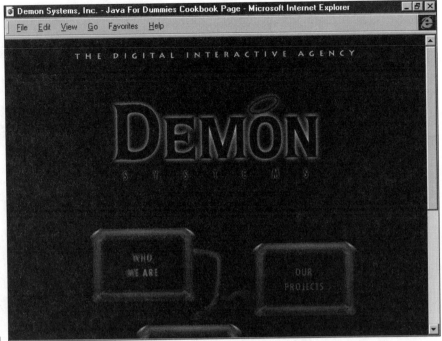

Figure 7-11:
Web pages
can contain
any number
of applets.

To find out all about using HTML to position images, check out *HTML For Dummies,* 3rd Edition, by Ed Tittel and Steve James (IDG Books Worldwide, Inc.). Personally, I think that *HTML For Dummies* is the perfect complement to this book — the cream for your Java coffee!

Close encounters

Although you can easily position applets one right after the other, sometimes you need to get your applets closer together. For example, to give the illusion of a single, larger applet, you may need to have several applets appear side by side or one on top of the other with absolutely no space between them.

Consider the image shown in Figure 7-12. You have no idea by looking at this image that it's composed of several smaller images pressed closely together. Here, different parts of the image are animated by separate applets that all work together to give the appearance of a single image that has various "moving" parts. Specifically, different parts of the image are animated by applets, giving it the appearance of a scene from a movie: The lights flicker, fluids drip into the tubes attached to the poor fella's head, and he really seems to be in pain, writhing so. When you place the mouse in different parts of the image, different sounds are emitted and he twitches even more. Not only does it *look* as if he's in serious pain, but it *sounds* like it!

Figure 7-12:
This image is composed of four different applets, each performing a specific part of the animation.

The key to this illusion, of course, is getting each applet to display its section of the image right next to the others, with no visible space between the applets. To do this, you must use an applet that provides these animation capabilities but doesn't place anything between the image and the edges of the applet (such as a 3-D bevel, which gives the appearance of a button by placing a thin border or a space around the animation). In addition, the HEIGHT and WIDTH attributes that you specify for each applet must match exactly the size of the images they use; otherwise, the fact that you're using several different applets becomes painfully obvious when you load the page (see Figure 7-13).

To find out the exact dimensions of your images, use a graphics program. Any graphics program worth its salt enables you to easily find out the size of an image.

One other thing you must do is enter each <APPLET> tag, one right after the other, ensuring that no other tags come between them. If a <BR> tag, for example, appears between each <APPLET>, each applet appears on its own line. You want line breaks to occur only where it makes sense for the overall image — after the second applet, in this case.

Figure 7-13:
If you don't configure your applets properly, or if they weren't meant to be positioned side by side, the effect can be ruined.

Give me some space!

Although pressing applets close together is useful when it comes to creating the illusion of a larger, seamless image or animation, sometimes you want just the opposite effect — to control the space between your applet and the items around it (text, images, or other applets).

The ALIGN attribute

Because applets are integral portions of Web pages, you must have some degree of control over where they appear on the page in relation to the other elements around them. In particular, you may need to place an applet in a page that has text in it.

Thankfully, you can use the `<APPLET>` tag's `ALIGN` attribute to do just that. In fact, you have nine options at your disposal:

- ✔ `ALIGN=left`
- ✔ `ALIGN=right`
- ✔ `ALIGN=top`
- ✔ `ALIGN=texttop`
- ✔ `ALIGN=middle`

✔ ALIGN=absmiddle

✔ ALIGN=baseline

✔ ALIGN=bottom

✔ ALIGN=absbottom

When specifying ALIGN=left or ALIGN=right inside the opening <APPLET> tag, the text following the applet is arranged accordingly — either to the left or right of it. When the applet is on the left, the text appears to the right. Conversely, if your applet is aligned to the right, the text appears to the left, as shown in Figure 7-14.

Note that all subsequent text continues to flow in this manner until you force it to stop. To return the text to its previous state (the way it was aligned before your <APPLET> tag appeared in the source code), you must specify a *line break* at the point at which you want text to start flowing normally again. The break tag <BR>, discussed in Chapter 5, accepts a CLEAR attribute that allows you to specify how the remaining text will flow. CLEAR can be LEFT, RIGHT, or ALL. To set the text back to a normal flow, simply provide the following line-break tag immediately before the text you want to return to normal:

```
<BR CLEAR=ALL>
```

The best way to find out how each of the ALIGN attribute values affects the alignment of your applet is to test each one. It's easy enough. All you have to do is provide one of the nine possible values immediately following the ALIGN attribute. For an idea of how each affects the positioning of your applets, see Figure 7-15.

Keep in mind that ALIGN is just one of several attributes you can use with the <APPLET> tag. (See Chapter 5 for a listing of each attribute you can use.) Don't forget to include these attributes in the opening <APPLET> tag, as follows. They won't do you any good if they're outside the tag! The following line of HTML illustrates the proper way to include attributes inside the opening <APPLET> tag — notice how the CODE, HEIGHT, WIDTH, AND ALIGN attributes appear after the word APPLET but before the greater-than character (>):

```
<APPLET CODE="LivingLinks" HEIGHT=100 WIDTH=345 ALIGN=top>
```

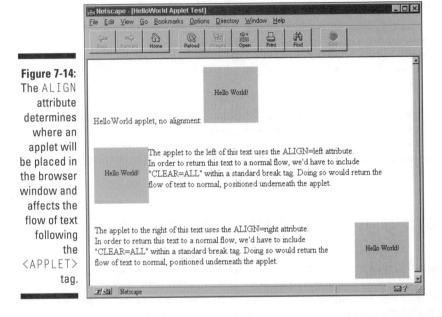

Figure 7-14:
The ALIGN
attribute
determines
where an
applet will
be placed in
the browser
window and
affects the
flow of text
following
the
<APPLET>
tag.

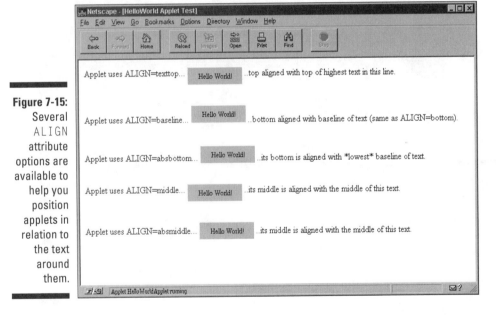

Figure 7-15:
Several
ALIGN
attribute
options are
available to
help you
position
applets in
relation to
the text
around
them.

Giving your applets elbow room with VSPACE and HSPACE

You can gain even more control over your applet's position relative to the text around it by using the VSPACE and HSPACE attributes. VSPACE specifies how much space appears vertically (above or below) around your applet. HSPACE, on the other hand, specifies the amount of horizontal space (from left to right) around your applet.

Whether you use them alone or in combination with the ALIGN attribute (covered in the preceding section), using HSPACE and VSPACE is a wonderful way to ensure that your applets appear with the amount of space around them that you want. For an example of how these attributes are used, see Figure 7-16.

Testing your Java-powered pages

After you insert the <APPLET> tag into your Web page, you need to test the results. To do so, simply save your newly created HTML code and open it using a Java-savvy browser. If all goes according to plan, a gray box appears exactly where the applet will be displayed, and in a few moments, the applet begins running.

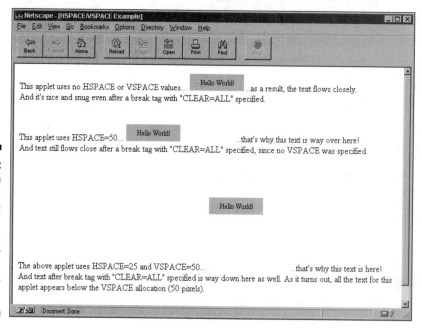

Figure 7-16:
Use the
HSPACE
and
VSPACE
attributes
to give your
applets a
little elbow
room.

Of course, things don't always go according to plan. If the applet doesn't appear, give it a few more seconds and then panic — something may be wrong. To know for sure, keep your eye on the status area of the browser window. If you see a message that says the applet couldn't be loaded, it means that the applet file couldn't be found. In this case, one of three things is going on:

✔ The applet file (or JAR file, if one is specified using the ARCHIVE attribute) isn't in the same directory as your Web page (assuming that you're working with a server-bound applet).

If the applet file is serialized, it requires the OBJECT tag instead of CODE, and will most likely have the *.ser* file extension. If the applet is traditional, and doesn't take advantage of serialization, it will use the CODE attribute and will have the *.class* extension. Be careful to use the correct attribute for your applet and make sure the applet file (whether traditional, serialized, or included in a JAR) is where it should be.

✔ The CODEBASE attribute is incorrect or you're not currently connected to the Internet (assuming that you're working with a distributed applet).

✔ The applet file or JAR is unavailable (in the case of a distributed applet) or possibly corrupt (if the file is in the same directory as your Web page).

Before assuming the worst, double-check that your <APPLET> tag references the applet by name exactly, matching all uppercase and lowercase letters. In the case of distributed applets, make sure that the URL is also entered exactly. In most cases, it's simply a matter of a typo or two, and you'll be back in action in no time. Simply fix the error, save the change in your source file, and reload it in your browser. If the applet still doesn't work, make sure that Java is enabled for your browser — if it's not, you'll never see the applet. (Chapter 3 tells how to find out whether Java is enabled on your browser, and how to turn it on if it isn't.)

If Java is enabled and your tag is constructed exactly, but the applet doesn't work, the file may be corrupt. (Or in the case of distributed applets, the server on which it resides may not be available; try again later. If the problem persists, use e-mail to contact the individual who made the applet available and explain your dilemma — the applet may have been moved or renamed without you knowing.) In some cases, the archive may not have made it across the wire intact. In this case, you have to download the applet and start anew.

If the applet loads okay but the status area reports that the applet couldn't initialize itself, chances are the <APPLET> tag isn't properly configured. Perhaps the parameters you provided aren't valid or the support files (sound files and graphics, for example) aren't available. Make sure that everything is where it belongs and make any necessary changes. Then reload your page and see if it flies. If it doesn't, you might be the victim of piggish browser (one which gobbles down the first <APPLET> tag you feed it but refuses to recognize any changes that you make to the tag unless the browser itself is quit and restarted)— which is easy to remedy — or the issue may run deeper still. Consult Chapter 17 for details on the most common errors you'll encounter and how to resolve them.

Chapter 8

Preparing to Customize Your Applets

In This Chapter

▶ Configuring applets to suit your needs

▶ Tweaking <PARAM> tags

*T*hink of each Java applet as a zippy little sports car. When you first slip into the driver's seat, the car seems to have been built just for you. Sooner or later, though, you want to add your own personal touches. These personal touches may be as insignificant as a set of beaded seat covers or a pair of fuzzy dice, or as radical as a racy paint job, tinted windows, monster tires, and chrome rims.

The extent to which you can customize your car depends on two factors:

✔ **Your car:** How much can it be customized?

✔ **Your resources:** Do you have the cash, the equipment, and the skills required to turn your Volkswagen Rabbit into a makeshift Dodge Viper?

The same concerns apply to customizing your Java applets:

✔ **Your applet:** Does the applet support customizing?

✔ **Your resources:** Do you have the support files, the software, and the HTML skills required to customize your applet, in essence turning a run-of-the-mill applet into a Web page wonder?

Tune-Up or Overhaul?

As with automobiles, you can customize most applets to some extent. Other applets, however, are *infinitely* customizable. You can spend months souping up these puppies and barely scratch the surface of their capabilities. Just as different cars appeal to different drivers, your Java applet requirements will vary from the applet requirements of your neighbors in the cyberhood. Your applet may work great right out of the box, or it may require regular maintenance to keep pace with your demands.

Depending on the applet itself, you may be able to customize any or all of the following attributes:

- Images
- Sounds
- Text
- Colors
- URLs

While Chapter 9 tells you everything you need to know to add these features, you must first determine what features the applet you're using actually supports. To do this, you need to find (and then consult) the documentation that came with the applet — you need to get your hands on the owners manual.

Do You Have an Owner's Manual?

The most important thing you can get your hands on, aside from the applet itself, is an owner's manual. Not the kind that comes with a new car or with the software programs you run on your computer, mind you, but something similar. In order to customize an applet, you need a guide that tells you what the applet can do and how the applet can do it. Sometimes an applet comes with the documentation you need. Unfortunately, this isn't always the case.

If you don't have documentation, you may have to connect to the Web and see how others have hooked up the applet. Although looking at customized HTML source code is just fine in many cases, it doesn't give you much to go on. Simply looking at the <APPLET> tag that someone else has constructed (see Chapter 7 for details) gives you no detailed information about the internal workings of the applet. At best, you get a general idea about how the applet works and enough information to start fiddling around with it on your own. At worst, you may never learn how to configure the applet to its fullest extent. Consider, for example, the LivingLinks applet.

You can find LivingLinks (the applet used in this example and throughout this chapter) in the Cool Beans! directory of the CD-ROM that comes with this book. For details on how to find LivingLinks on the CD-ROM, refer to Appendix A. If you want to work through the examples in this chapter, now is the perfect time to copy this applet to your personal computer.

Here's the <APPLET> tag for the LivingLinks applet as it's used in the Who We Are button on the top left of the Demon Systems "CookBook" page, included on CD-ROM:

```
<APPLET CODE=LivingLinks.class WIDTH=214 HEIGHT=140>
    <PARAM NAME=imagesDir VALUE="console/who/">
    <PARAM NAME=imagesName VALUE="who">
    <PARAM NAME=imagesExt VALUE="gif">
    <PARAM NAME=imagesCount VALUE="5">
    <PARAM NAME=URL VALUE="http://www.demonsys.com/who.html">
    <PARAM NAME=backgroundImage VALUE="console/who/top.gif">
    <PARAM NAME=backgroundColor VALUE="black">
</APPLET>
```

From the preceding code, you can see that the LivingLinks applet uses images. The big tip-offs, of course, are the four parameters beginning with the word "images"! But what does each parameter correspond to? Without any documentation to tell you, such as the LivingLinks documentation provided in the next chapter, you have to monkey around with these settings. Assuming that the applet and its associated Web page are already on your hard drive, tinkering with the settings isn't too tough. Just open the folder or directory that contains these files on your computer and begin exploring. (See Chapter 6 for more information on how to get an applet to your computer.)

By opening up the folder and taking a look around, you can see right off the bat that the only things it contains are an HTML file that uses the preceding <APPLET> tag, the applet it refers to (LivingLinks.class), and a directory called console, shown in Figure 8-1.

Figure 8-1: To figure out how to configure your <APPLET> tag, look inside the folder containing the applet.

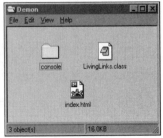

Keep in mind that all applets end with the .class extension, even though you don't have to include that extension when referencing the applet. (Java Archive files, or JARs, are another matter — more on those in the section entitled "The JARing truth.") In fact, you don't even need to use quotes around the applet name — quotes are used to surround text items inside the tag that have spaces in them, and applet names never have spaces (at least not in the foreseeable future, thanks to the way applets are compiled during the development process). As a result, each of the following four examples is an acceptable way to reference an applet:

```
CODE="LivingLinks"
CODE=LivingLinks
CODE="LivingLinks.class"
CODE=LivingLinks.class
```

Although Macintosh users always see the .class and .html extensions on filenames (and all other extensions, for that matter), these extensions may be hidden from Windows 95 users.

A feature of Windows 95 allows all extensions to be hidden, keeping them out of your way. As a result, you may eventually rip out your hair in frustration trying to track down files by extension. If you can't see the filename extension, how can you be sure which is myFile.html, myFile.class, or any other myFile file? Although different icons are generally used to represent each type of extension, the only surefire way to find out a file's document type is to actually open the file and see whether it contains the information you're looking for. To unhide the filename extensions, do the following:

1. **From Windows Explorer, choose View⇨Options.**

   The Options dialog box opens.

2. **Uncheck the Hide MS-DOS File Extensions For File Types That Are Registered checkbox.**

   Filename extensions are displayed from that point on.

In the LivingLinks example, you have very little documentation to go on regarding how the applet may be used except the `<APPLET>` tag itself. By closely examining the tag inside the HTML file, you see that one of the parameters, `<PARAM NAME=imagesDir VALUE="console/who/">`, actually specifies an image directory. The next logical step is to open the path that the directory points to (first open *console,* and then open the *who* directory inside it) and see what's inside. All you find, in this case, is a number of images, because the `"imageDir"` parameter does nothing more than point to a directory containing images.

On further examination of the contents of this folder (see Figure 8-2) and the remainder of the `<APPLET>` tag, it's clear that yet another parameter, `<PARAM NAME=imagesName VALUE="who">`, corresponds to the files inside of it. By

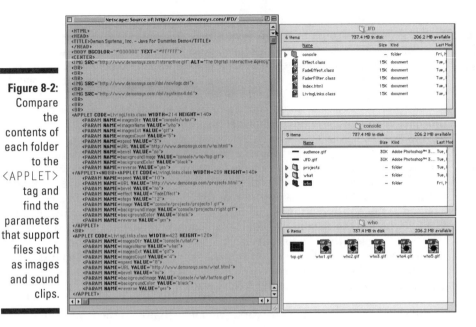

stepping through the code and trying to relate each parameter to the files that come with an applet, you can deduce quite a bit about the parameters and how you may customize them to your personal preferences.

In this example, notice that a total of four parameters are used to supply the applet with the series of images it will use in the animation. Although you can't tell just by looking at the applet's parameters that the animation is created by flipping through each image in the series (which produces the illusion of movement), you usually won't know anyway exactly what an applet does merely by looking at the HTML source code. There's a much easier way.

To find out exactly what an applet does when properly configured, simply use a Java-savvy browser to open the HTML file provided with the applet! In this case, the images inside the folder are animated on-screen. By opening the HTML file and seeing the animation in action, you know what the applet does and you have a better sense of each of the parameters. For example, if you have any doubt as to whether the applet is using the files in the images directory, just open the files with a graphics program to confirm your suspicions. Because you can see the animation running, you know right away whether these are the images that were used, further cementing your confidence in how a corresponding <APPLET> tag is constructed.

Not every applet you get off the Web comes with an example HTML page that shows the applet in action; sometimes all you get is the applet file and nothing more! Therefore, be careful to note where you get each applet (bookmarking is the fastest and most reliable way) and save to your computer for later reference any HTML source-code pages that use the applet. In this way, you can use source code on your computer to find out how the <APPLET> tag is constructed, and you can connect to the site later to see the applet in action, if necessary. For details, see Chapter 6.

You don't have to use a graphics program to open the images associated with an applet. Instead, you can use the browser itself. After all, browsers know how to display images contained in Web pages. All you have to do is choose File⇨Open and make sure that the file type (appearing in a pop-up menu at the bottom of the dialog box) is set to open *any* file, not just HTML files (which is the default). As long as the image you try to open is in the GIF or JPEG format (the two formats supported by Java and almost all browsers), your browser will have no problem displaying it. If the file isn't in one of these two formats, however, the browser tries to pass off the file to a helper application (see Chapter 5 for details on helper applications).

And so, after a little detective work, you know that with the LivingLinks applet you can specify a directory containing the images you want to display, the first name and file extension of each image, and the total number of images to use in the animation. By doing nothing more than hunting around the <APPLET> tag, you can now configure a similar applet for your own animation (see the next section).

Souping It Up

Some applets require that you follow specific rules for naming the files used with the applet. These rules, or *naming conventions,* help the applet decide what to do with the files you give it. How do you find out what the naming convention for a given applet is? You have to read the documentation, ask someone who uses the applet, or experiment a little.

Take the LivingLinks applet as an example. LivingLinks uses a naming convention that requires all images used in an animation to have exactly the same name (*myFace,* for example) with the addition of a number indicating their respective sequence in the animation (1, 2, 3, 4, . . .). In addition, each image must have the same extension (such as .gif or .jpg). Knowing this, I can use any images I want in an animation, as long as I name them accordingly. For example, I can put any number of myFace images (myFace1.gif, myFace2.gif, myFace3.gif, and so on) in a directory called narcissist, as shown in Figure 8-3, and expect LivingLinks to find them, as long as I set the corresponding parameters (imagesDir, imagesName, and imagesExt). But how many images will LivingLinks load? Ah, yet another parameter to be aware of: imagesCount.

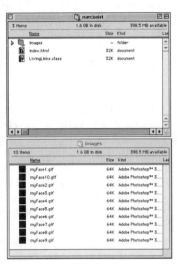

Figure 8-3:
You can configure an applet to use your own files, as long as you tweak the `<APPLET>` tag accordingly and use the file naming conventions it expects.

Although figuring out all these parameters without documentation would be difficult, it is possible to do so if you have a sample applet to work with (LivingLinks applet parameters are discussed in considerable detail in the next chapter). If not, hang it up: You'd be lucky to guess any one of the parameters, let alone all four! In this case, all you have to do is tweak the `<APPLET>` tag as in the following example and ensure that the directory containing the ten images of your face (named myFace1.gif, myFace2.gif, myFace3.gif, myFace4.gif, and so forth as shown in Figure 8-3) is located in the same directory as the Web page containing the tag and the LivingLinks applet.

```
<APPLET CODE=LivingLinks.class WIDTH=200 HEIGHT=150>
<PARAM NAME=imagesDir VALUE="images/">
<PARAM NAME=imagesName VALUE="myFace">
<PARAM NAME=imagesExt VALUE="gif">
<PARAM NAME=imagesCount VALUE="10">
</APPLET>
```

Of course, because all applets know how to deal with both GIF and JPEG images (see Chapter 9 for details on using images with applets), your images actually don't have to be in the GIF format as they were in the original example. Instead, you can further customize the applet by providing your images in JPEG format. If you are using JPEG images instead, you set the `<PARAM NAME=imagesExt VALUE="gif">` parameter to the .jpg extension, the default extension for files stored in the JPEG format:

```
<PARAM NAME=imagesExt VALUE="jpg">
```

Be sure to use the proper lowercase and uppercase letters for any parameter that you supply; myFace.gif is not the same as myFace.GIF, nor is myface.gif the same as myFace.gif! Java applets are sensitive to character case, so be precise when supplying parameters and naming any files they use. This is true for all parameters, not just images.

The animation looks about the same whether you use JPEG or GIF images, depending on how much compression is applied to your images (see Chapter 6). Changing the format that an applet's images are stored in isn't the type of customization that has the same visual impact on the applet as does changing the actual images used in the animation. However, by using a different set of images each time you weave this applet into your pages, you can produce radically different results from the same applet.

When customizing applets, you're really changing the way the applet looks, sounds, and feels. Although the look and the sound are pretty obvious, the feel of an applet is a little more elusive. Although the images an applet displays or the sounds that it plays are obvious and concrete, its feel is less tangible. An applet's *feel* is how the applet interacts with the Webber (see Chapter 1 for details on interactivity).

Merely changing the type of image format you use doesn't affect the overall *look* of the applet as much as it impacts the applet's *feel*. This type of customization may make using the applet more convenient (for example, if your images are already in a particular format), but the effects can run much deeper than that. If the format you choose significantly alters the total *weight* (the combined size of each file, discussed in detail in Chapter 6) of the material that must be transferred from the Web to the browser, you can radically alter the feel of the applet. And this, in turn, can effect how much or how little folks appreciate your Java-powered pages.

After all, which applets are more appealing to you, those that load quickly and begin doing something right away (such as an animation or playing sound), or those that take forever to download the files they need and then run sluggishly when they finally execute? By customizing an applet with your own sound and image files, you have the final say in how much material comes down the wire, and, ultimately, how taxed the applet is when it begins to use these files.

More is not always better

When selecting images for an animation, avoid including too many images or images that are too large in physical dimensions or storage requirements. In addition to taking a great deal of time to download, using many images (or a few very large ones) often adversely affects the applet. Applets have to struggle to draw each image on-screen fast enough, which may result in rough, jerky animation.

As a general rule, keep the total amount of material (images, sounds, text, and anything else your pages contain that must be downloaded to the browser) to 250K or less. Exceptions to this rule exist. For example:

✔ Using larger pages is justified if you provide enough information to give visitors something to view immediately while the rest of your material comes across the wire.

✔ 250K may be far too much for your page, depending on the speed of your Web server and its connection to the Internet (which together determine how fast your page can deliver the material to Webbers).

Of course, the only way you can know for sure whether the amount of information on your Web page is too little, too much, or just right is to upload the whole ball of wax to the Web (after you've crafted it on your personal computer) and then test it rigorously! For details, see Chapter 10.

The JARing Truth

The LivingLinks example used throughout this chapter includes a plain and simple <APPLET> tag, one that conforms to the original Java standard. Some applets are distributed in Java Archives, known as JARs for short (Chapter 5 has more on JARs). JAR files help you manage applets (especially if those applets are comprised of a bunch of class files), and can greatly decrease the amount of time it takes for an applet to transfer over the Web to the end user's computer — *JAR files* are compressed archives containing any number of files that the applet needs to run properly, and so are generally about half the size they are when not compressed.

While everything I've written so far in this chapter applies to traditional (non-JAR) applets, the concepts also apply to applets compressed into JARs. The LivingLinks applet, for example, is available on the CD-ROM that accompanies this book, both in traditional and JAR form. Both forms of this applet support the same PARAMs, and are exactly the same in that respect. The only difference between the two, in fact, is that the JAR version contains all the .class files, which enables you to deal with only one small archive rather than many different class files.

To use this version of the applet, or any other applet that uses a JAR file, for that matter, you need to supply the appropriate name of the JAR when specifying the ARCHIVE attribute in the opening <APPLET> tag. For example, to use the JAR version of LivingLinks rather than the traditional one, specify the following opening <APPLET> tag:

```
<APPLET CODE=LivingLinks.class ARCHIVE=LivingLinks.jar
          WIDTH=200 HEIGHT=150>
```

With this opening <APPLET> tag in mind, then, the following code is a complete <APPLET> tag constructed for the JAR version of LivingLinks:

```
<APPLET CODE=LivingLinks.class ARCHIVE=LivingLinks.jar
          WIDTH=200 HEIGHT=150>
<PARAM NAME=imagesDir VALUE="images/">
<PARAM NAME=imagesName VALUE="myFace">
<PARAM NAME=imagesExt VALUE="gif">
<PARAM NAME=imagesCount VALUE="10">
</APPLET>
```

Everything but the new ARCHIVE attribute is exactly the same as it is in the traditional version of the applet. The only difference here is that the archive contains all the classes that make up the LivingLinks applet, meaning that you don't have to bother with each class file individually. Just make sure that the LivingLinks.jar file is in the same directory as your Web page, and you're good to go!

JAR-style applets aren't supported in all browsers. As a result, any applets that you weave into your Web pages really should be traditional (non-JAR) if you expect all makes and models of Java-savvy browsers to see 'em! While traditional applets can be viewed by any Java-savvy browser, no matter how new or old, only the latest and greatest Java-savvy browsers can deal with JAR files.

In Chapter 13, I explain how to weave both styles of applets into a single page by using JavaScript, allowing your pages to dynamically display the appropriate version for each browser that visits (that is, traditional applets for older browsers, JAR-style applets for newer ones). However, unless you take the time to specifically support both types of applets (as I explain in Chapter 12), I highly recommend sticking with the traditional applets because they're supported by all versions of Java-savvy browsers.

While both versions of the LivingLinks applet support exactly the same features, the same isn't necessarily so with other applets. In truth, many applet developers add extra capabilities to their JAR-style applets. To find out what features any applet supports, whether traditional or JAR-style, you must consult the documentation that comes with the applet. To find out how, read on.

The Right Stuff

If it's so easy to figure out applet parameters just by examining the `<APPLET>` tag and tweaking the tag to suit your needs, why bother with real documentation? In today's ultra-sophisticated world of mouse-driven programs, clicking around to explore the various features should be enough, right? Nope! Unlike many of the software programs on your computer, you can't just click on an applet, select an Options or a Preferences menu, and configure the applet to your liking. At least, you can't today unless you spend a hefty sum of money on a "visual Web page development tool," such as Netscape's Visual JavaScript or RandomNoise CODA, which takes the burden off of you. However, these programs are pretty darned expensive (several hundred dollars, which translates roughly into a hundred or so cups of coffee at Starbucks), and generally are difficult to learn. For the time being, you're much (much!) better off learning how to tweak `<APPLET>` tags manually by typing applet parameters yourself. Hey, that's how real Web developers do it anyway! We don't need no stinkin' visual tools!

In the near future, Web page generation tools will come down drastically in price and become even easier to learn. Until then, however, it's a good idea to configure your applets by using plain old HTML. Of course, there's nothing to stop you from downloading a free trial version of these visual tools. To find a few useful links to visual Web development tools that also support Java, see `www.mantiscorp.com/java`.

So what's the big deal with tweaking `<APPLET>` tags manually by typing? Does typing in applet parameters manually also mean that you need documentation? Unfortunately, yes. Because you don't have a nice, comprehensive set of visual controls for setting parameters, you really have no idea exactly which parameters an applet accepts or which values you can supply for those parameters. Perhaps you're thinking, "No big deal — I'll just sneak a peak at the HTML source code to see how to configure my applets."

That's just fine, if you don't mind eating ice cream from the bottom of a cone. Consider the LivingLinks applet. By peaking at the `<APPLET>` tag provided earlier in this section, you were able to figure out a few parameters this applet uses and what those parameters correspond to. As a result, you can now configure that applet to animate your very own images, making for an infinite number of cool pages. As long as you supply different images each time you configure the tag, each animation will look different and so, too, will your pages. Pretty nifty, considering this feat took all of ten minutes to figure out, huh?

But by looking only at the `<APPLET>` tag, you miss out on some of this applet's other juicy options:

✔ Did you know that LivingLinks has an option to reverse the animation when it reaches the last image, yo-yo style?

✔ Did you know that you can change the speed of the animation in response to the mouse? The animation can run at one speed when the mouse is outside the applet and at an entirely different speed when the mouse is inside. Did you even know that you could set a speed for the applet, or are you plenty happy with the default speed?

✔ Did you know that you can supply a background image, which optionally can be tiled end to end like wallpaper, on which your animation will be displayed?

✔ Did you know that you can link sounds to the animation, adding an entirely different dimension to the applet? You bet. Not only that, but you can specify sounds to play based on the mouse position! You can have a Yanni soundtrack play when the mouse is outside the applet, and then burst into your favorite Beastie Boys tune when the mouse moves inside.

✔ Did you know that this applet allows you to loop sounds, instead of having them stop after they're done playing? In fact, you can even specify a timer for the sounds, if you don't want them looping immediately from start to finish. Instead, you may prefer to have sounds played once every ten seconds. And, yes indeed, you can set up a timer for more than one sound, and even mix sounds to play on top of each other rather than having each play by itself. Thus, you can have Yanni, the Beastie Boys, Sinatra, and Sting all jamming at once. You won't see that on pay-per-view.

✔ Did you know that you can choose different special effects to apply to a single image instead of just flipping through a bunch of slightly different-looking images as an animation? You can specify just one image and have it fade in and out, have different colors inside the image blink on and off, or have the whole image melt, warp, or shatter! No kidding; LivingLinks supports special effects that you can specify through a parameter.

✔ Did you pick up on one of the most wicked-cool features of the product: multiple-choice hyperlinks? Absolutely. Before LivingLinks, the Web supported only one link per image; you click on a hyperlinked image and navigate to the single URL associated with that link. One image, one link. But with LivingLinks, you can specify any number of URLs to appear in a pop-up menu for the Webber to choose from!

Buddy, you're eating your ice cream cone from the bottom. LivingLinks is a rich, decadent treat, with scoop after scoop of luscious ice cream loaded with your favorite toppings! But by looking only at the <APPLET> tag, and not the documentation for the applet, you have no idea what the applet is really capable of. Instead, you get a small taste of its potential — a trickle of flavor leaking out of the bottom of the cone.

Sure, as you visit more and more pages on the Web that use a particular applet, such as LivingLinks, you learn more about the applet and how to configure the features it offers (such as animation, sound, colors, interaction with Webbers, and so forth — see Chapter 9 for more details). But that's a slow, painful process. And how do you know when you've learned all there is to know about the product?

Instead, why not take a look at the menu, so to speak, and see exactly what ingredients you have to work with? By looking at the documentation, you know the capabilities of your applets right from the get-go, giving you all the ingredients you need to whip up sumptuous, irresistible Web pages.

Menu, Please

Configuring an applet without checking its documentation is like ordering food without looking at a menu. Aside from looking at the <APPLET> tag on other pages, the best you can do is guess at the names of parameters you *think* the applet might accept. And that, my friend, is a complete shot in the dark. You're better off playing the lottery.

Unlike standard software programs, such as your word processor, spreadsheet, and graphics packages, documentation for applets doesn't come in printed form. Instead, the information you need in order to make the most of these tiny programs comes electronically — usually as a Web page or a plain text file. Although there's no standard way of organizing applet documentation, what you get almost always has two major parts to it: a usage guide and a parameter listing.

Usage guide

An applet's *usage guide* is really nothing more than a description of what the applet can do, and may be as detailed or abstract as the author of the applet wants. Some applets are thoroughly detailed, explaining each and every facet of the mini-program and how you can weave it into your pages. Other user guides may be nothing more than a paragraph or two summarizing the applet's capabilities, perhaps even leaving some features out for you to discover on your own by looking at the parameter listing (see the next section).

But in almost all cases, the user guide includes a sample <APPLET> tag to get you started. And in the case of documentation that appears in Web page format, the applet may actually be running right then and there. Personally, this is my favorite form of documentation; not only do you get the information you need to use the applet, but you also see the applet running at the same time (see Figure 8-4). What a bargain!

Parameter listing

Although a usage guide is a real help, a comprehensive *parameter listing* is essential. Along with the name and description of each parameter, these listings usually tell you what values (strings or numbers) each parameter accepts and what constitutes a legal entry. Without such a listing, you have no idea what parameters to insert in the ⟨APPLET⟩ tag.

For example, some parameters that accept string values take a URL, whereas others expect the name of an image. A parameter that accepts numbers, on the other hand, may require whole integers in a certain range (1–100, for example), or decimal values (such as 1.5353). And in the case of those parameters that accept more than one value, you often are told what *separator character* to use in between each value you supply. Although the most popular separator is a pipe (|), some applets ask that you use a colon, semicolon, comma, or even spaces to separate each value (see Chapter 5 for details on parameters and values).

Just as usage guides vary from applet to applet, the way in which parameters are listed varies, too. Some programmers document their parameters by using little more than a list, as shown in the following code, whereas others use a table format (shown in Table 8-1 at the end of this chapter). Of course, the form really isn't all that important — having the information is what counts! As long as you get your hands on a comprehensive parameter listing (one that covers all parameters the applet uses), you have all you need to customize the applet.

Although a quick glance at Table 8-1 (all the way at the end of this chapter) gives you all the information you need concerning the parameters of the LivingLinks applet, this program is so comprehensive that understanding exactly what each parameter does is difficult. As a result, this applet is an ideal candidate for a comprehensive user guide in Web page format, where examples of the applet can execute alongside the documentation.

The following example is a list of parameters from the Celebrity Painter applet, provided (courtesy of Jeff Orkin) on the CD-ROM that comes with this book:

```
<APPLET CODE=CelebrityPainter.class WIDTH=300 HEIGHT=200>
<PARAM NAME=brush1 VALUE="Drew Barrymore">
<PARAM NAME=brush2 VALUE="Jim Carrey">
<PARAM NAME=brush3 VALUE="Bill Clinton">
</APPLET>
```

As you can see from the preceding list, you can add as many celebrities as you want. To add celebrities, follow these steps:

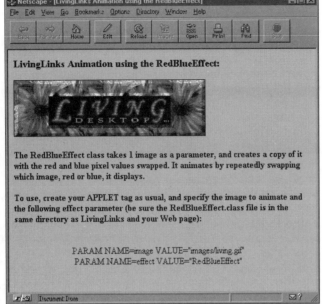

Figure 8-4:
Documen-
tation
provided in
Web page
format often
contains
embedded
applets,
allowing
you to see
first-hand
what is
being
discussed.

1. **Add a parameter that includes the next sequential brush number and a name string.**

   To add a David Letterman brush, insert the line `<PARAM NAME=brush4 VALUE="David Letterman">`.

2. **Provide a 160 x 200 JPEG image of the celebrity, with a filename that matches the name string, but with no spaces.**

   For example, place a 160 x 200 JPEG image called DavidLetterman.jpg in the same directory as the Celebrity Painter applet.

3. **Provide a 40 x 50 JPEG image of the celebrity, with a filename that matches the name string, but with no spaces and the characters BR at the end.**

   For example, place a 40 x 50 JPEG image called DavidLettermanBR.jpg in the same directory as the Celebrity Painter applet.

The Celebrity Painter applet figures out the file names based on the preceding naming convention. You specify the name string `"David Letterman"`, and the applet knows to look for DavidLetterman.jpg and DavidLettermanBR.jpg. Celebrity Painter's documentation describes these special naming conventions.

Although applets such as LivingLinks and Celebrity Painter are complex enough that both a usage guide and a parameter listing are necessary, some applets are much easier to understand. For example, you really don't need a usage guide to figure out the Marquee applet (also provided on this book's CD-ROM). Because the Marquee applet uses a relatively small number of parameters, just a quick glance at the parameter listing gives you a pretty good idea of what the applet can do. Here's an example of the Marquee applet being used to scroll the message `"Hello World!"` across the screen:

```
<APPLET CODE="Marquee" WIDTH=500 HEIGHT=24>
<PARAM NAME="shift" VALUE=2>
<PARAM NAME="delay" VALUE=20>
<PARAM NAME="font_face" VALUE="geneva">
<PARAM NAME="font_size" VALUE="20">
<PARAM NAME="font_italic" VALUE="no">
<PARAM NAME="font_bold" VALUE="yes">
<PARAM NAME="back_color" VALUE="255 255 255">
<PARAM NAME="text_color" VALUE="0 0 0">
<PARAM NAME="marquee" VALUE="Hello World!">
</APPLET>
```

The JAR-style version of Marquee, as you may guess, supports exactly the same suite of parameters, yet requires that you properly specify the archive attribute in the opening <APPLET> tag, like so:

```
<APPLET CODE="Marquee" ARCHIVE="Marquee.jar" WIDTH=500
        HEIGHT=24>
```

And, just as with the traditional version of this applet, you're free to exclude the quotes when specifying either CODE or ARCHIVE (and CODEBASE, if you choose to use this attribute — see Chapter 7 for details). Just be sure to enclose inside quotes the PARAM names and values that you supply if a space character is needed (such as the space between Hello and World in the marquee PARAM). Or, play it on the safe side and enclose all PARAM names and values in quotes:

```
<APPLET CODE=Marquee ARCHIVE=Marquee.jar WIDTH=500
        HEIGHT=24>
<PARAM NAME="shift" VALUE=2>
<PARAM NAME="delay" VALUE=20>
<PARAM NAME="font_face" VALUE="geneva">
<PARAM NAME="font_size" VALUE="20">
<PARAM NAME="font_italic" VALUE="no">
<PARAM NAME="font_bold" VALUE="yes">
<PARAM NAME="back_color" VALUE="255 255 255">
<PARAM NAME="text_color" VALUE="0 0 0">
<PARAM NAME="marquee" VALUE="Hello World!">
</APPLET>
```

Keep in mind, however, that the CODE and ARCHIVE names aren't always the same. It's up to the applet developer to choose names for the class file(s) and JARs (assuming JARs are used) — Chapter 5 has more on this. It's entirely possible, for example, to have an opening <APPLET> tag such as the following:

```
<APPLET CODE=Marquee ARCHIVE=ABC.jar WIDTH=500 HEIGHT=24>
```

Because there's no law saying the CODE and ARCHIVE names must be the same, you often run into JARs that don't have the same name as the class file that you must specify in the CODE attribute. In fact, it's entirely possible to have more than one JAR for a single applet. In this case, you must separate each JAR with a comma when constructing the opening <APPLET> tag, as the following theoretical example illustrates:

```
<APPLET CODE=Marquee ARCHIVE=ABC.jar, XYZ.jar, Yentil.jar
        WIDTH=500 HEIGHT=24>
```

The traditional (non-JAR) Marquee applet provided on CD-ROM is made up of two class files, Marquee.class and MarqueeFile.class, both of which are required in order for the applet to run properly. The JAR version of Marquee, on the other hand, requires only one file: Marquee.jar. If you wish to use the non-JAR version of Marquee, be sure to place both Marquee.class and MarqueeFile.class in the same folder as the Web page in which you weave the applet. To use the JAR version of Marquee, on the other hand, you need only place Marquee.jar in the folder containing your Web page. For more details on weaving the Marquee applet into your Web pages, see Chapter 9.

Defaults: If you don't say it, I will!

In some cases, certain parameters must contain a value to properly configure an applet. For example, an applet that does nothing more than display a scrolling message, such as Marquee, requires you to provide it with the text to scroll. But what if you don't?

Take, for example, the following configuration for Marquee:

```
<APPLET CODE="Marquee" WIDTH=500 HEIGHT=40>
</APPLET>
```

In this example, no parameters are used at all! Fortunately, the Marquee applet falls back onto *default* parameters that allow the applet to run even when you don't give it the proper information. Exactly what an applet does when you don't supply it with a required parameter is up to the programmer who created it; in the case of Marquee, it scrolls a little message across the screen to tell you that the applet wasn't properly configured (see Figure 8-5).

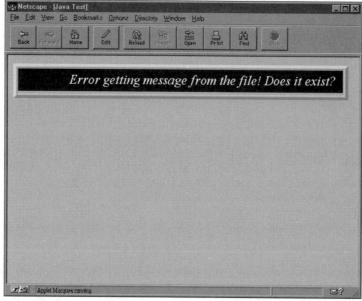

Figure 8-5:
If you don't
properly
configure
this applet,
it tells
you so!

LivingLinks, on the other hand, can't do much of anything if you don't at least supply it with an image (or a number of images) to animate. In this case, LivingLinks doesn't use a default image — instead, it displays an error message in the browser's status area to let you know something went wrong (see Figure 8-6).

In fact, many applets use the status area to keep you informed in case something goes wrong. As a result, be sure to keep your eye on this part of the browser each time you test your applets. Not only do applets use this area to display messages, but the browser itself does too. If, for example, the browser has difficulty locating, downloading, or executing an applet, it displays a message in the status area to let you know there is a problem.

Not all applets list the default values that they use when you don't supply your own values. As a result, the only way to know what happens is to actually omit a parameter and see how the applet reacts when executed. Because every applet is different, you never know for sure what will happen until you try it. In the case of ticker-tape applets, for example, some may not even run if you omit the text that is to be scrolled. However, even those that run are likely to display completely different messages as their default.

Params that need params are the luckiest params in the world

As with people, some parameters just can't live without constant companionship. That is, some parameters require that one or more other parameters be specified at the same time. You can find examples of these codependent parameters in both the Marquee and LivingLinks applets.

Figure 8-6:
Most
applets use
the status
area of
the browser
to report
problems.

Error message

Short of checking these parameters into group therapy, you have no way of dealing with them individually. If you specify a codependent parameter, you must also supply its companion parameters when constructing the applet tag. Depending on the applet itself, the number of dependents will vary.

LivingLinks is an example of an applet that has several codependent parameters, as shown in Table 8-1 (at the end of this chapter). The most critical of LivingLinks' codependent parameters are the ones that specify a series of images to animate. To animate a series of images with LivingLinks, you must configure four different parameters: imagesDir, imagesName, imagesExt, and imagesCount. These four parameters are all codependent; all four must be specified in order to give the applet enough information to find the images to animate. The following snippet of HTML code shows each parameter as it might appear in your Web page:

```
<PARAM NAME=imagesDir VALUE="images">
<PARAM NAME=imagesName VALUE="myLogo">
<PARAM NAME=imagesExt VALUE="gif">
<PARAM NAME=imagesCount VALUE="5">
```

Not all codependent parameters are required

Although LivingLinks won't run unless all four of the preceding codependent parameters are configured properly, other codependent parameters aren't as critical. An example of a codependent parameter that isn't required for LivingLinks to run properly is the `bevelWidth` parameter. Used alone, this parameter doesn't add (or subtract) anything from the LivingLinks applet. It's powerless without the parameter it depends on: `bevel`. However, `bevel` is *not* a codependent applet: You can use it by itself, as in the following line of code:

```
<PARAM NAME=bevel VALUE="yes">
```

If you use the `bevel` parameter alone, you have to settle for the default bevel: a thin, 2-pixel edge surrounding the applet to give it the appearance of a button. But you can add the `bevelWidth` parameter to make the bevel thicker (or even thinner). The following line of HTML code, when used with the preceding one, places a 5-pixel, 3-D bevel around the applet:

```
<PARAM NAME=bevelWidth
    VALUE="5">
```

Unlike some codependent parameters (such as those used to specify a series of images to animate), LivingLinks doesn't produce an error message if you use the `bevelWidth` parameter without the `bevel` parameter in tow. The applet works just fine, but it won't display a bevel.

If you omit any one of the preceding four parameters, LivingLinks won't know exactly what files to use. Without all four parameters, none of the images appear on-screen, and an error message (`Error Loading Images`) appears in the status area of the browser, as shown in Figure 8-6. It's very important to make certain that you supply every required codependent parameter so the applet can do its job.

Plug-in support

Some applets support what are known as *plug-ins* — special files that extend an applet's capabilities. Although plug-ins are most often associated with graphics programs, such as Adobe Photoshop, applets can also be designed to take advantage of plug-in modules.

Using a plug-in adds new functionality or features to an applet that it doesn't already have. In the case of LivingLinks, plug-ins provide special animation effects that the applet alone doesn't know how to perform. You can, for example, use a plug-in called Fade to give your LivingLinks animation a *fade* effect, allowing it to fade in and out, much the way a television show fades to black before going to commercial.

Plug-ins really are just little programs, much like applets, that come with their own set of parameters. Depending on the plug-in, you may have to supply a number of additional parameters to configure it properly, or no parameters at all. As with applets, it's entirely up to the developer of the plug-in to decide what parameters you must use to configure it. As a result, plug-ins often come with their own documentation telling you how to use them. The documentation for the Fade plug-in, for example, is a short description of the face effect and the parameters it accepts:

```
<PARAM NAME=effect VALUE="FadeEffect">
<PARAM NAME=image VALUE="images/logo.gif">
<PARAM NAME=steps VALUE="25">
<PARAM NAME=backgroundColor VALUE="white">
```

Fade requires one image and the number of steps to fade to the background color you supply in the backgroundColor parameter. Fade makes a number of copies of the image, as determined by the steps parameter, in which each copy is a step closer to the background color. Fade then animates these faded images by rotating back and forth through each of them.

Plug-ins generally are written by programmers other than the ones who wrote the applet itself; the whole idea behind plug-ins is to allow other developers to extend the functionality of the applet to meet their needs. Typically, plug-in authors are given credit for the work they do. To see the credits for LivingLinks' plug-ins, for example, place your mouse over the running applet for a few seconds and keep your eyes on the status area of your browser window.

Because plug-ins come with their own set of parameters, you need to supply them in the <APPLET> tag just as you do the parameters for the applet itself. Take, for example, the LivingLinks Fade plug-in effect. When you use this plug-in, you specify its parameters right alongside the applet's parameters:

```
<APPLET CODE=LivingLinks.class WIDTH=209 HEIGHT=140>
<PARAM NAME=speed VALUE="10">
<PARAM NAME=URL VALUE="http://www.demonsys.com/
          projects.html">
<PARAM NAME=effect VALUE="FadeEffect">
<PARAM NAME=steps VALUE="12">
<PARAM NAME=image VALUE="console/projects1.gif">
<PARAM NAME=backgroundImage VALUE="console/right.gif">
<PARAM NAME=backgroundColor VALUE="black">
<PARAM NAME=reverse VALUE="yes">
</APPLET>
```

The preceding tag comes from another button on the Demon Systems Web site — Our Projects. The complete page this tag comes from is provided as a "CookBook" example on the CD-ROM that comes with this book if you want to see it in person!

LivingLinks has no idea what the "steps" parameter means; it's unique to the Fade plug-in. This is true for most plug-ins — the parameters they use are usually independent of those used by the applet. As a result, plug-ins often don't use the same name for parameters as those used by the applet itself. Or if they do, both the applet and the plug-in share whatever value you supply. For example, if both an applet and its plug-in accept a parameter named steps, any value you supply for this parameter will be used by both the applet and the plug-in. Of course, how each uses the parameter is up to its respective developer; steps doesn't have to mean the same thing to both!

Several LivingLinks plug-in effects are provided on the CD-ROM that comes with this book, with others available on the *LivingLinks* support site (www.mantiscorp.com/LivingLinks). For details, see Appendix A.

Because each parameter has a unique name, the order in which you supply parameters doesn't matter at all! So although the following parameter example is more difficult to read than the one that follows it, they work just the same.

```
<PARAM NAME=backgroundColor VALUE="white">
<PARAM NAME=steps VALUE="25">
<PARAM NAME=image VALUE="images/logo.gif">
<PARAM NAME=effect VALUE="FadeEffect">
```

The parameters this plug-in uses come after the plug-in is specified:

```
<PARAM NAME=effect VALUE="FadeEffect">
<PARAM NAME=image VALUE="images/logo.gif">
<PARAM NAME=steps VALUE="25">
<PARAM NAME=backgroundColor VALUE="white">
```

Personally, I prefer to group my parameters logically: I place codependent parameters with the ones they are dependent on, and supply plug-ins last, followed by whatever parameters they require. This makes constructing the <APPLET> tag easier, and also helps to make the source code of the Web page in which the applet appears easier to read.

Table 8-1   **The LivingLinks Applet Parameters**

Parameter	Description	Default	Dependent on	Example
imagesDir	A URL (absolute or relative) pointing to a directory containing images to animate.	None	imagesName, imagesExt, imagesCount	"images/ logos/ mantis/"
imagesName	Base name of each image in the animation series.	None	imagesDir, imagesExt, imagesCount	"mantisLogo"
imagesExt	The extension of each image in the animation series.	None	imagesDir, imagesName, imagesCount	".gif" or ".jpg"
imagesCount	The number of images in the animation series.	None	imagesDir, imagesName, imagesExt	5
image	A URL (absolute or relative) pointing to a single image to animate by using a plug-in effect (see effect). May be in GIF or JPEG format.	None	None	"images/ logos/ Logo.jpg"
imageTop	Top-corner coordinate where the animation should appear within the applet.	Centered in applet	Image (or image series)	100
imageLeft	Left-corner coordinate where the animation should appear within the applet.	Centered in applet	Image (or image series)	20
effect	When specified, the plug-in effect file(s) must reside in the same directory as the LivingLinks applet.	Each effect may use its own parameters.	None	"Fade"
resize	If set to "yes", applet is resized to the size of the animation, regardless of the HEIGHT and WIDTH values specified in the <APPLET> tag.	"no"	None	"yes"

(Note: The current version of Netscape does not support dynamic resizing such as this.)

(continued)

Table 8-1 (continued)

Parameter	Description	Default	Dependent on	Example
speed	Speed of the animation. Higher values result in faster animation (see `inSpeed`).	1	Image (or image series)	45
URL	Internet address where animation will send users when they click on it.	None	Image (or image series)	`"www.anywhere.com"`
links	List of destination URLs (and descriptions of each) to appear in a pop-up menu when the mouse is clicked inside the animation.	None	Special Format: `name = url` Separator: | (pipe character) `"Mantis Home page = www.mantiscorp.com"`	`Java For Dummies = www.mantiscorp.com/JavaForDummies`
poster	Image to display while others in a series load.	First image in animation series	None	`"images/Image logos/mantis-Logo5.gif"`
background Color	Background color of the applet, specified as a color's name or hex value.	None	None	`"white"`
background Image	URL (absolute or relative) pointing to a GIF or JPEG background for animation.	None	None	`"images/backgrounds/paper.jpg"`
background Tile	If `"yes"`, the background image is tiled end to end like wallpaper. If `"no"` (the default), the background image is *not* tiled.	`"no"`	background Image	`"yes"`
random Delay	Provides support for "randomness" between frame painting, allowing users to create animations with non-precise, or random, frame rates (particularly useful for creating blinking "neon light" animations). A random delay value (in milliseconds) from 0 to `randomDelay` generated between every frame, resulting in random frame rates.	0	None	15

Parameter	Description	Default	Dependent on	Example
clear	If "yes", animation is cleared before each image is displayed.	"yes"	Image (or image series)	"no"
reverse	If "yes", animation images are animated forward, and then backward (1,2,3,4,3,2,1,2,3...) If "no", animation loops (1,2,3,4,1,2,3,4,1,2,...).	"no"	Image (or image series)	"yes"
bevel	If "yes", a 3-D bevel is drawn around the applet, giving it the appearance of a button (See bevelWidth).	"no"	None	"yes"
bevelWidth	Width of the 3-D bevel drawn around the applet.	2	bevel	5
inSpeed	Speed of animation when the mouse is inside the animation (See speed).	Same setting as speed	None	100
inMessage	String shown in the browser status bar when the mouse is in the animation.	URL if	URL or links specified, "LivingLinks" if multiple-choice links are used	"Click me, baby..."
soundDir	A URL (absolute or relative) pointing to the directory containing AU/uLaw format sounds (.au files).	None	None	"sounds/horns/"
outSound	String containing any number of uLaw format sounds (.au files) to be played when the mouse exits the applet; sounds are separated with | (pipe character) and no spaces.	None	soundDir	"horn.au| whistle.au| bang.au"
inSound	String containing any number of uLaw format (.au files) to be played when the mouse enters the applet; sounds are separated with | (pipe character).	None	soundDir	"horn.au| whistle.au| bang.au"

(continued)

Table 8-1 (continued)

Parameter	Description	Default	Dependent on	Example
outSound Loop	If "yes", out sounds loop when played (See outSound).	"no"	outSound	"yes"
inSound Loop	If "yes", in sounds loop when played (See inSound).	"no"	inSound	"yes"
outRandom Sound	If "yes", out sounds are selected randomly, rather than played in the specified sequence (See outSound).	"no"	outSound	"yes"
inRandom Sound	If "yes", in sounds are selected randomly, rather than played in the specified sequence (See inSound).	"no"	inSound	"yes"
mixSounds	If "yes", sounds are mixed instead of playing one at a time.	"no"	inSound or outSound	"yes"
clickStop Sound	If "yes", clicking inside the applet stops all sounds (clicking inside the applet again turns the sounds back on).	"no"	inSound or outSound	"yes"
outSound Timer	Number of seconds to wait before replaying the out sound (See outSound).	None	outSound	5
inSound Timer	Number of seconds to wait before replaying the in sound (See outSound).	None	inSound	45

Chapter 9

The Main Ingredients: Customize to Taste

*A*lthough some applets work exactly the way you want them to right out of the box, most Java users want to customize their applets by using their own images, sounds, and text. To customize a Java applet to your liking, you need to get under the hood and tinker with things a bit. When it comes to customizing applets, you have six main ways to go about it:

✔ Using images

✔ Using sounds

✔ Using text

✔ Using color

✔ Using URLs for navigation

✔ Using data files

Some applets may support customization in all six categories; others may support just a few kinds of customization, or perhaps only one. And there are those applets you can't customize at all!

Although each applet is different, all applets use images, sounds, text, color, URLs, and data files in a similar fashion. As a result, when you know how to customize one applet by using these features, doing the same with other applets is usually a breeze. The most you have to do is find out what parameters to specify, and you're home free.

Looping and reversing animation

Consider the LivingLinks applet. By default, when the last image, or *frame,* in the animation is drawn, LivingLinks starts anew with the first one. As a result, the animation plays from start to finish and repeats itself continuously. This behavior, known as *looping,* is extremely useful, and thus is often the default for applets that are capable of animating images.

In many cases, you have the option of *reversing* the animation instead of looping it. By reversing an animation, you prevent it from repeating the sequence when the last frame is reached. Instead of starting over with the first image and looping through each one in the same order again, the applet reverses the order in which it displays the images.

For example, an animation loop consisting of five frames displays each in order (1, 2, 3, 4, 5),

and then repeats itself when it reaches the last frame (1, 2, 3, 4, 5). An animation with the reverse option, however, starts out in the same fashion (1, 2, 3, 4, 5), but reverses direction when the last frame is reached (4, 3, 2, 1), rather than repeating the same sequence it started with. Each time the last frame in a sequence is displayed (either frame 1 or frame 5, in this case), the direction reverses.

Even if looping is the default for an animation applet, the applet may also support the reverse option. To get the reverse effect from the LivingLinks applet, use the following parameter:

```
<PARAM NAME=reverse VALUE="yes">
```

Cooking up Images

Without a doubt, images are the most compelling way to enhance a Web site. Although many Java applets allow you to use images, merely displaying these images is no big deal; the exciting part lies in animating them. And depending on that applet, you may have several ways to bring your images to life.

Frame-based and single-frame animation

The most impressive use of images is through animation, an effect you can accomplish in a few different ways. Perhaps the most popular animation method is to "flip through" a number of individual images, as you would a cartoon flip-book, where each image in the series differs slightly from the previous one (see Figure 9-1). This technique, sometimes called *frame-based animation* (where each image is like a frame in a cartoon), can produce wonderful results, depending on the images you choose.

Figure 9-1:
Frame-
based
animation
creates the
illusion of
movement.

Although animating a series of images can be quite impressive, it's also a tremendous bandwidth hog! Every image in the sequence must be sent over the wire, consuming time and money in the process (see Chapter 6 for details on bandwidth issues). *Single-frame animation,* on the other hand, uses only one image to get the job done. Rather than flipping though a sequence of images to produce the illusion of movement, this technique actually alters the image you specify to produce a desired effect.

Take, for example, the LivingLinks Fade plug-in effect, first mentioned in Chapter 8. LivingLinks is a powerful multipurpose animation applet provided on the CD-ROM for you to use in your own Web pages. The LivingLinks applet itself can animate a series of images by rapidly flipping from one to the next to produce the illusion of movement. You can also use LivingLinks in combination with any of a number of plug-in files (such as Warp, Shatter, Fade, and Kaleidoscope) that modify a single image to produce special effects.

Therefore, when you use LivingLinks in combination with the Fade plug-in effect, you only specify one image for the applet to use. Working hand-in-hand with LivingLinks, the plug-in makes several copies of the original image and then modifies each copy by adding progressively deeper shades of the color that you specify in the backgroundColor parameter (see Figure 9-2).

Keep in mind that every applet handles parameters differently. Although single-image animation in LivingLinks is accomplished using the applet's image parameter in conjunction with a plug-in effect (such as Fade), other applets use different parameters to get the job done and might not use plug-ins at all. As a result, it's important to read the documentation and review the parameter list for every applet that you use in order to know how to properly construct its <APPLET> tag.

Fading an image is only one of a number of things possible by using single-frame animation. Terribly cool effects, such as warping, melting, shattering, and more are all possible; all you have to do is get your hands on the applet or plug-in that makes these effects possible.

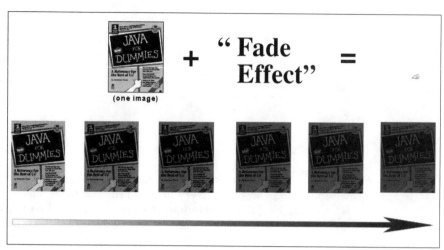

Figure 9-2:
Single-image animation produces the illusion of movement by modifying the same image.

A few plug-in effects are provided with LivingLinks on the CD-ROM that comes with this book, such as Fade, FireWorks, Raindrop, Warp, Shatter, and Twist. If these alone don't satisfy your craving for cool effects, you can always get the latest and greatest plug-ins right off the Net at www.mantiscorp.com/LivingLinks

The need for speed

To control the appearance of an animation, most applets (at least those that deal with animation) offer a *frame rate* parameter. Regardless of whether the animation is produced using a series of images or is generated on the fly using a single image, the speed at which the animation operates is known as the animation's frame rate. The idea is quite simple: A period of time may pass before each new frame in the animation is drawn on-screen.

A slow frame rate results in an animation that moves slowly. For example, a frame rate of 5 frames per second, or 5 fps, means that a total of five new images are drawn in the space of a single second. Higher frame rates result in faster animation. A rate of 15 frames per second, for example, is three times faster than one of 5 frames per second.

The frame rate you choose for your animation depends on the overall appearance you're trying to achieve and is largely dependent on the images or effect that you use. If the frame rate is too slow, the animation won't appear to be realistic. If it's too fast, the animation may become little more than a blur. To find out what's right for your animation, experiment with different frame rates.

How fast is too fast?

In the United States, television broadcasts are displayed at 30 frames per second, whereas other parts of the globe use slightly slower frame rates. The term *full motion* describes any animation (or broadcast) that approaches 30 frames per second (24 fps is usually the cut-off to qualify as full motion). Unfortunately, most computers aren't powerful enough to display more than 10 to 15 frames per second! Keep this in mind when specifying a frame rate for your animation; if you're lucky enough to have a computer capable of displaying full-motion animation, remember that almost everyone else is limited to 10 to 15 frames at best (if that).

In general, try to keep the speed of your frames as low as possible so that they can play back with ease on a wide range of systems. Depending on the applet you're using and the machine it's running on, frames in an animation may be skipped if either the computer or the applet can't keep up with the rate you specify. To reduce the risk of skipped frames, keep the frame rate low (10 frames per second is a good number to aim for).

Some applets don't use the words "frame rate" to refer to the parameter that controls the speed of animation. LivingLinks, for example, calls this parameter "speed" instead. The lower the speed, the slower the animation. You can, in fact, set two different speeds for the animation you create with this applet: *inSpeed* and *outSpeed*. These parameters correspond to the location of the user's mouse, allowing the user to interact with the animation by moving the mouse in and out of the applet (see Table 8-1 at the end of Chapter 8).

Depending on the browser you're using, changing the frame rate (or any parameter for that matter) may not affect the applet unless you quit the browser and start it again. In many cases, once an applet has executed, the browser won't recognize any changes you make to the ⟨APPLET⟩ tag, even if you click on Reload. As a result, you can change all the parameters you want and still see the exact same applet in your browser, leading you to believe that there's a problem with the applet when in fact the browser's at fault.

If you're a Netscape Navigator user, you can try a few tricks to force Navigator to display applets with their new parameters before pulling the plug and restarting the program from scratch. The first trick is to hold down the Shift key and press the Reload button at the same time. This forces a reload of the page. However, due to the finicky nature of Navigator, the page doesn't always reload the files from the server, but instead simply gets them from the disk cache.

A better solution is to clear the cache by using the Clear Disk Cache and Clear Memory Cache options — choose Edit⇨Preferences⇨Advanced⇨ Cache. As with the previous trick, however, this doesn't always work with Navigator, although Microsoft's Internet Explorer browser is usually responsive to such maneuverings. But take heart; there are a few other ways to force the browser to recognize your changes, although they are a little more complicated to explain. For a detailed account of how you can force your browser to accept your applet parameter changes, point your Web browser to www.mantiscorp.com/java and look for the Manhandling Java-Savvy Browsers hyperlink.

Sizzling Sounds

Although animating images is by far the most popular way to spruce up Web pages, sounds are another wonderful way to inject life into otherwise dead content. You can easily add sound to your Web pages by using LivingLinks, which offers a number of ways to play sounds. As with most applets that use sounds, to customize LivingLinks in this way, all you have to do is provide your own sound files and set the appropriate parameters to tell the applet where they're located (see Table 8-1 at the end of Chapter 8 or check out the LivingLinks examples provided on the CD-ROM).

Java applets that support sound do so by using a very specific AU format combined with a special compression scheme known as uLaw (pronounced "mu-law"), as described in Chapter 6. Sounds in this format have the .au extension. As a result, anytime you see a file with this extension specified in an <APPLET> tag (or anywhere else, for that matter), you know it's a sound file.

Unfortunately, Java applets are quite rigid in the AU format they can use. As a result, you must first convert sounds of other formats to this format if you want to use them with your applets. Here's how:

1. **Downsample the sound (that is, reduce the amount of data used to represent the sound) to 8 kHz.**

   If you recorded the sound from CD, then it probably was originally sampled at 44.1 kHz — CD quality. Notice how huge the original sound file is? Of course, this will never work within the bandwidth constraints of the Internet. Downsampling the sound to 8 kHz will drastically reduce the file size. The tradeoff is that the sound quality will also be drastically reduced. To downsample a sound, all you have to do is save it in the uLaw format; all excess sound information is removed automatically from the file.

2. Reduce the file to mono and 8 bits.

This refers to how many channels the sound uses (stereo has two channels, mono uses only one) and how many bits per channel you'll be using. Don't worry too much about what all that means — it basically comes down to the fact that you'll end up saving more disk space. Depending on the software utility you use, you may or may not have options for converting a sound to a mono 8-bit form. If you're a Windows user, you have these options when saving (or exporting) sound files with the GoldWave utility that's provided on the CD-ROM that comes with this book. If you're a Mac user, the uLaw program provided for that platform enables you to simply save a sound file in the uLaw format; the program automatically converts the file to a mono channel 8-bit format.

3. Save the file in NEXT/Sun AU (.au) format with uLaw compression.

As with each of the preceding steps, how you execute this step depends on the utility you use. Most sound-conversion tools enable you to specify precisely what format you convert a given sound file to, while others (such as the Macintosh uLaw conversion utility provided on this book's CD-ROM) choose a format for you. To find out for sure, you should consult the documentation that comes with the utility. (If you choose to use one of the utilities provided on the CD-ROM, you will find documentation in a text file along with the utility or built directly into the tool via a Help command.)

You're done! It seems like a lot of work, but the effort is well worth it; there's nothing quite like a powerful, thumping background soundtrack when you visit a Web site.

Adding and changing sounds

If an applet supports sounds, as does the LivingLinks applet provided on the CD-ROM, you can easily add your own sounds by using the proper parameters. This process is very similar to adding images; you must tell the applet where to find your sound file and exactly what it's named. If you give it that much information, an applet will be able to find and play your sounds (assuming, of course, that it was designed to play sounds in the first place — you can't get blood from a stone, or sound from an applet that doesn't know how to deal with it).

What an applet does with sounds is completely up to the programmer who created it in the first place. Some applets simply play a sound you give it, and that's that. Others may give you more control, such as being able to play a sound repeatedly (see the "Looping sounds" section in this chapter), or may even allow you to play a number of different sounds.

Again, when it comes to sound, all you have to do to customize an applet is tell it what sounds to use, and where the sounds are located. Of course, the parameters you use to do this depend on the applet itself and the extent to which it handles sound. While some applets do nothing but play or loop the sound (or sounds) you specify, some are a little more complex and can use sounds for different purposes.

This is true with the LivingLinks applet, which can be told to do nothing more than play a sound when it first runs, or much more. If you want to, you can configure this applet to play different sounds depending on the position of the mouse. If the mouse is outside the applet, the sounds you specify in the outSound parameter play. If the mouse moves into the applet, the sounds you specify for the inSound parameter play. By default, the sounds are played in the order you specify, but as an alternative, you can tell LivingLinks to randomly choose the sounds it will play.

Just as with the images the LivingLinks applet uses, you must specify in which directory the sounds can be found. However, you don't have to be so precise and ridged about the individual names of the sound files, as you can use different names for each:

```
<PARAM NAME=soundDir VALUE="sounds/">
<PARAM NAME=outSound VALUE="Orbit.au|boo.au|clang.au">
<PARAM NAME=inSound VALUE="Car
            Horn.au|fitebell.au|gong.au">
```

When specifying multiple sounds with LivingLinks, do not include any spaces before or after the | (pipe character) separator; otherwise, only the first sound will play.

In the preceding snippet of HTML code, sounds have been specified for the "in" and "out" positions of the mouse. Each will be played in the order that they are supplied, unless you explicitly tell the applet to choose the sounds supplied in each category at random. When the last sound in a category is played, the sequence begins again from the beginning. However, you might not want them to play in order. Instead, you might prefer that the sounds be selected at random:

```
<PARAM NAME=outRandomSound VALUE="yes">
```

Here, the sounds corresponding to the "out" position of the mouse will be selected at random, while those that are played in response to the mouse moving inside the applet are still played in the order they are specified. You can, however, tell the applet to choose these at random as well:

```
<PARAM NAME=inRandomSound VALUE="yes">
```

By default, most applets simply play sound from start to finish and then stop. If this is what you want to occur, then you're finished setting the parameters. However, if you want the sound to repeat, resulting in a continuous soundtrack that repeats itself over and over, read the following section on looping sounds.

Looping sounds

Most applets that support sounds allow you to loop those sounds just as you can loop images (see the sidebar "Looping and reversing animation" earlier in this chapter). By default, most applets simply play sound from start to finish and then stop. However, if you want the sound to repeat, looping is the only way to go.

Several examples of Web pages that use looping sounds are provided on the CD-ROM that comes with this book, each powered by the LivingLinks applet (versatile little applet, no?).

Adding sound looping to this applet is just a matter of setting the appropriate parameter. This, in fact, is true for all applets that support sound looping — if the sounds an applet plays don't loop by default, you have to set a parameter to tell the applet to do so! If you don't, the sounds will never loop. Of course, the parameter you use will vary from applet to applet, and so you must consult the documentation that comes with the applet or nose around for an example of the applet in action.

Depending on the applet, more than one sound loop may be specified. With LivingLinks, for instance, you can loop the "in" and "out" sounds independently of one another, because a parameter is supplied for each:

```
<PARAM NAME=inSoundLoop VALUE="yes">
<PARAM NAME=outSoundLoop VALUE="yes">
```

Actually, looping isn't the *only* way to repeat sounds. Some applets, like LivingLinks, enable you to play a sound based on a timer. Technically speaking, applets that loop sounds have no way of pausing for a period of time before playing the sound again (due to a limitation in the Java programming language). As a result, if you want to repeat a sound at a certain interval (such as every 30 seconds), you have to use a timer; a standard loop doesn't give you such control.

Sir Mix-a-Lot

Due to the way the Java programming language works, most applets that support sound also enable you to mix sounds. When an applet plays more than one sound, *mixing* allows them all to play at once.

Mixing sounds is a capability that's built into the Java language itself, and not something the programmer has to spend any time figuring out. In fact, it takes more effort to keep track of which sounds are playing, stopping each one before the next can begin, than it does to mix sounds. As a result, mixing sound is par for the course.

Of course, mixing may be something you don't want, and so some applets turn this feature off until you request it. LivingLinks, for example, won't mix sounds until you set the mixSounds parameter. Other applets, however, mix sounds by default until you turn the mixing parameter off! That's one more good argument for getting your hands on documentation for the applets that you use; no hard-and-fast rule exists for enabling or disabling the mixing of sounds.

A healthy dose of sounds is provided on the CD-ROM that comes with this book, along with utilities to help you convert your own files for use with applets. For details, see Appendix A.

Sprinkling on Text

Applets that support text usually let you specify the font face (TimesRoman, Courier, and so on), point size (10, 24, 72, and so on), and style (such as plain, bold, or italics) in which the text will be displayed. The Marquee applet, for example, lets you specify all three:

```
<APPLET CODE="Marquee" WIDTH=250 HEIGHT=30>
<param NAME="shift" VALUE=3>
<param NAME="delay" VALUE=5>
<param NAME="font_face" VALUE="courier">
<param NAME="font_size" VALUE="16">
<param NAME="font_italic" VALUE="yes">
<param NAME="font_bold" VALUE="yes">
<param NAME="back_color" VALUE="255 255 255">
<param NAME="text_color" VALUE="0 100 0">
<param NAME="marquee" VALUE="Howdy! I'm scrolling...">
</APPLET>
```

Although ticker-tape applets such as Marquee use these types of settings to display text as it scrolls across the screen, you can do many other things with the text in your applets:

✔ The LivingLinks applet, for example, supports a plug-in effect known as WildWords. This plug-in animates the text you provide by drawing each character in a slightly different location on the screen in a variety of colors and speeds. As a result, the text you specify comes to life, dancing up and down as if hopped-up on caffeine. And rightly so — it's full of Java.

✔ An applet that displays bar charts, for example, may allow you to choose the text that appears for each element in the chart; a spreadsheet applet may allow you to choose the size and style of the font in which its numbers will appear.

✔ Some applets let users select items from a menu. A good example of this type of applet is Celebrity Painter, which lets you specify the name of the "brushes" to use when painting. To choose a different brush, you simply make a selection from a menu. Because each brush in the menu is customizable, you can specify whatever names you want (see the Celebrity Painter example earlier in this chapter).

As always, the developer of the applet decides what parameters you can and can't configure. And, as always (again), the only way to find out what you can do with an applet is to read the documentation that comes with it. However, as a general rule, those applets that allow you to specify text also allow you to specify the characteristics of the font in which the text will appear.

Don't go crazy when choosing a font face for your applets! Not every computer has the same fonts installed on it as your computer, so the text on your pages may not appear to others the same way it does to you. Be conservative with your font choices and pick those available across a wide range of systems. Times Roman, Courier, and Helvetica are good examples of fonts that are installed on many users' computers. For details, see Chapter 6.

Pouring on Color

Many applets, especially those that deal with text, enable you to set parameters to control the color of content that appears on-screen (such as text, background, buttons, and other visual elements that an applet may utilize) . The Marquee applet provided on the CD-ROM that comes with this book, for example, lets you set the color of the scrolling text and the color of the banner on which the text scrolls. LivingLinks, on the other hand, doesn't deal with text itself (although plug-ins can provide a variety of text capabilities). As a result, this applet only allows you to set the background color on which an animation is displayed. Other applets, depending on what they do, may provide different color settings that you can customize through <PARAM> tags.

Because all applets are different, the approach each takes to dealing with colors will differ. The most user-friendly of applets, however, lets you specify color by name:

```
<PARAM NAME="anyColorSetting" VALUE="black">
```

The "anyColorSetting" parameter in the preceding code isn't a real parameter — it's just an example. To find out the proper parameters for your applets, consult the documentation.

Contrast the preceding tag with one from an applet that requires you to specify colors by using three numbers to represent the separate red, green, and blue components of a color:

```
<PARAM NAME="anyColorSetting" VALUE="255 255 255">
```

Here, each number is used to specify how much or how little red, green, or blue to mix into the overall color. By specifying how much of each color to use, you can get just the right shade of color you're looking for (if you have the patience to figure it out!). This method of representing color is called the *RGB model* — you tell the applet how much *r*ed, *g*reen, and *b*lue to mix together to produce the final color.

In this example, the color specified is created by using exactly the same amounts of red, green, and blue: 255. As a result, the color you end up with is white. White?! But in kindergarten you learned that mixing together the same amount of red, green, and blue results in black — what gives? Unfortunately, all you ever needed to know about colors you did *not* learn in kindergarten.

Computers work the opposite of finger paints. Instead of taking a blob of paint and putting it on a piece of paper, your computer shoots out three beams of colored light (a red beam, green beam, and blue beam) from behind your monitor. At an astonishing rate, each *pixel* (dot) on your monitor is, in turn, lit up from behind by the beams of light. Depending on how much intensity of color each beam contains, the pixel that is lit up will be a different color. Basically, your computer is mixing the beams of light to make a color.

Actually, not all computer monitors display color by shooting three beams of colored light at the pixels; there are a few different ways to go about creating color on-screen. But in the end, they all mix light together to come up with the colors that you see.

Because all computers create color by mixing light (not absorbing light, as finger paints do), combining the same intensity of red, blue, and green produces white, not black. To create black using the RGB model, you have to lower the intensity of each beam of light to nothing:

```
<PARAM NAME="anyColorSetting" VALUE="0 0 0">
```

In the RGB model, the highest value you can supply is 255, and the lowest is 0 (sorry, no negatives!). As a result, black is always formed by zero values for red, green, and blue, and white is always formed by lighting up the pixels so much that you can't see any color (255, 255, 255). With this in mind, you can create a nice shade of gray by taking the middle ground — not too light, not too dark, but right in the middle:

```
<PARAM NAME="anyColorSetting" VALUE="128 128 128">
```

Cool, huh? But what if you want other colors, say a nice bright red? Well, then all you'd have to do is specify the red component at 100 percent, and the others at zero:

```
<PARAM NAME="anyColorSetting" VALUE="255 0 0">
```

Got a case of the blues? Just turn up the knob on blue, and dim the others to nothing:

```
<PARAM NAME="anyColorSetting" VALUE="0 0 255">
```

And, of course, if you're after a nice, soothing green, try this value:

```
<PARAM NAME="anyColorSetting" VALUE="0 255 0">
```

You can make a less intense shade of each color merely by reducing the amount of light used from 255 on down. The lower you go, the darker the color becomes. If you want to create other colors, all you have to do is add different amounts of red, green, and blue. How about a nice shade of pink? Aqua? Sky blue? Okey-doke:

- ✔ **Pink:** `<PARAM NAME="anyColorSetting" VALUE="255 192 203">`
- ✔ **Aqua:** `<PARAM NAME="anyColorSetting" VALUE="0 255 255">`
- ✔ **Sky blue:** `<PARAM NAME="anyColorSetting" VALUE="135 206 235">`

Armed with the RGB color model, you can now set any color you want for the Marquee background and the text that scrolls across it. How about forest green on hot pink? Coming right up:

```
<APPLET CODE="Marquee" WIDTH=250 HEIGHT=30>
   <PARAM NAME="shift" VALUE=3>
   <PARAM NAME="delay" VALUE=5>
   <PARAM NAME="font_face" VALUE="TimesRoman">
   <PARAM NAME="font_size" VALUE="12">
   <PARAM NAME="font_italic" VALUE="yes">
   <PARAM NAME="font_bold" VALUE="yes">
   <PARAM NAME="back_color" VALUE="255 105 180">
   <PARAM NAME="text_color" VALUE="39 134 34">
   <PARAM NAME="marquee" VALUE="Am I an annoying ticker
           or what?">
</APPLET>
```

Throwing a hex wrench into the works

The RGB color model makes sense, even though it may take a little getting used to. But you're in for a doozie with some applets. A few cruel applet developers in the world like to think that you spend as much time behind the soft glow of a scientific calculator as they do. These heartless souls create their programs to accept colors using hexadecimal numbers.

Because I care about you, I'm not even going to try to explain these nasty little numbers. Black and white are no problem to represent in hexadecimal form, but things get pretty ugly from then on. Here's just a sample:

black	000000
red	ff0000
green	00ff00
blue	ffffff
pink	ffc0cb
aqua	00ffff
sky blue	87ceeb
hot pink	f0fff0
forest	228b22

If you've dealt with hexadecimal numbers before, this all makes perfect sense. Technically, these numbers are represented in hexadecimal triplet form: Each component for red, green, and blue is represented with a separate hexadecimal value. However, if this representation is new to you, it's not worth trying to figure out. Instead, what you need is a utility or chart to convert the color you're looking for into hexadecimal triplet form. Fortunately, one exists at the following URL:

www.mantiscorp.com/java

Connect to this site, and look for a hyperlink called Color Chart. Here, you'll find a table containing a wide range of colors, giving you a name, RGB color, and hexadecimal triplet setting for each. Save yourself the pain and agony of dealing with hexadecimal numbers — if you ever run into an applet that requires them, come here for help. Heck, for that matter, download the chart to you computer — that way, you'll always have it handy, just in case you need to convert from RGB to hexadecimal in an emergency. Hey, it could happen.

Mac users have a nifty shareware utility called WebColor 2.0, created by Patrick Bores. With this utility, you can use the Mac's standard color wheel to select colors and receive the corresponding hexadecimal value. WebColor is available on most shareware archives and at www.shareware.com

Cookin' with URL

Depending on whom you talk to, you'll hear URL pronounced either as a word, "earl" (sounding slightly like "oil" with a southern drawl), or by sounding out each letter in the acronym ("U-R-L," which stands for Uniform Resource Locator, described in Chapter 1).

However you say it, URLs have one purpose in life: to locate information on the Web. Every item that lives on the Web has a unique URL associated with it. Web pages, image files, sound files, data files, and everything else that exists on the Web has its very own URL. As a result, you can always find whatever you're looking for as long as you have its URL.

Because applets live on the Net, it's no surprise that many of them accept URLs as parameters. Typically, applets use URLs in one of three ways:

- To find files on the Web
- To find directories on the Web
- To navigate the Web

As with every other parameter that you specify, URLs must match the item they refer to exactly. If you want to provide your applet with a file that exists at www.mantiscorp.com./java/images, for example, then that's exactly what you must type, including all punctuation, and using all lowercase letters.

Although some applets don't deal at all with URLs, others make heavy use of them. The LivingLinks applet, for example, has several parameters that accept URLs. One of these, in fact, is actually named URL (see Table 8-1 at the end of Chapter 8). Another parameter, links, allows you to specify multiple URLs instead, each separated by a pipe character (|). Both of these parameters are used for navigational purposes, and both come into action when the Webber clicks on the applet.

But this applet uses several more URLs to access directories and files. You can provide URLs to tell LivingLinks in what directory on the Web it will find the sounds and images you tell it to use. Or you can use a URL to load just one image for the animation, if you prefer. You can also use a URL to specify an image to use as a background, on top of which the animation will appear. As with many applets, LivingLinks is chock full of parameters that accept URLs:

```
<PARAM NAME=links VALUE= "Mantis Homepage = http://
www.mantiscorp.com | For Dummies Homepage = http://
          www.dummies.com">
<PARAM NAME=soundDir VALUE="sounds/animals/mammals/">
<PARAM NAME=imagesDir VALUE="images/mantis/">
<PARAM NAME=backgroundImage VALUE="http://
          www.mantiscorp.com/images/mantoid.gif">
```

As with most applets, LivingLinks accepts both relative and absolute URLs (see Chapter 5). This means that you can refer to files and directories residing inside the same directory as the applet itself or one halfway around the world! But before you go nuts hooking up your applets to use files from a distant directory, keep in mind that an applet can only access files that reside on the same server as its own. Although this may seem like a contradiction ("Why give me the ability to use a full URL if I can't use files other than my own?"), it solves a problem with relative URLs in many applets: Unlike standard HTML, many applets don't allow you to use relative URLs that point to files in a higher directory than the one in which the Web page exists; you can only point to files residing in the same directory as the Web page or one located in a subdirectory. With an absolute URL, however, you can pinpoint any file on your Web server, regardless of where it's located in relation to the Web page or applet.

As a security precaution, the creators of Java made it impossible for applets to load files from anywhere else but the Web server from which they come (see Chapter 7). This means that all URLs you specify to access files or directories must point to somewhere on your own Web server. Fortunately, the same isn't true for URLs used to navigate the Web; for these, any URL will do. In LivingLinks, for example, all but the URL and links parameters must come from your Web server.

Dicing Data Files

Although most applets allow you to specify all the information they need right inside the <APPLET> tag by using parameters, others require (or give you the option to use) data files instead. *Data files* are nothing more than, well, files full of data! What the data consists of, however, is another story.

Just as applets differ in what they do, how they look, and the parameters they accept to get the job done, they also differ in what data they expect to find inside their files (assuming, of course, that they even use data files). Applets that track the stock market, for example, use data files that have stock market information inside of them. Applets that display pie charts and graphs, however, expect entirely different data.

So where do the data files come from that some applets allow you to use? Again, this depends on the applet. Applets that use images and sounds are the most common, and they may come with their own image and sound files. But if you really want to customize these applets, you can supply your own data files. You can even use a graphics page or a sound utility to create your own sounds and images.

You can usually use a <PARAM> tag to tell the applet where to find its data files, although some applets (such as Marquee) require that the file reside in the same directory as the applet itself.

Text data files

Marquee is an example of an applet that gives you the option of using a data file to obtain the text that it will scroll:

```
<APPLET CODE="Marquee" WIDTH=400 HEIGHT=34>
<PARAM NAME="shift" VALUE="2">
<PARAM NAME="delay" VALUE="20">
<PARAM NAME="font_size" VALUE="24">
<PARAM NAME="font_italic" VALUE="yes">
<PARAM NAME="font_bold" VALUE="yes">
<PARAM NAME="back_color" VALUE="255 255 240">
<PARAM NAME="text_color" VALUE="72 61 139">
<PARAM NAME="marquee_file" VALUE="bible.txt">
</applet>
```

The preceding example shows a Marquee applet that uses the file bible.txt — a file that happens to reside inside the same directory as the Web page that uses it. Other applets allow you to use URLs to point to data files.

A few examples of text files (jokes, famous quotes, horoscopes, fortune cookie messages, and Bible verses) are included, along with the Marquee applet, on the *Java For Dummies,* 2nd Edition, CD-ROM. Of course, you can always add to these files or create your own — just make sure that you save the files you intend to use with Marquee in the plain text format.

Marquee uses the file you specify to randomly choose one line of text to display. But for the applet to know when it has reached the end of a line, you have to be sure to place a carriage return at the end — just press Return (or Enter), and voilà — a new line begins. This certainly isn't any big feat, but so many text editors automatically wrap text around to the next line when you reach the end of a line that you may rarely type a carriage return. If you omit carriage returns, Marquee thinks that what you entered is just one giant piece of text and displays the whole thing.

This carriage return requirement for Marquee is exactly the type of thing you need to be careful of when dealing with data files, and why reading the documentation that comes with your applet is crucial. If the creator of the applet hasn't provided any documentation, you may have to wing it and try to figure out the file format yourself. If you have an existing file, you'll probably have no problem. Simply open the file with a text editor and see how it's organized. Then you can try to create your own by using the same basic layout of the original one, and see if it flies. It may take a few tries and some patience, but you'll probably figure it out in time.

If you don't at least have a data file to work with, then you may as well be driving down a winding country road at midnight with your headlights off. If the format of the data file is complex, you'll end up driving though fields and into trees, perhaps never to find the road again. Instead, get your hands on the documentation for the applet if you can. It's a lot less painful.

Sound and graphics data files

LivingLinks is an example of an applet that allows you to use image and sound files (which are data files that happen to contain sound and images) that exists elsewhere; all you have to do is supply the appropriate parameters. Most applets specify sound and image files with URLs. But keep in mind that, for security reasons, the URLs you supply must always point to a file that resides on the same server as the applet itself (see the preceding section on URLs and Chapter 7 for details). This means that any data files you specify for your applets must reside on the same server as the one your applet lives on.

When you're dealing with graphics and sound, all you have to do is save what you've created to a file in the right format — GIF or JPEG format for images, AU/uLaw format for sounds (see Chapter 6 for details). The program you use to create the file takes care of all the details of organizing the information in the correct format. In fact, that's all a *format* really is; it's just a way of organizing information.

Chapter 10

Bringing Your Applet to Life on the Web

In This Chapter

▶ Creating an applet directory structure on the Web

▶ Uploading Java-powered Web pages, applets, and support files

▶ Testing applets that live on the Web

Although Java-powered Web pages reside on your personal computer during the developmental stages (see Chapter 6), you'll eventually want to place them on the Internet for everyone to enjoy. After all, what good are Java-powered pages if you're the only one who can access them?

Luckily, when you have your applet-powered pages running in a local environment (that is, pages that reside on your computer, not on the Web), you're only a hop, skip, and a jump away from placing them on the World Wide Web. In essence, you simply create an exact copy on the Web of the folders (directories) in which your local pages exist and then transfer the files on your computer to their new home on the Web. These remote folders are basically exact copies of the local ones on your personal computer that contain your Java-powered pages and the applets that are embedded in them. That's really all there is to it.

Here's the rub: You have to use a special software program to create the folders you need on the Web, and then use that same software program to actually upload all the files that your applets require into the corresponding Web-based folders. Dealing with folders and files on the Internet is a bit more complicated than doing so on your personal computer. But after you get the basic process down, you'll be whipping up Java enhancements to your Web site in no time.

Taking Your Pages to the Web

To move from creating Java-powered pages for your local system to hooking up those pages for the world to enjoy, you create a remote directory structure — a Web-based copy of the folders located on your local computer system that contain your Java-savvy pages. Your Web site must have the same directory structure as your personal computer. Don't worry, you don't have to duplicate your entire hard-disk directory structure, just those parts of it that your applets use.

Web pages and the applets embedded in them typically reside in the same directory. Quite often, however, an applet requires support files (such as sound or graphics files) that are stored in different directories. For example, sound files may be stored in a directory called *audio,* and graphics files may be stored in a directory called *images.* Depending on the capabilities of the applet and on your own personal organization style, subdirectories containing support files often are located inside the directory that contains the Web page and the applet (see Figure 10-1).

Figure 10-1:
Support files usually live in sub-directories in the same directory as the applet and Web page.

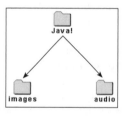

When you create a directory for the Web, you need to ask yourself the following questions:

- ✔ Does your Web page reside inside the same directory as the applets it uses? If so, you need to create only one directory on the Web in which to upload the page and any applets embedded in it.

- ✔ Do the Web page and the applet reside in separate directories? In this case, you have to create two directories on the Web, one for each file.

- ✔ If the applet requires support files, does the applet look for these files inside the same directory as the applet or in separate directories (such as an images or audio directory)? If the applet looks for the files in separate directories, you must create these directories.

Although this may sound like a lot to worry about, it's really not. When you have the applet running on a Web page locally (that is, running on a page that's located on your own computer — not one that's actually located on the Web), most of the work is behind you. You don't have to go far to know exactly what directory structure you'll need on the Web because the Web directory should be an exact mirror of the one you created locally. When you know which directories you need, creating them on the Web is a snap — something you can do in four short steps:

1. **Establish an FTP connection to your Web server (enter a password if one is required to log on to the server).**

2. **Determine the location (URL) for your Java-powered Web pages.**

3. **Create the main directory that will contain your Web pages.**

4. **Create each subdirectory that the applets require for their support files.**

Making the Connection

To create a directory on your Web site, you must first establish a connection to the Web server on which your site is hosted by using the *File Transfer Protocol* (FTP), the standard protocol used for sending files across the Internet (see Chapter 1 for information about protocols). A Web server is simply a special-purpose computer, connected to the Internet, that is responsible for hosting — *serving* — Web pages to browsers (the basis of all client-server relationships, which the Web is part of, as described in Chapter 1). If you've uploaded files to the Web before, you already know the ropes. If not, don't worry; it's almost as easy as browsing the Web. You need only three things:

- An FTP tool
- The FTP address of your Web site
- The password needed to access your site via FTP

Without an FTP tool, you can't put up your site on the Web. Without the FTP address of your Web server, you have nowhere to put your site. Without a password, you'll be turned away when you get there. But when you have all these things, you have the horse to ride on, the directions to the kingdom, and the keys to unlock the door when you arrive.

Choosing an FTP tool

If you've created Web pages before, chances are that you used an FTP tool to copy them from your personal computer onto your Web server. If this is the case, feel free to use the same FTP tool to create a directory structure on the Web and upload your pages and Java files. It really doesn't matter what FTP tool you use because applet files don't require special treatment when zooming across the Net.

You can use whatever FTP tool you want, but for the purposes of this discussion, I use the WS_FTP utility that is provided on the CD-ROM that comes with this book. If you're a Windows user who doesn't already have an FTP tool, I recommend that you use the WS_FTP utility because all the screen shots and examples in this chapter are based on it. (For details on how to install WS_FTP, see Appendix A.) If you're a Macintosh user, on the other hand, I suggest using the wonderful Fetch utility. Although this utility isn't provided on this book's CD-ROM, a hyperlink to it is available at www.mantiscorp.com/java, so you can download it with your Web browser.

Obtaining your FTP address

Don't mistake the URL of your Web site with the FTP address that you use to upload files to the Web! Heavens, no; these are two different beasts altogether. URLs are Web addresses, which are something Web browsers use to locate sites on the World Wide Web. FTP addresses, on the other hand, are what FTP tools use to locate servers, directories, and files on the Internet. In a limited sense, Web browsers make use of FTP addresses; the browsers can download the files to which an FTP address points, just as an FTP tool does. But FTP tools also enable you to upload files to the Web, assuming that you have the FTP address of the site to which you want to upload the files.

FTP addresses are usually either a series of words separated by periods, such as ftp.haviland.com, or a series of numbers separated by periods, such as 201.345.34.2. Although both forms are equally effective, words are usually easier to remember. The form you use depends on how your Web site has been configured by your Internet Service Provider (ISP) or Web server administrator (read on to find out about Web server administrators).

Because you'll be using an FTP tool to create directories and to upload files, you need to supply your Web server's FTP address to the tool. But how do you know the FTP address for your Web server?

The most straightforward way to obtain the FTP address of your Web server is to call your *Web server administrator.* This individual, or group of individuals, is responsible for keeping your Web server up and running. How you locate this person or group depends largely on how your Web site was established:

TECHNICAL STUFF

Why you need an FTP tool in the first place

Why must you bother with an FTP tool when you have a perfectly good Web browser? After all, Web browsers already know how to deal with the File Transfer Protocol (FTP), right? Well, sort of.

Unfortunately, Web browsers are designed to *get* information off the Web, not *put* information up there! When you visit a Web page, your browser retrieves the information contained (or referenced) in the page and downloads it for your viewing pleasure. How that information gets transferred really doesn't matter to your browser because it can accommodate just about every available protocol, including FTP (see Chapter 1 for more details on protocols).

When you create pages to publish on the Web, the information must travel in the opposite direction. To publish on the Web, you must create directories that didn't previously exist and then upload files into them. This process isn't something typical browsers are equipped to do, but it's something every FTP tool does quite well.

In time, all Web browsers are likely to include capabilities for both browsing and publishing. In fact, Netscape Navigator Gold and the Composer component of Netscape Communicator already feature the capability to upload files to the Web. Unfortunately, neither product is as flexible as an FTP tool when it comes to creating directories and uploading files. For this reason, you need to spend a little time getting comfortable with an FTP tool.

✔ If your Web site is provided through an Internet Service Provider (ISP) and you have access to the files residing in the account using FTP, you call the ISP directly. If you're not sure whether you have FTP access, give your service provider a holler and explain that you want to upload files to the Web. Your service provider can help you out and give you the details you need to access the account via FTP.

✔ If you don't have access to Web files via FTP or if your employer maintains the Web site internally, calling the ISP directly won't get you anywhere. In this case, you have to track down someone in your company who is responsible for granting access to the Web server.

✔ If you connect through a commercial online service such as America Online, CompuServe, or Prodigy, you have to use the tools provided for those services. In this case, contact the good people at technical support for your service and explain what you're doing — they'll give you all the information you need to get your Web site up and running.

You should note, however, that some commercial online services don't offer Java-savvy browsers to their members! This doesn't mean that the pages developed by these site members can't be Java-powered, mind you, it just means that viewers can't see them in action when using the service's built-in browser. Luckily, such service providers do allow their members to configure their account for use with Java-savvy browsers, such as Netscape Navigator and Internet Explorer.

After you track down the powers that be, explain that you want to create directories for and upload Web pages to your server. Make sure that the person you talk to understands that you'll be publishing Java-powered pages, to be made available for World Wide Web access. Although it shouldn't make a difference whether or not you're uploading Java-powered pages, it's always a good idea to ask your service provider for their advice; you may have to follow special rules, such as where you can place the files or what types of applets you can use, or they may be able to offer some time-saving advice. Regardless, be sure to let your service provider know what you plan to do; one question now can save you hours of aggravation later on.

Before your Web server administrator tells you what FTP address to use, be prepared to provide detailed account information to confirm your access privileges. Web server administrators commonly require details such as your username and password before furnishing you with an FTP address. However, assuming that you have the authority to create Web pages on the server, you shouldn't have to spend more than a few minutes on the telephone with the administrator before you have an FTP address.

You can always request your FTP address by using electronic mail, assuming that you have your Web server administrator's e-mail address. But if you use e-mail, don't send sensitive details of your Web server account (such as the password) unless you're 100 percent certain that the transmission is *secure* — that is, that what you type will be encrypted, rendering the message completely unreadable from the moment it leaves your computer until it reaches the person to whom you're sending it. Most e-mail systems are unsecure, so unless you know otherwise, assume that yours is, too.

Getting your FTP password

In addition to an FTP address, you need a password in order to put your page on the Web. When your Web server administrator gives you your FTP address, be sure to ask for your password as well. In most cases, this password is the same as the one you provide to the administrator to validate your access to the Web server in the first place. But depending on how your Web server is administrated, you may get a separate password to use when connecting files to the server with FTP.

Generally, you can't access a Web server via FTP without a password. And for good reason; after you have the FTP address and password for a site, you can add and remove files and directories at will! If no password were required, anyone with an FTP tool would be able to alter your Web site.

Imagine how surprised you would be to wake up one morning and find all the text on your home page replaced with dirty limericks: "There once was a man from . . .".

When you have a password, access to your site is much more secure. As long as you don't give out your password or send it though insecure e-mail, you're at low risk for sabotage. But the more people who know your Web server password or the more you transmit it through insecure e-mail messages, the more likely you are to become the victim of a practical joke or outright destruction of your site.

As a general rule, you should change your FTP password every few months. Don't make the mistake of choosing an obvious password, such as your name, the name of your pet, or your license plate number. Be sure to choose an obscure word that only you can easily remember, something that others won't be able to guess even if they know you. Including a few numbers in your password makes it more difficult for others to guess.

Firing up your FTP tool

With your Web site FTP address and password in hand, making the connection is a cinch. You simply launch your FTP tool as you would any other program and enter the address to which you want it to connect.

The process of connecting to a site and uploading or retrieving files via FTP is often called *FTPing* by those in the know, as in "I'm FTPing to my site. I'm hip." Toss that bit of Internet jargon around from time to time, and you're sure to impress friends and family alike.

The way you enter the FTP address varies depending on which tool you use. If you happen to use WS_FTP, as I do in this chapter, you simply enter the address in the Host Name box, as shown in Figure 10-2. In fact, you may be able to enter the password at the same time you enter the FTP address, as I've done here, killing two birds with one stone. If your FTP tool doesn't allow you to enter a password along with the address, don't worry: You get your chance when your FTP tool tries to make the connection.

Connecting to a Web site via FTP is very similar to using a browser, with the exception of the password. When using FTP to connect, you supply both the address for the site and the password, and the tool does the rest. You merely click on the OK button or your tool's equivalent (look for Connect, Go, Do It!, or something similar) and sit back for a few seconds.

The FTP tool attempts to make a connection to the address you give it and prompts you for a password (if you haven't already provided one). Assuming that you enter the correct address and password, the FTP tool displays a

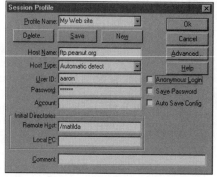

Figure 10-2:
Entering
an FTP
address
and
password
using
WS_FTP.

list of all the directories and files located inside the top-level directory of your site (a top-level directory contains a site's home page, along with all sub-directories the site may be comprised of; because Web sites are unique creations, the names of sub-directories found in top-level directories vary greatly). If this doesn't happen, make sure that you've entered the information exactly as your Web server administrator gave it to you, matching all uppercase and lowercase letters.

Many FTP tools assume that you're already online when you use them and report an error if you aren't! In this case, you have to get online before you start your FTP tool. The easiest way to do this is to start your Web browser. When your browser begins to load a page from the Web, you're online, and your FTP tool will be able to make its connection. After you've transferred the files as described below (see the section entitled "Uploading the files," in this chapter), you can close your FTP tool and your browser.

Although FTP tools are similar to browsers in many ways, they are nowhere nearly as graphical and elegant in their presentation of information. Remember that Web browsers go to great lengths to hide the mess of directories and files behind a visually pleasing display of graphics, text, and hyperlinks. FTP tools do just the opposite: They allow you to view the bare-boned site, as it existed on your personal computer — you're *supposed* to see all the directories and files so that you can navigate through them as you would on your own computer (see Figure 10-3).

Depending on the FTP tool you use, you may be able to save your site's address and password as a permanent *bookmark* for easy access the next time around. But be careful; if someone else uses your computer (or if your computer isn't located in a secure area), you're in danger of others accessing and altering your site. All someone has to do is launch the FTP tool and select the bookmark for your site to have full access to the directories and files!

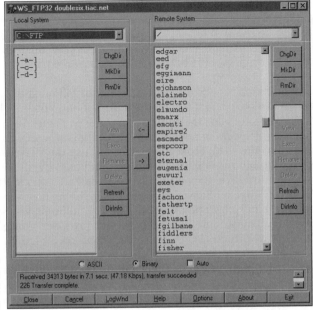

Figure 10-3:
With an FTP tool, you can see each site's directories and files.

Finding Your Own Little Piece of the Web

Where on your server you put your Java-powered Web page is largely a personal issue. Unless the page happens to be the home page for your entire site, it can go just about anywhere you choose and be named anything you want. If you're uploading the home page for your site, however, you don't have a choice about the location or the name of the file.

Typically, your home page *must* be located in the top-level directory of a Web site, and it must be named index.html (or index.htm, if the Web server your site is running on doesn't support filenames having more than three characters in the extension). You should receive your top-level directory when your Web server administrator gives you your FTP address, or navigate to it once connected if you don't automatically log in to that directory.

Giving your pages a home

Don't take lightly the task of choosing the name or location of your Web pages. Unless you're uploading these pages to the Web temporarily (for example, just to see whether you can or for testing purposes only), assume that you're choosing each page's final destination. The reason for this assumption is simple: Where you place the page dictates the URL others will use to access it!

Suppose that your name is Matilda and that your Web site's home page is accessible on the Web by using the URL www.peanut.org/matilda. If you were to enter the URL www.peanut.org alone, you would most likely get the home page for your Internet Service Provider — not your own site. You need to enter www.peanut.org/matilda to get to your home page.

When you FTP into your site, however, the FTP tool will most likely take you to your top-level directory (matilda, in this case). If not, you may have to specify an initial directory for the tool to use (refer to Figure 10-2, in which WS_FTP is shown with *matilda* specified as the initial directory to open when it connects to the site). From there, you can use the FTP tool to navigate deeper, into additional directories within your site, or perhaps move up one directory level to see the directories of all other Web sites maintained by your Internet Service Provider (see the nearby sidebar, "Sneaking around"). In fact, depending on what FTP address your administrator gives you, you may come in at your service provider's base level and then have to navigate directories to get to your matilda directory.

Regardless of what directory the FTP tool initially takes you to, you want to end up in the directory that contains the home page for your site. Depending on how your FTP tool is configured and the information your service provider gives you to make the connection, you may go directly to your main directory or you may have to navigate a bit to get there. If you aren't sure where this directory is located, take a look at the URL for your home page, which is the starting point for your site. In this example, the URL is www.peanut.org/matilda, which means that you want to FTP into the matilda directory on the www.peanut.org server. If you're having problems finding your home directory, don't panic. A simple call to your service provider's technical support team is all it takes to get back on track.

Sneaking around

Depending on how your Internet Service Provider handles security issues, you may or may not be able to use FTP to access the files of other Web sites on your server. If you do have access, it's likely to be *read-only* access: You can download files from these sites to your local computer, but you can't delete them or upload your own (except when you're dealing with your own directory). However, with read-only access, you're free to roam around and grab files that might be confidential! Though doing so may be tempting, don't — most service providers can see (to use Sting's words) every step you take and every move you make.

Be aware that if you can poke around other people's sites, they can do the same to yours. If this is the case, don't put anything confidential on your server unless the material is encrypted with a password. This way, even if someone does grab sensitive information off your site, that person won't be able to read it. Contact your Internet Service Provider for details on security and what tools your provider recommends to password-protect files on your site.

Keep in mind that Web addresses and FTP addresses are two different beasts. To connect to the `www.peanut.org` server, you may use an FTP address that bears no resemblance whatsoever to this URL. The FTP address you use may consist of numbers separated by periods, such as `234.35.35.6`, or names separated by periods, such as `ftp.peanut.org` or `doubletree.hotdog.com`.

Branching out with other pages

Any pages (in addition to your home page) that you add to your top-level directory have the same URL but with a slash followed by the filename tacked on to the end. For example, if you upload your resumé into the top-level directory and name it resume.html, the URL to access this page directly is `www.peanut.org/matilda/resume.html`.

Placing all your pages in the top-level directory isn't an efficient way of organizing your site. Think of your Web site as nothing more than a hard disk available to the world. Do you place all your files in the top-level directory of your hard disk? Certainly not; you create subdirectories that contain files, and often other subdirectories below that. Your computer's hard disk is organized using a hierarchy of directories, beginning at the top level and spreading out like the roots of a tree when depicted graphically, as in Figure 10-4.

Typically, you create subdirectories for your Web pages with an FTP tool by following a simple, three-step process that's similar to the way in which you create directories on your hard disk:

Figure 10-4:
Web sites, much like a personal computer hard disk, are organized in a hierarchy that resembles tree roots.

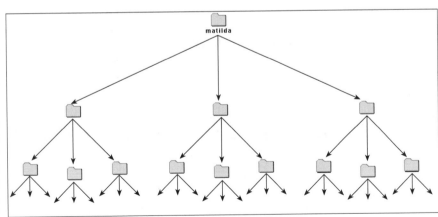

1. **Open the directory on your Web site that you want to place the new subdirectory in.**

2. **Issue a Create Directory command.**

3. **Give your new subdirectory a name.**

Because your Web site is really nothing more than a hard disk connected to the Internet, you should feel free to organize it however you want, adding new Web pages and directories as you see fit. You may, for example, want to store your Java-powered pages in a directory called coolstuff, located one level down from the top-level directory. If this directory doesn't already exist, use your FTP tool to create it (see the section "Structuring Your Web Page Directory," later in this chapter). Or you may want different directories to contain different pages. It's up to you to choose where your pages will find a home on the Web.

Now, suppose that the Java-powered page you are about to upload is named waltzing.html. By placing this file inside the coolstuff directory, you change the URL to `www.peanut.org/matilda/coolstuff/waltzing.html`. This address is the one you give to friends, relatives, colleagues, and anyone else you think may want to learn how to waltz Matilda-style.

If you give out your page's URL and then move or rename the page, the integrity of your site suffers. Webbers hate to go through the hassle of typing a URL only to see the all-too-familiar `File Not Found` message rather than the Web page they were anticipating. If a page in your site is accessible only through hyperlinks in other pages at your own site rather than directly through a URL, the consequences of moving it aren't as drastic (assuming you update all your hyperlinks accordingly). But even then, what if Webbers have bookmarked your page for fast access later on? When you move or rename a page, all bookmarks to that page instantly become invalid. To keep Web surfers happy and keep them coming back to your site, minimize the likelihood that you'll want to move or rename your pages later — carefully consider where to put your pages and what to name them *before* you put them on the Web.

Structuring Your Web Page Directory

How you structure your Web site's directory is a decision you should make when you first weave the applets into the pages on your hard disk (see Chapter 7). When you're ready to upload your Java-powered pages to the Web, the directory structure should be pretty much set. Here are just two things to consider when creating your directory structure:

✔ Even with the simplest of applets, you'll likely want to create a sub-directory or two to hold the support files. Do you *have* to? Certainly not. However, if you keep all your sound files in one directory, and your images in another, you'll always know where to find the support file you need. This assumes, of course, that the applet itself is flexible enough to allow you to place support files where you want them.

- LivingLinks, for example, is flexible enough that you can place any of your sound or image files wherever you choose.

- Marquee, on the other hand, is not so accommodating: The text files you use with this applet (to randomly supply a scrolling message) must reside inside the same directory as the applet itself. With Marquee, you don't have the luxury offered by LivingLinks of choosing where you want your files to reside.

As always, every applet is different when it comes to the things it will or won't allow you to do.

✔ Sometimes, different applets may need to access a single sound file, or all your applets may need to use a single image file, such as a trade-mark image. In either case, you may want to place all your sounds and images into two centrally located subdirectories that all your applets can access.

Again, this assumes that the applet allows you to choose where such files will reside. Some applets do (LivingLinks, for example) let you choose while others don't (such as Marquee, which is very inflexible when it comes to the location of the text support files it can utilize).

Remember that applets are creatures of habit. In most cases, the Java-powered pages you configure on your personal computer expect the *exact same* directory structure after you upload them to the Web. If, for example, you've configured an applet on your hard disk to use sound files located in a directory called audio that resides in the same directory as the page itself, the applet looks for this exact directory when it lives on the Web. You're free to choose where the page is located, but you must organize any support files required by the applets in that page in exactly the same way they were organized on your hard disk. If the audio directory on the Web, for example, doesn't exist in the same location relative to the page on the Web as it does on your hard disk, how will your applet find it?

An exception to the rule requiring that your hard disk directory match your Web directory comes into play when you use the CODEBASE attribute. In this case, the applet doesn't reside in the same directory as the Web page in which it appears. You may not even need a directory structure on the Web — if the applet resides on a server other than your server, it can't use your files anyway. However, if CODEBASE points to an applet residing on your own site, you have to take care to arrange the directories and files it uses accordingly. CODEBASE can be a tricky little devil to master, so I suggest avoiding it until you're comfortable with the whole process of creating Java-powered pages and uploading them to the Web. For more details about CODEBASE, see Chapter 7.

You can think of the upload process merely as copying a directory from your hard disk to the Web server. That's really all that's happening. Therefore, all the sub-directories and files your page relies on must be in their same relative positions after they're uploaded as they were on your hard disk. To make life easier, most FTP tools let you upload an entire directory from your hard disk to the Internet, including all subdirectories and files it contains. WS_FTP and Fetch, for example, take care of the whole issue of subdirectories by allowing you to copy everything wholesale. These two tools can automatically create subdirectories for you and upload the appropriate files into those subdirectories as you (and your applets) would expect.

For more information on creating subdirectories for support files, please read the (appropriately named) section "Creating subdirectories for support files," later in this chapter.

In many cases, the directory for your Web page already exists, so you can move right on to uploading the page itself or creating any subdirectories the page requires. The following list describes some situations in which you don't have to worry about creating a Web page directory:

- ✔ If the page is a home page, use the top-level directory that your administrator gave you when you established your FTP address. In those cases in which you're replacing an existing Web page with your red-hot Java version, this Web page directory will be in place already.

- ✔ Even if you're uploading a brand-spanking-new page, the directory in which you ultimately want it to reside may already exist. For example, you may (for some reason) want to store all your pages in your top-level directory. In this case, you don't need to create a directory for your Web page.

However, if the directory in which you intend to place your Web page does not exist already, you must create it by using your FTP tool. In this case, simply navigate to the directory in which the new subdirectory should appear and invoke your FTP tool's Create Directory command.

Suppose that I want to upload a Java-powered page called lightning.html to my company's Web site (www.mantiscorp.com). Furthermore, I want to place this page inside a directory called storms, that is located inside a directory called weather, which is located in the site's top-level directory. In this case, when all is said and done, the URL to the page becomes www.mantiscorp.com/weather/storms/lightning.html.

What if the storms directory doesn't already exist? Clearly, I have to create the storms directory, perhaps along with the weather directory if that one doesn't exist either. If I have to create both, I navigate to the top-level directory and create the weather directory first. After creating weather, I navigate into weather (by choosing Open) and create the storms directory. If weather already exists, I can simply open weather and create storms.

How you create a directory depends on the FTP tool you use, but the concept is pretty much the same regardless: You click a button or choose a menu item to tell the browser to create a directory, and then you give the new directory a name. With WS_FTP, for example, one click on the button named MkDir does the trick. With Fetch, you choose Directories⇨Create New Directory. In both cases, as soon as you choose the command, you must then type a name for the new directory (see Figure 10-5).

Figure 10-5:
With WS_FTP, the local hard drive ("Local System") appears on the left, and the Web server ("Remote System") is on the right. To create a directory on the server, click the MkDir button.

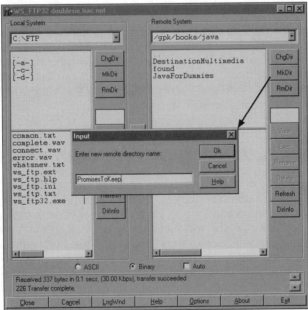

If your FTP tool supports bookmarks, you may want to consider bookmarking the main directory for each of your Java-powered pages. Doing so saves you from the hassle later of manually navigating into directories; simply choose a bookmark and you rocket straight to the corresponding directory.

With the main directory for your page in place, you're faced with a decision: Create the rest of the directory structure or upload the support files that should go inside the storms directory. This is another one of those personal choices — either option is fine.

I prefer to create the entire directory structure first and then upload the various files that each will need. In this way, if I happen to change my mind at the last minute about where the main directory for the page should be located, I have to delete only the directories I've created thus far. However, if I've also uploaded the files for each directory, I have to delete these files too.

To delete a file or directory by using an FTP tool, select the file or directory you want to delete and issue a Remove (or Delete) command. How you issue this command varies from tool to tool; some use a button, others a menu command. Although all FTP tools allow you to delete items, many don't let you delete a directory that contains files. If you're having problems deleting a directory, open it up and delete any files that are inside; then try again.

To remove a directory by using the WS_FTP tool, for example, highlight the directory you want to blow away and then click the RmDir button. To remove a file, highlight the file and press Delete. With Fetch, you use menu items rather than buttons. This tool uses a single menu item to delete both files and directories. Highlight the file or directory you want to delete and choose Remote⇨Delete File or Directory.

Creating subdirectories for support files

After you create the directory for your Web page and the applets it contains (both reside in the same directory, unless you use the CODEBASE attribute discussed in Chapters 5 and 7), you must also create any subdirectories that an applet requires for its support files. Any subdirectories you create will, of course, be merely a reflection of those the applet used when it was originally configured on your hard drive (see Chapter 7 for details). Remember, you're simply copying a directory from your hard disk to the Web server. You must be sure to maintain the same directory structure on the Web as the one the applet-powered page used on your hard disk.

Although manually creating a directory structure on the Web, as described here, isn't difficult, it does take time and concentration. If you have the choice, consider transferring everything to the Web at one time by using your FTP tool, as described earlier. If your FTP tool supports such a thing, as both WS_FTP and Fetch do, all directories, files, and subdirectories are uploaded for you. Just be sure to use the correct transfer mode, as described in this section, and you'll be all set.

Typically, applets require only a few subdirectories at most. These subdirectories store the support files, such as graphics and sound files, that the applet uses. Where these subdirectories are located in relation to the main directory depends entirely on the capabilities of the applet and how you've configured the ⟨APPLET⟩ tag (described in Chapters 5 and 7). Because many applets allow you to reference support files relative to the applet itself or the Web page in which it is embedded, you should create the subdirectories accordingly:

- ✔ If an applet loads files relative to itself, the subdirectories you create to hold these files should reside in the same directory as the applet.

- ✔ If the applet loads files relative to the Web page, on the other hand, the subdirectories and the files they contain must be created in the same directory as the page.

Suppose that your Web page embedded the LivingLinks applet by using the following ⟨APPLET⟩ tag:

```
<APPLET CODE="LivingLinks" WIDTH=150 HEIGHT=75>
<PARAM NAME=imagesDir VALUE="images/">
<PARAM NAME=imagesName VALUE="button">
<PARAM NAME=imagesExt VALUE="gif">
<PARAM NAME=imagesCount VALUE="5">
<PARAM NAME=speed VALUE="10">
<PARAM NAME=backgroundColor VALUE="white">
<PARAM NAME=reverse VALUE="yes">
<PARAM NAME=soundsDir VALUE="audio/">
<PARAM NAME=inSound VALUE="harp.au">
</APPLET>
```

Because the LivingLinks applet loads files relative to itself and not to the page in which it is embedded, each of the directories specified in the preceding tag (and the files they contain, of course!) must be located in the same directory as the applet. However, in this case, because the applet and Web page reside in the same directory anyway, you don't have to do anything special — just create the directories and upload the files into them, and you're done. So how can you tell whether the applet and the page must reside in the same directory? Take a close look at the opening ⟨APPLET⟩ tag.

In the previous code example the ⟨APPLET⟩ tag doesn't use the CODEBASE tag attribute (described in Chapter 5) so the Web page and applet must reside in the same directory. As a result, the images directory specified for the imagesDir parameter must also be located inside the same directory as the Web page. The same goes for the audio directory. All the directories and files this ⟨APPLET⟩ tag specifies are located in the same directory as the page itself because the CODEBASE attribute isn't used to specify otherwise.

However, the files this applet uses don't *have* to be in subdirectories inside the same directory as the applet. That's just how this particular tag was constructed. Because the directories are specified by using relative URLs, they're expected to be located relative to the applet. If, on the other hand, an absolute URL were used instead to specify a directory, the files this applet uses could be located elsewhere. Consider, for example, the following:

```
<PARAM NAME=imagesDirVALUE="http://www.mantiscorp.com/
    graphics/logos">
```

In this case, an absolute URL is used to specify the directory the images come from. As a result, the images are loaded from the logos directory, which is a subdirectory located inside the graphics directory on the Mantis Web server. But because an applet can access files only from its own server, the server on which the applet reside, the LivingLinks applet in this example has to be located somewhere on the Mantis server as well. If the applet resides on a different server, for example, it can't load images residing on the Mantis Web server. As a result, the applet doesn't run properly!

If this subject seems confusing, just remember these three things:

- If a tag doesn't specify CODEBASE, the applet and the Web page must reside in the same directory.

- In most cases, applets load files relative to themselves. But if CODEBASE isn't used, the way the applet loads the files is a moot point because the applet and the Web page are in the same directory anyway!

- Some applets, such as LivingLinks, let you use absolute URLs to load files. In such cases, files can come from anywhere on the same Web server as the applet itself resides, and the files don't have to be located relative to the applet.

However, the graphics and sound files this applet uses are a different story. Because the HTML code in the preceding example specifies a unique directory for each type of file (images for graphics and audio for sounds), you must create these subdirectories. But where?

First, check to see whether the HTML code specifies *where* these directories should be located, using an absolute location such as www.peanut.com/matilda/images. If, as in the preceding example, the code does not specify the directory location, you have to find out more about the applet. Specifically, you have to know whether the applet looks for the images in directories that are relative to the directory where the applet is located or in directories relative to the location of the Web page. How do you find this information? Usually, you have to check any documentation that came with the applet, or ask the applet's author.

In this particular HTML code example, you don't need to worry about where the images and sounds this applet uses are located. Because this applet's code doesn't contain the CODEBASE attribute, you know that the applet and Web pages are located in the same directory. If the CODEBASE attribute were used, then the applet and Web page would be located in separate directories.

✔ If your <APPLET> tag doesn't contain a CODEBASE attribute (indicating that the applet class files — or JAR files if they're used — and Web page reside in the same directory), all you have to do is create the subdirectories in the Web page's directory. Simply navigate into the directory where you plan to put the Web page and applet, issue a Create Directory command once for the audio and again for the images directories (to replicate the directory structure on your hard disk), and pat yourself on the back. Your entire directory structure is complete.

✔ If your <APPLET> tag uses CODEBASE, you have to create the images and audio subdirectories in the appropriate directory: Either the one the applet resides in or the one the Web page resides in (which one depends on how the applet was created — and to find that out, you have to consult the applet's documentation, as explained in Chapter 8).

Uploading the files

After your directory structure is complete, you can upload the files that your page requires into their respective locations. This step is a breeze, because all you have to do is navigate to the directory in which you want the file uploaded and then select the button or choose the menu option that begins the transfer. Some tools, such as WS_FTP, don't even require the use of a button or menu — by simply double-clicking a file displayed in the Local System window, the upload begins.

Of course, this process can be tedious when uploading a bunch of files, so you may opt to highlight them all and upload 'em together. With WS_FTP, simply highlight the files and then press the arrow button pointing to the side of the window in which the Web server files are displayed. With Fetch, you have to choose the Put Folders and Files option from the Remote menu and then select the files to upload by using a standard Macintosh file dialog box.

Regardless of whether you upload all files at once or one at a time, you must be sure to do one very important thing: Use the current transfer mode. Files are uploaded to the Web in different ways, or *modes,* depending on the type of information they contain. When dealing with Java-powered Web pages, be sure that you upload the applet and any non-text support files it uses (data files are typically in text format) by using a non-text transfer mode, such as the *binary* mode. Text transfer modes are designed to ensure that text files are uploaded to the Web with carriage returns and line breaks preserved. That system is great for text files, but quite another story for the applet and its non-text support files.

When in doubt, choose the *raw* transfer mode, if it's available. This mode railroads the file through your modem, over the phone lines, and onto the Internet without treating it in any special way.

A potential side effect of uploading files to the Web is the mangling of filenames, which usually is experienced only by Windows 95 users who are transferring files with an outdated FTP tool. When this type of tool gets through with your perfectly good filename, you wind up with a shortened name and extension — and a worthless applet. If this happens to you, you must wait until the transfer is complete and then rename the file to what it should be. Even if you don't use Windows, or if you use a Windows FTP tool that preserves filenames during transfers, you should always double-check all the filenames of your support files after transferring them to the Web. Then, fire up your Java-savvy browser and enter the URL of your Web page. If all goes according to plan, your page loads and comes to life as it did on your computer. If you experience difficulties, consult Chapter 17.

Shaking Out the Bugs

After you upload a Java-powered Web page to the Internet, along with all the Java files it requires (class or JAR files, and any support files such as sounds and images), chances are that you'll actually want to see it in action. But then again, maybe not. Perhaps you're the type of person who's simply too bashful to drink in the splendor of your own Java creation? Well, don't be, friend. Sit back and admire your Web masterpiece.

In reality, something will probably go wrong somewhere in the process. Although the plain-old HTML pages that you spin into a Java-powered work of art may look like a million bucks when you view it on your computer hard drive, a lot can happen on the way to the Web. Plainly put, chances are high — really high — that something will go awry as you try to upload your creation to the Internet. And until you figure out what it is that goes wrong, you can't fix it and therefore can't give your applet a nice, happy home on the Web.

Of course, I'm clearly assuming that *something* will go wrong *somehow*. Don't make me the bad guy here; I'm really not a doubting Thomas by nature (or a doubting Aaron, for that matter). The truth is that I've been around the block a few times (shhh, my mom doesn't know) when it comes to getting Web pages to really work on the Web. It's one thing to weave an applet into your page when the page and applet reside on your computer. It's quite another to upload the whole shebang to the Web for everyone to see.

But, hey, you're no ordinary person. You're charming, good looking, and smell great. How could anything go wrong? That's what we're going to find out. C'mon!

Testing, testing

The only way to know for sure if your Java-powered page is uploaded to the Web fully intact is to actually view it with a Java-savvy browser. To do so, simply fire-up your browser and type in the URL leading to your page. If all goes according to plan, your baby will appear bright-eyed and full of life. However, you're dealing with computers after all, so don't expect things to go according to plan the first few times around. Instead, pay attention to the status area of your browser as the page loads.

When testing your Java-powered pages, there are two areas on your browser to pay particular attention to:

✔ Status area

✔ Java console

What, when, where and why: The status area

The *status area* is used to display short messages related to the task at hand. If you move your cursor over a hyperlink in a Web page, for instance, the address of that link appears in the status area. In this way, the status area is used to help you better understand what that link is all about (assuming that such an address is actually of interest to you. At the very least, it's helpful to know if clicking the link will take you to an entirely different site on the Web, or merely take you a little deeper into the same site you're already visiting).

The status area typically is located in the lower-left corner of your browser window. If your browser's status area isn't visible, make sure you make it visible — you may be surprised how often folks forget that a status area even exists, simply because it isn't visible.

Thankfully, Netscape Navigator doesn't allow you to hide the status area. Older versions of the browser did, however, and so does Internet Explorer 4.0 — although Explorer uses the term "Status Bar" instead of status area — to enable the status area when using these browsers, make sure the item named status area (or Status Bar) located under the View menu has a check mark next to it.

While the status area is used to provide helpful pieces of information regarding the links on a page, it's also used by the browser to inform you of problems the browser may be having while attempting to run an applet. If the browser can't find the applet files that a Web page needs, for example, the status area displays an `applet not found` error. Assume for a moment that you uploaded a LivingLinks-powered Web page to the Internet, but didn't upload the LivingLinks class files. In that case, browsers can't find the applet files that your page requests, and displays a message in the status area that states something along the lines of `applet LivingLinks not found`.

Even if an applet runs just fine, it may take advantage of the status area to tell you important things when it is running, such as `Click now and subscribe to the Pickle of the Month Club`. Clearly it's a good idea to watch the status area for useful messages when first viewing your applet. In fact, the LivingLinks' `inMessage` parameter allows you to display any message that you need in the status area, as users moves their mice over the applet that's running (see Chapter 8 for details on the `inMessage` parameter, and all other parameters supported by the LivingLinks applet).

The status area is useful for viewing short pieces of information, such as an `applet not found` message when the browser fails to find the applet you specify in the `CODE` parameter of your page's `<APPLET>` tag. Sometimes, however, the information in the status area just isn't enough. If your Java-powered page fails to run when uploaded to the Web (or when you're viewing it locally on your own computer, for that matter), there's a good chance that the information displayed in the status area simply won't be informative enough. If this is the case, it's time to turn to your browser's Java console.

Finding consolation in the Java console

Most Java-savvy browsers on the market today allow you to open a *Java console* window to view the inner workings of applets. The Java console window has a great deal of leg room when it comes to screen real estate. Unlike the status area, which is very small and can accommodate only brief messages, the Java console is an independent window that browsers and applets alike can use to display messages of any length to the user.

The Java console window looks just like any other window (see Figure 10-6) that you may see on your computer. But this window is especially for Java applets, and contains information directly related to the applets running inside the Web pages you visit. If you have problems getting your Java-powered Web page to run after uploading it to the Internet, and the status area doesn't contain descriptive-enough messages to help you solve the problem, turn to the Java console. Here, you're much more likely to find detailed information related to the problem at hand.

Of course, finding out how to actually display the Java console window can be problem in its own right. Because all browsers are a little different, each has a different command for opening the Java console. Just poke around for a little while, and you should find a command with the word "console" in it.

Regardless of how you manage to open the Java console for your particular browser, be sure to take a peek at it if you have problems with your Java-powered pages. Between the Java console and the status area, you have all the information you need to figure out why your carefully sculpted Java-powered masterpiece falls apart when it hits the Web. And after you have a

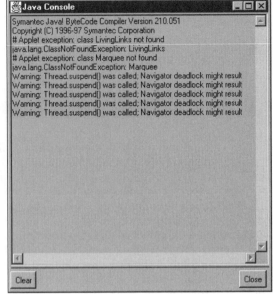

Figure 10-6:
A browser's
Java
console
window is
used to
relay
detailed
applet
information
to Webbers.

few rounds of the fascinating game I call "assessing the askew applet" under your belt, you'll probably come to find that most problems with Java-powered pages are the result of only a handful of mistakes, listed in the next section.

Band-aids and bubble gum

Fortunately, most mistakes of this sort fall into the "band-aids and bubble gum" category: They don't take much effort to fix and can make you and your browser happy in a few short moments.

Upload upheaval

The most common mistake you'll likely make when uploading your Web page, applets, and support files to the Web is one just about everyone makes the first few times: they forget to upload one piece or another of the puzzle.

When you first begin creating Java-powered Web pages, you may forget to upload an image that an applet needs, or a sound file, or even an applet itself. If you're working with a traditional applet that is comprised of more than one class file, chances are good that you'll overlook one of those class files when uploading. JAR files make this omission much less likely because all of the classes are bundled together in one easy-to-swallow package, but some applets require several JAR files, and it's easy to forget to upload one of these essential ingredients. This is especially true when you're dealing with support files that reside in their own directory. The more files an applet requires, and the more directories these various files may span (one directory for images, and another for sound, for example), the greater your chances of making a mistake and entirely omitting a file or even an entire directory.

When you work with LivingLinks or Marquee for the first time, take extra care to upload all the class files associated with these applets. Marquee, for example, requires that both the Marquee.class and MarqueeFile.class files reside in the same directory on the Internet to work properly. LivingLinks, on the other hand, requires only the LivingLinks.class file if you do *not* take advantage of a special effect (such as Fade, Warp, Shatter, Blur, and so forth). If you use a special effect, however, you must also upload the corresponding Effect.class file, along with any class files that make up the special effect itself (such as Fade.class and FadeFilter.class, in the case of the Fade special effect). Neglecting to upload all the necessary class files is the leading cause of applet failure, and nothing to be ashamed about. Just give your Internet directory a careful look-see before throwing your hands up in disgust, and you'll probably realize that a class file or two is missing.

Fortunately, fixing this problem is easy enough. All you have to do is use your FTP tool to compare the structure and contents of every directory associated with your Java-powered page. Simply ensure that all files residing on your local hard drive have been uploaded to the Internet, and that each file resides in its proper corresponding folder on the Net, and you'll be just fine.

Netscape Navigator features a Page Info command in the View menu. When you select this item (View⇨Page Info), the entire directory structure of a Web page displays, giving you a comprehensive overview of the various filenames and locations of files (even applets!) that a page uses. If you have difficulty figuring out what files you've uploaded to the Web, or want to take a closer look at the structure of your Java-powered page, give Page Info a whirl.

The name game

Another leading cause of applet failure lies in the naming of the files after they've been uploaded, something I like to call the "name game."

Assuming that you've successfully uploaded to the Web all the files that your page requires, your applet should run like a charm. If it doesn't, take a closer look at the name of each file involved. In many cases, an FTP will shorten (or *truncate*) a file name during the upload. What was once

LivingLinks.class becomes LivingLi.cla, while MarqueeFile.class mysteriously becomes MarqueeF.cla, effectively blowing your hopes of Java bliss out of the ether.

In these cases, you'll actually need to rename the files on the Internet by using your FTP tool (every FTP tool enables you to rename a file that you upload. Simply select the file and click on something like the Rename button). If a name is supposed to be LivingLinks.class, by gosh that's what you need to rename it! The same goes for all support files — any file associated with an applet must have exactly the same name when it lives on the Internet as it does when living on your own personal computer. If your LivingLinks applet expects to use an image named MyBigNose.gif, then you need to make sure that file resides on the Internet in the corresponding folder that it was in locally (such as images), and that it has exactly the same spelling and case.

If I sound a bit harsh about naming your Internet-bound files exactly as they appear on your local computer, it's just because I care. I've seen far too many loved ones hurt as a result of improper file naming, and can't bear to see you go through the same pain. Seriously.

Get off my case

Some FTP tools tend to change the case of the characters in filenames: LivingLinks.class is not the same as livinglinks.class, or even LIVINGLINKS.CLASS, for that matter!

Most FTP tools have settings that let you specify what to do with file names during uploads. If your file names are constantly being cut up, or the case of the names changes, hunt around in the settings of your FTP tool to see if it has options for disabling such features. Many years ago, it was acceptable to truncate file names or change the case when a file was uploaded, especially when uploading to DOS-based Web servers, which can't handle long file names. But today, things are different. Java-savvy browsers (and the applets that run inside of them) expect file names to be precise in both length and case. And so should your FTP tool.

Case matters, my friend, even when it comes to file extensions (like .class, .gif, and .jpg), and your browser will be the first to complain when it tries to find an image called MySmallEars.gif, if that's what the applet requires, yet only MySmallEars.GIF is available (or vice versa; an applet may be configured to use images having the .GIF extension, in which case images having the .gif extension simply won't due). You may be able to understand that the extensions .GIF and .gif are really the same thing when it comes to describing an image format, but your browser isn't so smart. Here, you'd either have to rename the file's extension to .gif, or configure the applet to look for MySmallEars.GIF instead of MySmallEars.gif, and things would be just ducky.

Major surgery

While the majority of problems you may experience when trying to get your Java-powered pages to live on the Web fall into the "band-aids and bubble gum" category, as described in the previous section, sometimes you won't be so lucky.

On the road to nowhere: Uploading files to the wrong directory

In some cases, you realize only after uploading an entire directory of files to the Web that you've mistakenly uploaded them to the wrong place. If, for example, you've uploaded all of your images into the wrong directory (the sound directory, for example, or even the directory the applet itself resides in, which is a problem if the images must reside inside their own directory) there's nothing you can do except delete the ones now on the Internet, move to the correct directory, and try again. Don't be ashamed. It happens to everyone now and again, even after a few years of working with Java (am I blushing?).

Dangerous dancing: The transfer mode two-step

In other cases, you may turn blue trying to figure out what's wrong with your Java-powered Web page, because nothing obvious is actually wrong. If all the files your page requires are uploaded to their proper directories, and the files are properly named, as are the directories themselves (a directory named images is not the same as one called image — that little "s" counts!), it can be truly maddening to figure out what's wrong. Everything looks exactly as it should, but the browser complains that it can't find the applet files or support files even though you know they are there. What gives?

If this is the case, chances are exceedingly high that you've uploaded your files to the Internet using the wrong file transfer mode. File transfer modes, as explained earlier in this chapter, tell your FTP tool how to break apart a file, send it over the network, and reassemble it on the other end. Think of your FTP tool as a primitive transporter of sorts, just like you'd see in any self-respecting science fiction movie (except without the big metal door and psychedelic lights). If your transporter isn't set to the right mode, things can get ugly. Did you ever see the modern remake of *The Fly* staring Jeff Goldblum? Enough said. When you use the wrong mode, you have no choice but to blow away the files you've already uploaded (that is, delete them) and try again. Simply delete the corrupted files off the Internet by using your FTP tool, and upload the original files from your hard drive once again. But this time, make sure your FTP tool's file transfer mode is properly set (see Chapter 17 for advice on setting file transfer modes for various types of files).

Finding a new home

In the worst situations, you may find out only after you've jumped through a number of fiery hoops that your problem runs much deeper than simply renaming a few files or having to upload a file you forgot to include in the first place. You might, amazing as it may seem, actually find out that your Web site doesn't support Java in the first place!

Although it's very rare, there are some Internet Service Providers (ISPs) out there that don't allow Java-powered pages to run from the Web space they supply. In this case, there's really nothing you can do but look for another service provider, one that actually supports Java (check out the AT&T WorldNet ISP kit provided on the CD-ROM that comes with this book; I personally guarantee that this ISP supports Java).

The same may even be true if you're using a corporate or educational Web site; your company or school may not want you to use Java. Because Java is powerful, it places extra demand on the computers that run a Web site (they're known as *hosts*). Not only does the computer hardware have to work a little harder when dealing with Java, so do the network pipes that connect the Web site to the Internet itself; they have to deliver more information than typically associated with a plain, old-fashioned Web page.

Also, the staff running the Web site has to work a little harder to support Java. Hey, something this cool doesn't come for free — somebody, or many bodies, have to support it! As a result, there are ISPs, companies, and even schools that don't want you to use Java because Java-powered pages are more demanding than their sad, naked little friends. Traditional Web pages are much less complicated to deal with and are much less difficult to support than those with Java. But then again, they're much less exciting. Much less powerful. Much less everything, as far as millions of people are concerned.

And so, if you find yourself in a situation where your Java-powered Web pages are in need of a Java-friendly Web host, be sure to ask the quintessential question before you dive in: "Do you support Java?" If the answer is no, move on, dear friend.

Part III

A Sip of JavaScript without the Bitter Aftertaste of Programming

The 5th Wave   By Rich Tennant

"How's that for dynamic content?"

In this part . . .

*P*art III shows you how to add another flavor of Java to your Web page — JavaScript. Find out what a scripting language is and how it differs from more complex programming languages (like the one used to create applets). This parts tells you where to find JavaScripts, how to customize them for your own use, and how to insert them into your Web page's source code. You also find out how to give your page a double-shot of Java, combining Java applets with JavaScript to get the most out of your Web pages.

Chapter 11

JavaScript: A Horse of a Different Color

*I*f you've spent any amount of time on the World Wide Web lately, you've certainly heard of Java. After all, this hot new technology is all the rage, and the buzz of the computer industry. In fact, Java is so hot, you're reading a book about it!

Though you may be hip to Java, perhaps having already woven an applet or two into your own Web pages, JavaScript is a horse of a different color, something you may not have even heard about until now. In comparison to Java, which burst onto the Web scene in 1995 and took it by storm, JavaScript is the baby of the Java family.

JavaScript is so new, in fact, that you may not have a clue about what it is or what it can do, even though it's changing the face of the Web almost as radically as Java itself.

Introducing JavaScript

JavaScript is a *scripting language* for the World Wide Web, developed by Netscape Communications Corp. and Sun Microsystems, Inc. (see Figure 11-1). Perhaps you've heard of these companies before? If not, brace yourself: Together, they're changing the way people learn, work, and play.

When it was first introduced, JavaScript held enormous promise for scripting Java applets, but it was only a promise. As of today, though, JavaScript is capable of scripting applets in the latest browsers. When used within these new browsers (Netscape Navigator and Internet Explorer 4.0), JavaScript can activate applets, and even fully interact with them after they are running.

With older Java-savvy browsers, however, JavaScript can only activate applets — interacting with applets isn't possible. If you stop and think about this for a moment, it becomes clear that the most powerful features of JavaScript are available only within the most powerful browsers, meaning the scripts will "break" when loaded by older browsers. Fortunately, there's a way around this, as you find out in Chapter 13, "Combining Applets and Scripts."

In Chapter 13, you see how you can use simple scripts to "sniff" browsers, enabling you to determine the exact browser types and versions that visit your pages. Using this information, a JavaScript-enabled Web page can dynamically accommodate any type of Java-savvy browser out there: Old browsers are fed only the scripts and applets they can handle, while newer browsers are given the more advanced scripts and applets.

What's a scripting language?

Although Java — a full-blown programming language meant to be used by experienced software developers — is enough to cause even Arthur Fonzarelli to lose his cool, JavaScript is a scripting language that even Potsy can handle. In terms of difficulty, scripting languages fall somewhere between markup languages, such as HTML, and full-blown programming languages, such as Java (as shown in Figure 11-2). Scripting languages provide much more than the capability to prepare documents for electronic publication, yet are not nearly as powerful as true programming languages. Scripting languages are, in essence, mini-programming languages for the average (dare I say "normal"?) person.

Figure 11-2:
In terms of complexity, scripting languages fall between markup languages and programming languages.

Actually, scripting languages fill a void left by programming languages. While programming languages are used to *create* software products (such as word processors, spreadsheets, Web browsers, applets, and the like), scripting languages let you, the end user, *control* such programs. In fact, a *scripting language* is defined as a relatively easy-to-use programming language that allows the end user to control existing programs.

Think of the relationship between the two kinds of languages this way: A software engineer creates a program using a programming language like Java, and you get to control the program using a scripting language like JavaScript. All you do is create a little list of things you want the program to do, a *script* if you will, and the program obeys. Pretty cool, huh?

Have you ever used a *macro* in a spreadsheet (as shown in Figure 11-3)? If so, you've used a specific type of scripting language. Macros, which have been available in spreadsheets since the dawn of number-crunching time, outline a list of predetermined steps that the spreadsheet performs when that macro is invoked — making macros little more than special-purpose scripts.

The great thing about scripting languages is that they save you time and money. You can play a script back any number of times without having to re-create any of the steps involved. Suppose, for example, that you design a script to create backup copies of all the files (word processor, spreadsheet, graphics, and so on) that you created within the past week. You only have to create the script once. From then on, you can activate the script whenever you want, and it automatically backs up all the files that were created in the past seven days. In fact, you can even set the script to execute automatically at the end of each work week, if you're so inclined, saving you from having to do so manually.

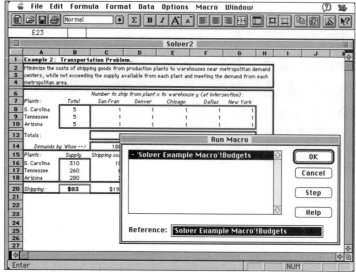

Figure 11-3:
Macros are
little more
than
special-
purpose
scripts.

Who needs JavaScript?

Before JavaScript was born, you had very little control over the interaction
between your Web pages and the Webbers who used them. Sure, you could
weave applets into your pages, but applets alone don't give you the ability
to *precisely* control the interactivity your pages offer. For the most part,
applets are just little programs that you plug in to make your pages look and
sound cool.

Cool is good, no doubt about it. But with applets, your pages are at the
mercy of the developer who wrote the applets. The best you can do is
customize an applet by setting parameters in HTML (see Chapter 8). However, you can't make an applet do something it wasn't intended to do. If the
developer didn't give the applet certain capabilities, no amount of parameter tweaking is going to make it do what you want it to do!

As a result, you may find yourself saying, "My Web page would be so killer if
it could only. . . ." But with HTML and applets alone, you don't always have
the degree of control you need to create such a site. Unless you have
JavaScript, you can only do two things: write the applets yourself or (more
likely) gripe, gripe, gripe.

A script by any other name would smell as sweet

Whether they're called macros, scripts, or even scriptable agents, the concept is the same: You, the end user, can control a program using a relatively easy programming language. If you're an online old-timer, meaning you were wired before commercial online services and the Web took over the networked world, chances are you used terminal emulation software. And if you used terminal emulation software, chances are you've seen scripts in action. Procomm, Blast, MacTerminal, MicroPhone, and just about every other commercial terminal emulation package ever created allowed you to record your steps for automatic playback later on. These recordings, whether or not you realized it, were actually scripts.

HTML is too little; applets are too late

The problem with using just HTML and applets is quite simple: HTML is static, offering no capability whatsoever to change a page once it is created, and applets arrive in your hands too late for you to have any say about how they behave. Applets are created by someone else, meaning that you get whatever the developer wanted, not necessarily what you may want!

If standard HTML were truly dynamic, you personally could create the pages you long for. Better yet, if you could hang out with a Java developer, munching chocolate and downing Mountain Dew into the wee hours of the morning, you could ensure that the applets you use behave exactly as you want them to. Unfortunately, HTML isn't dynamic. After a page is created in HTML and placed on the Web, all fonts, links, colors, and everything else are etched in digital stone. And, sadly, most developers aren't likely to invite you over for an all-nighter as they whip up the latest and greatest versions of their applets. At best, you can drop an e-mail to request that a feature be added to your favorite applet, but that's about it. So what's a cutting-edge Web page author such as yourself to do (short of spending years mastering a difficult programming language like Java)?

Use JavaScript, that's what. This is precisely where JavaScript fits into the Web page puzzle. Using JavaScript, *you* can create dynamic, interactive Web pages, without learning how to program Java language applets from scratch, or having to bribe other applet developers with your homemade tuna casserole. Save yourself the pain and embarrassment on both fronts: JavaScript is the key.

Dynamic HTML: Tomorrow's heir to the throne

Today, standard HTML is static. Eventually, however, it will become dynamic. Even as I write this, developers are making new improvements to HTML that give it some of the dynamic capabilities that JavaScript now offers.

However, *dynamic HTML* as a standard is far from being a reality today. Sure, there are proprietary flavors of dynamic HTML available this very moment, but they're not part of the standard (meaning there's no guarantee that browsers will support them in the future). In due time, the standards body that governs HTML will adopt dynamic capabilities similar to those seen with JavaScript, at which point you'll be able to work wonders with standard HTML, and be certain that all modern browsers will be able to handle it. But until that day comes, you have no choice but to weave nonstandard scripts into your Web pages.

What Does JavaScript Require?

Writing Java applets from scratch requires a host of special software programs intended for use by experienced software developers, but JavaScript is much less demanding, and more akin to HTML in its requirements. Actually, if you're already creating Web pages from scratch, typing HTML code directly into a document, and saving the result as a plain text file, you have everything you need to write JavaScript.

Unless you enjoy the tedium of creating Web pages from scratch, I strongly suggest using a graphically-oriented Web-page authoring tool such as Netscape Navigator Gold or the Netscape Composer component of Communicator (trial versions of both Navigator Gold and Composer are available through Netscape's home page at www.netscape.com) or Microsoft FrontPage (a trial version of which is available at www.microsoft.com/frontpage).

These powerful Web page development tools enable you to create sophisticated Web pages by using your mouse instead of entering the HTML code manually with a text editor. And, because these tools understand JavaScript, you can enter and edit scripts directly, meaning you don't need to bother with a text editor at all. Such tools can save you hours of work, and perhaps even your sanity, because they spare you from having to deal with HTML directly. With Web-page authoring tools such as these, creating smashing Web pages is no more difficult than using your word processor. Oh, the joys of technology.

A text editor

If you intend to create your own scripts or to customize scripts created by others, you need a *text editor* — any program that enables you to change the contents of a text file.

✔ Windows 95 comes with its own text editor called NotePad. Nothing special, mind you, just a plain text editor.

✔ Macintosh users can use the SimpleText application (shown in Figure 11-4) that comes with every Mac that rolls off the assembly line. Yep, SimpleText is simple all right — no doubt about it. But it's just fine for creating script.

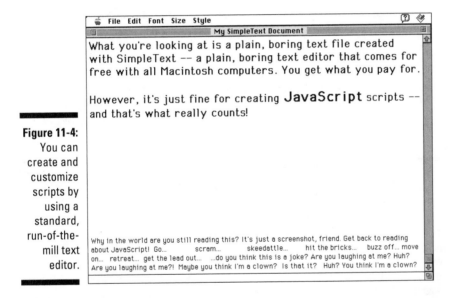

Figure 11-4: You can create and customize scripts by using a standard, run-of-the-mill text editor.

Any ol' text editor will do, actually — including the one you use to write HTML, or even your word processor. (If you use a word processor to edit HTML and JavaScript, remember to save the file as a text file rather than as a word processor document.) The reason you need a text editor is simple: JavaScript scripts are nothing more than plain text! That's right: Scripts are written and stored as plain, ordinary, everyday text. Nothing glamorous or special about it. Just text.

A JavaScript-savvy browser

JavaScript and Java are *not* the same thing, although they share the same gene pool. Just because your browser supports Java doesn't automatically mean that it supports JavaScript, and vice-versa. Just as you need a Java-savvy browser to run Java applets, you need a JavaScript-savvy browser to run JavaScript.

If a browser is Java-savvy, it's likely to be JavaScript-savvy as well. The reverse isn't true, however. Because JavaScript is a different technology than Java, browsers commonly support JavaScript but not Java; in fact, this is the case with Netscape Navigator 2.0 for the Macintosh. As a result, Macintosh users using Navigator 2.0 must get their hands on either Navigator 3.0 (www.netscape.com) or Internet Explorer 3.0 (www.microsoft.com/ie), at the very least, if they want to access both Java and JavaScript through one browser — a move that I highly recommend.

Better yet, Macintosh users should check out the latest version of both browsers. At the time of this writing, version 4.0 of both Netscape Navigator and Microsoft Internet Explorer are in the wings, and should be available by the time you read this. Windows users, on the other hand, can get their mitts on either right now — version 4.0 of both browsers are available today.

Optional: Visual JavaScript

Netscape Visual JavaScript is a cutting-edge visual development tool aimed squarely at folks who want to weave JavaScript magic. Unfortunately, Visual JavaScript is expensive and somewhat complicated to learn, and isn't something I recommend to the casual scripter.

You can always download a trial version of Visual JavaScript from Netscape's homepage (www.netscape.com) and give it a test-drive. In doing so, you get a chance to work with this wonderful new tool without having to shell out serious bucks from the get-go. Should you decide that Visual JavaScript isn't really for you after all, you don't have to do a thing: Just stop using it. That's the beauty of trial software — you get to try it out free of charge, and you only pay for it if you want to keep it. What could be better? (Aside from not having to pay at all and still getting to keep it, that is.)

A whole lotta patience

In addition to a text editor (or graphical Web page or JavaScript editing tool) and a JavaScript-savvy browser to test the script with, you need one more thing to create JavaScript: the patience of Job. JavaScript isn't easy to learn, and it's considerably more complicated to use than HTML. In fact, JavaScript can be, by most accounts, an utter nightmare to understand. At least initially.

If you're a type-A personality, I suggest a shiatsu massage immediately before and after each attempt to create a script, followed by an hour or two soak in a sensory-deprivation tank, just to be on the safe side. If you're a type-B personality, not easily frustrated or prone to go off the handle after hitting a few walls, a box of chocolates and a soda or two should do you just fine.

If you're using this book, you don't need to worry about losing your senses and running screaming into the street. I intend only to show you how to *use* and *customize* existing scripts, not how to program new scripts from scratch! In fact, there's no way (short of calling in a miracle or two from the Big Guy) that you could actually learn how to become a proficient JavaScript programmer in the three chapters I have set aside for the subject. If you want to write scripts from scratch, you need an entire book on the subject. Might I suggest *JavaScript For Dummies,* 2nd Edition, by Emily A. Vander Veer (IDG Books Worldwide, Inc.)? It's just the ticket if you want to really master scripting. In this book, you start out nice and slow, so that you can decide for yourself whether you want to dig deeper into JavaScript.

Why torture yourself? I recommend you start with the easy stuff: reading, using, and customizing existing scripts. There's no reason, practically speaking, that you must become a JavaScript programmer to weave JavaScript into your Web pages. Instead, take what others have done and apply it to your own pages, personalizing as needed. If, having done this, you want to create your own scripts from scratch, go for it! You'll have a strong base to start from, and the process of mastering the language won't be nearly as daunting.

Even though this book won't turn you into a master JavaScript programmer (I'll leave that to *JavaScript For Dummies*), you still need a goodly amount of patience to customize scripts. Weaving existing scripts into Web pages is a cinch, but customizing them is another matter entirely. When you customize a script, you dig in and change what the original developer created to make the script fit your needs. As a result, you must peer into the guts of a script, ripping out what you don't need, sewing in what you do. It's not a pretty sight, so prepare yourself.

TECHNICAL STUFF

Clash of the scripting Titans: JScript versus JavaScript

Microsoft has its own version of JavaScript called *JScript*. Microsoft was forced to invent JScript from scratch because Netscape wouldn't turn over the internal secret recipe for JavaScript in the time frame it had originally promised. Because Microsoft wanted to build support for JavaScript into Internet Explorer sooner rather than later, the company decided to create its own flavor of JavaScript by mixing up its own secret recipe. As a result, JavaScript and JScript aren't 100% compatible!

Some of the bells and whistles that JavaScript includes don't work in a browser that supports only JScript (such as Internet Explorer). JScript also has a few tricks of its own that JavaScript can't perform. Sadly, you must straddle both worlds for the time being, until JScript and JavaScript are 100% compatible. This won't happen for a few more years (if it ever does happen, actually), so you're forced to play a balancing act with your scripts, as Chapter 13 illustrates.

Why Bother?

If JavaScript is so difficult, why bother with it? For starters, JavaScript may be difficult to learn, but it's easy to *use!* Just include a script between an opening `<SCRIPT>` tag and a closing `</SCRIPT>` tag, and you're done. (If you're curious about why JavaScript and Java require different HTML tags to be woven into Web pages, read the sidebar "Why use two tags rather than one?") At this level, using JavaScript is as easy as weaving the simplest applets into Web pages. *Customizing* scripts, however, is a different story.

When you customize a script, you actually change it. In essence, you reprogram the script to do what you want. How little or how much you alter the script depends on your needs, and how close the original script comes to fulfilling those needs. In some cases, the task is no more difficult than configuring `<APPLET>` tag parameters; at other times, altering a script gets much hairier. Luckily, how much you alter a script depends entirely upon you.

You may find that you rarely, if ever, have to bother with customizing a script. After all, thousands of scripts are out there on the Web for the taking. All you have to do is find the ones that fit your needs, and you're all set. But even if you do have to get under the hood from time to time, tinkering with a script's innards until it does what you need, you'll probably find the process worthwhile. When you can use existing scripts and customize them to fit your needs, your Web site will never lack for truly compelling content.

(This assumes, of course, that you first obtain permission from the original owner of the scripts before you weave them into your pages — it would be a shame to admire your compelling site from behind bars!)

If you're interested in learning how to customize scripts, take a tour of the CD-ROM that comes with this book (see Appendix A). On the main Web page of this CD-ROM is a link named "Customizing JavaScript" that shows you exactly how to customize scripts. In fact, you'll see precisely how to hook up and tweak scripts that come for free on the CD-ROM, meaning that you no longer have to guess what the examples look like in real life: The "Customizing JavaScript" chapter on your CD-ROM is actually a Web page containing real scripts!

HTML is dead; JavaScript is alive!

The difference between standard HTML pages and those injected with JavaScript is like the difference between night and day. Standard HTML is static, dead, incapable of creating anything more than inanimate hyper-media documents (as shown in Figure 11-5). With a solid dose of JavaScript, however, Web pages actually *interact* with their readers, rather than just look pretty and provide basic hyperlink capabilities.

This dynamic nature of JavaScript gives Web pages the ability to react to user input like a real program. For example, by using JavaScript, you can create buttons on pages that do something when visitors to your site click

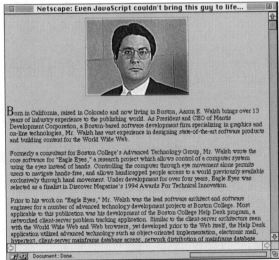

Figure 11-5: Standard HTML produces static, lifeless Web pages.

them. Perhaps the buttons open a new window and display another Web page inside, an image, or maybe an applet. It's all up to you. Here are just a few of the ways that JavaScript can enable Webbers to interact with your Web page:

- ✔ You may choose to arrange a set of buttons in a certain order and have them work together to form a basic calculator.

- ✔ You can display a brief questionnaire in a pop-up window that the user must complete to receive something from you for free, or to travel any further into your site.

- ✔ Instead of a full-blown questionnaire, you may prefer a simple Confirmation dialog box with Yes and No buttons corresponding to whatever message you choose to have the user agree to before going any further.

Perhaps interacting with the user isn't really what you want to do. Maybe you want a few special effects to appear when Webbers come to your page. How about a nice fade-in, from one color to the next? Maybe you want to scroll a message in the status area of the browser or directly on the Web page, as with the popular applet ticker tapes that abound. Or maybe you want to display the current date and time in your page. With JavaScript, all this and more is possible (as shown in Figure 11-6).

Figure 11-6:
JavaScript delivers dynamic, interactive content, bringing your Web pages to life! (Trust me on this one — the page shown here is definitely not dead; it's alive and kickin'.)

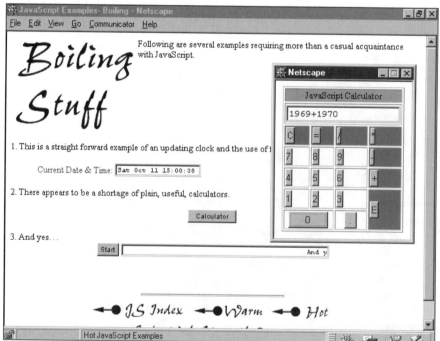

You may be thinking, "Hmmm . . . I've seen a lot of this stuff in Web pages already, sometimes accomplished by an applet, other times using what looks like standard HTML." Most of these feats can be and are being accomplished without JavaScript. None of these feats, however, are possible with standard HTML. What you're seeing in many cases is a technology known as the *Common Gateway Interface* (CGI). CGI looks like HTML and can accomplish some of the same things as JavaScript and applets, but CGI has its downside.

CGI is a bear; JavaScript is a gentle bear

Before Java and JavaScript burst onto the Web, the only way to create even marginally interactive pages was through use of the Common Gateway Interface, known to millions simply as CGI. In fact, until the past year or so, every time you filled out a form (such as a search engine), clicked a button, typed in any information, or navigated by selecting different areas inside one image (an *image map*) on the Web, you were using CGI.

Although CGI produces satisfactory results, JavaScript gives you better results with much richer levels of interaction at a fraction of the time and hassle. CGI lets you get simple information from the user, such as entry form information, but CGI doesn't provide live feedback to the user. When users click a button, the CGI form sends information to the server, which sends back updated information. A CGI form is just as dead as an HTML page, though the CGI form *appears* to be interactive. JavaScripts genuinely interact with users, responding as they click buttons, enter information, and move the mouse around.

Programming in CGI makes JavaScript look like a walk in the park! If you're hesitant to undertake JavaScript, don't even think about CGI; it's an absolute bear to learn. Sure, if you want to take full advantage of JavaScript, it can be a bear too. But JavaScript is a cuddly, warm, gentle bear, one you'd be happy to share a sticky bun with on a chilly winter day. CGI is a bloodthirsty, feverish, crazed bear with fangs the size of steak knives. Run for your life!

Java is a nightmare; JavaScript is a dream

If you're interested in writing your own applets, JavaScript is the perfect introduction. Because you must learn the complex Java programming language in order to create an applet from scratch, you're much better off taking the easy road paved by JavaScript and creating scripts instead.

Although the Java language isn't so difficult to learn if you're an experienced programmer, to the uninitiated, Java is an utter nightmare! JavaScript, by comparison, is a dream to learn — you don't have to be an experienced programmer, or a programmer at all for that matter, to use JavaScript.

For example, consider the following piece of JavaScript:

```
document.write("The Current Date and Time: "+Date())
```

TECHNICAL STUFF

Why use two tags rather than one?

If you were the kind of kid who always kept the class late in grammar school, asking questions that stumped even the teacher, you may be wondering, "Why not have just one tag, say, <JAVA>, and have the browser tell the difference between the two after it looks inside?"

If you must know, smarty pants, the reason there are two tags is due to the disparate development cycles the two technologies took. Java, developed entirely by Sun Microsystems, made its way to the Web quite a while before JavaScript. It was Sun that dreamt up the <APPLET> tag, making it the standard tag for embedding applets into Web pages. Netscape, on the other hand, developed JavaScript in large part without Sun's help.

By the time JavaScript finally shipped, the Java-savvy version of Netscape had been out and around the block a few times. The only way the original crop of Java-savvy browsers can recognize an applet is through the <APPLET> tag (the most modern browsers can see applets by using HTML 4.0's new <OBJECT> tag, as discussed in Chapter 5 and Appendix B). Although creating a universal <JAVA> tag that could contain either applets or scripts would be possible, the millions of older Java-savvy browsers in use today wouldn't be able to deal with it — they're capable of viewing applets only though the <APPLET> tag. Some older browsers can't even deal with scripts because they predate the <SCRIPT> tag!

Creating a whole new generation of browsers that use only the <JAVA> tag (or something similar) would leave older browsers in the cold. And when you consider that tens of millions of users would be unable to see applets and scripts embedded with these new tags, merely suggesting this idea amounts to what I fondly call a *bonehead move.* So the world is destined to continue using the <APPLET> tag to weave in applets, and the <SCRIPT> tag to weave in scripts. At least for now.

Applets are players; JavaScript is the coach

The only way to control an applet without JavaScript is to configure `<APPLET>` tag parameters using HTML. And the only way to change a parameter without JavaScript is to physically change the HTML into which the parameter is woven, and then upload the page to the Web again. Even then, the applet only acts according to its preset parameters. Yes, you can change the parameters by changing the HTML page, but you cannot *dynamically* change an applet's parameters as visitors are viewing the page. Not without JavaScript, that is.

With JavaScript, you can dynamically alter your applets. Great. So what does that mean? Imagine being able to change any applet parameter you want in response to something a Webber does. For example, say that you have an animation applet embedded in your page. Without JavaScript, you can only configure the applet's parameters so that the applet is just the way you want it, and then upload the applet to the Web. When Webbers visit the page, the animation plays according to your configuration, and will continue to play this way until you change the parameters and upload a new page.

With JavaScript, however, it's a whole different ballgame. Because JavaScript can dynamically control applets, your Web pages can change on-the-fly and in response to Webber activity. The following are just a few of the tricks you can do with Web page animation, thanks to JavaScript and a "scriptable" applet (such as the LivingLinks applet supplied on your CD-ROM):

✔ Have the applet animate very slowly at first, and then speed up over time.

✔ Reverse the animation direction by playing the animation backwards if Webbers place their mouse pointers in a certain area of the applet that you define.

✔ Change the actual images being animated, just for the heck of it or in response to the Webber's activities. You could, for example, use JavaScript to feed the animation different images depending on where Webbers move their mouse pointers.

But that's not all! JavaScript allows you to string together applets, enabling you to call any number of them into action, each applet keyed off one another's actions. For example, your animation applet can — at a time you specify — kick off another animation in a different part of the page. When the second animation is finished, it may trigger another applet, one that does something entirely different. And, thanks to JavaScript, you'll be able to control how the applets and scripts on a page work together, effectively making you a conductor in charge of a symphony of applets.

Of course, these things I just described are possible only with applets that understand how to take orders from a script. LivingLinks, for example, is fully *scriptable* — it understands how to take orders from a script, so you can do all these things and more with it. However, the Marquee applet, included on this book's CD-ROM, doesn't understand a thing about scripting; you'll sooner get blood from a stone than you will get this applet to respond to JavaScript commands.

To see a few examples of the LivingLinks applet being dynamically controlled by JavaScript, fire up your browser and visit www.mantiscorp.com/javascript/.

With this single line of JavaScript embedded in it, your Web page displays the current date and time (as shown in Figure 11-7). Although this line of JavaScript may look a little strange to you now, being your first introduction to the language, consider the following Java code, which accomplishes exactly the same thing, as far as your page is concerned:

```
import java.util.Date;
import java.awt.Graphics;
public class HelloWorld extends java.applet.Applet {
  public void init() {
    resize(150,25);
  }
  public void paint(Graphics g) {
    Date today = new Date();
    g.drawString("Date and Time:" + today, 50, 25);
  }
}
```

Yep. That is genuine Java code. If you really want to know what each line of this code does, check out *Java Programming For Dummies,* 2nd Edition, by Donald J. and David Koosis (IDG Books Worldwide, Inc.). But you can tell already that Java is much more complex than JavaScript.

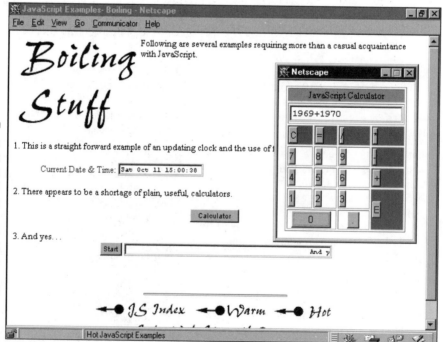

Figure 11-7: JavaScript is a breeze compared to writing Java applets; this little script clock was created with just one line of JavaScript.

Whereas I can explain the single line of JavaScript to you in a paragraph or two, helping you make sense of the Java language would consume several pages of text. Sure, experienced programmers scarf down mass quantities of Java code as if it were Jolt cola fresh from the cooler, but nonprogrammers are hard-pressed to swallow (let alone digest) even the simplest examples.

No, if you want to get the most out of your Web pages without surrendering your life to dweebdom and getting a computer science degree, JavaScript's the only way to go. JavaScript goes down nice and easy, at least once you learn the basics, and, unlike too much Java, JavaScript won't keep you up all night.

JavaScripts are easy to find!

Unlike applets, which you must somehow get your hands on before you can use them (see Chapter 7), JavaScript scripts are out in plain sight. By their very nature, being nothing more than plain text, scripts are part of the HTML page in which they are embedded. To see the complete source code of a script, you need only view the source of the Web page (see Figure 11-8).

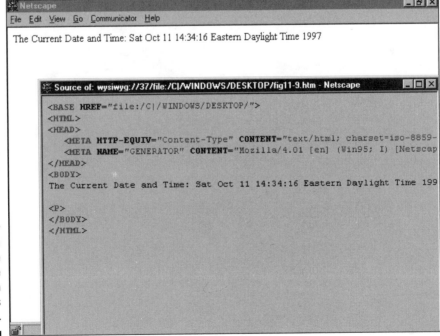

Figure 11-8:
To view the source code of a script, you need only view the source code of the page in which it is embedded.

The only way to know whether you can reuse a JavaScript just as you find it (that is, without significant modifications) is to look at the script itself. Authors who don't want you to reuse their scripts usually include a copyright within the script. If, on the other hand, they want you to make use of their work, they may include a statement in the script that says, "Take it, it's yours!" If you don't find a message telling you to go ahead and use a script, or a copyright telling you not to, the decision is up to you. Personally, I always get permission to use a script unless the script tells me to take it. You know, it's better to be safe. . . .

Because you can see scripts, you can save them to your own computer, where you're free to tinker with them as you want. It's always a good idea to ask permission of the original author before making use of a script in your own pages, but you're free to examine its source code without so much as a word of thanks. This is, in fact, a big advantage of scripts over applets: You can't see the source code for an applet, nor can you download the applet to your computer without the permission of the author. And if the parameters of an applet aren't provided, you have no way of knowing how to customize it! The open nature of scripts makes looking at the work of others an ideal way for you to learn more about the process of writing scripts yourself.

Chapter 12

Weaving JavaScript into Your Web Pages

- -

In This Chapter

▶ Getting to know the <SCRIPT> tag

▶ Searching for scripts

▶ Adding scripts to your Web pages

▶ Hiding scripts from non-Java browsers

▶ Avoiding common <SCRIPT> tag problems

▶ Dealing with functions

- -

*W*hereas Java applets are tiny, high-powered programs that software programmers write in the Java language, a *script* is really nothing more than one or more English-like commands that appear inside a standard Web page for browsers to follow. Because scripts consist of nothing but text, they are more accessible than applets — you can easily find scripts and add them to your own pages, customize them to fit your needs, or even write your own from scratch. All it takes is a little know-how — know-how that begins with the <SCRIPT> tag.

A Script Is Born

Just as applets are created somewhere by someone, JavaScript scripts don't just happen; somebody writes them. And just as applets vary in terms of what they do, scripts also widely vary in function.

Although JavaScript is an easier language to understand than Java (which is used to create applets), it's still complicated and intimidating until you get used to it. In fact, I won't even pretend to try to show you how to create your own scripts — that would take a whole book! In fact, a whole book is indeed dedicated to JavaScript. If you're looking to move beyond the use of existing scripts to becoming fluent in JavaScript, check out *JavaScript For Dummies,* 2nd Edition, written by Emily A. Vander Veer (IDG Books Worldwide, Inc.).

Don't worry; you may never have a reason to write your own scripts from scratch, because you can customize what others have already created. If knowing that you can simply customize scripts created by others weren't good enough, in many cases you don't even need to do that — tons of scripts are offered for free, ready to be plopped right into your own Web pages without requiring that you get under the hood and fiddle around with the script's innards. Whether you decide to customize a script or use it as is, you need to add it to your pages by using the <SCRIPT> tag.

Introducing the <SCRIPT> tag

Ladies and gentlemen, children of all ages, I now give you the tags that make adding scripts to Web pages possible. Please put your hands together and give a good old-fashioned welcome to the opening and closing <SCRIPT> tags:

```
<SCRIPT attributes>
</SCRIPT>
```

Not exactly the show-stopper you were expecting? They may not make you gasp in amazement, but the opening <SCRIPT> and closing </SCRIPT> tags are truly the stars of the JavaScript show — without them, you can't add scripts to your Web pages. No matter how you slice it, if you want to add JavaScript to your pages, you have to go through these two tags. Or, to be more precise, JavaScript must go between these two tags:

```
<SCRIPT attributes>
Here, inside the opening and closing script tags, is where
        the JavaScript code goes.
</SCRIPT>
```

The opening and closing <SCRIPT> tags merely tell the browser that what comes between them is script, not standard HTML. Without these tags, the browser would try to treat the script as HTML, which would cause some real problems. These tags do little else other than ensure that browsers treat the script that comes between them properly. The script is what really does all the work. Like most bigwig bosses in the world, the <SCRIPT> tags just make sure that the work that needs to get done does, in fact, get done. But who actually does the work?

Although the `<SCRIPT>` tags are critical, no doubt about it, the lines of JavaScript code that come between those tags are what JavaScript is really all about. This code includes the various commands that tell browsers what to do and how to do it.

You may have, depending on the script, as few as one line or as many as hundreds of lines of code inside the opening and closing `<SCRIPT>` tags. How big a script is depends on what the script does. A simple script, such as one that displays the current date and time, may consist of only one or two lines of code; more complex scripts (a few of which make cameo appearances in Chapter 13) can span several pages.

Because scripts vary greatly, depending on what they do, the line or lines of code that come between the opening and closing `<SCRIPT>` tags also vary greatly. Sometimes you can make sense of what's going on merely by reading each line. At other times, you won't have a clue about what's happening. But don't worry: You really don't have to know what's going on to use a script in your own pages. All you have to do is construct the opening and closing `<SCRIPT>` tags and then place inside them the lines of code that make up the script. It's a snap after you get the hang of it.

The unsolved mystery of JavaScript attributes

One of the most interesting (if not downright mysterious) aspects of JavaScript has to do with the attributes that may be included in the opening tag. As with applet attributes, discussed in detail in Chapter 5, JavaScript attributes are simply keywords within an opening `<SCRIPT>` tag that change the way browsers treat that tag. According to the formal, official, straight-from-the-horse's-mouth JavaScript documentation (that is, the documentation provided by Netscape), you may supply two attributes inside the opening `<SCRIPT>` tag: `LANGUAGE` and `SRC`. But (here's the weird part), although you're free to supply either or both of these attributes when creating your `<SCRIPT>` tags, original JavaScript-savvy browsers, such as Netscape Navigator 2.0 and Internet Explorer 3.0, ignore them both!

That's right — despite being part of the formal JavaScript documentation, the original crop of JavaScript-savvy browsers totally ignore the `LANGUAGE` and `SRC` attributes. However, both of these attributes are supported by the most recent crop of browsers (Netscape Navigator 4.0 and Internet Explorer 4.0) and so there's incentive to understand what each attribute does and how (and when) to use them.

Do you speak my language?

Today, the most important of the two <SCRIPT> tag attributes is LANGUAGE. Even though this attribute isn't used by older JavaScript-capable browsers, you should take care to include it in all of your scripts anyway. This attribute is especially important for today's most modern JavaScript-savvy browsers — or, to be more accurate, today's script-savvy browsers.

Although JavaScript was the only game in town when it was originally introduced to the Web, JavaScript is no longer the only scripting language to choose from (see Chapter 11 to find out more about scripting languages). Today, alternatives to JavaScript, such as Microsoft's JScript and Visual Basic Script, have burst on the scene and are vying for your browser's attention.

In anticipation of this recent outpouring of diverse scripting languages, the makers of JavaScript long ago decided to give you a way to tell browsers which scripting language you're actually using: The LANGUAGE attribute. Naturally, the most popular scripting language in use today is JavaScript, simply because it was the first out of the gate. But time has a way of changing leadership in the Web area! Because JavaScript already has serious competition, and other scripting languages are on the way, make sure that all the JavaScript scripts that you use are clearly identified as such. To tell a script-savvy browser which type of script falls between your opening and closing <SCRIPT> tags, all you have to do is set the LANGUAGE attribute to "JavaScript":

```
<SCRIPT LANGUAGE="JavaScript">
Some nifty JavaScript code goes here.
</SCRIPT>
```

Of course, there's nothing to prevent you from omitting the LANGUAGE attribute, except your own conscience. Can you really sleep at night knowing that you didn't bother to inform all possible script-savvy Web browsers that you're using JavaScript? If so, perhaps you're the same kind of person who doesn't bother to deal with income taxes, figuring that they won't come back to haunt you later on? Think again, bucko!

Not only will leaving off the LANGUAGE attribute alienate those browsers that expect to find the scripting language specified, but future browsers may even refuse to recognize scripts that aren't explicitly identified as being written in a specific scripting language. Because the official word from Netscape is that all opening <SCRIPT> tags must set the LANGUAGE attribute to identify the type of script being used ("JavaScript", in this case), you would be wise to do so!

In the future, the LANGUAGE attribute may be used to tell browsers not only in which language a script is written but also which *version* of a scripting language is used. Although JavaScript is relatively fresh from the oven, it has already undergone major changes, and it's just a matter of time before another new-and-improved version of the language is developed. You can expect JavaScript to keep maturing, with new versions being released for years to come. To differentiate between the various versions of the language that will eventually be released, Netscape may even mandate that future releases of JavaScript be identified by using the LANGUAGE attribute (for example: LANGUAGE="JavaScript2.0", LANGUAGE="JavaScript3.0", and so on).

A source of aggravation

Whereas the LANGUAGE attribute may save your script from short-circuiting when viewed by modern script-savvy browsers, the SRC attribute may keep *you* from short-circuiting! The SRC attribute, which stands for *source,* was not supported initially by script-savvy browsers. Today, however, you may use the SRC attribute with Netscape Navigator 4.0 or Internet Explorer 4.0.

With these browsers, you can provide an SRC attribute that specifies a URL pointing to a file containing the JavaScript code you want to execute. With older browsers, however, you have no choice but to provide that JavaScript code right then and there, between the opening and closing <SCRIPT> tags. Writing out JavaScript code inside the tag is no problem for short-and-sweet scripts, but it's a royal pain in the attribute with scripts that span more than a half-dozen lines or so.

The longer the script or the more scripts you have in a page, the more cluttered and difficult it is to understand the HTML code. What was once reasonable, easy-to-read HTML code can quickly become a nightmare containing so much JavaScript code that you must scroll for what seems like an eternity to get though it all. When you have to include all that JavaScript code between your <SCRIPT> tags, page maintenance becomes much more difficult than it should be. You may spend more time swimming though line after line of JavaScript than you spend enhancing your pages.

The solution to this potential travesty of code justice lies in the SRC attribute, which enables you to separate your HTML code from your JavaScript code. Although this miraculous SRC attribute isn't supported in older script-savvy browsers, you're free to use it as long as the browser viewing your page is either Netscape Navigator 4.0 (or later) or Internet Explorer 4.0 (or later).

Although you can use the SRC attribute with modern browsers, it's not supported at all by older JavaScript-savvy browsers, meaning that any scripts pointed to by SRC won't run under older browsers. To deal with this situation, you can either forego the SRC attribute altogether and imbed all of your scripts inside the Web page itself, or you can use a *sniffer* script to determine exactly what browser is being used each time a Webber visits your page and then construct a new <SCRIPT> tag on the fly based on this information. In this way, older script-savvy browsers can be supported by simply using a little sniffer script to determine exactly what type of browser is visiting and constructing the rest of your attribute based on this information: Older browsers will receive script that doesn't make use of the SRC attribute, while newer browsers can be told to use the SRC attribute. To see how this is done, refer to the "Bait and Switch: Browser Sniffing" section found in Chapter 13.

To use the SRC attribute with today's latest and greatest browsers, all you have to do is provide a URL, either absolute or relative (see Chapter 5 for details on absolute and relative URLs), that points to the text file containing the JavaScript code you want to execute:

```
<SCRIPT SRC="MyScript.js">
</SCRIPT>
```

Quick! Hide! It's a non-Java browser

Aside from the inclusion of opening and closing <SCRIPT> tags, the most important thing to remember when constructing a tag for JavaScript is that not all browsers understand how to deal with JavaScript. In fact, millions of Webbers are still using old browsers that don't have a clue when it comes to JavaScript. Not only that, some Webbers with perfectly fine JavaScript-savvy browsers actually "turn off" this capability, or never turn it on in the first place, making it impossible for them to see JavaScript in action (imagine the nerve!). For all intents and purposes, such browsers are considered by your Web pages to be the same as older, JavaScript-ignorant browsers. It's a pity, actually, but it happens to millions of Webbers every day. They hit the Web with browsers that can't (for one reason or another) understand JavaScript.

When a non-JavaScript browser encounters a JavaScript-powered page, it displays what amounts to garbage instead of executing the script. As a result, your well-designed pages look like a junkyard to folks who don't use JavaScript-savvy browsers. The trick is to hide the JavaScript code from these types of browsers. If a non-JavaScript browser can't see the JavaScript in a page, it won't display the garbage. In essence, you'll sweep this unreadable garbage under the rug when non-JavaScript browsers come to visit.

Unlike the <APPLET> tag, the <SCRIPT> tag doesn't support an area for alternate HTML. For details on alternate HTML, see Chapters 5 and 7.

So how can you hide your JavaScript from script-ignorant browsers and still allow JavaScript-savvy browsers to do their magic? The answer lies in *comments*.

Making a comment

Standard HTML enables you to hide the code of your pages merely by placing an exclamation point (!) immediately inside a beginning less-than (<) character. This hidden text is referred to as a *comment*. For example, if you want to document your HTML code with a little bit of information to remind you when the page was last updated, all you have to do is place a comment somewhere, such as:

```
<! This page was last updated on February 14th >
```

Because browsers know to skip over the entire tag thanks to the exclamation point that comes immediately after the opening less-than sign (<), this line doesn't interfere with regular HTML code. Instead, these types of comments are only for your benefit; they mean nothing to browsers. That is, comments *meant* nothing — until JavaScript was invented.

Commenting on JavaScript

To hide scripts from non-JavaScript browsers, you must surround the entire script with a special comment tag that begins with a less-than sign, an exclamation point, and two hyphens (<!--) and ends with two forward slashes, two hyphens, and a greater-than sign (//-->). Anything that comes in between, such as a script, is ignored by non-JavaScript browsers. But browsers that do know how to execute JavaScript realize that what's inside the comment tag isn't something to be ignored. Not at all. Instead, JavaScript-savvy browsers know that a script falls between these special comments and therefore treat it with all the love and attention that it justly deserves.

To hide JavaScript from standard browsers while making it available to those in the know, all you have to do is surround the script with these special comment tags. However, most folks just getting started with JavaScript forget this little nugget of helpful information, and usually omit these special comment tags even though they're a cinch to add. Before I show you how to use these special comment tags to hide your scripts from browsers that don't understand JavaScript, take a gander at the code below that you can use to display the current date and time inside a Web page. I've intentionally neglected to hide this script from non-JavaScript browsers:

```
<SCRIPT LANGUAGE="JavaScript">
todays_date=new Date();
document.write("The Current Date and Time: ")
document.write(todays_date)
</SCRIPT>
```

The preceding script is fine for all JavaScript-savvy browsers, but standard browsers are useless when it comes to scripts; they display garbage instead. Take a look at Figure 12-1 if you don't believe me — it shows the little date-and-time script through the eyes of a standard browser. Pretty ugly, indeed.

Figure 12-1:
If you don't hide scripts from standard browsers, they display garbage when they reach the script code.

To remedy the problem, just surround the JavaScript code that appears between the opening <SCRIPT> and closing </SCRIPT> tags with the special comments previously described:

```
<SCRIPT LANGUAGE="JavaScript">
<!--
todays_date=new Date();
document.write("The Current Date and Time: ")
document.write(todays_date)
//-->
</SCRIPT>
```

These comments hide the script from non-JavaScript browsers, as shown in Figure 12-2. You may notice, however, that the comments appear *inside* the opening and closing <SCRIPT> tags. If the comments didn't appear there, your attempt to hide the script from non-JavaScript browsers would fail because the comments would actually hide the tags that tell script-savvy browsers, "Hey, a script is right here — check it out!" Non-JavaScript browsers ignore the <SCRIPT> tags anyway, but you don't want script-savvy browsers to ignore these tags.

Figure 12-2:
When you hide scripts inside comments, non-JavaScript browsers don't bother trying to display the scripts.

That's all there is to it. As long as you precede the actual script code with `<!--` and end it with `//-->`, the script code remains hidden from all standard browsers but is still available to JavaScript-savvy browsers. If you omit these special tags, however, you create a mess when non-JavaScript browsers try to treat this special JavaScript code as standard HTML code. Believe me, it's not a pretty sight.

If you want to save yourself time and effort, all you have to do is use the following snippet of HTML code as the basis for all scripts you weave into your pages. Just save the following code in a plain text file, and then copy it the next time you add a script:

```
<SCRIPT LANGUAGE="JavaScript">
<!--
//-->
</SCRIPT>
```

By using this code snippet as the template for all scripts you weave into your pages, you prepare for the future (`LANGUAGE="JavaScript"`) while also accommodating the past (`<!--` and `//-->`).

The JavaScript Is Out There

Unless you plan to write your own scripts from scratch, a daunting task if you've never dealt with a scripting language (see Chapter 11), you have to rustle up a few scripts to add to your pages. Luckily, the Web is crawling with scripts; all you have to do is find them.

Although scrounging up a few scripts for your pages is a cinch if you're surfing the Web in search of them, you can save time and online charges by using the scripts in the Cool Beans! folder of the CD-ROM that comes with this book. There, you find several scripts that you can use to liven up your pages, as well as links to even more scripts. The examples I use in this chapter come straight from scripts on the CD-ROM, so you can follow along with the same applet or apply the skills to applets you find yourself. (See Appendix A for details on using the scripts that come with the *Java For Dummies,* 2nd Edition, CD-ROM.)

Whether you get your scripts from the Net or the CD-ROM, you have to do one thing before you even can see JavaScript in action, let alone create your own JavaScript-powered pages: You must turn JavaScript on! No, this doesn't involve mood music or a candlelit dinner (although you're free to try). To turn on JavaScript, you first need to fire up your JavaScript-savvy browser and make sure that the JavaScript option is enabled (see the next section).

Turning on JavaScript

Before you waste your time looking for scripts, take a moment or two to make sure that your browser is JavaScript-savvy, and that JavaScript support is actually *enabled,* or turned on. Even if you're using the most script-savvy browser in the world, it won't matter a bit if you haven't actually enabled JavaScript (described in Chapter 3).

By placing a check mark inside either the Enable Java or the Enable JavaScript check box, you enable each feature, respectively. Because Java and JavaScript are two different technologies (described in detail in Chapter 11), you can enable or disable each one independently of the other. For the ultimate Java experience, however, you should be sure that both options are selected to get the most out of Navigator when it comes to viewing Java-powered pages.

Regardless of the computer you use, after you enable the JavaScript feature on your JavaScript-savvy browser, it's just a matter of surfing the Web or working your way through this book's CD-ROM to find script-powered pages that tickle your fancy.

Searching for JavaScript

How can you tell whether a page is enhanced with scripts, applets, or both? Whenever you come across a Web page that is alive in some way (whether it's through dancing, animated buttons, moving text, sounds, or some form of interactivity), there's a good chance that the page is powered by Java. But the real question is whether the magic is performed by scripts, applets, or some other, non-standard technology.

Java isn't the only game in town when it comes to bringing Web pages to life, although it is by far the most popular. Other non-standard technologies also deliver dynamic content, such as Netscape and Microsoft's suite of non-standard HTML tags, plug-in browser enhancements offered by both Netscape Navigator and Internet Explorer, and Microsoft's ActiveX technology (the closest in capability to Java, although still a distant second in terms of popularity and power). For my money, however, and for millions of other Webbers' money, Java's the clear winner: With the one-two punch of applets and scripts, Java packs a wallop that would bring George Foreman to his knees.

To find out what's going on behind a Web page, take a gander at the HTML source code. In Chapter 7, I discuss what's going on behind the scenes with applets, but what about JavaScripts? When hunting down applets, you look for pages containing the ⟨APPLET⟩ tag, so it should come as no surprise that when hunting down JavaScript, you look for a ⟨SCRIPT⟩ tag.

To find out whether a page is JavaScript-powered, simply view its HTML source code and then invoke your browser's Find command (see Chapter 6 for details on viewing source code and searching through it for tags). When the Find dialog box appears, type the word **script** and begin your search by clicking on the Find Next button.

To save time, don't worry whether the letters you use are uppercase or lowercase when typing **script.** Web page authors can use any case they want when entering tags (some use all uppercase, others use lowercase, and still others use a mixture of the two), so you would have no idea which case to search for. Cover all your bases in one fell swoop by making sure that the Match Case option in the Find dialog box is disabled; then type in whatever case you prefer.

If a page contains scripts, your search of the HTML source code is likely to turn up the opening tag for the first script (see Figure 12-3). But be careful — your browser's Find feature shows you every occurrence of the word *script*, regardless of whether it's a ⟨SCRIPT⟩ tag. A page containing information about playwrights and stage actors, for example, will probably result in several matches when you search for the word **script**. But this doesn't mean that they're ⟨SCRIPT⟩ tags — you're more likely to find a hyperlink to the script for *Hamlet* than to find a JavaScript tag!

If you find matches for the word *script* that have nothing to do with JavaScript, simply move on. Click on the Search button again, telling your browser to find the next occurrence of the text you're looking for. Keep going until you find a ⟨SCRIPT⟩ tag or reach the end of the source code.

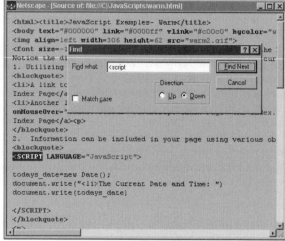

Figure 12-3:
To find the
JavaScript
code in a
Web page,
simply
search
through its
HTML
source
code for
opening
`<SCRIPT>`
tags.

If you're really pressed for time or if the page you're looking at contains the word *script* in a context that has nothing to do with JavaScript, you can search for **<script** instead. By including the opening less-than sign (<) of the tag, you ensure that only JavaScript tags will be found. However, don't use the corresponding greater-than sign (>) that signals the end of a tag. As with `<APPLET>` tags, `<SCRIPT>` tags may contain extra information, called *attributes,* that comes before the end of the tag. If you search for **<script>**, you will find only tags that have no attributes associated with them. (For details on tags and attributes, see Chapter 5.)

Adding Self-Contained Scripts to Your Web Pages

The most basic scripts you can find are those that exist entirely inside the opening `<SCRIPT>` and closing `</SCRIPT>` tags. Although a number of scripts are broken up into little pieces, called *functions,* and are woven into different parts of a Web page (see "Of Form and Function," later in this chapter), many scripts are entirely self-contained and exist inside a single set of `<SCRIPT>` tags. With the exception of code that doesn't need `<SCRIPT>` tags (see the preceding section), these self-contained scripts are the easiest to add to your own pages.

Adding self-contained scripts to your pages takes just a few easy steps:

1. Find the script to add.

2. **Copy the script (or save it to your computer).**

3. **Add the script to your page.**

Finding self-contained scripts

Finding scripts is easy — all you have to do is go out on the Web and hunt around for a while (see the section "The JavaScript Is Out There," earlier in this chapter, or see Chapter 16 for details). The key to finding scripts is recognizing whether the script you're dealing with is indeed self-contained.

To find out whether a given script is self-contained, you must take a closer look at the HTML code for the entire page and pay special attention to the JavaScript code that falls between the opening <SCRIPT> and closing </SCRIPT> tags. Scripts that aren't entirely self-contained reference functions that are located toward the top of the HTML source code for the page in which they appear.

The following script, for example, is completely self-contained. It doesn't rely on any external functions at all; what falls between the opening and closing <SCRIPT> tags (and the tags too, unless you plan to type them yourself) is all that you need in order to use this script in your own pages:

```
<SCRIPT LANGUAGE="JavaScript">
<!--
todays_date=new Date();
document.write("The Current Date and Time: ")
document.write(todays_date)
//-->
</SCRIPT>
```

The next script, however, references a function called display_clock. As a result, you must copy both the script and the display_clock function into your Web page for this script to work properly:

```
<SCRIPT LANGUAGE="JavaScript">
<!--
document.write("Here's a cool clock: ")
display_clock(todays_date)
//-->
</SCRIPT>
```

Unfortunately, it's tough to tell just by looking at a script whether it makes use of a function, as these two examples illustrate: Which one uses the function? If I didn't tell you, it would be tough to figure out — at least until you have more experience with JavaScript. Sometimes, what you see looks like a function call, but isn't; at other times, you would swear that the script is self-contained even though it may rely on a function to get the job done.

The only surefire way to find out whether a script relies on a function is to add the script to your page and then load it in a JavaScript-savvy browser. If the browser displays the script, it doesn't use functions. If, however, the browser displays an error message telling you that something in the script is not properly defined, then a function is missing. (For details on tracking down functions, see the section "Of Form and Function," later in this chapter.)

Copying scripts

After you've found a script that you want to add to your own page, all you have to do is copy the entire <SCRIPT> tag and paste it into your own HTML source code. Of course, you could also type the entire thing from scratch, but why bother? By simply copying and pasting it, you save both time and aggravation — and no typos!

To copy a script, just highlight it with your mouse and choose Edit⇨Copy. Or, if you want to save a little time, you can press the appropriate key combination instead (Ctrl+C if you use Windows or ⌘+C for the Macintosh). But be sure to get the whole thing! If you don't copy the *entire* script, it won't work when you add it to your page. To make sure that you copy the whole script, simply highlight all the code appearing between the opening <SCRIPT> and closing </SCRIPT> tags *and* the tags themselves (see Figure 12-4) before issuing the Copy command.

If you want to, you can save to your personal computer all the HTML source code for the page rather than just copy the script itself. In fact, this is the easiest way to deal with scripts that use functions. (See the section "Of Form and Function," later in this chapter.) For details on saving HTML source code to your personal computer, see Chapter 7.

Pasting scripts

After you copy a script, the only thing left to do is to paste it into your own HTML source code. For example, look at the script shown earlier in Figure 12-3. After you copy the script, you can add it anywhere you want within your Web page by simply pasting it (choose Edit⇨Paste or press Ctrl+V if you use a Windows system, or press ⌘+V if you use a Macintosh). In fact, you can add the script to several different pages if you want; all you have to do is paste it into the HTML code for each page in which you want it to appear. Or you can add the same script in many different places inside a single page. Again, it's just a matter of pasting the code wherever you want the script to appear.

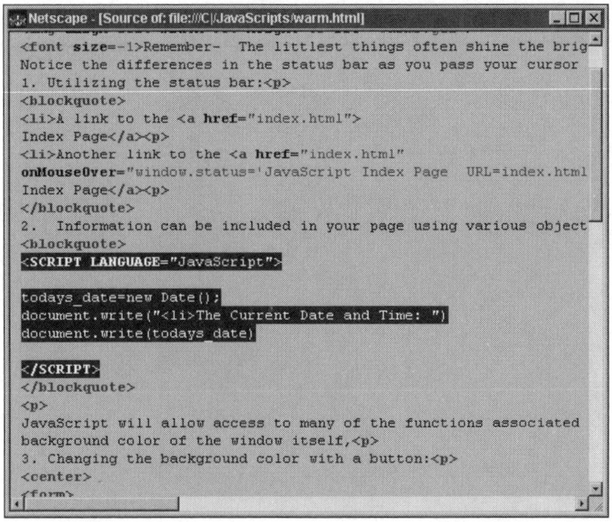

Figure 12-4:
When
copying a
script,
highlight
everything
that comes
between the
opening
<SCRIPT>
and closing
</SCRIPT>
tags
(including
the tags
themselves).

```
Netscape - [Source of: file:///C|/JavaScripts/warm.html]

<font size=-1>Remember-  The littlest things often shine the brig
Notice the differences in the status bar as you pass your cursor
1. Utilizing the status bar:<p>
<blockquote>
<li>A link to the <a href="index.html">
Index Page</a><p>
<li>Another link to the <a href="index.html"
onMouseOver="window.status='JavaScript Index Page   URL=index.html
Index Page</a><p>
</blockquote>
2.  Information can be included in your page using various object
<blockquote>
<SCRIPT LANGUAGE="JavaScript">

todays_date=new Date();
document.write("<li>The Current Date and Time: ")
document.write(todays_date)

</SCRIPT>
</blockquote>
<p>
JavaScript will allow access to many of the functions associated
background color of the window itself,<p>
3. Changing the background color with a button:<p>
<center>
<form>
```

Of course, you could also type the script from scratch. Either way, you must be sure that the opening and closing <SCRIPT> tags are present, along with every line of JavaScript code that comes between them. For example, to add a script that inserts the current date and time in your page, just place the following lines of JavaScript into your HTML source code. Whether you paste them in or type them is your business; just get them in!

```
<SCRIPT LANGUAGE="JavaScript">
<!--
todays_date=new Date();
document.write("The Current Date and Time: ")
document.write(todays_date)
//-->
</SCRIPT>
```

Don't worry if this block of code looks confusing at the moment. For now, the only thing to concern yourself with is adding the script to your HTML source code. Presumably, you already know what the script does — after all, you've gone through the effort of looking through Web pages (or pages on the CD-ROM) to find something that appeals to you. In this case, the script doesn't do anything terribly fancy (see Figure 12-5). All you have to do is paste or type the script into the page and then save the page.

Reload; then reload again

Whereas applets can be frustrating to configure because browsers tend to grab the first set of parameters they see and refuse to accept new ones (see Chapters 6 and 16 for details), you can easily alter a script and immediately

Figure 12-5:
The script in this example displays the current date and time.

see the changes in your script-savvy browser. Applets require that you either quit and rerun the browser or use a few tricks to get the browser to see the changes you make. Viewing your altered scripts, on the other hand, is a simple process:

1. **Make your changes.**

2. **Save the HTML source code by choosing File⇨Save.**

3. **Switch to your browser.**

4. **Choose Reload.**

As long as you've opened the Web page already with your Web browser, pressing the Reload button (discussed in detail in Chapter 3) after saving the changes you've made to the code forces the browser to look at the page anew, reflecting any changes you make to it.

Reloading isn't as critical now as it is when you customize scripts (which the digital "Customizing JavaScripts" chapter provided on this book's accompanying CD-ROM shows you how to do), but it's helpful to know that you don't have to restart your browser to see changes you make to the HTML source code.

To err is human, but your browser is unforgiving

Browsers expect HTML code (and, in the case of JavaScript-savvy browsers, the actual script code) to appear in an exact way. Consequently, you must be terribly precise when entering scripts into your Web pages, which is why I strongly recommend that you copy and paste scripts whenever possible. As soon as you start to type, you run the risk of making a mistake and throwing the browser into a rage.

Watch your comments

Although the addition of comments to your JavaScript code doesn't affect the way a script looks in a JavaScript-savvy browser, chances are pretty high that you'll make a mistake along the way at some point (and mistakes throw browsers into a tantrum). For example, the following script looks okay, at least at first glance:

```
<SCRIPT LANGUAGE="JavaScript">
<!--
todays_date=new Date();
document.write("The Current Date and Time: ")
document.write(todays_date)
//-->
</SCRIPT>
```

But take a closer look at the special comment that begins after the opening `<SCRIPT>` tag. This comment should be `<!--`, not `<!`, which is a common mistake to make if you're accustomed to using `<!` comments in your HTML code. But the browser doesn't think so, and it'll be the first to tell you in no uncertain terms, as Figure 12-6 attests.

Whenever a JavaScript-savvy browser encounters a script that it can't understand or an improperly formatted pair of `<SCRIPT>` tags, it displays an alert box with an error message like the one in Figure 12-6. Although the

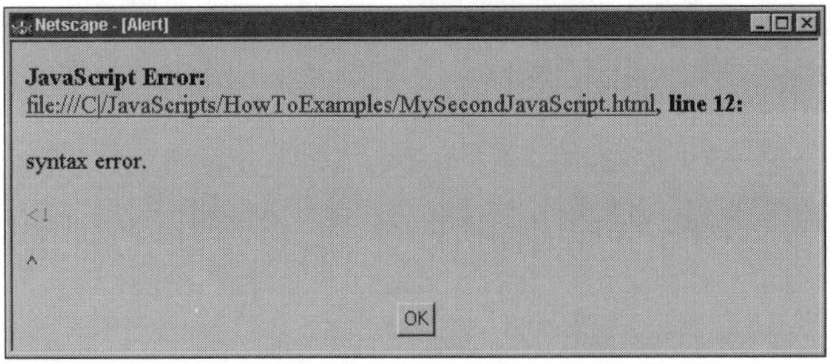

Figure 12-6:
Script-
savvy
browsers
tell you
when they
encounter
incorrect
script code.

Netscape - [Alert]

JavaScript Error:
file:///C|/JavaScripts/HowToExamples/MySecondJavaScript.html, **line 12:**

syntax error.

<!

^

OK

messages your browser displays aren't very helpful in most cases, they give you a rough idea of the problem and the line number in which it was found. This line number corresponds to the entire HTML source code file, not just to the lines of code in the script. This means that you actually have to start at the *top* of your HTML document and count down the number of lines until you reach the one with the problem. (In this example, because the error occurs on line 12 of the HTML file, you count down 12 lines from the top of the file to find the problem.)

When you add comments to scripts, be sure that no lines of JavaScript code are included with the comment. For example, consider the following:

```
<SCRIPT LANGUAGE="JavaScript">
<!-- todays_date=new Date();
document.write("The Current Date and Time: ")
document.write(todays_date)
//-->
</SCRIPT>
```

The preceding script may look okay to humans, but browsers would spit it up faster than last month's leftovers. Because the first line of JavaScript code (todays_date=new Date();) appears on the same line as the first comment (<!--), the browser ignores it. And, because it thinks that every-thing on that line is a comment, your browser doesn't see what you or I can plainly recognize as JavaScript code. As a result, an important line of code is missing from the script — a problem the browser is more than happy to tell you about (see Figure 12-7).

Omitting one or the other comment, typing them incorrectly, or including JavaScript code on the same line causes the browser to lose its mind when it comes upon the script and to complain that something is terribly wrong. The only way to satisfy the browser is to fix the error and reload the page. A simple task, yes, but something you can avoid altogether if you take care to enter the script properly in the first place.

Figure 12-7:
Be careful not to place JavaScript code on the same line as a comment.

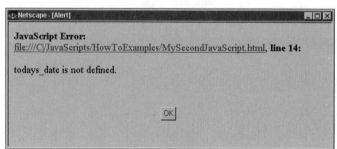

Netscape - [Alert]

JavaScript Error:
file:///C|/JavaScripts/HowToExamples/MySecondJavaScript.html, **line 14:**

todays_date is not defined.

OK

Picky, picky

Browsers aren't just picky about the comments surrounding JavaScript code — they're picky about everything. All browsers, both standard ones and their JavaScript-savvy relatives, expect the text they find inside Web pages to be precise; they're terribly unforgiving.

In both of the following script examples, a simple typing error is the problem. To you and me, typos aren't a big deal. But to the browser, they're a major calamity. If a browser encounters the following snippets of code, it tosses up an alert window telling you that it doesn't have a clue about what's going on. Clearly, you must fix the typing error and reload the page.

Can you tell what's wrong with the following example?

```
<SCIRPT LANGUAGE="JavaScript">
todays_date=new Date();
document.write("The Current Date and Time: ")
document.write(todays_date)
</SCRIPT>
```

The opening <SCRIPT> tag has been misspelled (SCIRPT rather than SCRIPT). Now try this one:

```
<SCRIPT LANGUAGE="JavaScript">
todays_date=new Date();
document.write("The Current Date and Time: ")
document.write(todays_date)
<\SCRIPT>
```

Here, the closing tag has been preceded with a backward slash (\) rather than the required forward slash (/). Again, it's not something you or I would lose our cool over, but the browser goes nuts and tosses up an alert telling you that it can't go on (browsers are very dramatic)! You must fix these types of problems before the script will run properly.

The same goes for the code that falls between the opening <SCRIPT> and closing </SCRIPT> tags; every line must be entered correctly or else the browser panics. In particular, you can't mix uppercase and lowercase letters, unless that's exactly how the script is written. (Note, however, that the <SCRIPT> tags can appear as all uppercase, all lowercase, or a combination of both — I use all uppercase just to make my HTML pages easier to read, although lowercase or a mixture of both is just fine.)

Tricks of the trade

Scripts can be difficult to make sense of, especially when you have several scripts in a page or long scripts that take up more than just a few lines of code. Although you really don't have much control over how long your JavaScript is or how many scripts you need to use on a page, you can always take advantage of the SRC attribute to place scripts in their own files, as described earlier in this chapter (see the sections "The unsolved mystery of JavaScript attributes" and "A source of aggravation" for details), or better yet, you can take advantage of comments to help make sense of the scripts that do appear in your pages.

Because the entire line on which a comment appears is ignored by JavaScript-savvy browsers, you can place additional information on these lines to help you (and others who look at your JavaScript) identify the code. In the JavaScript example that inserts the date and time, for example, you may find it helpful to identify in the first comment line what the script does:

```
<SCRIPT LANGUAGE="JavaScript">
<!--=============== Begin Clock ===============
todays_date=new Date();
document.write("The Current Date and Time: ")
document.write(todays_date)
//=================== End Clock =================-->
</SCRIPT>
```

Because JavaScript-savvy browsers ignore everything on the line that begins with <-,not — and the line that begins with //, you can add text to help separate the block of JavaScript code from the rest of your HTML code. In the preceding example, I've used a bunch of equal signs (=) to set this script apart from any standard HTML code that might surround it. To help identify what the script does, I added a brief but descriptive bit of text (Begin Clock and End Clock).

Of course, you're free to do whatever works for you when you format comments. But whatever you choose, be sure that the first comment begins with <!-- and the last comment begins with // and ends with -->, although you're free to put anything in between these two special comments, as shown in the preceding and following examples:

```
<SCRIPT LANGUAGE="JavaScript">
<!--=========================================
todays_date=new Date();
document.write("The Current Date and Time: ")
document.write(todays_date)
//=========================================-->
</SCRIPT>
```

or

```
<SCRIPT LANGUAGE="JavaScript">
<!--————————
todays_date=new Date();
document.write("The Current Date and Time: ")
document.write(todays_date)
//————————-->
</SCRIPT>
```

Of Form and Function

Very simple scripts, such as the one in the preceding section, are entirely self-contained, but most scripts that do anything worthwhile are composed of several pieces of JavaScript code that work together. The various pieces that may make up a script are called _functions_ because they typically perform a specific task or function.

The main reason for using functions is quite simple: Code that exists inside <SCRIPT> tags is executed only once — when the page loads. Functions, on the other hand, are little bundles of JavaScript code that don't execute until they are called into action. They simply hang out, waiting for the chance to run. Unlike code in <SCRIPT> tags, functions can be executed any number of times by any number of scripts in a page. Think of a function as a reusable chunk of JavaScript code.

Functions are the cornerstone of flexible, robust scripts. When a programmer is perusing a script and comes upon a chunk of code that might be useful at a later time, perhaps by an entirely different script, he or she typically turns it into a function. As a function, the code becomes universally available to all scripts in a page and may be called into action when needed.

A good example of a function is a working clock. Unlike the date-and-time example shown earlier in this chapter, a clock that actually displays the passing of time is a little more complex to create. Whereas the display of the current date and time takes only a few lines of JavaScript code, a clock that keeps track of time takes a great deal more effort. Because this type of clock may be used in a few different places in a page, perhaps simply to show the current date and time or as the basis for a timer ("You've spent 5 minutes at this page — aren't you done yet?!"), it is a good candidate for a function.

When you turn JavaScript code that comprises the clock into a function, any script in the page can use it at any time. You don't have to write a new clock each time you want to use it. With this in mind, you can begin to see how functions save a great deal of time and greatly reduce the number of lines of JavaScript code.

Functions are available only to scripts that exist in the same page. If you want to use a particular function in more than one page, you have to place that function on each page. This placement takes a little extra effort because you have to copy and paste the function into each page that uses it, but it beats adding the entire code each time you want to use the function. Even if a page uses a function 100 times, for example, only one copy of the function needs to be in the page. Of course, 100 *function calls* would then appear in the page, but these are composed of only one line of code, whereas the function itself may take up any number of lines.

So how do you know whether the script you are copying uses a function, and what do you do if it does? Ahh, now you're getting to the heart of the matter.

Does a script use a function?

Figuring out if a script uses a function is easy: Just copy and paste the code between the <SCRIPT> tags as usual and add it to your Web page. Then save the newly altered HTML source code and load it into your browser. If the script doesn't use a function, it will run just fine. If the script makes a function call, however, your browser will have a fit because you didn't copy the function(s) for it to use.

If you copy script that uses a function, your browser displays an error message like the one shown in Figure 12-8. This message just tells you that the script tried to call a function that wasn't in the page or, more accurately, your feeble attempt to pilfer the function failed. The important thing to note is the name of the function displayed in the alert window (display_clock, in this particular case) — it's the function that you must go back and find and then add to your page.

Heads up

Because functions are available to any script in a page, they must appear early in the HTML source code. This placement gives the browser a chance to see the function before it is called and to put the function aside until it is really needed. Script programmers typically place their functions between opening <HEAD> and closing </HEAD> tags, which are standard HTML tags that are among the first to appear in Web page source code.

Figure 12-8:
If a script
calls a
function
that isn't in
the same
page, this
error
message
tells you so.

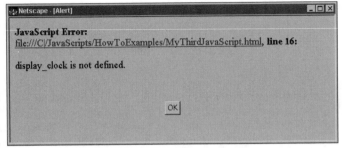

Because functions must be defined before the scripts that use them, look for functions at the top of the Web page. Alternatively, you can search for functions by name by using the browser's Find command (discussed earlier in this chapter). However you go about finding them, you surely will recognize functions when you run into them. They're hard to miss because the first word of a function is actually *function!*

The clock example I've been talking about in this chapter isn't a make-believe function that I concocted merely to illustrate a point. Heavens, no — the clock function is very real, and even provided in the Cool Beans! directory of the CD-ROM that comes with this book (see Appendix A for details on locating files on this CD-ROM). To add the clock to your own Web page, copy the following function:

```
function display_clock(){
document.write('<font color=blue size=-1><form
          name=current_time>Current Date ')
document.write('&amp; Time: <input name=date size=20
          value=""</form></font>')
begin(document.current_time)
}
```

But take a closer look at the JavaScript code that makes up this function. See anything interesting? If this is your first encounter with JavaScript, it all looks pretty strange, but what's going on here is significant. The last line of code inside the *function block* (the chunk of code that makes up a function, which is contained inside the opening and closing curly braces {}) is calling another function. You may not be able to make much sense of this code now, but all you really need to understand is that functions can call other functions. In this case, the display_clock function calls another function named begin.

So how do you know which script functions contained in a Web page to copy and which to ignore? In all honesty, you don't. The best you can do is find the function you think is needed and copy the entire amount of code it contains. You should copy every single function that happens to reside within the same opening and closing <SCRIPT> tags as the one you were originally looking for.

Because functions are created with JavaScript, they must be contained inside opening and closing <SCRIPT> tags, as the preceding functions illustrate. You can think of functions as reusable scripts because that's really what they are. As such, all you have to do is copy the entire chunk of code — everything between the opening and closing <SCRIPT> tags, including the tags themselves — and paste it into your own HTML code. By transferring the whole thing — lock, stock, and barrel — you get everything you need.

For example, if you see the display_clock function within a page of the CD-ROM that comes with this book (or in the wild, as the case may be), the function likely appears in the HTML source code of a page as follows:

```
<SCRIPT>
<!--
var current_time
function begin(x){
count=x; time_out=window.setTimeout("display_date()",1000)
}
function display_date() {
count.date.value=new Date();
        time_out=window.setTimeout("display_date()",1000)
}
function display_clock(){
document.write('<font color=blue size=-1><form
        name=current_time>Current Date ')
document.write('&amp; Time: <input name=date size=20
        value=""</form></font>')
begin(document.current_time)
}
//-->
</SCRIPT>
```

Figure 12-9 shows the preceding chunk of JavaScript code as it appears on one of the pages in the CookBook directory of the CD-ROM that comes with this book (see Appendix A for details on locating scripts on this CD-ROM).

Function names don't have to be all lowercase, nor must they contain an underscore (_), as the ones in this example do. Programmers are free to name their functions whatever they want (within reason), so you find function names of all shapes and sizes. Although this programmer chose to

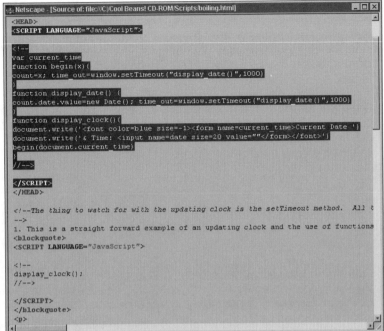

```
Netscape - [Source of: file:///C|/Cool Beans! CD-ROM/Scripts/boiling.html]
<HEAD>
<SCRIPT LANGUAGE="JavaScript">

<!--
var current_time
function begin(x){
count=x; time_out=window.setTimeout("display_date()",1000)
}
function display_date() {
count.date.value=new Date(); time_out=window.setTimeout("display_date()",1000)
}
function display_clock(){
document.write('<font color=blue size=-1><form name=current_time>Current Date ')
document.write('& Time: <input name=date size=20 value=""</form></font>')
begin(document.current_time)
}
//-->

</SCRIPT>
</HEAD>

<!--The thing to watch for with the updating clock is the setTimeout method.  All t
-->
1. This is a straight forward example of an updating clock and the use of functions
<blockquote>
<SCRIPT LANGUAGE="JavaScript">

<!--
display_clock();
//-->

</SCRIPT>
</blockquote>
<p>
```

Figure 12-9:
You usually can find functions at the top of the Web page HTML code, often inside `<HEAD>` tags.

name the various clock functions `display_clock`, `display_date`, and `begin`, another programmer may have chosen entirely different names, such as `Clock`, `Date`, and `Start`.

Adding functions to your own pages

After you find the functions a script uses, just copy and paste them into your own page. The easiest way to do this is to copy the entire chunk of code in which the function appears (as described in the preceding section) and paste it into the `<HEAD>` tags of your own page. If your page doesn't have `<HEAD>` tags, you can either add them or simply place the functions somewhere at the top of your page. As long as the functions appear before they are used, they will work just fine.

Keep in mind that functions can call other functions, which means that you have to copy *all* the functions triggered by a script. In the clock example, you need to copy three functions. Some scripts use fewer functions, some more. Although the three functions in this example all appear inside the same pair of `<SCRIPT>` tags, they didn't have to — each could have been inside its own set of `<SCRIPT>` tags or even intermingled with other functions that have nothing to do with the clock. As a result, you must track down all the functions a script triggers and add them to your page, even if they don't appear inside the same set of `<SCRIPT>` tags.

TIP

If you don't like reading through the code of each function to see whether it relies on other functions, you can always let your browser tell you which functions are missing. Simply copy the functions you think a script needs, save the changes to your HTML code, and then reload the page. If a function is missing, the browser tells you so. Then you can go back and look for it by name.

After you paste a function (or set of functions) into your Web page HTML code, you can call that function from within any other `<SCRIPT>` tag. To call the JavaScript clock function used in the examples in this section, for example, all you need is the following chunk of code:

```
<SCRIPT LANGUAGE="JavaScript">
<!--
display_clock();
//-->
</SCRIPT>
```

This simple little script calls the `display_clock` function and displays it on the Web page, as shown in Figure 12-10. Because the clock is a function, you can call it anywhere in the page you want the clock to appear.

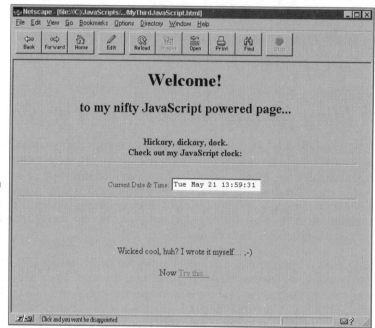

Figure 12-10:
This clock comes to you courtesy of a JavaScript function.

Chapter 13

Combining Applets and Scripts

- -

In This Chapter

▶ Weaving applets and scripts into the same page

▶ Executing applets from scripts

▶ Synchronizing applets and scripts

▶ Sniffing around browser versions

▶ Putting applets, scripts, and beans together

- -

lthough Java applets and JavaScript are two different technologies, they can peacefully coexist in Web pages:

✔ Applets bring your pages to life with animation, sound, and other forms of executable content.

✔ Scripts give you the ultimate control when it comes to handling user interaction.

Alone, each of these technologies greatly enhances standard Web pages. Together, however, they usher in a completely new generation of Web pages: finely tuned, totally interactive content — true multimedia on the Web.

With standard HTML, you can control certain aspects of an applet's behavior, depending on how the applet is designed, by using parameters (see Chapters 8 and 9 for details). Although using applet parameters help you to customize the images and sounds that your applet uses, this approach is rather limited when you want to create dynamic Web content. For the most part, applets are a *plug-and-play* technology: You plug 'em into your pages, and they play (run) whenever someone loads the page.

Scripts, on the other hand, aren't as powerful as applets when it comes to handling animation and sound and creating whizzy, compelling content. In fact, I have yet to see a script anywhere that is nearly as slick as some of the better applets on the Web. But JavaScript excels in a very different way — flexibility. Because scripts are little programs that you can modify to suit your needs, you have the power to customize them in ways you can't customize applets. On the off chance that you can't find a script that comes close to what you need, you can always create one from scratch.

Combined, applets and scripts deliver enormous power and flexibility to your Web pages. You have all the thrill-a-minute content that applets deliver integrated with the sophisticated user interaction that JavaScript offers. These two technologies have just recently been introduced to each other, but they promise to remain fast and strong friends.

Coexisting in Cyberspace

Using applets and scripts in the same page is a breeze — it doesn't require anything special. You merely weave the appropriate tags into your HTML code (using <APPLET> tags to add applets and <SCRIPT> tags to add scripts, as explained in Chapters 7 and 12, respectively).

Scripts and applets, side by side

The Web page in Figure 13-1 uses two scripts and one applet. The scrolling text immediately above the Christmas tree image was created using a script, as was the date-and-time text in the lower-right corner of the image. The image, on the other hand, is displayed by using the LivingLinks applet, which is included on this book's companion CD-ROM for you to use in your own pages.

Figure 13-1:
This Web page uses both scripts and applets to keep visitors abreast of what's going on at the site.

Page courtesy of Toys For Tots (www.toysfortots.org)

If HTML is a nightmare to you, take a deep breath, grab the smelling salts, and head to Chapters 7 and 12 to read more about <APPLET> and <SCRIPT> tags. If you're not comfy dealing with standard HTML, you can turn to Chapter 5 or get on the horn and order a copy of *HTML For Dummies,* 3rd Edition, by Ed Tittel and Steve James (IDG Books Worldwide, Inc.).

To really get the most from applets and scripts, you should know enough about HTML to understand what's going on here.

Because browsers process (or *execute*) tags in the order in which they appear in HTML code, the preceding chunk of code ensures that the page first displays the scrolling text script, followed by the applet, and then the date-and-time script.

JavaScript functions are an exception to the rule that browsers execute tags in the order in which they appear in the code. JavaScript functions are never executed unless they're called from inside a <SCRIPT> tag or in response to an event (see Chapter 12 for details). Even though the scrolling text functions appear at the top of this HTML code, they aren't executed until the browser later encounters the following line of JavaScript code:

```
scroll_text()
```

Executing applets with scripts

The capability to run applets and scripts side by side, as illustrated in the preceding example, is all well and good, but the real kicker is when scripts actually execute and dynamically control applets. Yes, you can design your scripts to execute applets in response to user interaction. You can even create scripts that finely control the various aspects of running applets, changing at will how your pages look and act and how they respond to user activity, giving your site the highest degree of interactivity possible on the Web today.

For example, consider the following snippet of HTML code. It doesn't look like much, but it packs quite a punch:

```
<FORM>
Would you like to see a neat Java applet?
<input type="button" name="button_one" value="Yes!"
onClick="window.open('animation.html', 'new_window',
          'width=315,height=175')">
</FORM>
```

The preceding code creates an input form consisting of nothing more than the text "Would you like to see a neat Java applet?" followed by a Yes! button (see Figure 13-2).

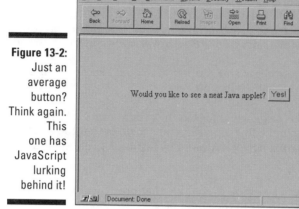

This is no ordinary form, mind you; it's a JavaScript-powered form. The JavaScript used in this page is really an *event trigger*. When the user clicks on the Yes! button ("onClick"), an event is triggered, which in turn opens a new window (window.open) that displays a Web page (animation.html) containing both JavaScript code and an animation applet. This Web page, although interactive in real life, is frozen in time in Figure 13-3.

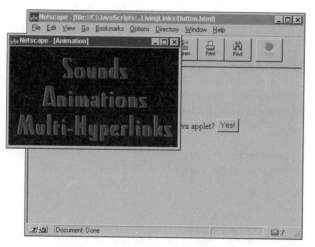

The script in this new page sets the background color to black while the applet runs through a slick little animation. The HTML code is pretty simple. Here's the complete HTML source code for the entire page:

```
<HTML>
<TITLE>Animation</TITLE>

<SCRIPT>
document.bgColor = "black"
</SCRIPT>

<APPLET CODE=LivingLinks WIDTH=299 HEIGHT=155>
<PARAM NAME=image VALUE="images/features.gif">
<PARAM NAME=effect VALUE="RedBlueEffect">
<PARAM NAME=speed VALUE="15">
<PARAM NAME=backgroundColor VALUE="black">
<PARAM NAME=soundDir VALUE="audio/">
<PARAM NAME=inSound VALUE="bongoDrums.au">
<PARAM NAME=inSoundLoop VALUE="yes">
</APPLET>
</HTML>
```

Seeing this page in action is cool, but the real point here is that an applet is executed in response to an event. Although this example executes when a user clicks a button, you can use many other events to trigger the execution of applets and script functions.

For a complete bells-and-whistles tour of the many ways you can combine Java applets with scripts, point your Web browser to www.mantiscorp.com/javascript. There, you can see the end result of such a combination and copy the code for your own use.

Synchronizing Your Applets and Scripts

Figure 13-1, near the beginning of this chapter, shows an example of a scrolling-text script that is entirely independent of the applet beneath it. In fact, the snippet of HTML source code that created this display is just that: Two scripts and an applet completely independent of each other.

Even the code example in the preceding section (the Yes! button) has nothing to do with true communication between scripts and applets. In that example, a script merely creates a new window and tells the browser to display the animation.html file inside it. This file happens to contain a script and an applet, which the browser displays in the window just as if the page had been accessed directly with your browser instead of by way of a hyperlink. No real interaction takes place between the script and the applet.

What if you want your applets and scripts to work in tandem? For example, what if you want a script's scrolling text to correspond to the applet's image below it? Suppose that you want a half-dozen or so different images displayed on-screen, one after the other, while a text message about the current image scrolls above it. When your forest-ranger applet runs, for example, you want the corresponding text (Where's Yogi?) to scroll above it. In short, you want the applet and script to be *synchronized* with each other.

Unfortunately, many applets and scripts can't easily be synchronized — at least not today. In the future, when more applets are designed with JavaScript in mind, things will change. The LivingLinks applet provided on the CD-ROM that comes with this book, for example, is fully scriptable. It's designed specifically for use with JavaScript, and has a great number of scriptable features. LivingLinks, however, is an exception to the rule; in many circumstances, you have only two choices for synchronizing applets and scripts: Script it or hack it.

When the original crop of Java-savvy browsers hit the Web, scripts didn't know diddly about applets. Scripts running in these older browsers, millions of which are still used to navigate the Web today, know exactly what the user is doing and what's going on with the Web page as far as standard HTML is concerned (background and text colors, what hyperlinks are in the page, what URLs have been visited, where the user came from before stopping by, and stuff like that), but they don't have a clue about applets. Now, however, JavaScript is fully aware of applets and is capable of sending them messages that control their behavior. As long as the scripts and applets are viewed using a browser that knows how to deal with the more advanced capabilities of scripts and applets (such as Netscape Navigator 4.0 or Microsoft Internet Explorer 4.0) and the applet itself is scriptable (such as LivingLinks), you can weave pages that are as dynamic and interactive as the best traditional (non-Web) software products available today.

Specifically, you can write scripts that execute, control, and terminate applets. The applets in a Web page become, in essence, objects that scripts can communicate with, just as scripts communicate with any other object (see the link to Customizing JavaScripts that is provided on this book's companion CD-ROM for information about JavaScript objects). When this communication occurs, JavaScript becomes the coach and the applets act as players under its control, as explained in detail in Chapter 11.

Are you talking to me? Huh? Are you talking to me?!

Even though images of Robert DeNiro always run through my mind when I think about scripts talking to applets, the interaction is relatively painless, assuming that you're running a newer browser, such as Netscape Navigator 4.0 or Microsoft Internet Explorer 4.0, with both Java and JavaScript capabilities enabled as described in Chapter 3.

The trick to getting scripts to talk to applets lies in the `<APPLET>` tag — specifically in the `NAME` attribute (see Chapter 5 for details). Using this attribute, you can give the applets in your page a name that scripts can use to talk with them. For example, the following `<APPLET>` tag is exactly the same as the one shown earlier in this chapter (in the section "Executing applets with scripts"), with the sole exception of the `NAME` attribute:

```
<APPLET CODE=LivingLinks WIDTH=299 HEIGHT=155 NAME=Bob>
<PARAM NAME=image VALUE="images/features.gif">
<PARAM NAME=effect VALUE="RedBlueEffect">
<PARAM NAME=speed VALUE="15">
<PARAM NAME=backgroundColor VALUE="black">
<PARAM NAME=soundDir VALUE="audio/">
<PARAM NAME=inSound VALUE="bongoDrums.au">
<PARAM NAME=inSoundLoop VALUE="yes">
</APPLET>
</HTML>
```

In this example, the applet has been named *Bob*. Now that it has a name, Bob can be controlled by a script. Just place the Bob object in a JavaScript variable — a name that you use in JavaScript to identify a piece of information, in this case an applet — and you can then use and abuse the applet. In the following line of code, because I've created a script variable named `bobTheApplet` to which I've assigned the applet object, I can use the variable to communicate with the applet:

```
var bobTheApplet = document.Bob
```

Not so stinkin' fast!

Armed with the most current crop of Java-savvy browsers and the preceding information, you're set to synchronize your scripts and applets, right? Well, there *is* one more little detail — you have to know what messages, or commands, the applet understands. Just as you must know what parameters an applet accepts to configure the applet properly, you must also know what commands the applet uses to communicate with scripts. Finding these details is a no-brainer; if an applet can communicate with scripts (that is, if it's a *scriptable* applet), all the information you need is included with the documentation that comes with the applet (see Chapters 7, 8, and 9 for details on applet documentation).

The messages that an object understands are also known as *methods;* you *invoke the method* of an object when you send it a message. Java programmers may be interested to know that JavaScript can access all public methods of an applet, whether or not the applet was designed to be scriptable. You can therefore invoke any public method of an applet, whether or not the developer of that applet intended it to be used with JavaScript. Of course, if an applet's methods aren't documented, you are in the dark regardless — you can't invoke methods unless you know their names!

Even though you can control all applets to a certain degree by using scripts (you can execute and terminate them by using the standard `start()` and `stop()` messages supported by all applets), applets designed with JavaScript in mind from the onset are infinitely more flexible. These applets will do your bidding, provided that you write the script properly!

With JavaScript, you can access an applet's scriptable messages whenever you want. You can then orchestrate how an applet behaves and finely tune its behavior in response to a Webber's behavior. You're the puppet master; you call all the shots. For example, to change the speed at which the LivingLinks images are displayed, just insert this line of JavaScript:

```
bobTheApplet.setSpeed(100)
```

Or to stop playing sounds that may be pumping away, use this line of JavaScript:

```
bobTheApplet.stopSounds()
```

Depending on what messages an applet understands, the possibilities are truly staggering. With the right applet and a dash or two of JavaScript, your pages have the potential to become as sophisticated and powerful as any commercial piece of software on the computer store shelf, if not more so. LivingLinks alone, for example, can create sophisticated multimedia pages that include interactive games, virtual worlds, interactive music videos, and other wildly impressive features.

To see what folks are doing with LivingLinks and JavaScript and to get ideas and code for your own site, point your Web browser to `www.mantiscorp.com/javascript`

Even though scriptable applets are wonderful and the Web will soon be full of them, not all applets are designed to work with JavaScript. As a result, you'll probably have to synchronize your scripts and applets the old fashioned way: by hacking a solution any which way you can. Sometimes, however, depending on what you're trying to do, even scriptable applets won't do the trick.

TECHNICAL STUFF

Arguing with your messages

Many messages that you send to objects require parameters, or *arguments*. If a message requires no arguments, you send it by using dot notation and by including an empty set of parentheses at the end:

`object.message()`

When a message requires arguments, as many do, you must supply the arguments inside the parentheses in whatever order the message dictates. Furthermore, the arguments you supply with a message must be in the proper form (or *data type*, to use the official term). For example, messages that expect *Boolean arguments* (a "true" or "false" value) require that you supply the proper Boolean values when calling them. Some messages expect "true" or "false" Boolean values, and others (such as LivingLinks) expect "yes" or "no" values instead. Depending on the message, either of the following Boolean arguments may be correct:

`object.message("true")`

`object.message("yes")`

If you're dealing with a message that expects an integer argument, on the other hand, you must supply an integer (a whole number) between the parentheses. Here's an example of a message with an integer as an argument:

`object.message(143)`

Likewise, you must give a string to messages that require a string argument:

`object.message("Are you lookin' at me?")`

Some messages take multiple arguments, in which case you must be careful to supply each one in the proper order. If, for example, a message requires a string, integer, and Boolean, in that order and separated with commas, you must supply them accordingly:

`object.message("Are you lookin' at me?", 23546, "true")`

When supplying arguments, never put spaces between the object and the dot, the dot and the message, or the message and the first argument parenthesis:

Correct:

`object.message(124)`

Incorrect:

`object. message(124)`

`object .message(124)`

`object.message (124)`

Consider, for example, an attempt to synchronize the LivingLinks applet with the scrolling-text script, as discussed earlier in this chapter. A problem still exists, even though LivingLinks is indeed scriptable: None of the messages that LivingLinks understands helps you synchronize the images it displays with the text that you want to correspond with those images! The problem is straightforward: The LivingLinks applet is designed to display images used in an animation one right after the other, resulting in the illusion of movement. You can slow the animation down by setting the speed parameter to 1 (or calling setSpeed(1) with JavaScript), but you can't stop the applet from moving to the next image of the animation entirely and then control when the next image will be displayed. If you could, things would be a little easier. You would simply time how long each text item takes to scroll across the screen and then go to the next image when the time is up. But you can't.

There's no easy way to resolve this sticky synchronization problem, but you can hack a reasonable solution that will keep most folks satisfied. And hacking, as you'll soon learn, is something you'll probably come to rely on if you plan to live on the cutting edge of Web development.

Getting started on the same foot

The applets and scripts on your page are on different schedules from the get-go. Because applets typically use images and sounds, they take much longer to load than do scripts (which are nothing but plain text). As a result, the scrolling-text script in the preceding example loads and executes right off the bat, while the LivingLinks applet is still loading images. You need to postpone the scrolling text until the LivingLinks applet has finished loading, but because you have no way to find out for sure when the applet has finished loading, all you can do is make a reasonable guess. But even the best guess doesn't always work, because different people connect to the Web at different speeds. What may take two minutes to load on one person's computer may take only a second or two on another computer.

For starters, you can provide different Web pages for different connection speeds — let visitors to your site choose which speed to view pages: People with fast connections will, naturally, choose the option that gives them the information with little or no delay; people with slower connections, on the other hand, will choose a slower route.

Of course, this isn't a very elegant solution. It not only disrupts the flow of your site by requiring Webbers to make a choice when they enter but also requires you to maintain more pages than you would need to otherwise. But even though this solution isn't ideal, plenty of sites already ask you if you want to go *graphics-heavy* or *graphics-light*. This is just another way of asking at what speed you're connecting.

Staying in synch

At the heart of the problem of synchronizing applets and scripts is that many applets don't allow you to find out when they're finished loading images. For those that do let you know, your synchronization job is practically done; first, you consult the applet's documentation to find out the name of the JavaScript method used to tell you when the images have finished loading, then you simply write a little script that hangs out until that method indicates that the image(s) is loaded and then kicks off the scrolling text. You just have to insert some artificial delays into your scrolling-text script.

For starters, you need to postpone the scrolling for some predetermined amount of time. This part is a cinch — JavaScript has a built-in function you can call to postpone scrolling. Simply call setTimeout, and tell it which function to execute when the time you give it expires (scroll_Text, in this case). But don't mistake the timer value you provide as representing seconds; setTimeout expects the number you give it to be in *milliseconds!* You have to experiment with the values to get the proper timing mix, but the idea is simple. Rather than call scroll_text immediately, you call it after a certain amount of time has passed:

```
<SCRIPT>
<!--————— Call Scrolling Text function ————
setTimeout("scroll_text()", 1000)
//—————————————————————————————-->
</SCRIPT>
```

Thanks to setTimeout, you can postpone the scrolling text for a predetermined amount of time. But there's still the problem of not being able to synchronize the messages that scroll by with the images that appear underneath it. Suppose that you must synchronize three images with three different text messages. If you aren't worried about synchronizing everything, you can just scroll one message right after another (assuming that you are using the scroll_it script — see the "Customizing JavaScript" link that appears on the CD-ROM that accompanies this book for details on using this script):

```
<SCRIPT>
<!--————— SCROLLING TEXT FUNCTION ————
var display_text = "This is message 1 - it says something
                about the first image..."
+ "This is message 2 - it says something about the second
                image..."
+ "This is message 3 - it says something about the third
                image..."

var out = " "; var place = 60;
var meter;

function scroll_text(){
for (meter = 0; meter < place; meter++){
out += " "
}

if (place >= 0)
out += display_text
else
out = display_text.substring(-place,display_text.length)
```

(continued)

(continued)

```
document.scroll_form.field.value = out
out = " "
place—
if (place < -(display_text.length)){
place = 60
}
setTimeout('scroll_text()', 100)
}
//——— End Scrolling Text >———-->
</SCRIPT>
```

This <SCRIPT> tag works just fine if you don't mind the text scrolling by faster than the images. To ensure the images appear in sync with their appropriate message, however, you have to do one of two things:

- Speed up the animation
- Slow down the scrolling text

Although you can speed up LivingLinks, what about applets that don't support this luxury? In this example, you can do two different things to slow down the scroll_text script:

- Tweak the setTimeout('scroll_text()', 100) line of code to provide a larger time-out value
- Insert *dead space* between the individual text messages

Slowing down the text by using setTimeout may do the trick. But what if, to stay synchronized with the images, you have to slow down the text so much that the entire scrolling effect is destroyed? Text that inches sluggishly across the screen looks pretty silly. In this case, you may choose instead to insert a little time interval between each message that scrolls by, without changing the speed of the scrolling text:

```
var display_text = "This is message 1 - it says something
               about the first image..."
+ "                                              "
+ "                                              "
+ "This is message 2 - it says something about the second
               image..."
+ "                                              "
+ "                                              "
+ "This is message 3 - it says something about the third
               image..."
+ "                                              "
+ "                                              "
```

By simply inserting spaces between the messages, you ensure that the whole scrolling process takes longer. In the preceding example, the first message scrolls by, followed by a bunch of spaces (which look like nothing at all to the user — it looks as though the first message has just gone off the screen as the Webber waits for the next one to come by), and then the second message scrolls by. After that one, another set of spaces scroll by, and then the third and final message comes out. And, just to keep the timing of the whole thing consistent, more spaces scroll by before the entire process is repeated.

No, this may not be the most desirable way to get the job done; life would be much easier if you could use JavaScript to find out when the applet finishes loading and then begin scrolling the text. But in many cases, applets aren't scriptable, so you must find a way to use what you do have (JavaScript) to get the job done. That's hacking for you!

If you're not in the mood to type the scripts that appear in this chapter (I don't blame you), then check out the CD-ROM that comes with this book. All the scripts found in this chapter are also included on your CD-ROM, so you can copy/paste them directly into your own Web page in a jiff. For details, check out Appendix A.

Bait and Switch: Browser Sniffing

Because JavaScript isn't fully compatible with JScript, there's a good chance that a feature of JavaScript that works like a charm under Netscape Navigator, fails miserably under Microsoft Internet Explorer, or vice versa. At best, you get an error dialog box explaining the problem. At worst, your browser may freeze or crash, and you even may need to restart your machine.

Sniff, Sniff. . .

There is a solution, however, to the JavaScript/JScript incompatibility problem — your scripts can *sniff out* each browser it encounters and supply each browser with the appropriate type of script that it requires. You can write a bit of script that detects — sniffs out — the make, model, and version of browser being used, and serves up an appropriate *real* script (one that does something interesting or useful, not mere sniffing), contingent on the information your script sniffs out.

Of course, the trick is to create your sniffer script using 100 percent compatible JavaScript, because you don't want it to break under any browser. But that's no problem, as the following basic sniffer script illustrates:

```
<SCRIPT LANGUAGE="JavaScript">
<!--
var browserType = navigator.appName;
var browserVersion = navigator.appVersion.substring(0,5);

document.write("You're running: " + browserType + " version
        " + browserVersion);
//-->
</SCRIPT>
```

This script doesn't do anything useful, really, except detect the make, model, and version number of the currently visiting browser and then display that information on the browser window, as shown in Figure 13-4. But that information is what you're after. With a little spit and polish, you can actually turn the preceding bare-bones sniffer into something worthwhile:

```
<SCRIPT LANGUAGE="JavaScript">
<!--
var browserType = navigator.appName;
var browserVersion = navigator.appVersion.substring(0,1);

if (browserType == "Microsoft Internet Explorer") {
  if (browserVersion >= "4"){
    document.write ("You're using a new version of Internet
          Explorer!");
  }else{
    document.write ("You're using an old version of
          Internet Explorer.");
    }
}

if (browserType == "Netscape"){
  if (browserVersion >= "4"){
    document.write ("You're using a new version of
          Netscape!");
  }else{
    document.write ("You're using an old version of
          Internet Explorer.");
    }
}

if ((browserType != "Netscape") && (browserType !=
        "Microsoft Internet Explorer")) {
  document.write ("You're NOT running Navigator OR Ex-
          plorer!!");
```

```
}

//-->
</SCRIPT>
```

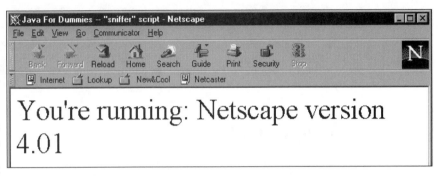

Figure 13-4:
The
bare-bones
sniffer
script
merely
displays the
visiting
browser's
make,
model, and
version.

Building on the basic sniffer script, this example actually checks to see what
type of browser the Webber is using, and then displays an appropriate
message. The first important thing this script does is test the `browserType`
variable to find out whether Netscape Navigator or Internet Explorer is
being used — if so, the `browserVersion` variable is then tested to see if the
browser's actual version number is equal to or greater than four
(`browserVersion >= "4"`). The results of this test determine what text
the script will display in the browser. This assumes, of course, that the
Webber is actually using either Internet Explorer or Navigator. If not, the text
`"You're NOT running Navigator OR Explorer!!"` is displayed, and no
attempt is made to determine the actual browser version.

With the previous bit of script, you can determine exactly what type of
browser is being used, and serve up custom content based on that knowledge. All you have to do is place the JavaScript code inside the `if ( )`
clause that identifies the Netscape Navigator browser, and your JScript code
inside the `else ()` clause. In this way, Netscape Navigator receives only 100
percent pure JavaScript code, and Microsoft Internet Explorer is fed 100
percent JScript code, like so:

```
<SCRIPT LANGUAGE="JavaScript">
<!--
var browserType = navigator.appName;

if (browserType == "Microsoft Internet Explorer") {
```

(continued)

(continued)

```
   JSCRIPT GOES HERE!
}


if (browserType == "Netscape"){
   JAVASCRIPT GOES HERE!
}


//-->
</SCRIPT>
```

It's just what the doctor ordered when dealing with sticky script that isn't entirely compatible between the two browsers.

Sniffing out JARs

Similar to the sniffer scripts in the previous section, you should try to support both the older and newer browsers when it comes to using JARs (Java Archives).

Consider the following script-sniffing example:

```
<SCRIPT LANGUAGE="JavaScript">
<!--
var browserType = navigator.appName;
var browserVersion = navigator.appVersion.substring(0,1);

var jarString = 'Supports Jar Files';

var originalString = 'Does Not Support Jar Files';

if (browserType == "Netscape" || "Microsoft Internet
         Explorer"){
   if (browserVersion >= "4"){
      document.write (jarString);
      }else{
      document.write (originalString);
   }
}else{
   document.write (originalString);
}
//-->
</SCRIPT>
```

This sniffer script still doesn't do much — it decides only whether the browser in question is Netscape Navigator or Microsoft Internet Explorer, and whether the browser is new enough to support JARs. If it is new enough, the string `Supports Jar Files` is displayed in the browser. If it's either of the two browsers, but not current enough to deal with JAR files, the string `Does Not Support Jar Files` is displayed. If the browser is not Navigator or Internet Explorer, nothing is displayed.

Keeping the fact that older Java-savvy browser don't support JAR files in mind, consider the following sniffer script created specifically to support both Java 1.0 and Java 1.1 browsers. Using both versions of the Marquee applet that are supplied on this book's CD-ROM, this script dynamically serves up the appropriate <APPLET> tag depending on what browser comes a-calling:

```
<SCRIPT LANGUAGE="JavaScript">
<!--
var browserType = navigator.appName;
var browserVersion = navigator.appVersion.substring(0,1);

var jarString = '<APPLET CODE=Marquee
         archive=MarqueeClasses.jar WIDTH=400
         HEIGHT=34><param NAME=shift VALUE=2><param
         NAME=delay VALUE=20><param NAME=font_size
         VALUE=24><param NAME=font_italic
         VALUE=yes><param NAME=font_bold VALUE=yes><param
         NAME=back_color VALUE="255 255 240"><param
         NAME=text_color VALUE="72 61 139"><param
         NAME=marquee VALUE="Hello! Welcome to my JAR-
         POWERED homepage...""></APPLET>';

var originalString = '<APPLET CODE=Marquee WIDTH=493
         HEIGHT=26><PARAM NAME=font_face
         VALUE=TimesRoman><PARAM NAME=font_size
         VALUE=22><PARAM NAME=font_italic
         VALUE=yes><PARAM NAME=text_color VALUE="255 0
         0"><PARAM NAME=marquee VALUE="Mantis Marquee: Am
         I scrolling, or what? Wheeeee!! "><B> This line
         is alternate HTML — if you can read this, you
         don't have a Java-savvy browser!</B></APPLET>';

if (browserType == "Netscape" || "Microsoft Internet
         Explorer"){
    if (browserVersion >= "4"){
      document.write (jarString);
      }else{
```

(continued)

(continued)

```
        document.write (originalString);
    }
}else{
    document.write (originalString);
}
//-->
</SCRIPT>
```

In this example, I've crammed two complete ⟨APPLET⟩ tags into one sniffer script! The entire ⟨APPLET⟩ tag for the JAR version of Marquee is stuffed into the jarString variable, while the original non-JAR ⟨APPLET⟩ tag is stored inside the originalString variable. The appropriate variable is then dynamically sent to the browser using the document.write() command depending on what version the browser is. The result, as you can see in Figures 13-5 and 13-6, is dramatic: Browsers receive only the ⟨APPLET⟩

Figure 13-5:
Java 1.1 browsers can be dynamically supplied with a JAR-style applet.

Figure 13-6:
Original Java 1.0 browsers must be sent traditional (non-JAR) applets.

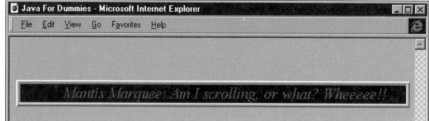

tag that they can understand. No more, no less.

Because Version 4.0 of both Netscape Navigator and Internet Explorer are the only browsers in widespread usage that support JAR files, I've only accommodated them. However, if I wanted to support HotJava as well, I could just as easily have modified the actual "sniffer" portion of the script to look like this:

```
<SCRIPT LANGUAGE="JavaScript">
<!--
var browserType = navigator.appName;

var browserVersion = navigator.appVersion.substring(0,5);

document.write("You're running: " + browserType + " version
           " + browserVersion);

var jarString = 'Supports Jar Files';

var originalString = 'Does Not Support Jar Files';

if (browserType == "Netscape" || "Microsoft Internet
           Explorer"){
   if (browserVersion >= "4"){
      document.write (jarString);
      }else{
      document.write (originalString);
   }
}else{
   document.write (originalString);
}
//-->
</SCRIPT>
```

If you want to find out more about JavaScript and JScript and their incompatibles, I strongly suggest going to the source. Turn to Netscape's own JavaScript developer's guide (developer.netscape.com) to find out all the grisly details of this language, or to Microsoft's JScript site to learn about that scripting language. You may also want to take a peek at Chapter 16 of this book, which lists the best JavaScript sites around. Finally, you might considering sashaying on over to your nearest bookstore and leafing through a copy of *JavaScript for Dummies,* 2nd Edition by Emily Vander Veer (IDG Books Worldwide, Inc.). Who knows? You might even walk out with it (just be sure to pay first).

Applets and Scripts and Beans, Oh My!

Although it's cool and very useful to sniff browsers in order to customize the type of scripts and applets the respective browsers receive, there is another potential use for sniffing just around the corner: JavaBeans.

JavaBeans, or simply *beans,* as they're often called, is a new feature introduced in Java 1.1 that has yet to be fully incorporated into today's Java-savvy browsers. Beans are actually software components written in the Java language that are much like little, self-contained applets. The big hoopla surrounding beans lies in their capability to be easily reused in a variety of ways — beans are essentially software Legos that developers can string together in a great many ways for a great many purposes. Instead of being forced to write a custom program to perform a specific act, a developer can tap into the power of a pre-written bean to do the task (should one exist that actually performs the desired function).

JavaBeans are just getting started, though. By the time you read this, scores of beans will be available, free for the taking, or for a small charge. Unfortunately, they likely will be of use only to software developers, because beans aren't meant to be woven directly into Web pages. At least not yet.

In time, browser vendors may introduce special scripting capabilities into their products that will allow you, the Web developer, to take advantage of beans in the same way that professional software developers do. Wouldn't it be great to assemble your own applets by using nothing more than plain HTML and a smidgen or two of JavaScript? While tools abound that let software developers do just that, you will have to wait a while longer before beans are as easy to assemble into custom applets and weave into Web pages as are plain old-fashioned applets and scripts today.

If you want to get your hands on some of the more powerful JavaBeans tools now available, check out `splash.javasoft.com/beans/tools.html`. There, you will find a comprehensive listing of tools that are designed to give you point-and-click access to JavaBeans.

Part IV
The Part of Tens

The 5th Wave   By Rich Tennant

"We met on the Internet and I absolutely fell in looove with his syntax."

In this part . . .

Ah, the Part of Tens. What would a *...For Dummies* book be without it? Take a peek at the ten hottest Java-powered Web sites, the ten best places on the Internet to find Java help, the ten liveliest JavaScript sites, and the ten most common pitfalls of Java users around the world.

Chapter 14

Ten Places to Find Java Help on the Web

As you travel down the road toward Java nirvana, you'll no doubt have questions about this fascinating technology, perhaps even requiring help from time to time as your pages become more sophisticated. Naturally, the best place to find Java-related help is on the Web itself. In this chapter, you'll find ten (or so) of the best Java help sites out there, each of which contains even more links to Java-related resources and support sites.

JavaSoft

The home of Java, JavaSoft is the Sun Microsystems, Inc. business unit responsible for developing, marketing, and supporting Java technology. A ton of information related to Java is available here, including links to external Java sites. If you want to stay on top of this rapidly moving technology, visit often!

www.javasoft.com

Netscape Communications

What better place to find out about Java than from the company that helped make it a star? Here, you'll find plenty of Java-related information and links, as well as the most current versions of the world's most popular Java-savvy browser: Netscape Navigator.

`www.netscape.com`

Microsoft

No one said life was fair, so why should you expect Netscape to have all the fun? Microsoft has waged a fierce battle in an attempt to make away with Netscape's crown jewels: the Java-savvy browser market. But while they duke it out in true gladiator fashion, we're the ones who really make out like bandits. And why not? War is hell, so get what you can while the gettin' is good.

`www.microsoft.com/java/`

The IDG Books Worldwide Java Resource Center

IDG Books Worldwide, Inc., the leading publisher of computer-related materials (including the book you're reading now), is on the Web — and they're Java-powered! Visit the Java Resource Center often to find out all about IDG Books Worldwide's current Java titles and those coming down the pipe — and pick up applets and source codes while you're at it. At this site, you can find my regularly updated area, the Future of Java, where you can get the latest scoop (and plenty of links!) on this constantly evolving technology.

`www.idgbooks.com/rc/java`

JavaWorld

As Olivia Newton-John might say, "Let's get technical, technical. I wanna get technical, technical. Let me hear your Java talk!" To stay on the cutting edge of Java, visit the IDG *JavaWorld,* a Web-based magazine dedicated entirely to Java, in which you can find articles, applets, and source code written by professional Java developers and available for free.

    www.javaworld.com

Javology

Are you tired of weaving Java applets into Web page masterpieces? Have the nuts and bolts of Java got you down? Perhaps you long for a relaxing cup of coffee, a wee bit of Danish, and juicy gossip? Although you're on your own when it comes to coffee and treats, gossip I can deliver thanks to the Javology Web site. Tune in for the latest scoop, heavily slanted opinions, and deep background info on all those Java-hungry companies you've been hearing about. If you don't have the time to check in regularly, don't fret: Have the latest issue e-mailed to your desktop.

    www.javology.com/javology/

Yahoo!

One of the first search engines to catalog the Web, Yahoo! is the place to visit if you're searching for Java sites (or anything else, for that matter). Yahoo! not only allows you to search the Web for Java resources but it also organizes many of the better Java links for easy access.

Search:

    www.yahoo.com

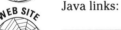

Java links:

    www.yahoo.com/Computers_and_Internet/Languages/Java

Java FAQ Archives

Frequently Asked Questions, or *FAQs,* are plain, old-fashioned text documents bursting at the seams with detailed questions and their corresponding answers — well worth consulting if you have a question that you think others may have asked before. Fortunately, you can visit the Java FAQ Archives site if your question is in any way related to Java. If you have questions about cheese, you'll have to look elsewhere.

    www-net.com/java/faq

JavaLife

Billed as "All The Buzz That's Fit To Click," *JavaLife* is an a e-mail publication that keeps you abuzz with useful and interesting Java-related news and events. As a *Java For Dummies* reader, your subscription to *JavaLife* is on the house, courtesy of Mantis Development Corporation (my company). Sign up for your free *JavaLife* subscription today; it's my way of saying thanks for reading this book.

    www.mantiscorp.com/javalife/

Chapter 15

Ten Rock 'n' Roll Web Sites for Finding Applets

In This Chapter

▶ Rock 'n' roll Web sites for finding Java applets

▶ Hip 'n' happening Java-powered Web sites

*W*hether you're new to Java or an old pro, you want to keep your Web pages flowing with fresh, innovative applets. Thankfully, you'll find no lack of applets on the Web — with your trusted Web browser at hand, you have everything you need to quench your thirst for Java. Here you'll find a bevy of Web sites (ten or so) overflowing with fresh and invigorating Java. Fire up that browser and take off!

Mantis Java Links

This master page provides links to all Java sites mentioned in this book — and many more sites — and keeps them up-to-date to ensure that you always have access even if those URLs change. In addition, all Cool Beans! applets are available for downloading through this site, including new ones that aren't on your CD-ROM. But perhaps the most tantalizing reason to fire up your browser and visit today is the free subscription to *JavaLife* that awaits. This exclusive digital publication delivers "All The Buzz That's Fit To Click" directly to your e-mail inbox, and is available free of charge to all Java For Dummies readers. All you have to do is ask, so don't be shy.

www.mantiscorp.com/java

LivingLinks

Want to add more special effects (*plug-ins*) to the LivingLinks applet provided on the Cool Beans! portion of this book's companion CD-ROM? How about more cutting-edge CookBook pages, giving you recipes for some of the hottest Java-powered sites on the Web? Perhaps you want to see how sites from around the world are using this state-of-the-art applet to turn standard Web pages into dynamic, living ones? Or maybe you just want to surf the Web using LivingLinks-powered buttons? If so, then this is the site for you!

www.livinglinks.com

Gamelan

The mother of all Java sites, Gamelan is a comprehensive Java repository with links to all things Java. You'll find links to tons of applets, information sites, help areas, and much, much more. If you can't find it on Gamelan, it probably doesn't exist.

www.gamelan.com

Java Applet Rating Service (JARS)

A repository with a twist: a rating system! This site has links to top-rated applets, as rated by a large panel of judges. When you look at the "JARS Top 1%" list of applets, you know that you're dealing with the cream of the crop.

But before you dive in, there are a few things you should know about this Java Applet Rating Service. First, it has no association with the compressed Java Archive files (JAR files) that I've talked about in this book. And second, you must enter the URL that follows this paragraph *exactly* as it is shown if you intend to wind up at the site I'm talking about. There's another site out there that uses a different mix of uppercase and lowercase letters (although it has the exact same address). If you don't type the address that follows in all lowercase characters, you won't end up where you really want to go!

www.jars.com

The Java Boutique

Let's see . . . the last time you went to a boutique it was most likely quite small, overpriced, and sported a funky-looking staff that gave off serious attitude. But then again, what did you expect from the real world?! Things are a little better in cyberspace, as the Java Boutique illustrates. True, the site may be small — housing just over 100 applets — but the applets are free and they all contain instructions for downloading and weaving them into your Web pages. What's more, there's a clear and refreshing absence of attitude. Now, if only pricey designer boutiques in the real world could be more like the Java Boutique. . . .

javaboutique.internet.com

The Java Centre

Located in the United Kingdom, The Java Centre (that's right, "centre," not "center!" — folks in the U.K. have swapped the "re" around just to make life interesting) is a watered-down version of the Gamelan site previously listed. That's not to say that The Java Centre isn't useful, heavens no! (Hey, some folks don't like strong coffee.) If Gamelan seems overwhelming to you, check out The Java Centre — it's visually appealing, well organized, and chock full of useful and exciting Java applets.

www.java.co.uk

Java Italian Site

Break out the linguine and clam sauce — it's time to celebrate! Java has been adopted by our friends in Italy, and you're invited to join in the festivities. Worried that you won't be able to scale the language barrier? Fear not. You'll be happy to know that the award-winning Java Italian site doesn't play favorites: It serves up a mean platter of applets, links, and resources in both English and Italian. Mamamia!

jis.rmnet.it

Applet Avenue

Had your fill of adding applets to your Web pages? Bored to tears with industry updates? Technical details making you crazy? Then why not rock down to Applet Avenue and have some fun? This site is dedicated to the best Java games out there. And let's be honest, don't you deserve the break?

`home.earthlink.net/~pdk82`

AltaVista

If you're hankering for that special applet, and can't track it down through any one of the previously listed sites, you can turn to the AltaVista search engine. Created and maintained by Digital Equipment Corporation (DEC), AltaVista has a leg up on its competition when it comes to Java: This search engine lets you find applets that have already been woven into Web pages by their exact name.

Thanks to this innovative feature, you can, for example, search for an applet named "FlyingPig" and be certain that only those Web pages contain a Java applet whose name matches exactly (including the precise mixture of upper- and lower-case characters) will be referenced. After all, when you're searching for "FlyingPig," anything less simply won't do.

`altavista.digital.com`

Chapter 16

Top Ten Scripts on the Web

In This Chapter

▶ Killer Web sites for finding JavaScripts

▶ Kickin' Web sites for finding JavaScript-related information and help

*J*avaScript offers more than meets the eye. As a scripting language, it's meant to provide you with a powerful mechanism to control browsers and applets; yet it's intended to be simple enough that you can get started with it immediately. For the ultimate experience in building dynamic, interactive Web pages, nothing else is like it.

Although JavaScript is a brand-new technology, you'll probably be amazed at how much JavaScript information you can find on the Web. Whether you're looking for fresh, innovative JavaScripts that can be plugged in to your pages directly or you run into problems or questions along your way to becoming a scripting expert, the ten (or so) sites listed in this chapter are worth visiting.

Of course, because these sites contain links to sites, rather than the actual JavaScripts, you'll find that some duplication exists. If you see a hyperlink to a JavaScript site in several locations, that site just may be something you would find interesting. Check it out.

Netscape's JavaScript Support Area

What better place to begin than the place that started JavaScript? This site offers everything from an overview of JavaScript and tips on authoring to hyperlinks to some of the best JavaScript examples available. If you want to learn more about JavaScript or just keep up with the buzz about this exciting new technology, this is the place to start.

```
developer.netscape.com
```

and

```
home.netscape.com/eng/mozilla/3.0/handbook/javascript
```

Mantis JavaScript Links

This master page provides links to many JavaScript sites, including all those mentioned in this book. The links are always up-to-date, so even if a URL changes, you can still access the site. In addition, all Cool Beans! JavaScripts and their source codes are available for downloading through this site, including ones that aren't on your *Java For Dummies,* 2nd Edition, CD-ROM. If you're looking for links, scripts, or new CookBook examples, this is the place to visit.

```
www.mantiscorp.com/javascript
```

Gamelan's JavaScript Site

Although this site was considered the runt of Gamelan's litter when it first debuted, it has grown up big and strong and made its parents proud. In fact, Gamelan's JavaScript site can stand on its own now and is the place serious JavaScript developers come first to see what others are doing and to offer their scripts to the world.

Hundreds of scripts are here for the taking, and more are added every day, along with JavaScript-related press releases, news and updates, links, "how-to" examples, help, and much, much more. Your folks raised you right, baby!

```
www.javascript.developer.com
```

JavaScript Index

This site — a virtual buffet of JavaScripts treats — can link you to everything from the latest JavaScript books and a collection of JavaScripts to Frequently Asked Questions (FAQs) and more. Well-organized and easy to navigate, this is a site you'll want to visit often: It's packed with useful links.

```
www.c2.org/~andreww/javascript
```

The Unofficial JavaScript Resource Center

Come one, come all — this site has something for everyone. Whether you're a novice, intermediate, or expert JavaScripter, you find tips and hints, scripts and code, and JavaScript links to suit your needs. Beginners love this site and advanced scripters may never outgrow it. This site may be an unofficial JavaScript resource center, but it's packed with so much information that you won't care that it's not endorsed by Netscape or Sun.

```
www.intercom.net/user/mecha/java/index.html
```

JavaScript World

This site snatched up several awards for Web site excellence while it was still a toddler, within two months of its startup. This sponsor-supported site is frequently updated with new scripts, links, and JavaScript chats. As a young site that is maturing every day by leaps and bounds, JavaScript World is worth checking in on every once in a while to see how it grows.

```
www.mydesktop.com/internet/javascript
```

24 Hour JavaScripts

If you're on the hunt for a hip, hot, and wild shot of JavaScript at 2:00 a.m., this is the site for you. 24 Hour JavaScripts is a 24,000-member (and growing!) organization dedicated to all aspects of JavaScript. If you really like the site, you can even make a few dolla's off of it — simply cut and paste their banner script code into your Web page and then sit and wait. If you can drive enough Webbers to their site, 24 Hour JavaScripts will send you a check in the mail — really! Who knows, perhaps 24 Hour JavaScripts can provide the funds you need for that espresso maker you've been eyeing lately?

```
www.javascripts.com
```

JavaScript FAQ - 411

Stuck with a JavaScript problem you just can't figure out? Tempted to post to the JavaScript newsgroup (see the next section) but afraid of sounding like a beginner? Check out this Frequently Asked Questions (FAQ) document first — perhaps your questions have been answered already! This FAQ is updated on a regular basis, using questions and answers posted to JavaScript newsgroups.

```
www.freqgrafx.com/411/jsfaq.html
```

JavaScript Newsgroup

So you still have questions, eh? You must be working on one heckuva script! But you don't have to feel alone or abandoned in today's digital world — many folks in the "cyberhood" are willing to help you make your dream site a reality. If the FAQ (see the preceding section) doesn't have the answers you need, turn to the JavaScript Newsgroup. You can think of a newsgroup as an electronic corkboard for the Web: Post your questions and concerns here and someone, somewhere, may just reply with the answer! The best way to thank those who help you out for their thoughtfulness is to answer someone else's posting whenever you can, with hopes that that person will answer someone else's, and so on, and so on.

```
news:comp.lang.javascript
```

JavaScript-Intro by Voodoo

Want to know more about JavaScript but aren't sure where to begin? Does the FAQ sound like gibberish to you, and the newsgroup appear too intimidating? If so, you may want to head to this well-referenced and highly-respected site. You're introduced to JavaScript one step at a time, and you can learn at your own pace.

```
www.webcomm.com/java/javascript/intro
```

Ask the JavaScript Pro

Is Dear Abby falling short of the mark? Have you stumped Ann Landers too? And what's up with Dr. Joyce Brothers? Her Ph.D. certainly isn't in computer science! So who can you turn to for honest, accurate advice to your most intimate JavaScript questions? To a JavaScript Pro, that's who.

But before you embarrass yourself by blurting out a question that you'd rather keep to yourself, you might first consider looking through the JavaScript Pro's database of previously asked questions. If you don't find what you need, then feel free to type in your own question and send it directly to the Advice Column.

But be forewarned: If you want a personal response, take the time to type in your e-mail address accurately, no matter how nervous you are or how sweaty your keyboard. Like any dedicated professional, the JavaScript Pro is far too busy to track down bad e-mail addresses!

```
www.inquiry.com/techtips/js_pro
```

JavaScript Technical Reference

You are beyond beginner. Beyond intermediate. You are an advanced JavaScripter: Da-ta-da! But you need reference materials and can't find them anywhere. Did your dog eat them? Who knows? You can blame it on the dog, but you still need to get your mitts on solid JavaScript reference materials. Fire up your browser and head to this site immediately, where you find gobs of JavaScript reference materials right on the Web. Get your information now — blame the dog later.

```
www.cs.uidaho.edu/~acm/javascript
```

Yahoo!

They don't call it Yahoo! for nothing. After checking out all the primo JavaScript links that this search engine offers, you'll be hollering like a hillbilly, too.

Search:

```
www.yahoo.com
```

JavaScript links:

```
www.yahoo.com/Computers_and_Internet/Languages/JavaScript
```

JavaScript Tip of the Week

If you're pressed for time and can only manage to squeeze out ten minutes a week to spend learning JavaScript, be sure to spend 'em here. Start or end your week with a fresh JavaScript Tip of the Week. Think of it as a power lunch of the zesty, cerebral, JavaScript type.

webreference.com/javascript

Chapter 17

Ten Technical Tragedies

*I*n this chapter, I discuss the ten most likely reasons why you're having trouble getting an applet or script to run properly — assuming that your browser can handle Java and JavaScript in the first place. Not having a Java-savvy or JavaScript-savvy browser (or not enabling these features on your browser) is the leading cause of applets and scripts failing to work properly. But that's an easy one to solve. Following are a few of the not-so-obvious technical hurdles you may have to clear on your path to developing Java-powered Web pages.

Missing or Misspelled Tags

HTML tags (explained in detail in Chapter 5) are the lifeblood of both applets and scripts. Misspelling a tag, or forgetting to include one altogether, will certainly cause your Java-powered page to flop. If you experience an applet or script failure, check your tags for the following mistakes:

✔ **Forgetting the opening or closing tag:** You must always open with `<APPLET>` or `<SCRIPT>` and close with `</APPLET>` or `</SCRIPT>`.

✔ **Spelling tags incorrectly:** Check for tag typos like `<APPLIT>` or `<SCRIPTS>`.

- ✔ **Using a backward slash rather than a forward slash:** Your closing tags should look like this: `</APPLET>` and `</SCRIPT>`, not like this: `<\APPLET>` and `<\SCRIPT>`.

- ✔ **Leaving off required tag attributes:** In all `<APPLET>` tags, you must at least specify `CODE`, `HEIGHT`, and `WIDTH` attributes. With the `<SCRIPT>` tag, you should always include the `LANGUAGE` attribute. Although older Java-savvy browsers run scripts even if the `LANGUAGE` attribute isn't specified, leaving this attribute off may cause your scripts to fail in the future as more scripting languages (such as VBScript, REXX, PYTHON, and scripts with equally cool-sounding names) spill out into the Web. Play it safe and include `LANGUAGE="JavaScript"` in all your `<SCRIPT>` tags that actually surround JavaScript code.

- ✔ **Neglecting to open and close all `<PARAM>` tags:** If you forget to begin your `<PARAM>` tags with an opening less-than sign (`<`), or neglect to close 'em with a terminating greater-than sign (`>`), you'll probably be sorry. Some Java-savvy browsers deal gracefully with a missing opening or closing tag, and will go on as if nothing is wrong. Others will flip out, refusing to run the applet, or may even crash. Don't gamble with the life of your applet. Properly open and close `<PARAM>` tags and you'll come up a winner every time.

Missing or Misspelled Information between Tags

What good are meticulously typed tags if the information inside them is full of errors and holes? If your tags look okay but your applet or script still fails to run, look a little deeper at the parameters and statements between the tags. It's time to pull apart the chocolate sandwich cookies and check out the creamy filling inside.

Applet parameters and JavaScript statements are case-sensitive! `"Speed"` is not the same as `"speed"`, `"http://www.mantiscorp.com/images/mantoid.gif"` is not the same as `"http://www.mantiscorp.com/images/Mantoid.gif"`, and `"potato"` is not the same as `"Potatoe"`.

Applets are configured using parameters, all of which you must supply in the form of a `<PARAM>` tag that has the following basic structure:

```
<PARAM NAME="the parameter name" VALUE="parameter's value">
```

Watch out for the following applet-killers in your parameters:

- ✔ Misspelling a parameter name or value or providing incorrect information in a value prevents your applet from getting what it needs to function properly.

- ✔ Omitting quotes from around names or values that contain spaces (or even one space) prevents your applet from getting the whole parameter. Browsers read only the characters up until the space and omit the rest.

- ✔ Including an extra quote (for example, `VALUE="This is the text for my ticker tape""`) is deadly and may even crash the browser!

- ✔ Using "curly quotes" rather than "straight quotes" prevents the browser from properly processing a parameter. However, because plain text doesn't support curly quotes, you shouldn't have a problem. If you happen to see curly quotes around a parameter, you're probably using a word processor to construct the tag. In this case, be sure to save the file as *plain text* before trying to load it in your browser.

- ✔ Omitting a required parameter (such as an image or series of images, in the case of LivingLinks) prevents an applet from executing or adversely affects its behavior if it does manage to run.

Scripts contain JavaScript statements between opening and closing `<SCRIPT>` tags. If these statements are misspelled or missing, the script doesn't work properly. Also, some scripts call functions (see Chapter 12) which must be defined early in the script (preferably in the `<HEAD>` section of the page) in order to work properly. If a script calls a function that doesn't exist or that contains errors, the script doesn't work properly. To make life easy on yourself, copy and paste scripts (and script functions) into your Web pages rather than type them yourself. You'll save time and drastically reduce the chance of errors.

Mistaken Identity: CODE and ARCHIVE Attributes

When working with JAR files (Java Archives), you may be tempted to assume that the name you supply for a `CODE` attribute is derived from the name specified in the `ARCHIVE` attribute. And while there usually exists a close relationship between the two, there's no law saying the two names must be identical. It's up to the developer who created the applet to choose a name for both the `CODE` and `ARCHIVE` attributes, so you shouldn't try to guess one or the other. Instead, consult the documentation that comes with each applet in order to correctly identify the proper `CODE` and `ARCHIVE` attributes.

For example, the JAR-style Marquee applet available on the CD-ROM that comes with this book requires the following opening `<APPLET>` tag:

```
<APPLET CODE="Marquee.class" ARCHIVE="Marquee.jar"
            WIDTH=500 HEIGHT=40>
```

Clearly there is a close relationship between the name supplied for both the `CODE` and `ARCHIVE` attributes. However, the company that created this applet (Mantis Development Corp. — that's my company) could just as easily have used different names (such as Marquee for the `CODE` attribute and PickleJuice.jar for the `ARCHIVE` attribute). Mantis simply chooses to make life a little easier on you by using the same names for both `CODE` and `ARCHIVE`, although other applet developers are under no obligation to do the same. Beware.

Jarring JARs

Although applets rarely require multiple JAR files, sometimes they do. If you haven't seen applets that use multiple JARs, you may forget to explicitly list each one in the `ARCHIVE` attribute. And even if you don't forget to specify each JAR individually, you may forget to place a comma between each one, like so:

```
<APPLET CODE="MyApplet.class"
          ARCHIVE="MyApplet.jar","MyApplet2.jar","MyApplet3.jar"
          WIDTH=50 HEIGHT=40>
```

Each of the three JAR files in this example is separated from the other with a comma, but no spaces! If you try to slip a space between the comma and a JAR file, you're asking for trouble. Some browsers can handle the space, others can't. Play it safe and remove all spaces between JAR files listed in the `ARCHIVE` attribute, and stick with commas only.

Missing Applet Files

Depending on how an applet is designed, it may or may not rely on more than one *applet file* to run. Applet files can be traditional class files (files with the .class extension), newer JAR files (Java Archives, which have the .jar extension), and serialized files (applet files that have been serialized, which typically sport the .ser file extension), all of which are discussed in Chapter 5. If you don't have the proper assortment of applet files for a given applet, you'll get nothing but grief.

The Marquee applet supplied on CD-ROM with this book, for example, comes in two forms: One is written using the original version of Java to hit the Web (Java 1.0), and another is written using the most current version of Java now available (Java 1.1). To distinguish between the two, I call the Java 1.0 version of the applet "traditional." If you want to weave this applet into a Web page that all Java-savvy browsers can use, you must ensure that you upload to the Web the two class files — Marquee.class and MarqueeFile.class — that make up the traditional version of this applet. If you wish to support *only* newer browsers, however, you need only weave the associated Java Archive file (Marquee.jar) into your <APPLET> tag using the new ARCHIVE attribute.

You can also opt to weave both into a single page in order to serve up the more efficient (and faster!) JAR version to newer browsers, while using the traditional class files when older Java-savvy browsers come knocking. To do this, use a smidgon of JavaScript to allow your Web page to "sniff" details about the browser used to view your page and then construct the appropriate <APPLET> tag (as described in Chapter 13). Just be sure that all files associated with both versions are uploaded to the Web: Marquee.class and MarqueeFile.class, in addition to Marquee.jar.

Unlike the traditional Marquee applet, which always requires two class files regardless of how you configure it in the <APPLET> tag, the LivingLinks applet (like many other applets) only requires multiple class files depending on how you use it. If you don't tap into the power of a special effect, for example, you need only upload the LivingLinks.class file. If you want to hook up a special effect plug-in such as Fade, however, you need to ensure that the Effect.class file is also uploaded, along with any class files associated with that particular effect — Fade.class and FadeFilter.class, for this example.

Relative URLs Starting with a Slash

Most applets cannot properly process relative URLs that start with a slash. You should always specify relative URLs without the leading slash. For example, when specifying a single image to use in a LivingLinks animation, the following tag is incorrect:

```
<PARAM NAME="image" VALUE="/images/logos/mantoid.gif">
```

Because the relative URL supplied as the value for the image parameter begins with a slash, the applet will never find the support file. Instead, leave off the initial slash:

```
<PARAM NAME="image" VALUE="images/logos/mantoid.gif">
```

Absolute URLs Pointing to Another Server

Unless an absolute URL is used for navigation, the file to which it points *must* reside on the same server as the applet. For security reasons, applets can access only files that reside on the same server as they do. If, however, a URL is used for navigation (for example, the URL and links parameters of the LivingLinks applet), it may point anywhere on the Web. This restriction applies only to URLs that are used to access files — images, sounds, data files, and any other file an applet may require. (Absolute and relative URLs are discussed in Chapter 5.)

Files Incorrectly Uploaded

Depending on the tool you use to upload files to the Web and on the mode in which you choose to upload the various files you need (the applet .class file, support files such as images and sound clips, and Web pages), one or more files may fail to make it to the Web server intact. Uploading files to the Web can be a tricky business the first few times you do it. You're almost certain to upload files incorrectly from time to time, rendering them useless after they arrive.

The key to a successful upload lies in choosing the correct *transfer mode* for each file you are uploading. This mode determines exactly how the file on your hard disk is broken up into tiny pieces, sent over the wire, and reassembled on the Web server. If you're unsure of what transfer mode to use, just figure out what type of file you want to upload and choose the corresponding transfer mode:

- Text files (Web pages, text-based support files, and scripts): Text
- Nontext files (applet files, sound files, and image files): Binary

When in doubt, choose the *raw* transfer mode if it's available. This mode just crams the file through your modem, over the phone lines, and onto the Internet without trying to treat it in any special way. As a result, this plain-vanilla approach is your best bet if you're not certain which mode to use.

If you're uploading from a Macintosh computer, don't use *any* of the Apple encoding methods (special upload modes for Macintosh files), such as Apple Single, BinHex, and MacBinary II. Instead, determine the type of file you're uploading (text or nontext) and stick with the appropriate corresponding transfer mode.

Another potential side effect of uploading files to the Web, which is experienced primarily by Windows folks using older uploading tools, is the mangling of filenames during the upload process. What starts out on your hard drive as LivingLinks.class may end up on the Web as livingli.cla, making it worthless as a support file unless you rename the file to what it should be (LivingLinks.class, in this case). Even if you don't use Windows or you happen to use a Windows tool that preserves filenames during transfers, you should always double-check every file's name after transferring it to the Web to make sure that it has *exactly* the same name on the Net as it has on your personal computer (including upper– and lowercase letters!).

Giant-File Overload

At times, it's tough to know for sure whether an applet is loading large files over the Web or is actually having problems running. To find out, take a look at the lights on your modem: If they're flashing, chances are the applet is busy receiving files from the Net. If not, and you're hanging out for an excessive amount of time, the applet may have *hung* or stalled out.

In the case of internal modems, you may have no way to know whether information is being transferred. Windows 95 users can check the status of their connection by double-clicking on the icon of a modem that appears on the right side of the taskbar. Mac users, however, don't have this type of indicator built into their operating system. If you need this type of tool, you may be happy to hear that a number of shareware tools are available for peeking at your modem connection. Check out the utilities section of your nearest Macintosh shareware archive, or use a search engine on the Web to look for such a program (see Chapter 4 for details about search engines).

As a general rule, try to keep the total amount of material on your Web pages (text, applets, support files, and sound clips, for example) down to 250K. If that's not possible, let Webbers know that the information on your site may take a while to download. Whenever possible, supply a message in the applet if you expect a lengthy file download. For example, with LivingLinks, you can specify a *poster image* (a placeholder image that appears on-screen while the rest of the images an applet uses are loading) that says something like "Quit your whinin', I'm downloading as fast as I can!"

Out of Memory

Mac users especially are susceptible to this problem: Netscape runs out of available memory and crashes or simply does not display your applets. This problem usually happens if you have a bunch of graphics or large applets running at the same time.

If you're a Windows user, you can remedy a RAM shortage by making sure that at least 50MB (megabytes) of free space is always available on your primary hard disk, although I'd recommend that you reserve even more (I like to keep 100MB or so free on my own system).

Because Windows uses the hard disk as *swap space* when it's low on memory (transferring the contents of RAM to an invisible *swap file* on the hard disk when it needs extra RAM), keeping a hefty amount of free space available ensures that you always have room on the hard disk even if real RAM is in short supply. This swapping process happens all the time in Windows, although things get really hot and heavy when a number of applications are all vying for the same chunk of RAM.

If you're a Macintosh user, you can allocate more memory to Netscape Navigator by highlighting the program's icon in the Finder and choosing File⇨Get Info. A dialog box appears, giving you an opportunity to set the memory requirements for the application. Depending on how much RAM you've installed (which you can easily find out by choosing About this Macintosh from the Apple menu), you can boost up the preferred memory allocation as much or as little as you want — but never lower it!

Part V
Appendixes

"SINCE WE GOT IT, HE HASN'T MOVED FROM THAT SPOT FOR ELEVEN STRAIGHT DAYS. ODDLY ENOUGH THEY CALL THIS 'GETTING UP AND RUNNING' ON THE INTERNET."

In this part . . .

This part contains a boatload of useful appendixes. Appendix A is your road map to the CD-ROM that comes arm-in-arm with this book — it contains all the information you need to locate the applets, scripts, sample CookBook Web pages, utilities, online-service information, and other good stuff included on the disk. Appendix B gives you a hint of what the future holds for applets and scripts, so you can prepare for the next major blast of Java.

Appendix A

About the CD

• •

*T*he CD-ROM included with this book contains a hefty amount of software to get you up and running with Java in no time flat. Designed for use with Windows 95 and Windows NT 4.0, Macintosh, and OS/2, this CD-ROM gives you a number of Java applets and scripts that you can weave directly into your own Web pages. In addition, the CD-ROM includes a bevy of utilities to help you get the most out of your Web travels, as well as a few utilities to help you convert your own images and sounds for use with Java.

Although the same applets and scripts are available regardless of what type of computer you use, the utilities aren't. If you're a Windows user, you'll find a number of utilities specifically for use with these systems; if you're a Macintosh user, you'll find a separate set of utilities altogether (OS/2 utilities are not provided). However, despite these differences, the end result is the same — the disc contains utilities to help you decompress files that you download from the Web, and utilities to help you convert sound and image files for use with your Java applets. This appendix is your guide to the CD-ROM, and it shows you how to install its contents on your personal computer.

System Recommendations

In order to successfully use the CD that comes with this book, I recommend the following:

- For PCs, Windows 95, Windows NT 4.0 (or greater), or IBM OS/2. For Mac OS computers, Mac OS 7.5 (or greater).

- 100MHz Intel Pentium processor (or compatible) for Windows-based systems, or a Motorola 68030 processor (a PowerPC processor is even better!) for Macintosh systems. A faster processor (133MHz, 200MHz, and so forth) will greatly enhance your Java experience, but is not absolutely necessary.

- 16MB RAM at a bare minimum (32MB, or more, is much better — you can never have too much RAM).

✔ At least 81 MB of hard drive space for Windows users, or at least 55 MB of hard disk space for Macintosh if you want to install the entire contents of the CD-ROM on your hard drive.

✔ A double-speed or faster CD-ROM drive.

✔ A Java-savvy browser (such as Netscape Navigator 3.0, or Internet Explorer 3.0 or greater) is necessary if you want to see the Java applets in action. You're free, however, to browse the CD-ROM without a Java-savvy browser, in which case any browser will do the trick (for details on installing the Java-savvy browser that comes on CD-ROM, see the "Client Software directory" section later in this chapter).

✔ A 14,400 bps or faster modem is necessary only if you want to visit the Web sites listed in this book.

✔ For PCs, a sound card is not required, unless you want to hear the audio played by many of the applets included on the CD-ROM. (All Macs come with built-in sound support.)

✔ A color monitor capable of displaying 256 colors (8bit) or more is highly recommended, although Java applets may run under any monitor configuration (even black and white!).

If you're uncomfortable with the technobabble jargon I've used to explain the recommended system requirements here, or are interested in getting the most out of your computer by upgrading what you have to a more powerful configuration, take a look at the *...For Dummies* book that corresponds to your computer: *PCs For Dummies, Macs For Dummies, Windows 95 For Dummies, Windows 3.11 For Dummies,* or *OS/2 For Dummies.*

How to Use the CD with Windows

On the CD are several folders containing loads of sample applets and some great software.

Before we get down and dirty, we need for you to perform a short test of your CD-ROM drive.

To test, pop the CD in your CD-ROM drive, and use My Computer mode or the Windows Explorer program to show the CD's contents.

The first thing you see are two folders named Long and Short. Open the Long folder and look for a folder named Client Software.

If you see the Client Software folder staring back at you, great. When we talk about the CD from here on, open the Long folder on the CD and fiddle with the CD from there. Users of the Long folder can skip to the section "The Ten-Minute Tour" now.

If you don't see the folder name "Client Software," then move to "Whoops . . . I don't see that folder name."

Whoops . . . I don't see that folder name

If you see a folder named CLIENTSO or CLIENT~1 in the CD test described at the start of "How to Use the CD with Windows," then you're one of a few readers who will need to copy most of the good stuff from the CD to your hard drive using the Short folder.

Some Windows 95 users may have a CD-ROM drive that can't open or use anything on the CD that uses a filename longer than the old DOS 8-character, 3-letter file extension limit (like MYFILE.TXT).

The Long folder contains the CD contents that we hope most of you can use right off the CD. If your CD-ROM drive can't see the long filenames on the CD, you can't use anything in the Long folder without odd error messages cropping up from Windows.

Fear not, for the Short folder has everything you need to make a copy of the CD on your hard drive, where you can access almost everything that's found on the CD (except the Internet sign-up software and the other useful utilities — we'll install that in a later section).

Moving the folders to your hard drive

To copy the sample applets and such to a folder named Java For Dummies 2E CD on your hard drive, follow these steps.

1. **Insert the CD in your CD-ROM drive, and open the Short folder on the CD.**

2. **Double-click the file ALL.EXE.**

   A message appears that tells you that the sample applet folders will be copied.

3. **Click the tiny message away.**

   The Unzip window appears.

4. **Click the Unzip button to copy the items.**

5. **Another tiny message appears that tells you that about 1129 items were copied. Click the message away, and then click the Close button in the Unzip window to wrap up.**

On your hard drive is a folder named Java FD 2E. Inside this folder is the Client Software, Support Files, and Cool Beans! folders, as well as the file Index.html and a few other small tidbits.

This process didn't copy the Goodies and Clients folder to your hard drive. You won't need to. The software can be installed from the CD. Time for you to go the section "The Ten-Second Tour."

Later on, you might twiddle a bit with the contents of the Cool Beans!, Support Files, and CookBook folders and have a need to reinstall a fresh copy of one of the folders. In the Short folder are additional installer files named roughly after these folders. To install them, follow the same instructions as above, but substitute COOKBOOK.EXE, COOLBEAN.EXE, or SUPPORTF.EXE in Step 2.

If you need to make a new folder copy but don't want to delete the contents of your original folder, be sure to type in a new folder name in the installer's Unzip window, or your original files may be erased.

How to Use the CD with a Mac

To install the items from the CD to your hard drive, follow these steps.

1. **Insert the CD into your computer's CD-ROM drive and close the drive door.**

   In a moment, an icon representing the CD you just inserted appears on your Mac desktop. Chances are, the icon looks like a CD-ROM.

2. **Double-click the CD icon to show the CD's contents.**

Like the Windows folks, you'll find a collection of files and folders. For a quick glimpse of what you'll find on the CD, move along to "The Ten-Second Tour."

The Ten-Second Tour

Because most folks like to dive right into new software products as soon as they get them home, I thought it'd be nice if I supplied a quick and dirty tour of the CD-ROM to get you going now, while saving you as much time as possible. Of course, you're free to jump ahead to the section "The Ten-Minute Tour" if you want to take things a little slower and savor each step it takes to appreciate your *Java For Dummies,* 2nd Edition, CD-ROM. Either way is fine by me. Hey, this is your book and CD-ROM; I'm just along for the ride!

Flipping through files

The following is a brief description of each of the files within the main directory of your CD-ROM (or the main directory installed onto your hard drive, as the case may be). A more detailed account of each follows in the next section, "The Ten-Minute Tour."

The Read Me file (README.txt or Read Me First)

README.txt is a text file that's essentially an electronic version of the appendix you are now reading. It's provided on the CD-ROM to help you find the applets, scripts, and utilities the disc contains without requiring that you reference this printed book. You can view the contents of this file with any text editor or word processor.

Index.html

Index.html is a Web page that serves as your electronic guide to the applets and scripts provided on the CD-ROM — Index html requires a Java-savvy browser to use it (see "Client software" later in this chapter for details on Java-savvy browsers). Whereas the README.txt file merely tells you where the applets and scripts are located on the disc, requiring that you manually locate them, opening Index.html with a Java-savvy browser takes you on an interactive tour — you'll actually see the applets and scripts in action. (This file doesn't, however, give you access to the utilities. You must access the utilities the old-fashioned way, as described in this appendix and in the README.txt file.)

Although Macintosh users always see file extensions (such as .html, .class, and .txt), Windows users may have this option turned off, making it difficult to distinguish between files of different types having the same name (such as LivingLinks.class and LivingLinks.html). If you're using a Windows system and the files on your CD-ROM don't have extensions, your computer has been instructed not to show file extensions. Not seeing file extensions doesn't affect your ability to use files, but you can always turn this option on, if you want to, by doing the following:

1. **From Windows Explorer, choose View➪Options.**

   The Options dialog box opens.

2. **Uncheck the Hide MS-DOS File Extensions For File Types That Are Registered check box.**

   Filename extensions are displayed from that point on.

Dashing through folders

Now for a bare-bones description of each of the subfolders within the main folder of your CD-ROM. A more detailed account of each subfolder appears in the next section, "The Ten-Minute Tour."

Client Software folder

In order to see Java in action, you must use a Java-savvy browser (such as Netscape Navigator 4.0 or Microsoft Internet Explorer 4.0). Without such a browser, the applets and scripts in a page will never come to life. You also need a connection to the Internet if you want to surf the Web or publish your own Java-powered pages. Although there's a good chance that you already have access to the Web, you may not be using a Java-savvy browser at the moment.

To help you get your hands on the most current crop of Java-savvy browsers, the Client Software or folder contains Internet Service Provider (ISP) setup software, a text file (ISP.txt), and a Web page (Browsers.html). Here's how to use these files:

- **If you don't have a connection to the Internet (and you want one):** AT&T WorldNet Service is a good ISP to try — it provides good Internet service and gives you a Java-savvy browser. Find more details in the section "The Ten-Minute Tour." If you want to shop around for other ISPs, open the ISP.txt file with any text editor or word processor to find the names and telephone numbers of a few nationwide services that can help.

- **If you already use the Web but don't yet have a Java-savvy browser:** Open the Browsers.html Web page and click on the hyperlink provided to bring you directly to the download area for Java-savvy versions of Netscape Navigator, Internet Explorer, and HotJava.

- **If you already have a connection to the Internet but your service provider doesn't allow you to publish your own Web pages:** Click on the ISP hyperlink in Browsers.html to find a nationwide provider that will allow you to publish your own Java-savvy pages.

CookBook folder

This folder contains a number of starter pages to help you generate ideas for your own Java-powered Web site. Using the applets and scripts provided on the Cool Beans! portion of the CD-ROM, CookBook pages are living examples of what you can do to kick your own pages into high gear with Java.

Although this folder provides a number of CookBook pages, you'll also find a hyperlink to CookBook pages on the Web. Between the pages you have on CD-ROM and the ones you can find in cyberspace, you'll never run out of great ideas for your Web site!

Cool Beans! folder

This folder contains two subfolders that are home to the coolest applets and scripts around:

- **Applets subfolder:** The Applets folder contains all the applets provided on the CD-ROM, along with examples of each applet in action. You can use the Index.html file (housed on the main level of this CD-ROM) to navigate through these applets, or you can open the Applets folder yourself and go straight to any of the applets you find inside of it. To use any one of these applets in your own pages, you must first copy the actual applet (a file with the .class extension, such as LivingLinks.class) and any support files it requires (image, sound, or data files) to your own computer. For details, see the section "The Ten-Minute Tour."

- **Scripts subfolder:** This folder contains a number of JavaScripts (and examples of each in action) that you can add to your own Web pages. Although the Index.html file provided on the main level of the CD-ROM gives you one-click access to the contents of this folder, you're free to open it yourself and explore its contents manually.

Goodies folder

Ah, the Goodies folder. This is where you can find a small arsenal of tools to help you get the very most out of your Web experience, whether you're a Windows or Macintosh user. Here are some of the handy utilities housed in this folder:

- Several of the most popular compression/decompression tools to ensure that you can access the files you download from the Web
- FTP tools to help you upload files to the Web
- Sound-editing and conversion utilities that allow you to use your own sounds with Java applets
- Image-editing software so you can create (or convert) your own graphics for use with Java
- "Customizing Javascripts" chapter

SupportFiles folder

Because the most compelling Java-powered pages usually contain graphics and sounds, this folder contains a number of animations and sounds that you can use in your own Java pages. In addition, a number of special data files (jokes, fortunes, horoscopes, quotes, Bible verses, and so on) are included for use with the Marquee ticker-tape applet provided on CD-ROM.

The Ten-Minute Tour

If you're comfortable installing software on your computer, or if you've already read the chapters that deal with weaving applets and scripts into your Web pages, a ten-second tour of the CD-ROM is probably all you need. But to really get the most this disc has to offer, you may want to set aside a few extra minutes to explore its contents and install the utilities it contains onto your system.

Index.html: Your interactive tour guide

When it comes to checking out the applets and scripts on the CD-ROM, there's no better approach than to open the main Index.html file with your Java-savvy browser. When you view it with a Java-savvy browser, the main Index.html file comes to life and provides you with links to all other pages on the disc. Simply open this file with your browser, and you'll be treated to sound, animation, and a ticker-tape welcoming you to the CD-ROM.

If you don't already have a Java-savvy browser, you need to get your hands on one to make full use of anything on the CD-ROM other than the utilities. Even if you plan to dig through the applets and scripts manually, you *must* have a Java-savvy browser and you must ensure that your browser has both Java and JavaScript enabled. (For details on obtaining and installing such a browser, see Chapter 3 or read about the Client Software directory in this appendix.) Without a Java-savvy browser, you won't be able to see the applets and scripts in action, and you won't have any idea what they're capable of.

Audio, updates, and animation

The first set of hyperlinks provided on the main Index.html file gives you access to audio files and animations that you can use with your own pages, as well as a direct link to the Web-based update to the CD-ROM. When you click on either the Audio or Animation links, you begin cruising around the various support files provided for use with your own pages (see "Support files" later in this chapter).

Clicking on the Update link, on the other hand, connects you to the official World Wide Web upgrade site for this disc. Here, you can find late-breaking additions that didn't make it on the CD-ROM at press time, plus upgrades to the applets and scripts that did make it. Of course, because this site is located on the World Wide Web and isn't a page on the CD-ROM, you'll need to be connected to the Internet to visit this site.

Applets and scripts

Sure, the first set of hyperlinks provided on the main Index.html file takes you to the support files area of the CD-ROM and provides you with access to the online update for this disc. But the real meat lies in the hyperlinks that follow. Note the following paragraph, which appears just below this first set of links:

> Create thrilling, compelling, and exciting Java-powered pages by using these **applets** and **scripts**. Cool pages will be linked from the *Java For Dummies,* 2nd Edition, official Web site. But we can't link you if we don't know you. So **drop** us a line with the address of your funky new Web pages; we'd love to check 'em out! Need ideas? Check **these** out. . . .

Pretend for a moment that the preceding paragraph isn't just plain old text, but rather *hypertext* — just as it is in the Index.html file. The bold, under-lined items are really hyperlink items; all you have to do is click on them with your mouse to see the pages they're linked to. A total of four links are available, but the last two aren't nearly as important as the first two, al-though the last two links give you a way to share your own Java-powered pages with fellow readers, and provide inspiration in the form of CookBook pages:

- The ***drop*** hyperlink simply brings up a pre-addressed e-mail message that you can use to send Mantis Development Corporation the URL of your Java-powered pages (assuming that you want to link your pages to the *Java For Dummies,* 2nd Edition, Web site established for this book).

- The ***these*** hyperlink sends you to the CookBook pages provided on the disc to give you inspiration while you create your own Java-powered pages (see the section entitled "CookBook" later in this chapter).

The ***applets*** and ***scripts*** links, however, are the real reason this CD-ROM was provided with this book in the first place!

Applets

Clicking on the ***applets*** hyperlink provided in the main Index.html file brings you to another Index.html file, this one residing in the Applets folder. If you want, you can always open the Applets folder on the CD-ROM yourself and then load the Index.html file located there into your Java-savvy browser.

By convention, the main Web file in any directory is named Index.html. This is because the main file in a directory often acts like an index (or a table of contents) for that directory. It's not uncommon, therefore, for an Index.html file to exist inside each directory, as is the case with this book's CD-ROM.

You can use the Applets Index.html file in two ways:

- You can open each directory manually and then open the Index.html you find there with a Java-savvy browser.

- You can just use the main Index.html to hyperlink to the other index files on the disc, as described in this section.

Personally, I prefer the second method. I find it faster and more convenient to load the main Index.html and click on the ***applets*** hyperlink than to bother opening the Applets directory and manually loading the index file inside of it.

Either way, you get a rather bland Web page, in comparison to the main Index.html, with a few more hyperlinks on it. Clicking on a link brings you to one or more demos of that applet, giving you an idea of how you might configure that applet for use in your own page.

If you want to see how the ⟨APPLET⟩ tag for a given example is constructed, just take a peak at the source code for that page (see Chapter 6 for details). In fact, because the CD-ROM contains everything you need to weave the applet into your own page, you can use the ⟨APPLET⟩ tags in any of these pages as the basis for your own Web pages.

Although you can add *scripts* to your own Web pages simply by copying and pasting the appropriate ⟨SCRIPT⟩ tags into your documents (see Chapter 12 and the section called "Scripts" further on in this chapter), copying the ⟨APPLET⟩ tag is only half the battle with applets: You also must copy the applet files (the .class files that the tag refers to) and any support files the applet requires. To do this, you need to open the Applets folder on the CD-ROM and copy to your personal computer the files that are used in the demo.

After you locate files in an applet demo that you want to use on your own page, copy the files to your hard drive and place them in the appropriate directory. Usually, you must copy the applet file itself (the .class file referred to in the CODE attribute of the ⟨APPLET⟩ tag) into the same folder as the Web page in which it will appear, and then place any support files (sound and images files, for example) in subdirectories inside that same folder. But, to be sure of what files you need to copy and where you need to place them for a given applet, you need to carefully examine the ⟨APPLET⟩ tag, as described in Chapters 8 and 9.

The easiest way to ensure that you're searching in the right place is to look at the location area of your Java-savvy browser, which tells you exactly what directory the current page is located in. If the location area of your browser isn't visible, simply make it visible (with Netscape Navigator 4.0, choose View⇨Show Location Toolbar; with Internet Explorer 4.0 choose View⇨ Toolbar⇨Address bar). To find out more about the different parts of your Java-savvy browser, read Chapter 3.

Of course, you can always copy an entire *demo folder* — the folder containing the Web page demo file, applet file, and all support files it may use — over to your computer and use that as the basis for your own Web page. Either way, you'll end up with all the necessary files on your own computer. To find out how to construct an ⟨APPLET⟩ tag, see Chapters 5 and 7. For help customizing an applet to suit your own needs, see Chapters 8 and 9.

Be sure to enable your browser's Java option. If you don't, you won't be able to see the applets in action. See Chapter 3 for details.

Scripts

Java comes in two flavors: applets and scripts. Cool Beans! contains both flavors for you to weave into your own Web pages as you see fit. To access the scripts provided on the CD-ROM, you can either click on the **_scripts_** hyperlink provided on the main Index.html page, or open the Scripts subdirectory (inside the Cool Beans! directory) and manually load the Index.html file located inside. Just as with applets, I prefer to use the main Index.html file because it's faster and more convenient.

The scripts on this disc are organized into four categories: _warm, hot, boiling,_ and _industrial strength._ These categories are used to organize the scripts according to how complex they are from a programmer's point of view. You don't have to know how to program in JavaScript to add any of these scripts to your page, but should you decide to _customize_ any of the scripts for your own needs, this arrangement helps you determine where to start. Begin with the warm scripts and work your way up from there. Of course, if you're not interested in customizing the scripts, you can cruise through all four levels in any order you want and choose scripts to add to your own pages, without a care in the world for how they are actually created. To find out how to add any of these scripts to your own Web pages, review the chapters that make up Part III of this book.

Although scripts can be a tad bit more complicated than applets to weave into your pages, you don't have to worry about copying over files to your personal computer as you do when dealing with applets. All you have to do is view the source code of the page that contains the script you want to add to your own page, and then copy the appropriate parts of it into your own HTML documents. You never have to bother digging around in the Scripts folder on the disc, unless you want to take a look at the images that appear on these pages.

Be sure to enable your browser's JavaScript option. If you don't, you won't be able to see the scripts in action. See Chapter 12 for details.

Support files

When it comes to creating your own Java-powered pages, chances are you'll want to customize the applets and scripts you use. The scripts provided on this disc don't use sounds or images (with the exception of the Industrial Strength page, which uses an image in a Fade example), but most of the applets do. And, as you cruise the Web looking for more applets and scripts to add to your pages, you'll come across others that also make frequent use of sounds and images. Because sounds and images are a great way to spruce up Java-powered pages, the _Java For Dummies,_ 2nd Edition, CD-ROM includes a number of sound and image files for you to use.

The Marquee ticker-tape applet provided on this CD-ROM gives you the option of using data files to display a scrolling message across the screen. To get you started, a handful of Marquee data files are provided in the SupportFiles folder. Look inside the Marquee_datafiles directory to find text files containing jokes, famous quotes, fortunes, horoscopes, and Bible quotes. Each file is also available in the Applets folder, inside the Marquee folder located there, but are included here as well for your convenience. Feel free to use the data files located in either directory — they contain the same information.

Audio support files

To listen to the various sounds provided on the disc, choose Audio from the main Index.html page. This opens the Index.html file located in the Audio folder, which itself resides in the SupportFiles folder. Or, if you want to, you can manually open the Audio folder (after first opening the SupportFiles folder, in which the Audio folder is located) and load the Index.html inside.

The Sound Index page contains hyperlinks to the various categories of sound provided on the CD-ROM. When you click on one of the hyperlinks, you see all the sound files in that category. To hear a specific sound, all you have to do is click on its name. Because these sound files are already in the format required for use with Java applets (see Chapter 6 for details), they're good-to-go. If you like a sound, just copy it from the CD-ROM to your personal computer and hook up the <APPLET> tag to use it (see Chapter 9 for help customizing applets for use with your own sound and image files).

In some cases, applets that use sound files grab onto the sound equipment in your computer and don't let go! As a result, the only sounds you can hear are those played by the applet itself. If this happens, clicking on the individual sound files will do no good — the browser can't play them because an applet has taken over the sound capabilities of your computer. In this case, the only way to resolve the problem is to actually quit the browser, and then launch it again. But this time, before loading any other pages, go straight to the Audio directory instead and open the Index.html file that it contains. This ensures that no other applets have a chance to execute first, preventing them from taking over the sound equipment in your computer.

To copy a sound file, just follow these steps:

1. **Open the SupportFiles folder on the CD-ROM.**

2. **Open the Audio folder.**

   Inside the Audio folder, you will find a folder corresponding to each sound category.

3. **Open the appropriate folder and locate the sound file you want to use.**

4. **Copy the folder over to your personal computer, inside the same directory as the Web page in which you want to use it.**

You're set, except for one minor detail. You have to construct the <APPLET> tag to make use of this new sound. But as long as the applet you're using supports sound files (such as the LivingLinks and PageSounds applets provided on the disc), it's just a matter of configuring the parameters of the applet properly (see Chapter 8 for details).

Animations

You probably have your own images for use with your Java-powered pages (such as your company's logo or a picture of your dog), but a handful of animations are provided on the disc just in case you're running low.

To see the animation examples in action, choose the ***Animations*** hyperlink from the main Index.html file. Alternatively, you can open the SupportFiles folder on the CD-ROM and then open the Animations folder. Inside the Animations folder is the same Index.html file to which the main Index.html file provides a hyperlink, which you can load into your Web browser. Whichever route you choose, you will see a number of hyperlinks corresponding to animations that the LivingLinks applet brings to life. (This applet is also provided on the CD-ROM — see "Applets," earlier in this appendix, for details.)

Clicking on a link brings you to a page that displays the corresponding animation. Because each animation is actually a series of images, the applet must load each image before the animation begins. Depending on how many frames (each image in an animation is known as a *frame*) the animation contains, this may take a minute or two. When all frames are loaded, the browser displays them one after the other, giving the illusion of movement. To see how these animations are configured using the LivingLinks applet, just take a look at the HTML code of each page (see Chapter 6). You'll see exactly how each <APPLET> tag is configured, and you can copy the code for use in your own page.

Of course, if you copy the <APPLET> tag code, you'll also need to copy the images that make up the animation. To do this, open the SupportFiles folder and then the Animations folder located inside of it. Here, you find a folder corresponding to each animation hyperlink shown back in Figure A-8. In each folder is an Index.html file and a LivingLinks.class applet file, so you can copy the entire folder to your computer and get everything you need to run the animation: Web page, applet, images, and all! Each animation is actually a series of images; you can use the individual images in your Web pages as well. Simply open the images with a graphics program and choose the one you want (each is slightly different from the previous one, giving the illusion of movement when displayed rapidly in sequence), then copy that one image file over to your personal computer.

CookBook pages

To get an idea of the things you can do with the applets and scripts provided in the Cool Beans! directory, take a look at the many CookBook pages. These pages are intended to jump-start your creative processes and get those Java juices flowing. To use these pages, simply choose the ***these*** hyperlink from the main Index.html file or open the CookBook directory on the disc and manually load the Index.html file you find there.

Although the images and sounds used in CookBook pages aren't available for use in your own Web site (unless explicit permission is given on the page itself), they'll give you an idea of what you can do with your own images and sounds. And because each of the applets and scripts used in these pages is provided on the CD-ROM, you can see how the corresponding `<APPLET>` and `<SCRIPT>` tags are formed simply by taking a peek at the HTML source code of the page (for details, see Chapters 6 and 12).

In addition to the CookBook pages provided on the disc, this page also contains a hyperlink to additional CookBook pages residing on the World Wide Web. In fact, if you want to have your own Java-powered pages made available on the Web as CookBook pages for others to use as inspiration, simply click the ***drop*** hyperlink on the main Index.html file and type in the corresponding URL. Or if your Web browser isn't configured to send e-mail, drop a message to `mantis@mantiscorp.com` using the software program you normally use to send e-mail. I'd love to see what you come up with and how you put the applets and scripts in the Cool Beans! directory to use on your own Java-powered pages. Don't be shy!

Client software

To use the Java applets and scripts provided on the CD-ROM, or any others for that matter, you'll need to get your hands on a Java-savvy browser. And to publish Java-powered pages on the World Wide Web, you must have access to the Internet through a service provider that allows you to publish Web pages.

If you don't already have a connection to the Internet, you might want to join AT&T WorldNet℠ Service, an ISP that provides you with a Java-savvy browser as well as some space to publish your Web pages. You have to pay for this service, so have a credit card ready as you install the software and sign on. You also need a modem connected to your computer. A 14,400 bps modem will work, but I recommend 28,800 bps or faster.

If you already have an Internet Service Provider, be aware that installing AT&T WorldNet Service software may change your current Internet connection settings.

Installing AT&T WorldNet Service from the Long folder on the CD (Windows):

1. **Open the AT&T WorldNet Service folder (located in the Client Software folder).**

2. **Open the Setup with Internet Explorer folder or, if you prefer using Netscape Navigator, open the Setup with Netscape Navigator folder.**

3. **Double-click the Setup.exe file to start installation, and then follow the on-screen instructions.**

Installing AT&T WorldNet Service from the Short folder on the CD (Windows):

1. **Open the WORLDNET folder in the Clients folder.**

2. **Open the IESETUP folder for Internet Explorer version of AT&T WorldNet Service or, if you prefer Netscape Navigator, open the NNSETUP folder.**

3. **Double-click the Setup.exe file to start installation and follow the on-screen instructions.**

Installing AT&T WorldNet Service on a Macintosh (Internet Explorer only):

1. **Open the AT&T WorldNet Service folder in the Client Software folder.**

2. **Double-click the Install AT&T WorldNet Service icon and follow the on-screen instructions.**

During registration, you may be asked for a registration code. If you are an AT&T long-distance service customer, type this registration code: **L5SQIM631.** If you use some other company to do long-distance calls, type **L5SQIM632.**

If you don't choose AT&T WorldNet Service, you may need to get your hands on a Java-savvy browser. For details on which Java-savvy browsers are available and how to obtain and install the most popular ones — Microsoft Internet Explorer 4.0 and Netscape Navigator 4.0 — take a look at Chapter 3. If, however, you want quick access to the various Java-savvy browsers on the market, load the Browsers.html file located in the Client Software folder. This page contains hyperlinks to the download areas of the various Java-savvy browsers currently on the market at the time this book went to print.

If the Internet Service Provider (ISP) you now use doesn't give you the ability to publish Web pages, or if you're in the market for a new provider (perhaps your current ISP's rates are too high?), check out the ISP hyperlink provided on the Browsers.html file. This link brings you to a comprehensive listing of service providers, and is the perfect starting place if you're shopping around for Internet access.

Goodies

In addition to the applets, scripts, and support files provided on the CD-ROM, you'll find a number of software utilities to assist you when browsing the Web and creating your Java-powered pages. Although the utilities you can use depend on the type of computer you run, they ultimately provide the same functionality.

To find the utilities for your system, open the Goodies folder on the CD-ROM. Inside, you'll find a number of utilities, each used for a different purpose. To understand what each is used for, read the brief descriptions that follow. For a more in-depth account of how to use a particular tool, simply read the documentation that accompanies it.

Because each utility is different in its system requirements, you should read the accompanying documentation provided with each *before* you install it on your system. Although most (if not all) of these utilities should run just fine on your system, it's a good idea to find out ahead of time.

- ✔ **If you use a Macintosh:** Some of the software has an installer icon in the folder on the CD that you double-click to get started. In other cases, you just drag and drop the folder containing the program from the CD to your hard drive.

- ✔ **If you use Windows:** You need to run the program's installer to copy the software to your computer. This program, usually named *installer* or *setup,* is inside the program's folder itself.

  To install a Windows program from the CD, follow these steps.

  1. **Insert the CD in your CD-ROM drive.**

  2. **Using Windows Explorer or My Computer, open the Long or Short folder (which folder you open depends on the results of your test in the section "How to use the CD with Windows").**

  3. **Open the Goodies folder.**

  4. **Open a program folder you want to use.**

  5. **Locate the program SETUP.EXE or INSTALL.EXE and double-click it to start installation. (There may only be a single item in some folders that you can double-click for the same results.)**

To find out exactly how to use any of these programs, you may want to invest a little more time reading the documentation that comes with each one (or using an associated Help menu when the program is running, if one exists). Because each of these utilities performs a different function, each comes with its own set of documentation. For an overview of each utility (to decide whether you even want to use it), skim over the section that's appropriate for your system.

✔ **Coda Trial (Windows and Macintosh):** Coda (RandomNoise) is a Java-based Web page editor that lets you create Java-based interactive Web pages. This trial version may limit its features or abilities.

Coda is a program written entirely in Java. Because Java is still a little buggy around the edges at present, make sure that you pay close attention to the program's system requirements. Coda may not work properly with Java 1.1 or higher (it was written with Java 1.0.2 in mind), and requires at least 16MB of free RAM with Windows 95 or 32MB with Mac OS *in addition* to what Windows 95 or Mac OS takes up for itself. Also, Coda installs the Microsoft Java 1.0.2 virtual machine on Windows and the Macintosh Runtime for Java (MRJ) 1.0.2 on Macintosh computers.

✔ **ConvertMachine (Macintosh):** ConvertMachine (Rod Kennedy) is a batch-processing utility to convert sound format files to a desired format. It performs one or more of the following tasks without requiring user interaction: decompression, resampling (sample rate conversion), mixing (stereo to mono), and compression. You don't need to worry about what format the file is in; all you do is specify the desired output format. Freeware.

✔ **DropStuff with Expander Enhancer (Macintosh):** This shareware utility (by Aladdin Systems) gives Macintosh users the ability to create StuffIt (SIT) archives by dragging and dropping files and folders onto the DropStuff icon. And thanks to the Expander Enhancer, users of Aladdin's StuffIt Expander (also provided with this CD-ROM) can expand virtually every compression format found online that was created by Macs, UNIX systems, and IBM PCs and compatibles. You can decompress SIT, ZIP, and TAR archives, which are the most common formats you'll probably encounter when surfing for applets.

✔ **GraphicConverter (Macintosh):** GraphicConverter (Lemke Software) is a powerful shareware graphic viewing and conversion program. You can also make retouches, perform batch conversions for Mac and PC graphic formats, and more.

✔ **Goldwave (Windows):** Goldwave is a comprehensive, digital audio editor that allows you to play, record, edit, and convert audio files on your Windows computer. In addition to the number of audio file formats Goldwave supports, it allows you to save sound files in a special *AU* format that is required by Java applets. To save files in this format, simply choose File⇨Export from Goldwave's menu, choose Sun (.au) from the Save Files as Type list box that appears, and then click on OK. For more details on using sound in your Web pages, see Chapter 6.

✔ **The Java Development Kit (Windows version 1.1.3, Mac OS version 1.02):** The Java Development Kit (or JDK for short) from Sun Microsystems provides you with the basics you need to create Java applets. Included with the installer for the JDK is an installer for the HTML-based documentation for the software. Note to Mac OS users: Your Mac may require additional software to run Java applets and programs outside of a Web browser. One option is the Macintosh Runtime for Java (MRJ) software, available from Apple Computer's Java Web site at `applejava.apple.com`.

Note: The JDK is © 1997 by Sun Microsystems, Inc., 2550 Garcia Ave., Mtn. View, CA, 94043-1100, USA. All rights reserved.

✔ **Paint Shop Pro (Windows):** Paint Shop Pro (JASC, Inc) is a graphics program that offers many useful features such as image retouching, painting, and image-format conversion. In addition to enabling you to create and save images in the two graphics formats supported by Java applets, GIF and JPEG, Paint Shop Pro supports transparent and interlaced GIF images (see Chapter 6 for details on the image formats supported by Java).

✔ **Sound Editor 1.2 (Macintosh):** Sound Editor (David Veldhuizen) helps solve some of the problems associated with recording sound from your Mac's Sound control panel (control panels are located in the Apple menu). This utility also enables you to copy and paste portions of a sound, mix sounds together, and create special effects, such as echoes and backwards sounds.

✔ **SoundApp:** SoundApp (Norman Franke) is an extremely powerful and free program that can play and convert a variety of sound formats. It understands the special Sun AU sound format required by Java applets, as well as many others including the following: SoundCap and Studio Session Instruments, SoundEdit, AIFF and AIFF-C, System 7 sound and .snd resource, QuickTime MooV (soundtracks only, including MIDI movies), NeXT .snd, Windows WAVE, MPEG audio, Sound Blaster VOC, Many varieties of MODs, ScreamTracker 3 module (S3M), Multitracker module (MTM), MIDI, Amiga IFF/8SVX, Sound Designer and Sound Designer II, IRCAM, and PSION sound.

✔ **SoundMachine:** This utility (from Rod Kennedy) allows Macintosh users to play many of the most common sound format sound files, such as AIFF, Windows WAV files, and AU files from the Internet. New versions of SoundMachine are made available through updates on the World Wide Web (see the software's documentation for the Web address), so you can stay up-to-date as more sound formats are invented.

✔ **StuffIt Expander for Macintosh:** StuffIt Expander (Aladdin Systems) expands archives from the most popular archive-based compression formats found on the Macintosh: StuffIt and Compact Pro, can also decode BinHex attachments from Internet e-mail and newsgroups. All non-encrypted archives created by any version of these products are supported, including files created with any member of the StuffIt family, such as StuffIt SpaceSaver, StuffIt Deluxe, StuffIt Lite, or DropStuff.

✔ **WinZip (for Windows):** WinZip (Nico Mak Computing) brings the convenience of Windows to ZIP-compressed files. This versatile utility is one of my all-time favorites; it allows you to decompress (*unzip*) and compress (*zip*) file archives in the ZIP format, and supports many other popular Internet file formats, such as TAR, GZIP, and UNIX compress. WinZip includes a powerful yet intuitive point-and-click, drag-and-drop interface for viewing, running, extracting, adding, deleting, and testing files in ZIP, LZH, and ARC files, including self-extracting archives. To install WinZip, simply copy the folder to your hard drive and then execute the winzip95.exe program (or, if you prefer, you can install it directly from the CD-ROM). Located in the Winzip folder.

✔ **WS_FTP:** The WS_FTP program (Ipswitch) is a file transfer protocol (FTP) utility for use with Windows computers. The user interface for this FTP client is designed with the novice FTP user in mind, yet is extremely powerful. With this program, you can upload your Web pages, applets, and support files to the Internet one at a time or all at once (assuming they reside in the same folder on your personal computer).

✔ **ZipIt:** ZipIt (Tom Brown) is a Macintosh program to decompress (*unzip*) and compress (*zip*) files in the ZIP format. To decompress a ZIP archive by using ZipIt, choose File⇨Open and then select the archive by using the dialog box that appears. After an archive opens, use the mouse or the Edit⇨Select All command to choose the items you want to extract, and then choose Zip⇨Extract to actually perform the decompression.

✔ **"Customizing Javascripts" chapter:** This special chapter on the CD-ROM tells you how to customize scripts — you can even see precisely how to hook up and tweak scripts that come for free on the CD. In order to read this chapter, you'll need to install Adobe Acrobat Reader, which is in the Reader folder inside the Goodies folder.

If You Have Problems (Of the CD Kind)

On the CD, I've tried my best to compile programs that work on most computers with the minimum system requirements. Alas, your computer may differ, and some programs may not work properly for some reason.

If you have any trouble seeing the applets on the CD-ROM come alive, you may want to consider upgrading to Netscape Navigator 4.0 or Internet Explorer 4.0. Earlier Java-savvy browsers — particularly those on the Macintosh platform — aren't as industrial strength in their handling of Java-powered pages. My advice: Upgrade as soon as possible.

The other two most likely problems are that you don't have enough memory (RAM) for the programs you want to use, or you have other programs running that are affecting the installation or running of a program. If you get error messages like Not enough memory or Setup cannot continue, try one or more of these methods and then try using the software again:

- ✔ Turn off any anti-virus software that you have on your computer. Installers sometimes mimic virus activity and may make your computer incorrectly believe that it is being infected by a virus.

- ✔ Close all running programs. The more programs you're running, the less memory is available to other programs. Installers also typically update files and programs. So if you keep other programs running, installation may not work properly.

- ✔ Have your local computer store add more RAM to your computer. This is, admittedly, a drastic and somewhat expensive step. However, if you have a Windows 95 PC or a Mac OS computer with a PowerPC chip, adding more memory can really help the speed of your computer and allow more programs to run at the same time.

If you still have trouble with installing the items from the CD, call IDG Books Worldwide Customer Service at 800-762-2974 (outside the U.S., call 317-596-5261).

Appendix B
To Java 1.1 and Beyond!

●●

*W*hen Java first burst onto the Web scene, it brought with it a non-standard HTML tag. In just a few years since it was introduced to Web page developers, the `<APPLET>` tag has become a close and intimate friend to millions. After finding its way into just as many Web pages, it's no surprise that Web page developers have come to appreciate, if not adore, the pure simplicity and raw power that the original `<APPLET>` tag delivers. But oh, the times — they are a changin'.

All of the latest browsers support Java 1.1 — the successor of the original Java. As you might expect, the `<APPLET>` tag itself was also updated when Java 1.1 arrived. Like ice cold water in our veins, many Java devotees were initially frozen in fear that their original arsenal of Java-powered pages would break under the new Java 1.1 `<APPLET>` tag.

Fortunately, their fears were unfounded. Sun Microsystems, the maker of Java, was clear-thinking enough to make the new `<APPLET>` tag backwards-compatible with the original `<APPLET>` tag. And, thanks to the cooperation of browser vendors, we can be sure that Java 1.0-powered pages run just fine under the newest wave of Web browsers.

The New Java 1.1 <APPLET> Tag

In fact, the new Java 1.1 `<APPLET>` tag is almost identical to the original one. Because it introduces only two new attributes, `OBJECT` and `ARCHIVE`, there's not too much to pick-up. And, because these attributes are necessary only when you attempt to weave special-purpose applets (applets that make use of these two new attributes) into your pages, chances are pretty slim that you have to work with either of the new attributes immediately.

In time, however, you'll probably find yourself taking advantage of the Java 1.1 `OBJECT` and `ARCHIVE` attributes of the `<APPLET>` tag. Luckily, there's not much to the new and improved Java 1.1 `<APPLET>` tag. As Chapter 5 explains, there are still only three required `<APPLET>` attributes, regardless of which version of Java your applet is created with.

Further along in this appendix is a formal definition, or template, of the Java 1.0 and Java 1.1 <APPLET> tag. The following <APPLET> tag definition is merely a generic template that gives you an overview of the various elements that comprise the tag itself. I've used the following formatting to help you:

✔ Attributes in bold are required, meaning every <APPLET> tag you construct must have them.

✔ Non-bold attributes are optional, meaning you only have to supply them if you want a desired effect (or if a specific applet requires them, such as applets that make use of PARAM attributes to specify parameters).

✔ The information you supply for each attribute is in italics, and will vary from applet to applet. This information you supply depends on the attribute you're using, and the applet itself.

✔ Attributes in brackets [ ] are available only with Java 1.1 applets, and only when specifically required by a particular applet. A Java 1.1 applet may not necessarily require these Java 1.1-specific attributes; it's up to the applet developer. Each applet that you use will be different in its application of these attributes.

```
<APPLET
  CODE = appletClassFile  ...or...  [OBJECT =
           serializedAppletFile]
  [ARCHIVE = archiveList]
  HEIGHT = pixels
  WIDTH = pixels
  CODEBASE = codebaseURL
  ALT = alternateText
  NAME = appletName
  ALIGN = alignment
  HSPACE = pixels
  VSPACE = pixels
>
<PARAM NAME = appletAttribute1 VALUE = value>
<PARAM NAME = appletAttribute2 VALUE = value>
    . . .
Alternate HTML (displayed by non-Java browsers)
</APPLET>
```

Spartan enough, don't you think? So do I, which is why I turn to Table B-1 and Table B-2 whenever I have a question about what an attribute is and what type of information it accepts. And so too, dear friend, should you.

Java 1.0 was the original McCoy; it was the first version of Java to hit the Web. As such, all Java-savvy browsers understand how to deal with the Java 1.0 <APPLET> tag attributes that appear in this table.

Table B-1	Java 1.0 <APPLET> Tag Attributes
Attribute	**Description**
REQUIRED	
CODE	Specifies the name of the applet file.
HEIGHT	Specifies the height of your applet, in pixels, as it will appear in the browser when displayed.
WIDTH	Specifies the width of your applet, in pixels, as it will appear in the browser when displayed.
OPTIONAL	
CODEBASE	Specifies the base URL for your applet (the applet class file). The applet must be located relative to this URL. If CODEBASE isn't specified, the applet is expected to reside in the same directory as the Web page.
ALT	Specifies the alternate text to be displayed by Java-savvy browsers that are incapable of executing the applet for whatever reason. Note that this text is seen only by Java-savvy browsers, as it falls within the opening <APPLET> tag, which all non-Java browsers skip over. If you want to communicate with non-Java browsers, do so using Alternate HTML.
NAME	Specifies the symbolic name of your applet, allowing other applets and/or scripts embedded in the same page to locate your applet by name. This attribute is used only when applets on a page communicate with one another (something most applets don't do), or scripts are used to dynamically control/alter applet behavior (a more common practice).
ALIGN	Specifies where your applet is placed on the page with respect to the text around it; it may be one of the following nine alignments: left, right, top, texttop, middle, absmiddle, baseline, bottom, and absbottom.
HSPACE	Specifies the horizontal space, in pixels, surrounding your applet.
VSPACE	Specifies the vertical space, in pixels, surrounding your applet.

Java 1.1 introduced several new features to the original version of Java. As a result, two new <APPLET> tag attributes are available that allow you to weave these sophisticated new capabilities into your Web pages. These new attributes, however, are available only when using browsers that support Java 1.1 (such as Sun's HotJava 1.0, Netscape Navigator 4.0, and Microsoft Internet Explorer 4.0). Older browsers ignore the new attributes entirely — your Java 1.1 applets won't run when viewed with a browser that only understands Java 1.0.

Table B-2	Java 1.1 `<APPLET>` Tag Attributes
Attribute	**Description**
ARCHIVE	Specifies one or more Java archives (JARs), assuming the applet actually takes advantage of JAR files (special-purpose archives introduced with Java 1.1). JAR files may contain images, sound files, and any other resource that the applet requires to operate properly. If multiple JAR files are required by the applet, they must be separated by a comma. This attribute works hand-in-hand with the required `CODE` attribute (see Table 1.1), because a Java archive may actually contain the class file specified with `CODE`. (The class file specified by `CODE` may alternatively reside outside the archive, depending on how the applet developer decided to implement the applet.)
OBJECT	This optional attribute specifies the name of a serialized applet file, as opposed to the non-serialized applet file (standard Java class), which is specified through the `CODE` attribute. Serialized applet files are an advanced feature of Java 1.1, and allow developers to store applet information in a way that makes it easy to send applets and their internal data over the network or save it to disc. Because serialized applet files are actually special versions of standard applets, the `CODE` attribute is not necessary when the `OBJECT` attribute is used. If the `CODE` attribute is used, however, the `OBJECT` attribute is not used. The best way to determine whether an applet uses `CODE` or `OBJECT` is to consult the documentation that comes with the applet, or peek at the `<APPLET>` tag contained in an example Web page, if available. However, because serialized applets typically have a .ser extension, as opposed to the standard .class extension that traditional applets have, you usually can determine if an applet supports the `OBJECT` attribute simply by looking at the applet's file extension.

HTML 4.0

Recently, the main organization governing World Wide Web standards — the World Wide Web Consortium (W3C) — released a new draft of the Hypertext Markup Language (HTML) 4.0. In addition to making standard HTML more powerful and flexible, HTML 4.0 focuses considerable attention on the area of executable content — Web page contents, such as applets, that are actually little software programs that run on your computer once downloaded. Plainly put, HTML 4.0 gives more control and flexibility when it comes to weaving applets (and any other form of executable content, such as ActiveX Controls) into your Web pages, thanks to the new `<OBJECT>` tag it introduces.

In fact, the <OBJECT> tag is expected to replace the <APPLET> tag wholesale; future browsers will allow you to weave applets into your Web pages by using the new <OBJECT> tag exclusively. Of course, this won't happen overnight. First, HTML 4.0 must become official, moving from the draft stage it is in now to a final, rock-solid version that browser vendors will support.

However, just building support for HTML 4.0 into all browsers won't banish the <APPLET> tag for good. Heck no! Remember, the entire world doesn't upgrade to the latest and greatest browsers as soon as they become available. In fact, some folks never upgrade at all. You can guarantee that tens of millions of Webbers will surf with outdated browsers for years to come. Hey, some folks won't upgrade to an HTML 4.0 browser until after the new millenium, in which case HTML will be old, old news (and so will our planet, if you believe the end of our world is tied to the year 2000, but that's another story, for another time . . . as long as it's told before midnight 1999).

The moral of the story here is pretty simple: Look before you leap. Go ahead and get a feel for new and cool features, such as the <OBJECT> tag, and even weave Web pages that take advantage of these features, but don't get caught up in the hype. If you want your Web pages to be available to the entire world of Webbers, you have to ensure that your pages are built with backwards-compatibility in mind.

Thankfully, Chapter 13 is all about backwards-compatibility. That chapter shows you how to weave wildly powerful Web pages that take full advantage of today's most advanced features, while supporting older, less sophisticated browsers. Thanks to Chapter 13, no Java-savvy browser shall be ignored, no matter how old or new, make or model. It is, I'd say, the most politically and technologically correct chapter in this book.

Meanwhile, there's no reason that you can't become comfortable with HTML 4.0's <OBJECT> tag right now. Hey, you'll probably want to use it sooner rather than later, if only to see what all the fuss is about. And so, without any further adieu, I give you the <OBJECT> tag in all its glory:

```
<OBJECT
  DECLARE    (declare but don't instantiate flag)
  CLASSID    (URL that identifies an implementation)
  CODEBASE   (URL specifying base path used to resolve rela-
             tive URLs specified by classid)
  DATA       (URL that is a reference to object's data)
  TYPE       (Internet content type for data)
  CODETYPE   (Internet content type for code)
  STANDBY    (message to show while loading)
  ALIGN      (positioning inside document)
  HEIGHT     (suggested height)
  WIDTH      (suggested width)
```

(continued)

(continued)

```
   BORDER    (suggested link border width)
   HSPACE    (suggested horizontal gutter)
   VSPACE (suggested vertical gutter)
   USEMAP    (reference to image map)
   SHAPES    (object has shaped hypertext links)
   NAME      (URL submit as part of form)
   TABINDEX  (position in tabbing order)
   >
```

Table B-3 describes the attributes found in the `<OBJECT>` tag — the potential successor to the `<APPLET>` tag.

Table B-3	HTML 4.0 `<OBJECT>` Tag Attributes
Attribute	*Description*
CODEBASE	This attribute, a URL, specifies the base path used to resolve relative URLs specified by `CLASSID` — it gives the base URL when the object requires code. If this attribute is not specified, its default value is the base URL of the current document. Not all rendering mechanisms require this attribute.
CLASSID	This attribute, a URL, specifies the location of a rendering mechanism.
CODETYPE	This attribute specifies the Internet Media Type (MIME type) of data expected by the rendering mechanism specified by `CLASSID`. This attribute is optional but recommended when `CLASSID` is specified because it allows the user agent to avoid loading information for unsupported media types. If no explicit value is given for this attribute, it defaults to the value of the type attribute.
DATA	This attribute specifies the URL leading to data that will be rendered.
TYPE	This attribute specifies the Internet Media Type (MIME type) specified by the data. This attribute is optional but recommended when data is specified because it allows the user agent to avoid loading information for unsupported media types. If no explicit value is given for this attribute, the user agent should attempt to determine the type of the data to be rendered.
DECLARE	When present, this Boolean attribute makes the current `OBJECT` definition a declaration only. The object must be created by a subsequent `OBJECT` definition referring to this declaration.

Attribute	Description
STANDBY	This attribute specifies a message that a user agent may render while loading the object's implementation and data.
ALIGN	This attribute specifies the position of the object with respect to its surrounding context. Its possible values are texttop, middle, textmiddle, baseline, textbottom, left, center, or right.
HEIGHT	This attribute specifies the height of the applet object, in pixels, as it will appear in the browser when displayed.
WIDTH	This attribute specifies the width of the applet object, in pixels, as it will appear in the browser when displayed.
TABINDEX	This attribute, an integer, specifies the position of the current element in the tabbing order for the current document. This value may be a positive or negative integer. The tabbing order defines the order in which elements will receive focus when navigated by the user via the keyboard. The tabbing order may include elements nested within other elements.
BORDER	This attributes specifies the width (in pixels only) of the frame around a table.
HSPACE	This attribute specifies the horizontal space, in pixels, surrounding the applet object.
VSPACE	This attribute specifies the vertical space, in pixels, surrounding the applet object.
SHAPES	When set, this Boolean attribute specifies that the object being defined is an image map. The contents of the OBJECT element will specify the active regions.
NAME	This attribute assigns a name to the control, and will be paired with the current value of the control if the element's value is submitted along with a form.
USEMAP	This attribute specifies a URL leading to a map defined by MAP and AREA (two additions to HTML 4.0 that allow client side image maps. Don't you just love living on the cutting edge?).

While the <OBJECT> tag may seem a bit confusing, if not downright over-whelming, don't toss up your hands just yet. As with most of the new powerful and flexible tags introduced since HTML was first invented, the <OBJECT> tag is meant to give you everything you need to get the most out of your executable content (Java applets, in our case). However, you're under no obligation to use all the bells and whistles; simply use what you need and ignore the rest. For example, consider the following applet example written using the traditional <APPLET> tag:

```
<APPLET CODE="Marquee.class" HEIGHT="40" WIDTH="500">
Sorry, but you can't see this neat ticker-tape style
        applet...<br>
Enable Java or upgrade your browser if it isn't Java-
        savvy!<br>
</APPLET>
```

This is a perfectly simple applet, and is easily rewritten using the `<OBJECT>` tag. As the following snippet of HTML 4.0 code illustrates, you merely replace `APPLET` with `OBJECT`, and `CODE` with a combination of `CODETYPE` and `CLASSID`:

```
<OBJECT CODETYPE="application/octet-stream"
  CLASSID="java:Marquee.class"
  HEIGHT="40" WIDTH="500">
Sorry, but you can't see this neat ticker-tape style
        applet...<br>
Enable Java or upgrade your browser if it isn't Java-
        savvy!<br>
</OBJECT>
```

Of course, the preceding two examples don't bother at all with parameters, a very common element of `<APPLET>` tags implemented by using the `PARAM` attributes. The following example builds on the original applet example by adding a few useful parameters via `PARAM` attributes:

```
<APPLET CODE="Marquee.class" HEIGHT="40" WIDTH="500">
<PARAM NAME="font_face" VALUE="Helvetica">
<PARAM NAME="font_size" VALUE="24">
<PARAM NAME="marquee" VALUE="Welcome to my page!">
Sorry, but you can't see this neat ticker-tape style
        applet...<br>
Enable Java or upgrade your browser if it isn't Java-
        savvy!<br>
</APPLET>
```

Because the `<OBJECT>` tag supports `PARAM` attributes in exactly the same way as the `<APPLET>` tag supports them, the conversion to HTML 4.0 is a slam-dunk:

```
<OBJECT
  CODETYPE="application/octet-stream"
  CLASSID="java:Marquee.class"
  HEIGHT="40" WIDTH="500">
<PARAM NAME="font_face" VALUE="Helvetica">
<PARAM NAME="font_size" VALUE="24">
```

```
<PARAM NAME="marquee" VALUE="Welcome to my page!">
Sorry, but you can't see this neat ticker-tape style
          applet...<br>
Enable Java or upgrade your browser if it isn't Java-
          savvy!<br>
</OBJECT>
```

One of the most beautiful features of the new `<OBJECT>` tag is its ability to create cascading levels of embedded content. Because different makes, models, and versions of browsers all have different capabilities, you can't always ensure that your most powerful applets will be visible to all. In fact, you must assume that your applet-powered pages will, at times, be viewed by non-Java browsers, or older Java-savvy browsers possessing less power than the most current crop. As a result, you have to accommodate them all by using a combination of alternate text and browser-sniffing scripts, as described briefly in the next section, "Browser Sniffing for Fun and Profit," or in detail in Chapter 13.

In HTML 4.0, the `<OBJECT>` tag takes a great deal of the burden off your shoulders. You can create Web pages that contain various levels of content, from the very complex to the extremely simple, from which the browser can choose what it's most comfortable displaying. In short, the `<OBJECT>` tag can be written in such a way that it acts like a menu at an all-you-can-eat buffet. Each browser that visits, in turn, can then pick and choose what they're most comfortable digesting. Oh, what a wonderful thing.

Consider, for example, the following few lines of HTML 4.0. Here I've nested, or cascaded, four different levels of `<OBJECT>` tags, starting with the most complicated (an applet class file) and ending with the most simplistic (plain old-fashioned "alternate HTML"). In between are two entirely different `<OBJECT>` tags: one for a MPEG movie, and another for an animated GIF. Take a look:

```
<OBJECT CLASSID="http://www.mars.com/mars.class">
 <OBJECT DATA="mars.mpeg" TYPE="application/mpeg">
  <OBJECT SRC="mars.gif">
   Sorry, you can't see diddly! Get a real browser...
  </OBJECT>
 </OBJECT>
</OBJECT>
```

A browser first encounters the applet definition. If it's comfortable dealing with applets, it loads and executes the one specified in the CLASSID. If not, the browser moves on to the next `<OBJECT>` tag. This time it sees the MPEG movie, and displays the movie if it's capable of doing so. If the browser can't display the movie, it then progresses to the animated GIF. Assuming it can't even display that (what a lame browser!), it displays the alternate text that is included.

While it may seem a bit much to deal with, it sure beats the alternative of writing JavaScript to sniff out the make, model, and version of browsers visiting your pages.

Browser Sniffing for Fun and Profit

While HTML 4.0 promises to do away with a great deal of the complexity now involved in supporting various levels of browsers, as the previous example illustrates, it'll be several years before you can rely on it. Because it will be a while before you can be certain that the vast majority of Webbers are using HTML 4.0 browsers, you have no choice but to use the browser-sniffing JavaScript presented in Chapter 13.

As this chapter illustrates, you can use scripts to determine exactly what browser make, model, and version is being used to view your pages. Armed with this information, you can then use a little more script to dynamically whip up exactly the level of HTML that particular browsers understand.

It might not be the perfect solution, especially if you don't like dealing with JavaScript, but it works like a charm. Sure, there's the potential that Webbers won't have JavaScript enabled when they visit your sniffer pages, but that's part of the challenge, as Chapter 13 explains.

Index

(continued)

Java™ Development Kit
Version 1.1.3 Binary Code License

This binary code license ("License") contains rights and restrictions associated with use of the accompanying software and documentation ("Software"). Read the License carefully before installing the Software. By installing the Software you agree to the terms and conditions of this License.

1. **Limited License Grant**. Sun grants to you ("Licensee") a non-exclusive, non-transferable limited license to use the Software without fee for evaluation of the Software and for development of Java™ compatible applets and applications. Licensee may make one archival copy of the Software. Except for the foregoing, Licensee may not re-distribute the Software in whole or in part, either separately or included with a product. Refer to the Java Runtime Environment Version 1.1 binary code license (www.javasoft.com/products/JDK/1.1/index.html) for the availability of runtime code which may be distributed with Java compatible applets and applications.

2. **Java Platform Interface**. Licensee may not modify the Java Platform Interface ("JPI", identified as classes contained within the "java" package or any subpackages of the "java" package), by creating additional classes within the JPI or otherwise causing the addition to or modification of the classes in the JPI. In the event that Licensee creates any Java-related API and distributes such API to others for applet or application development, Licensee must promptly publish an accurate specification for such API for free use by all developers of Java-based software.

3. **Restrictions**. Software is confidential copyrighted information of Sun and title to all copies is retained by Sun and/or its licensors. Licensee shall not modify, decompile, disassemble, decrypt, extract, or otherwise reverse engineer Software. Software may not be leased, assigned, or sublicensed, in whole or in part. **Software is not designed or intended for use in on-line control of aircraft, air traffic, aircraft navigation, or aircraft communications; or in the design, construction, operation, or maintenance of any nuclear facility. Licensee warrants that it will not use or redistribute the Software for such purposes**.

4. **Trademarks and Logos**. This License does not authorize Licensee to use any Sun name, trademark or logo. Licensee acknowledges that Sun owns the Java trademark and all Java-related trademarks, logos and icons including the Coffee Cup and Duke ("Java Marks") and agrees to: (i) comply with the Java Trademark Guidelines at java.com/trademarks.html; (ii) not do anything harmful to or inconsistent with Sun's rights in the Java Marks; and (iii) assist Sun in protecting those rights, including assigning to Sun any rights acquired by Licensee in any Java Mark.

5. **Disclaimer of Warranty**. Software is provided "AS IS," without a warranty of any kind. ALL EXPRESS OR IMPLIED REPRESENTATIONS AND WARRANTIES, INCLUDING ANY IMPLIED WARRANTY OF MERCHANTABILITY, FITNESS FOR A PARTICULAR PURPOSE OR NON-INFRINGEMENT, ARE HEREBY EXCLUDED.

6. **Limitation of Liability**. SUN AND ITS LICENSORS SHALL NOT BE LIABLE FOR ANY DAMAGES SUFFERED BY LICENSEE OR ANY THIRD PARTY AS A RESULT OF USING OR DISTRIBUTING SOFTWARE. IN NO EVENT WILL SUN OR ITS LICENSORS BE LIABLE FOR ANY LOST REVENUE, PROFIT OR DATA, OR FOR DIRECT, INDIRECT, SPECIAL, CONSEQUENTIAL, INCIDENTAL, OR PUNITIVE DAMAGES, HOWEVER CAUSED AND REGARDLESS OF THE THEORY OF LIABILITY, ARISING OUT OF THE USE OF OR INABILITY TO USE SOFTWARE, EVEN IF SUN HAS BEEN ADVISED OF THE POSSIBILITY OF SUCH DAMAGES.

7. **Termination**. Licensee may terminate this License at any time by destroying all copies of Software. This License will terminate immediately without notice from Sun if Licensee fails to comply with any provision of this License. Upon such termination, Licensee must destroy all copies of Software.

8. **Export Regulations**. Software, including technical data, is subject to U.S. export control laws, including the U.S. Export Administration Act and its associated regulations, and may be subject to export or import regulations in other countries. Licensee agrees to comply strictly with all such regulations and acknowledges that it has the responsibility to obtain licenses to export, re-export, or import Software. Software may not be downloaded, or otherwise exported or re-exported (i) into, or to a national or resident of, Cuba, Iraq, Iran, North Korea, Libya, Sudan, Syria, or any country to which the U.S. has embargoed goods; or (ii) to anyone on the U.S. Treasury Department's list of Specially Designated Nations or the U.S. Commerce Department's Table of Denial Orders.

9. **Restricted Rights**. Use, duplication, or disclosure by the United States government is subject to the restrictions as set forth in the Rights in Technical Data and Computer Software Clauses in DFARS 252.227-7013(c) (1) (ii) and FAR 52.227-19(c) (2) as applicable.

10. **Governing Law**. Any action related to this License will be governed by California law and controlling U.S. federal law. No choice of law rules of any jurisdiction will apply.

11. **Severability**. If any of the above provisions are held to be in violation of applicable law, void, or unenforceable in any jurisdiction, then such provisions are herewith waived to the extent necessary for the License to be otherwise enforceable in such jurisdiction. However, if in Sun's opinion deletion of any provisions of the License by operation of this paragraph unreasonably compromises the rights or increase the liabilities of Sun or its licensors, Sun reserves the right to terminate the License and refund the fee paid by Licensee, if any, as Licensee's sole and exclusive remedy.

IDG Books Worldwide, Inc., End-User License Agreement

READ THIS. You should carefully read these terms and conditions before opening the software packet(s) included with this book ("Book"). This is a license agreement ("Agreement") between you and IDG Books Worldwide, Inc. ("IDGB"). By opening the accompanying software packet(s), you acknowledge that you have read and accept the following terms and conditions. If you do not agree and do not want to be bound by such terms and conditions, promptly return the Book and the unopened software packet(s) to the place you obtained them for a full refund.

1. **License Grant.** IDGB grants to you (either an individual or entity) a nonexclusive license to use one copy of the enclosed software program(s) (collectively, the "Software") solely for your own personal or business purposes on a single computer (whether a standard computer or a workstation component of a multiuser network). The Software is in use on a computer when it is loaded into temporary memory (RAM) or installed into permanent memory (hard disk, CD-ROM, or other storage device). IDGB reserves all rights not expressly granted herein.

2. **Ownership.** IDGB is the owner of all right, title, and interest, including copyright, in and to the compilation of the Software recorded on the disk(s) or CD-ROM ("Software Media"). Copyright to the individual programs recorded on the Software Media is owned by the author or other authorized copyright owner of each program. Ownership of the Software and all proprietary rights relating thereto remain with IDGB and its licensers.

3. **Restrictions on Use and Transfer.**

   (a) You may only (i) make one copy of the Software for backup or archival purposes, or (ii) transfer the Software to a single hard disk, provided that you keep the original for backup or archival purposes. You may not (i) rent or lease the Software, (ii) copy or reproduce the Software through a LAN or other network system or through any computer subscriber system or bulletin-board system, or (iii) modify, adapt, or create derivative works based on the Software.

   (b) You may not reverse engineer, decompile, or disassemble the Software. You may transfer the Software and user documentation on a permanent basis, provided that the transferee agrees to accept the terms and conditions of this Agreement and you retain no copies. If the Software is an update or has been updated, any transfer must include the most recent update and all prior versions.

4. **Restrictions on Use of Individual Programs.** You must follow the individual requirements and restrictions detailed for each individual program in Appendix A: "About the CD." These limitations are also contained in the individual license agreements recorded on the Software Media. These limitations may include a requirement that after using the program for a specified period of time, the user must pay a registration fee or discontinue use. By opening the Software packet(s), you will be agreeing to abide by the licenses and restrictions for these individual programs that are detailed in the "About the CD" Appendix and on the Software Media. None of the material on this Software Media or listed in this Book may ever be redistributed, in original or modified form, for commercial purposes.

5. **Limited Warranty.**

   (a) IDGB warrants that the Software and Software Media are free from defects in materials and workmanship under normal use for a period of sixty (60) days from the date of purchase of this Book. If IDGB receives notification within the warranty period of defects in materials or workmanship, IDGB will replace the defective Software Media.

   (b) **IDGB AND THE AUTHOR OF THE BOOK DISCLAIM ALL OTHER WARRANTIES, EXPRESS OR IMPLIED, INCLUDING WITHOUT LIMITATION IMPLIED WARRANTIES OF MER-CHANTABILITY AND FITNESS FOR A PARTICULAR PURPOSE, WITH RESPECT TO THE SOFTWARE, THE PROGRAMS, THE SOURCE CODE CONTAINED THEREIN, AND/OR THE TECHNIQUES DESCRIBED IN THIS BOOK. IDGB DOES NOT WARRANT THAT THE FUNCTIONS CONTAINED IN THE SOFTWARE WILL MEET YOUR REQUIREMENTS OR THAT THE OPERATION OF THE SOFTWARE WILL BE ERROR FREE.**

   (c) This limited warranty gives you specific legal rights, and you may have other rights that vary from jurisdiction to jurisdiction.

6. **Remedies.**

   (a) IDGB's entire liability and your exclusive remedy for defects in materials and workmanship shall be limited to replacement of the Software Media, which may be returned to IDGB with a copy of your receipt at the following address: Software Media Fulfillment Department, Attn.: *Java For Dummies*, 2nd Edition, IDG Books Worldwide, Inc., 7260 Shadeland Station, Ste. 100, Indianapolis, IN 46256, or call 800-762-2974. Please allow three to four weeks for delivery. This Limited Warranty is void if failure of the Software Media has resulted from accident, abuse, or misapplication. Any replacement Software Media will be warranted for the remainder of the original warranty period or thirty (30) days, whichever is longer.

   (b) In no event shall IDGB or the author be liable for any damages whatsoever (including without limitation damages for loss of business profits, business interruption, loss of business information, or any other pecuniary loss) arising from the use of or inability to use the Book or the Software, even if IDGB has been advised of the possibility of such damages.

   (c) Because some jurisdictions do not allow the exclusion or limitation of liability for conse-quential or incidental damages, the above limitation or exclusion may not apply to you.

7. **U.S. Government Restricted Rights.** Use, duplication, or disclosure of the Software by the U.S. Government is subject to restrictions stated in paragraph (c)(1)(ii) of the Rights in Technical Data and Computer Software clause of DFARS 252.227-7013, and in subparagraphs (a) through (d) of the Commercial Computer– Restricted Rights clause at FAR 52.227-19, and in similar clauses in the NASA FAR supplement, when applicable.

8. **General.** This Agreement constitutes the entire understanding of the parties and revokes and supersedes all prior agreements, oral or written, between them and may not be modified or amended except in a writing signed by both parties hereto that specifically refers to this Agreement. This Agreement shall take precedence over any other documents that may be in conflict herewith. If any one or more provisions contained in this Agreement are held by any court or tribunal to be invalid, illegal, or otherwise unenforceable, each and every other provision shall remain in full force and effect.

AT&T WorldNet℠ Service

A World of Possibilities…

Thank you for selecting AT&T WorldNet Service — it's the Internet as only AT&T can bring it to you. With AT&T WorldNet Service, a world of infinite possibilities is now within your reach. Research virtually any subject. Stay abreast of current events. Participate in online newsgroups. Purchase merchandise from leading retailers. Send and receive electronic mail.

AT&T WorldNet Service is rapidly becoming the preferred way of accessing the Internet. It was recently awarded one of the most highly coveted awards in the computer industry, *PC Computing's* 1996 MVP Award for Best Internet Service Provider. Now, more than ever, it's the best way to stay in touch with the people, ideas, and information that are important to you.

You need a computer with a mouse, a modem, a phone line, and the enclosed software. That's all. We've taken care of the rest.

If You Can Point and Click, You're There

With AT&T WorldNet Service, finding the information you want on the Internet is easier than you ever imagined it could be. You can surf the Net within minutes. And find almost anything you want to know — from the weather in Paris, Texas — to the cost of a ticket to Paris, France. You're just a point and click away. It's that easy.

AT&T WorldNet Service features specially customized industry-leading browsers integrated with advanced Internet directories and search engines. The result is an Internet service that sets a new standard for ease of use — virtually everywhere you want to go is a point and click away, making it a snap to navigate the Internet.

When you go online with AT&T WorldNet Service, you'll benefit from being connected to the Internet by the world leader in networking. We offer you fast access of up to 28.8 Kbps in more than 215 cities throughout the U.S. that will make going online as easy as picking up your phone.

Online Help and Advice
24 Hours a Day, 7 Days a Week

Before you begin exploring the Internet, you may want to take a moment to check two useful sources of information.

If you're new to the Internet, from the AT&T WorldNet Service home page at www.worldnet.att.net, click on the Net Tutorial hyperlink for a quick explanation of unfamiliar terms and useful advice about exploring the Internet.

Another useful source of information is the HELP icon. The area contains pertinent, time-saving information-intensive reference tips, and topics such as Accounts & Billing, Trouble Reporting, Downloads & Upgrades, Security Tips, Network Hot Spots, Newsgroups, Special Announcements, etc.

Whether online or off-line, 24 hours a day, seven days a week, we will provide World Class technical expertise and fast, reliable responses to your questions. To reach AT&T WorldNet Customer Care, call **1-800-400-1447**.

Nothing is more important to us than making sure that your Internet experience is a truly enriching and satisfying one.

Safeguard Your Online Purchases

AT&T WorldNet Service is committed to making the Internet a safe and convenient way to transact business. By registering and continuing to charge your AT&T WorldNet Service to your AT&T Universal Card, you'll enjoy peace of mind whenever you shop the Internet. Should your account number be compromised on the Net, you won't be liable for any online transactions charged to your AT&T Universal Card by a person who is not an authorized user.*

*Today, cardmembers may be liable for the first $50 of charges made by a person who is not an authorized user, which will not be imposed under this program as long as the cardmember notifies AT&T Universal Card of the loss within 24 hours and otherwise complies with the Cardmember Agreement. Refer to Cardmember Agreement for definition of authorized user.

Minimum System Requirements

IBM-Compatible Personal Computer Users:
- IBM-compatible personal computer with 486SX or higher processor
- 8MB of RAM (or more for better performance)
- 15–36MB of available hard disk space to install software, depending on platform (14–21MB to use service after installation, depending on platform)
- Graphics system capable of displaying 256 colors
- 14,400 bps modem connected to an outside phone line and not a LAN or ISDN line
- Microsoft Windows 3.1x or Windows 95

Macintosh Users:
- Macintosh 68030 or higher (including 68LC0X0 models and all Power Macintosh models)
- System 7.5.3 Revision 2 or higher for PCI Power Macintosh models: System 7.1 or higher for all 680X0 and non-PCI Power Macintosh models
- Mac TCP 2.0.6 or Open Transport 1.1 or higher

- 8MB of RAM (minimum) with Virtual Memory turned on or RAM Doubler; 16MB recommended for Power Macintosh users
- 12MB of available hard disk space (15MB recommended)
- 14,400 bps modem connected to an outside phone line and not a LAN or ISDN line
- Color or 256 gray-scale monitor
- Apple Guide 1.2 or higher (if you want to view online help)
  If you are uncertain of the configuration of your Macintosh computer, consult your Macintosh User's guide or call Apple at 1-800-767-2775.

Installation Tips and Instructions

- If you have other Web browsers or online software, please consider uninstalling them according to the vendor's instructions.
- If you are installing AT&T WorldNet Service on a computer with Local Area Networking, please contact your LAN administrator for setup instructions.
- At the end of installation, you may be asked to restart your computer. Don't attempt the registration process until you have done so.

IBM-compatible PC users:
- Insert the CD-ROM into the CD-ROM drive on your computer.
- Select *File/Run* (for Windows 3.1*x*) or *Start/Run* (for Windows 95 if setup did not start automatically).
- Type *D:\setup.exe* (or change the "D" if your CD-ROM is another drive).
- Click *OK*.
- Follow the onscreen instructions to install and register.

Macintosh users:
- Disable all extensions except Apple CD-ROM and Foreign Files Access extensions.
- Restart Computer.
- Insert the CD-ROM into the CD-ROM drive on your computer.
- Double-click the *Install AT&T WorldNet Service* icon.
- Follow the onscreen instructions to install. (Upon restarting your Macintosh, AT&T WorldNet Service Account Setup automatically starts.)
- Follow the onscreen instructions to register.

Registering with AT&T WorldNet Service

After you have connected with AT&T WorldNet online registration service, you will be presented with a series of screens that confirm billing information and prompt you for additional account set-up data.

The following is a list of registration tips and comments that will help you during the registration process.

I. Use one of the following registration codes, which can also be found in Appendix A of *Java For Dummies,* 2nd Edition. Use L5SQIM631 if you are an AT&T long-distance residential customer or L5SQIM632 if you use another long-distance phone company.
II. During registration, you will need to supply your name, address, and valid credit card number, and choose an account information security word, e-mail name, and e-mail password. You will also be requested to select your preferred price plan at this time. (We advise that you use all lowercase letters when assigning an e-mail ID and security code, since they are easier to remember.)
III. If you make a mistake and exit or get disconnected during the registration process prematurely, simply click on "Create New Account." Do not click on "Edit Existing Account."
IV. When choosing your local access telephone number, you will be given several options. Please choose the one nearest to you. Please note that calling a number within your area does not guarantee that the call is free.

Connecting to AT&T WorldNet Service

When you have finished installing and registering with AT&T WorldNet Service, you are ready to access the Internet. Make sure your modem and phone line are available before attempting to connect to the service.

For Windows 95 users:
- Double-click on the **Connect to AT&T WorldNet Service** icon on your desktop.
  OR
- Select **Start, Programs, AT&T WorldNet Software, Connect to AT&T WorldNet Service.**

For Windows 3.*x* users:
- Double-click on the **Connect to AT&T WorldNet Service** icon located in the AT&T WorldNet Service group.

For Macintosh users:
- Double-click on the **AT&T WorldNet Service** icon in the AT&T WorldNet Service folder.

Choose the Plan That's Right for You

The Internet is for everyone, whether at home or at work. In addition to making the time you spend online productive and fun, we're also committed to making it affordable. Choose one of two price plans: unlimited usage access or hourly usage access. The latest pricing information can be obtained during online registration. No matter which plan you use, we're confident that after you take advantage of everything AT&T WorldNet Service has to offer, you'll wonder how you got along without it.

Explore our AT&T WorldNet Service site at http://www.att.com/worldnet.

Installation Instructions

• •

*I*n order to make use of the cool applets, scripts, and tools on the CD-ROM that comes with this book, you need to have a Java-savvy browser installed on your computer (see Chapter 3). For a detailed listing of all the wonderful treats and surprises on this CD-ROM, check out Appendix A.

Note: Use of the Java Development Kit is subject to the Binary Code License terms and conditions. Read the license carefully. By opening this package, you are agreeing to be bound by the terms and conditions of this license from Sun Microsystems, Inc.

For Windows 95

Step 1: Insert the *Java For Dummies,* 2nd Edition CD-ROM into your computer's CD-ROM drive.

Step 2: Double-click the My Computer icon located on your desktop.

Step 3: Double-click the icon for your CD-ROM drive (usually the D: drive).

Step 4: Double-click the index.html file for an interactive tour of the CD-ROM, or copy the specific files you want to install on your computer. (See Appendix A or the README.txt file on the CD-ROM for detailed instructions.)

For Macintosh

Step 1: Insert the *Java For Dummies,* 2nd Edition CD-ROM into your computer's CD-ROM drive.

Step 2: Double-click the CD-ROM icon that appears on your desktop.

Step 3: Double-click the index.html file for an interactive tour of the CD-ROM, or copy the specific files you want to install on your computer. (See Appendix A or the Read Me First file that comes on the CD-ROM for detailed instructions.)

YOUR ONLINE RESOURCE

WWW.DUMMIES.COM

Discover Dummies Online!

The Dummies Web site is your fun and friendly online resource for the latest information about ...*For Dummies*® books and your favorite topics. The Web site is the place to communicate with us, exchange ideas with other ...*For Dummies* readers, chat with authors, and have fun!

Ten Fun and Useful Things You Can Do at www.dummies.com

1. Win free ...*For Dummies* books and more!
2. Register your book and be entered in a prize drawing.
3. Meet your favorite authors through the IDG Books Author Chat Series.
4. Exchange helpful information with other ...*For Dummies* readers.
5. Discover other great ...*For Dummies* books you must have!
6. Purchase Dummieswear™ exclusively from our Web site.
7. Buy ...*For Dummies* books online.
8. Talk to us. Make comments, ask questions, get answers!
9. Download free software.
10. Find additional useful resources from authors.

Link directly to these ten fun and useful things at **http://www.dummies.com/10useful**.

For other technology titles from IDG Books Worldwide, go to **www.idgbooks.com**.

Not on the Web yet? It's easy to get started with *Dummies 101*®: *The Internet For Windows*®*95* or *The Internet For Dummies*®, 4th Edition, at local retailers everywhere.

IDG BOOKS WORLDWIDE

Find other ...*For Dummies* books on these topics:

Business • Career • Databases • Spreadsheets • Food & Beverage • Games
Gardening • Graphics • Hardware • Health & Fitness • Internet and the World Wide Web
Networking • Office Suites • Operating Systems • Personal Finance • Pets
Programming • Recreation • Teacher Resources • Word Processing • Sports • Test Prep

IDG BOOKS WORLDWIDE
BOOK REGISTRATION

Register This Book and Win!

We want to hear from you!

Visit **http://my2cents.dummies.com** to register this book and tell us how you liked it!

- ✔ Get entered in our monthly prize giveaway.
- ✔ Give us feedback about this book – tell us what you like best, what you like least, or maybe what you'd like to ask the author and us to change!
- ✔ Let us know any other ...*For Dummies* topics that interest you.

Your feedback helps us determine what books to publish, tells us what coverage to add as we revise our books, and lets us know whether we're meeting your needs as a ...*For Dummies* reader. You're our most valuable resource, and what you have to say is important to us!

Not on the Web yet? It's easy to get started with *Dummies 101®: The Internet For Windows® 95* or *The Internet For Dummies*, 4th Edition, at local retailers everywhere.

Or let us know what you think by sending us a letter at the following address:

...*For Dummies* Book Registration
Dummies Press
7260 Shadeland Station, Suite 100
Indianapolis, IN 46256
Fax 317-596-5498

BUSINESS AND GENERAL REFERENCE BOOK SERIES FROM IDG

COMPUTER BOOK SERIES FROM IDG